GW00992336

Between River and Sea
Encounters in Israel and Palestine

Also by Dervla Murphy:

Between River and Sea

Encounters in Israel and Palestine

DERVLA MURPHY

ELAND

First published by Eland in 2015
61 Exmouth Market, London EC1R 4QL

Text copyright © Dervla Murphy 2015

ISBN 978 1 78060 045 1

Text set by Antony Gray
Printed and bound in Great Britain by
CPI Group (UK) Ltd, Croydon CR0 4YY

To Andrew, with affection and admiration

Contents

Foreword

My personal memories of the creation of the state of Israel are opaque. For years the newspapers were full of related bombings, snipings, ambushes and occasional spectacular assassinations, interspersed with Commissions of Inquiry, Delegations, Conferences, International Reports and British White Papers, all seen through an ambiguous haze of public sympathy for and guilt about Jews per se. Pre-partition, as a juvenile Irish nationalist with rabid tendencies, I admired the anti-British Zionist militias and scorned as 'traitors' any Irishmen serving with the Palestine Police. However, by 1947 I had left the rabid stage behind and confusion was setting in. At that date the partition of Ireland still throbbed like an open wound and I remember my parents deploring the UN vote but I can't recall having strong feelings of my own. Adolescents are notably self-centred and I'd other things on my mind like Shakespeare and long-distance cycling.

As the years passed I remained lazy and hazy about what was misleadingly known as 'the Palestinian problem'; it seemed even more complicated than the various other twentieth-century problems. As a reviewer however, I gradually read more widely around the subject, and came to pay due attention to the Palestinian tragedy. I travelled to Israel for the first time in November 2008, and this book records three months spent there, and five months on the West Bank over the following two years. A visit to Gaza in the summer of 2011 has already spawned *A Month by the Sea: Encounters in Gaza* (Eland, 2013).

Individuals may be anti-Semitic, anti-Israel, anti-Zionist – or all three, or none of the above. I confess to being anti-political Zionism, therefore anti-Israel as the state is at present constituted. 'Political Zionism' is generally used to describe the movement specifically founded in the 1890s to settle European Jews as colonists on Palestinian land. Its original leaders were not devout believers but hard-nosed secularists adept at using Judaism to attract massive funding and the support of such statesmen as Arthur Balfour and David Lloyd George.

Dervla Murphy

Author's Note

This book is based on visits made between November 2008 and December 2010. Certain facts and figures may by now be out of date but for the majority of Palestinians no major economic or political changes have taken place and the military occupation has, in the interval, become more oppressive.

All personal names, apart from those of public figures, have been changed. For security reasons some place names have also been changed or not specified.

Nowadays acronyms seem to breed like fruit-flies, especially in the Middle East. In an otherwise clarifying analysis of post-Oslo developments I found the PLC, PLO, PNC, and PLA in every other paragraph and they all had frequent dealings with the CMIP, UPMRC, CDC, GUPT, ANERA, PNGO, PGFTU, PPER, and GUPTOT. Whereupon I decided to be kind to my readers (and myself) and abstain from all but the most familiar, of which a list may be found, along with a Glossary, at the end of the book.

Acknowledgements

Firstly, the Nameless Ones without whom this book could not have been written but who must remain nameless at their own request.

Mary Buchalter and Yvonne Jacobson provided pivotal introductions. Garry Kilgallen forwarded many illuminating 'documents' and 'attachments'. John Feighery maintained a steady flow of relevant newspaper cuttings. Jo Murphy-Lawless patiently printed out the numerous essential articles and essays I was too computer illiterate to find for myself. Toni Madden unearthed much hard-to-find information. Gwyn Daniels and Avi Shlaim provided invaluable advice and encouragement. Raja Shehadeh provided inspiration and much-needed moral support during my residence in Balata. Lovena Wilson took my twentieth-century TS into cyberspace and on the way disentangled horribly convoluted corrections and dodgy spelling with unrivalled skill. Steph Allen provided other skills without which my (and many other) books would be stillborn. Eland Publishing (i.e., Rose Baring and Barnaby Rogerson) performed heroic editorial deeds and dealt tolerantly with authorial crankiness. Finally, Rachel, Andrew, Rose, Clodagh and Zea spurred me on when the going got rough by making frequent anxious enquiries – 'How's the Book?'

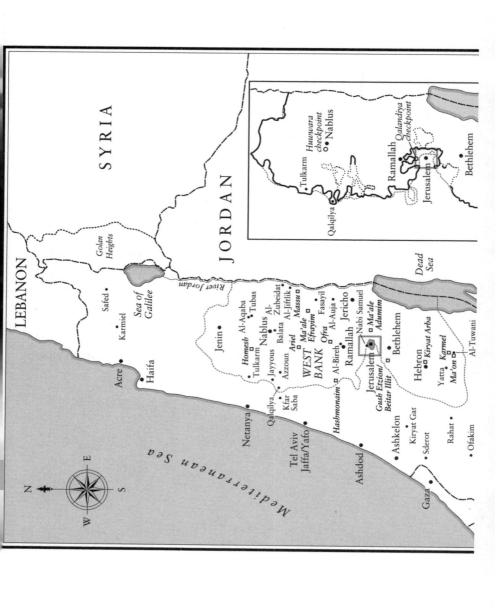

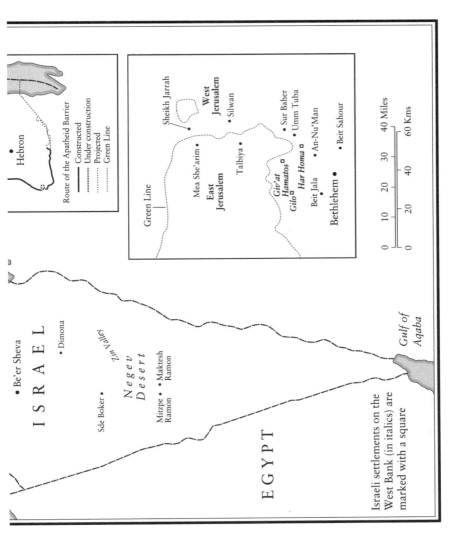

Israel and the Occupied Palestinian Territories
showing places visited by the author

A Palestinian international campaign for a one-state solution backed by a wide popular insurgence cannot be discarded if indeed the Palestinians come to the conclusion that a viable state is not in the offing for them.

SHLOMO BEN-AMI,
former Israeli Minister of Foreign Affairs and
leader of the Israeli negotiating team at Taba

I trust in you, when you return to your countries, to help us rid ourselves of these dishonest mythologies, of which we have become ourselves the victims.

YEHUDID HAREL,
Israeli human rights activist,
addressing an international writers'
gathering in Ramallah

PART ONE

CHAPTER 1

Mixed Company in Jaffa and Tel Aviv

On the evening of 4 November 2008, I boarded my night flight to Tel Aviv as Barack Obama was being elected – the first mixed-race President of the United States. All around me sat vocally Democratic young Americans, too excited to sleep, on their way to work with West Bank Palestinians. Such volunteers, known collectively as 'Internationals', may be of any age and are unpopular in Israel. Some undertake to protect schoolchildren from the Israel Defense Forces (IDF) or illegal settlers; and over the years a few have been killed and several seriously injured.

When we landed at 3.40 a.m., squeals of frustration filled the cabin; the Internationals' cell phones, so eagerly switched on, had failed to connect. But they didn't have long to wait; as we trooped into the vast Immigration Hall elevated TV screens were showing Barack Obama in victory mode. His devotees cheered and laughed and hugged each other: some even wept for joy. Most of the other passengers remained resolutely uninterested.

It's said that Israeli officials are inconsistent when interpreting rules and regulations. Before choosing an immigration queue I studied the four women officers in their bullet-proof kiosks. Two were young, attractive and apparently amiable, their colleagues were dourly middle-aged with an evident penchant for complications. In the queue on my left stood six Haredim – long bushy beards matching long ear-locks, wide-brimmed black hats and long black coats mentally anchoring them in some nineteenth-century shtetl. All carried the maximum of hand-luggage yet their clothes and shoes were shabby. Behind me a young Californian whispered, 'See how poor they are? They won't work. You'll notice some begging at traffic lights!' These government-subsidised ultra-Orthodox exasperate their tax-paying fellow-citizens. I wondered how the sextet would deal with female officials. Their Halacha (collected religious rules) forbids them to listen to women singing and their sacred literature, closely studied by every Haredi male, proclaims – among other things – that 'A woman is a sack full of excrement' (Tractate Shabbat, page 152). As they neared a kiosk one 'sack' was replaced by a man and the group at once exchanged their advantageous position for the end of his long queue.

Israel craves tourists but prefers them to arrive tidily packaged with pious or frivolous destinations: the Holy Places or beaches and discos. Solitary foreigners arouse suspicion and when my turn came the dialogue went like this:

Why you visit Israel? For a holiday. Which your group? I'm travelling alone. Who meet you outside? No one. You know who in Israel? No one. Tonight you stay where? In Jaffa. Where else you go? I don't know yet, I don't plan ahead. You have occupation, job, work? I write books. Books what about? About travels in different countries.

Suddenly a friendly smile replaced the officer's professionally stern expression. 'Now I understand your travel method! I hope Israel for you is exciting! I have no good English or I would like to read your books.'

So much for all those warnings about Israeli authorities being automatically hostile to foreign writers.

A ludicrously spacious Arrivals Hall, its ceiling almost out of sight, stretches beyond the customs barrier. This glittering new airport, self-described as 'ultra-modern', cost US$1 billion – though the Haredim are but one among Israel's several impoverished communities. In the far distance a brown-robed Franciscan was shepherding Spanish pilgrims to their coach. Then the Jerusalem-bound Internationals found their minibus taxi, leaving me alone.

Surprisingly, the Cambio office was open, staffed by a balding man with grey stubble, pale blue eyes, heavy jowls and a Russian accent. As my euros became shekels (at a rate of about 5 shekels to the euro) I asked about the US vote – by what percentage had Obama won? Frowning, the clerk consulted his computer but failed to find the figures. Then abruptly and vehemently he said, 'We don't like him, he'll make trouble for the whole world!' When I lingered, hoping to prolong our conversation, he pointedly picked up his newspaper.

I sat amidst the cafeteria's scores of plastic tables and chairs feeling slightly like a piece of statuary. Two teenagers – he tall and thin, she small and fat – were slumped behind the counter. Towards sunrise, when I asked them about train times, they shrugged and turned away.

At the adjacent railway station a down-at-heel young couple, pimply and pallid, were the only people in sight. They, too, seemed to resent being addressed in English, as did the elderly woman who had just unlocked the ticket booth.

That thirty-minute ride into Tel Aviv, through industrial estates and rubble-strewn wasteland, gives the newcomer a dreary first impression of Israel. We halted thrice to pick up workers and neatly uniformed schoolchildren – a glum lot, the juniors plugged into their iPods, the seniors yawning and eye-rubbing. On this early morning suburban service the majority must know one another yet no greetings or smiles were exchanged.

Tel Aviv dates from 1909, when the Jewish National Fund bought an expanse of low sand dunes three miles north of Jaffa; around the central station, overlooked by high-risery, one might be in any twentieth-century city. The few pedestrians ignored my 'Jaffa bus?' query and I remembered a London friend's warning. She had remarked that as a septuagenarian, bowed and white-haired, loaded with a dingy rucksack and carrying a few plastic bags, I was likely to be mistaken for a beggar. Happily bus signs are bilingual on tourist routes and quite soon I chanced upon the relevant stop. The No. 10 appears infrequently, the stop is unshaded and by 7.30 sweat was gently trickling down my face; even in November, Israel's coastal climate challenges me.

Of the five waiting passengers two were dark-skinned and crinkly-haired, sharing a cigarette and carrying tool-boxes. The others were teenage conscripts, each armed with a long weighty weapon. The slim blue-eyed girl, not much older than my eldest granddaughter, wore a flaxen waist-length pigtail and seemed at ease with her formidable gun. The gum-chewing youths sported those crocheted skullcaps that mark 'observant' Jews (or those wishing to seem so). Most Israeli males must do three years military training, their sisters two. The Haredim minority are exempted from this duty, as are Israel's Palestinian citizens (one-fifth of the population) 'for security reasons'.

On the crowded bus I sat beside an overweight youth, ginger-haired and freckled; a hair-clip kept his skullcap in place and he held his gun upright between his knees. Not all these weapons are unloaded; some carry rubber or plastic 'crowd-control' bullets which prove fatal only if fired maliciously or recklessly. Tentatively I asked this lad if he spoke English. 'Talk Hebrew!' he snapped while opening his cell phone.

Where Jabotinsky Street joins Tel Aviv's beach boulevard the conscripts were replaced by four Jaffa residents, young Palestinian women coming off their night-shift and laden with office-cleaning gear. In 1950 Tel Aviv and Jaffa were united, to the latter's detriment, in the Municipality of Tel Aviv-Yafo. Where I left the bus a giant multilingual billboard proclaims: 'JAFFA AGED 4000 YEARS' – scarcely an exaggeration. History (not legend or myth) records that in 1468BC Pharaoh Thutmose III conquered 'Yapu', a port city of such importance that its conquest was recorded on stone.

From a brand new sea-wall three short streets of shack-like huxter stores and family workshops converge on the 1906 clock tower, erected to mark the 25th year of Sultan Abdel Hamid II's reign. The twentieth century was relentlessly unkind to Jaffa. During the Arab Revolt (1936–39), this district of ancient dwellings and narrow laneways was dynamited by the British to make way for military vehicles. On 8 May 1936 a general strike had begun, reinforced by a boycott of British and Zionist goods and institutions. A month or so later, furious mobs turned on Jaffa's expanding communities of immigrant Jews, indiscriminately killing and looting. Other large areas of the Old City were then blown up, equally indiscriminately, 'to punish residents'. Subsequently the British had second thoughts and explained that those demolitions were part of an 'urban improvement project'. The Israelis' routine use of collective punishment – uprooting olive groves and orchards, razing homes and villages – is nothing new.

Beyond the comparatively modern (c.1814) al-Mahmoudiya mosque I wandered through a semi-slum of handsome but neglected nineteenth-century residences once occupied by prosperous Palestinians. Many have now been reclaimed by 'illegal' workers from the Occupied Palestinian Territories (OPT) who find poorly paid jobs on building sites. In 1947, UN Resolution 181 specified that Jaffa was to remain 'an Arab enclave'. Yet within weeks of the British withdrawal David Ben-Gurion noted in his diary: 'Jaffa will be a Jewish city. War is war.' Ten months later he boasted to the Knesset that 45,000 recent immigrants had been settled in Jaffa's 'abandoned' houses. As M. LeVine has noted, 'The city of Jaffa was then reimagined as a historically Jewish space, one that was "liberated from the Arab hands" as current tourist brochures put it.' I soon realised that most Israelis don't know how much the Nakba, the forcible emigration of Palestinians in 1947–8, altered the UN-approved Partition border. Not only Jaffa but Nazareth, Safed, Acre and Beersheba went to the victorious Zionists as a result of the 1949 Armistice Agreements.

Even now, this quarter of Jaffa retains an Arab flavour. Chai-khana boys carry glasses of tea on round little trays to merchants sitting outside their shops, stoking the day's first *narghile*. Many elders wear kaftans and *keffiyehs*. Mud ovens glow within bakeries where golden steaming loaves are stacked on high racks. I paused to watch a butcher, under surveillance by three cats, artistically arranging piles of offal at one end of his tree trunk chopping block, adding sprigs of greenery. Nearby a ragged, legless youth sat on the pavement, propped against a corner wall, receiving tiny coins from passers-by. I might have been a thousand miles from US-flavoured Tel Aviv.

My quirky hostel was an unmodernised early-nineteenth-century mansion with late-nineteenth-century plumbing. Pushing open a high, brass-embossed double door, I crossed a wide empty hallway, its floor and walls magnificently tiled, and climbed a curved, creaking stairway decorated by 1890s sepia studio portraits of pompous hirsute men and their demure womenfolk – all Palestinian Christians of the Greek Orthodox persuasion. On the landing a massive antiquated telephone squatted on a delicately carved rosewood table. With this museum piece I was to have numerous expensive and unproductive dealings.

The commonroom, formerly a salon, was lit by three tall arched windows and furnished with wooden trestle tables and benches, six computers and two mega-fridges for the use of self-catering guests. From the 'Reception' cubby-hole emerged a burly, bewhiskered Hebrew-speaking man who greeted me with a mechanical smile, was uninterested in my passport and offered no register to be signed. A wordless servant (mildly Down's syndrome) abandoned her bucket and mop to lead me past a dozen doors opening off a dark, uncarpeted corridor. At the end was an eccentric five-sided corner room; the brass bedstead's aesthetic appeal made up for sagging springs and a lumpy feather mattress. My vine-draped balcony – much bigger than the room – overlooked an entertaining flea-market. There one can buy anything from Bedouin stringed instruments to a five-foot, papier-mâché grinning chimpanzee, wearing a top hat, tails and boxer shorts; from an ibex-horn chandelier to a Victorian-era typewriter; from a set of six brass spice-weights fitting in a matchbox to a mahogany wardrobe bigger than a kitchenette.

I breakfasted off bread and bananas on the spacious hostel roof: an enchanting retreat, its low stone parapet fancifully carved. Cane chairs with tattered cushions furnished creeper-curtained nooks; sack-cloth awnings shaded coffee-tables provided with horse-hair stools for chess and backgammon players. Bulbous earthenware jars held flowering shrubs, their blossoms being stirred by a salty breeze. Cracked marble floor tiles matched the pale brown doves who cooed and strutted and fluttered around a gently splashing wrought-iron fountain.

Gazing beyond three slender minarets to a silver-blue sea, I reflected that never before had I arrived in an unknown country carrying so much emotional baggage, and feeling ill-at-ease rather than eagerly curious. A week later, in Jerusalem, a middle-aged Englishman (closely involved with Israel all his life) said, 'I believe you've a reputation for objectivity but one can't be neutral here. Yes, one must be fair and there's plenty to criticise on the Palestinian side. But honest observers and reporters *can't be neutral.*'

A short walk took me to a sad ancient district, long-since stripped of its authentic 'Arabness'. In the 1960s the Old Jaffa Development Company, working with the Municipality, sought advice from the architect Frank Meisler who later reminisced:

> I had seen villages in southern France where the local people had left for the city and artists had moved in and restored them. So from a property point of view I thought Jaffa wouldn't be a bad deal. People bought cheaply and renovated, an artists' colony appeared, the buses started arriving and the tourists came.

Many of Jaffa's 'abandoned' properties have become artists' homes and galleries, in several cased renovated by the original owners' sons, now living in faraway shacks and glad to work for a pittance on their ancestral homes. But old stonework needs expert restoration and some buildings are proving to be not such a good deal 'from a property point of view'.

On Fort Hill the museum and craft shops were closed for lack of tourists. Standing beside a simple stone monument I noted its inscription:

In everlasting Memory of the Restorers of the Jewish Yishuv in Yafo at the beginning of the nineteenth century.

Of the Founders of the Sephardic community who came from Turkey, the Balkans and North Africa as well as Ashkenazi immigrants and residents of the cities of Palestine who added their contribution to the independent life of building, agriculture, education, economy and trade.

Had it not been for the first core of the Jewish Yishuv in Yafo, we would not have lived to see the built-up city of Tel Aviv and all the settlements that surround it.

Signed: Rabbi Ben Zion Meir Hai Uziel, Chief Rabbi of Yafo and Tel Aviv.

Was this inscription in clumsy English (aimed at the US Diaspora) meant to paper over a crack?

Centuries before the birth of Christ, large Jewish communities flourished in Damascus, Baghdad and Cairo, their deep-rootedness in those cites proved by prodigiously long pedigrees. Among the North African families who arrived in nineteenth-century Jaffa were the Chelouches, jewellers and money-changers, who soon became rich enough to contribute significantly to Tel Aviv's creation. As Arabic-speakers, belonging culturally to the Middle East, these Mizrahi Jews, as they are known, in general adapted more easily to Jaffa life than the pioneering Yiddish-speaking Ashkenazim from eastern Europe – who scorned the Mizrahi for their loyalty to the corrupt Ottomans. In turn, the Mizrahi found the Ashkenazim lamentably lacking in dignity and in the diplomatic skills necessary for a Jewish community to advance under Muslim rule. In Jaffa it took the two communities more than a generation to achieve the sort of cooperation needed for the development of Tel Aviv.

'Yishuv', which simply means 'settler', has become synonymous with the pre-1948 Zionist 'pre-state'. Supported by Diaspora (mainly US) funding, and British advice, the Yishuv ran its own medical, educational and financial services for a quarter of a century. Its illegal army, the Haganah, was founded by Ze'ev Jabotinsky who wrote in 1926 – 'The Arab is culturally backward, but his instinctive patriotism is just as pure and noble as our own; it cannot be bought, it can only be curbed . . . by *force majeure.*' To ensure a future supply of force, Jabotinsky set up the

Betar, a junior branch of his Revisionist Party. In 1923 he noted: 'The only way to achieve a settlement in the future is total avoidance of all attempts to arrive at a settlement in the present' – advice consistently acted upon by Israeli governments.

Some 80% of the pre-1948 'ingathering' of Jews settled along the coastal plain, on territory never controlled by the Israelites in Biblical times. Political Zionism's early leaders were not enamoured of the indigenous Palestinians, whether Jewish or gentile. Therefore most chose to live in Tel Aviv, which acquired autonomous urban status in 1921, when still a mere straggle of settlements. It grew fast, absorbing nearby towns and becoming the headquarters for most Zionist military, political and cultural organisations. Its secular progenitors visualised it as a wholesome all-Jewish alternative to messily pluralistic Jerusalem. Their state was to be forward-looking, brisk and modern, neither inspired nor hampered by the Old Yishuv's quasi-mystical relationship with 'the City of David'. For esoteric theological reasons, Palestine's ultra-Orthodox native Jews were scandalised by Zionism's colonial ambitions and a minority still refuses to recognise the State of Israel.

Jaffa's unusual subterranean Visitors' Centre was closed, but an external wall-rack offered free brochures and maps. The effrontery of the Old Jaffa Development Company is literally breath-taking; while reading its brochures upsurges of rage impeded my aspiration. For example:

At the beginning of the British Mandate the port of Jaffa was the principal port of Israel and was also recognised as the port for Jerusalem. It was in Jaffa that conquering pilgrims and Jewish immigrants came each in their turn to settle in Israel. The Jews suffered from Arab persecution throughout the first part of the twentieth century; these attacks reached their most violent height at the moment of the creation of the State of Israel, towards the middle of the century. The defensive counter-attacks of the Jews put to rout the majority of Jaffa's Arabs . . . In 1960 the Old Jaffa Development Company, was given the mandate of saving the dignity of the ancient city and its glorious past from annihilation . . . Jaffa's Old City, with its past, its history, its architecture, its geographical location, its marvellous sunsets, its verdant footpaths, its narrow alleys, by daylight or by night, it awakens keen feelings in every visitor sensitive to its beauty and serenity.

With my own serenity in tatters, I wondered how many tourists know what really happened 'towards the middle of the century'? In December 1947 Irgun, the Zionist terrorist organisation, began systematically to terrorise Jaffa and its surrounding villages, the sort of campaign now described as 'ethnic cleansing'. Soon law and order had collapsed completely. The British forces, near the end of their Mandatory mission, were almost exclusively focused on self-preservation. The Palestinian leaders, characteristically disunited and disorganised, failed to restrain their enraged followers from looting, murdering and occasionally raping in retaliation for the destruction of their homes and fields. When the well-armed Zionists seized Jaffa's central al-Manshiya district the Palestinian commander, Michel al-'Issa, saw the futility of fighting on and asked the British to negotiate an agreement whereby Jaffa would become 'an open city', a shared space. The Zionists' rejection of this compromise left the Palestinians with no alternative but to sign a surrender, witnessed by Haganah representatives, on 13 May 1948. Next day the Mandate ended and, in accordance with UN Resolution 181, the British should have handed over to the Palestinian National Committee the keys of all Jaffa's public buildings. Instead, the Zionists secured those keys for themselves, showing how easy it is to defy UN Resolutions – a lesson heeded by all their successors.

On my sweat-soaked way back to the hostel I visited one of Jaffa's many little cambio offices where a young Israeli woman – anorexically thin and heavily made up – was being vivacious on her mobile. When I slid my euros under the counter's metal bars she stretched out a hand, not otherwise acknowledging my presence and continuing her conversation. Withdrawing the notes, I waited to be told that day's rate of exchange. But she talked on: why should my trivial business interrupt her social life? Muttering a rude phrase, I departed – and farther along the same street realised that not only youngsters have sacrificed their manners to the mobile. When I bought a plastic bowl in a shadowy, cavernous hardware store the elderly Palestinian merchant left his only customer standing by the till for ten minutes while he chuckled and exclaimed in response to an invisible friend.

On the roof-garden Hasan was awaiting me, leaning against the parapet rolling a cigarette. A short sturdy man, with luminous green eyes and wavy raven hair, he had been described by our mutual friend in

Dublin as, '. . . very remarkable, choosing to go home instead of making money in Europe'.

Hasan put it another way. 'I saw the academic life was not for me – too far from the action!' A graduate of Trinity College Dublin, he was now using his sociological skills as a 'Rehabilitation Officer'. He laughed, 'A silly label, I watch how you're thinking! And it's false. I rehabilitate no one, only keep a few kids out of gangs and within their families. I'm learning as I go. It's worth drawing kids into local politics, like al-Aqsa Association work. Drugs are more tempting when you're idle. In al-Aqsa we try to shame the government into giving back some of the mosques and cemeteries grabbed during the Nakba. Also some of the *waqfs* confiscated under the "Law of Absentee Property". My grandfather was one of those absentees, killed near the Green Line. In 1949 hundreds of starving farmers tried to slip back to their land by night, to harvest what they'd planted. The Zionists called them "infiltrators". No one knows how many were murdered, the policy was shoot to kill. But I tell the kids we shouldn't blame Holocaust survivors. They suffered in Europe what we suffered here – losing everything. *They* weren't the calculating colonisers. Most arrived not knowing they were displacing us.'

Elaborating, Hasan defined al-Aqsa Association as an offshoot of the Islamic Resistance Movement. 'You could say it's an ally or cousin of Hamas.' While promoting al-Aqsa's non-violent but verbally hard-hitting campaigns, Hasan detested Hamas's fanatical factions. He complained, 'They're competing with religious Zionism. Their Charter pretends the Caliph 'Umar ibn al-Khatab declared all of Palestine endowed as a *waqf* for Muslims till the Day of Judgement – making us sound like Jews hallucinating about Abraham and the Promised Land!' In exasperation, Hasan ground his cigarette butt under his heel. 'It's humiliating, Islam being so twisted. It's a kind of giving in to Zionism, playing their stupid game.'

I posited that political Zionism's Biblical game is far from stupid. Without it, would colonising the Holy Land have received such strong support from within what used to be Christendom? 'Anyway,' I added, 'it's no game for Jews who still believe in their myths. Which are marginally less absurd than belief in a virgin birth.'

Later, as we parted at the street door, Hasan said, 'What we've been talking about, it's not *history*, past stuff that doesn't matter. Our refugees' children and grandchildren are still refugees and now their great-grand-children are being jailed for stoning the IDF. Don't just visit Israel. Go live on the West Bank to *see* how it is. And tomorrow I'll show you bits of Jaffa not for tourists.'

At sunrise, strolling to the harbour between renovated Arab mansions and a long strip of shrubbery, I came upon an improbable sight: thirty-eight breakfasting cats. Cats of every shape, colour, age and coat-length, all being fed by a wrinkled, faded blonde, her bicycle and trailer parked nearby. Each cat had its double dish for meat and biscuits. I stood still, counting, at first unobserved by the human. Then a tardy trio arrived and as more dishes were being filled my presence was noted. This remarkable woman spoke English with a slight German accent and her greeting was curt. Beyond informing me that she fed some forty cats twice a day she declined to discuss matters feline. This deflated me; a cyclist with a cat fixation should have proved a kindred spirit . . .

The harbour quay was overlooked by semi-ruined, fortress-like sand-stone warehouses – sternly handsome buildings, soon to be demolished. Here fishermen sold their night's catch to mixed groups. The Jaffa residents seemed intent on a bargain, the servants from Tel Aviv house-holds sought expensive calamari, sea trout, mullet. Some arguments were complicated by a Russian fisherman's halting Hebrew. When one haggle became a loud exchange of insults I caught the eye of a young woman who smiled and moved closer to ask, 'Where you from?'

Marie was a homesick Filipino, newly arrived in Tel Aviv, employed by a rich family. Her purchase made, we walked together by the water's edge where fish were being swiftly gutted and nets slowly mended while countless cats deftly extracted the tastiest organs from amidst the guts. Marie was well-informed. 'For the Israelis it's new,' she said, 'having people like me to work. It's because they don't trust Palestinians any more. My parents said I shouldn't come because Israelis are cruel to Palestinians. Then my friends here already told me this is a better place than Arab countries, because Israelis don't ill-treat us. But it's a sad place when you're new. The family don't look at me like a person, I'm like a machine, same as the hoover. I'm here only one week. When I find other Filipinos it'll be OK. I'm not overworked, I get fair time off. And my parents are joyful to get the money even if it's Israeli!'

We parted at the No. 10 bus-stop on Yerushalayim Avenue.

Later, Hasan and I walked to his home district, Ajami, through the sadly inactive port area. My companion complained about the municipality's longing to develop the port 'as a tourist and recreation site' in what Simone Ricca calls 'a cheap, promotional-type post-modern style'. In opposition are the Society for the Protection of Nature in Israel and a group of eminent Israeli architects.

Hasan recalled a few victories by local activists. One project, Midron Yafo, part-sponsored by the Jewish Agency, planned to extend the coastal area available to developers by dumping tens of thousands of tons of Tel Aviv's garbage in the sea and bulldozing numerous handsome nineteenth-century Arab mansions, despite their being habitable. When Midron Yafo was defeated in the 1980s the Jewish Agency suggested Project Renewal, a neighbourhood renovation scheme from which the Ajami mosque had benefited despite its undeserved reputation as 'a haven for terrorists'. 'But that was in my childhood,' said Hasan, 'just before the first Intifada. It couldn't happen now. Things are only getting worse, year by year.'

Strolling close to the hissing wavelets, we paused to glare at the Peres Center for Peace, then only half-built but already colossal and crudely intruding on an ancient Muslim cemetery. At each gable end prominent notices publicised the names of its US sponsors.

I mentioned the young New Jersey couple, on their way to a Tel Aviv Business Management conference, who had sat beside me in Heathrow's departure lounge. When the wife asked, 'Are we going to a new continent?' her husband hesitated before replying, 'I guess not, I figure Israel's in Europe.'

Hasan was not amused. 'That's how Zionists want it – being seen as part of the "civilised" West deserving protection from savage Islamic terrorists!'

A steep ascent from the shore, through a run-down suburb of late-Ottoman terraced houses, gave us an overview of 'new' Jaffa's disjointed sprawl. There were few people around and the traffic was light. In May 1948 Jaffa's population was about 100,000 Muslim, 70,000 Christian, the rest Jews. Fourteen months later the Palestinians were fewer than 4,000. 'And now,' said Hasan, 'we're about 22,000 and half of us have to fit into some relatives' space. This is part of the "dispossession" policy, the plan to "relocate" us. All over Israel, from the '60s to the '80s, we couldn't get permits for new houses or even repairs. Old places need attention but when owners dared to repair without permits Amidar claimed demolition rights. The most unlucky people, like my mother, had to *pay* for a demolition because they broke the law!'

On the flight from London two Internationals had told me about Amidar, a government-run housing company empowered to issue eviction orders. Supposedly it provides subsidised and rent-controlled housing for all Israelis but its major stockholders are the Jewish National Fund and the Jewish Agency. Therefore non-Jewish citizens are boycotted.

Now we could see, in the near distance, luxury apartment blocks looming over rickety Palestinian homes lining pot-holed, litter-smothered streets. The less expensive apartments cost US$350,000. 'Ajami is at a transitory stage,' explained Hasan. 'Lately state land has been sold to private developers and more than 500 families are living with eviction orders. It's a fragmented community, always twitchy because of demolitions or being "illegal".' (A sardonic tone inserted the quotation marks.) 'Not many are what's called Salafist – not yet. But refugees who've trickled back are fierce anti-Zionists, more than the '48-ers who stayed on. Some try political activism in a muddled way and that bothers the '48-ers who mostly keep their heads down. While I was in Ireland drugs spread fast from Tel Aviv's tourist beaches and now crime's nearly as bad as Dublin!'

One of Hasan's innumerable cousins ('Only my grandmother knows how many we are!') had invited us to lunch. 'Jawdat' sounded a suitable name for this forceful leader of the Jaffa Popular Committee Against Housing Demolition, a '48-er who did not keep his head down. He lived in one of a row of detached, breeze-block cubes shadowed by a ten-storey apartment tower. Its four rooms could have comfortably accom-modated his immediate family – a strong-featured wife, as forceful as himself, and three bouncy small children. This however was an extended-by-misfortune family, including Jawdat's mother, a widowed sister and her two children (also small and bouncy), an alarmingly asthmatic first cousin, two adolescent orphans bequeathed by a more distant cousin and Musa, a seriously disabled great-uncle. In 1988 an IDF bullet had damaged his spine as he walked home through a 'disorder'.

'We can sit outside,' said Hasan, leading me through the chaotic living-room to a minuscule yard, its privacy ensured by sheets of battered corrugated iron. Here four plastic chairs surrounded an improvised coffee-table – an upturned baby's bath. Only Musa spoke English. When he had been carried out to sit beside me he apologised for the lack of shade and pointed to a central tree-stump. 'The army made us cut it down. It gave tons of figs. They said snipers could use it.' He leant forward slightly while Munira, Jawdat's wife, was fixing a cushion behind his back. Then he continued, thoughtfully, 'There's some good people in the IDF. "Refusniks", they call themselves. They won't do military service in our Occupied Territories. They go to jail instead.'

I felt a sudden easing of tension within myself – and then a surge of gratitude. In situations where injustice prevails, unembittered individuals can do a lot for the harrowed outside observer.

Hasan and Jawdat were arguing vigorously. When Munira reappeared with four coffees, Hasan translated. The cousins disagreed about how best to obtain free legal aid for destitute, eviction-threatened families. 'This matters,' said Hasan. 'Some cases have loopholes but only lawyers can find them.'

A little later, Munira spread a tea-towel on the 'table' before serving us with garlic-laden lentils, salty goats' cheese, chard, thick yoghurt, hot flat bread, real orange juice.

My companions were Obama-sceptics. 'He makes all sorts of sweet promises,' said Musa, 'as medicine against the Bush poison. But he's only one man. Even if he wanted to, he couldn't beat the Israel Lobby.'

It surprised me to hear that before the first Intifada began in 1987 this street had been 'mixed' – and peacefully so. 'Then,' Musa sadly recalled, 'anger came over us like a wave.' Within a month, several of their Jewish working-class neighbours ('quiet helpful people') were murdered. The animosity generated then never abated. And it increased after the Oslo Accords when Shin Bet recruited informers throughout the district.

'People forget,' continued Musa, 'that before Zionism Jews lived safe in Palestine. They were few but they belonged, like us and the Christians. Saying religion is the problem is wrong. Politicians made it the problem. Before Zionism, Jews were nobody's enemy.'

On our way home I commented on Musa's fluent English and discovered that for four years he had worked in England as a stone mason. 'He was first of nine children and came home for the younger ones when the parents died of typhoid.' Hasan added, 'Did you notice he's like me? *Not* a simple old-style nationalist! It's true Palestine wasn't a *nation* taken from us. Under the Ottomans it was part of Syria. I go crazy thinking about how it might have been if only Jews *really* needing a home were let in. It could have been peaceful, funded by the billionaire Jews who wouldn't live here for diamonds – even now! We could have settled together, us gaining from the refugees' know-how about farming, finance, science and so on. But Zionism was never about sharing.'

My plan to stay on a kibbutz in the Negev, before visiting Jerusalem, amused Hasan. 'So you're going back to the beginning! You'll be among dinosaurs – take care what you say, some are dangerous . . .'

Before dawn, at the famed Abulafia bakery – founded in 1879 and long known as 'the gate of Jaffa' – I chose a warm golden roll stuffed with mushroom, chopped egg and *za'atar*. Then I sat on the sea wall, above a calmness of colourless water, awaiting that magical second when the first dazzling sliver of sun seems to rest on the horizon before swiftly becoming an orb. Several two-man fishing boats were approaching the harbour where, it is said, slaves unloaded cedars from Lebanon to build Solomon's temple. (Archaeologists can find no trace of this structure but we won't let that spoil the story.) Palestine's twenty-first-century land surface would be unrecognisable to those pharaonic troops who captured Yapu in 1468BC – yet every cloudless morning, if up early enough, they saw exactly what I was now seeing. Jaffa's antiquity over-excites the imagination and to me that link, spanning 3,476 years, seemed worthy of reverence. I've always been able to empathise with certain forms of sun-worshipping.

As I turned towards Tel Aviv devout men, mainly elderly, were leaving Jami'a al-Bahr. This Mosque of the Sea rises austerely above clustering trees, within spray-reach of the waves; close by is the much larger but now little used Armenian Church of St Nicolas. Behind rises an artificial hill, created half a century ago when tons of builders' rubble (the remains of Palestinian homes) were planted with grass and named the Sir Charles Clore Park in honour of a (selectively) philanthropic British Jew. It has since been renamed HaPisgah Gardens. Nearby, archaeologists have exposed traces of Egyptian, Greek and Roman activities. As Keith Whitelam explains, 'In the 1950s and 1960s archaeology became more than an amateur pastime, it was a national obsession . . . and helped to forge a sense of shared identity among a disparate population.'

On the beach I walked close to the water and met a few panting

joggers, a multitude of cats – often surrounded by kittens – and many
dog-walkers equipped with state-of-the-art harnesses and canine toys.
Not for nothing had *Newsweek* recently included Tel Aviv among its
Top-Ten Tech Cities. The cats and dogs ignored each other, a display
of tolerance not replicated when my own pack of terriers is being
exercised.

My Tel Aviv day had been planned around three introductions
provided by Eva, an Anglo-Jewish friend and supporter of Independent
Jewish Voices. This newish organisation hopes to counterbalance the
staunchly pro-Israel Board of Deputies of British Jews (founded in 1760)
by reminding gentiles that, in Eric Hobsbawm's words, 'There are Jews
who do not agree that the only good Jew is one who supports Israel.'

First on my list was Ruth, an impoverished Holocaust survivor who
had suggested 'coffee any time after ten'. Echiel, a Cairo-born Mizrahi
professor, was free at lunch time and Anna and David, an affluent
middle-aged Ashkenazi couple (both medical consultants), were able to
do 'drinks at sundown'.

Eva had told me Ruth's story. In 1937 she saw her parents being
taken away to what she later realised was a death-camp. As a seriously
emotionally damaged twenty-five-year-old she arrived in Israel from a
Displaced Persons' camp and soon married another survivor, even more
damaged; he hanged himself within a year of their daughter's birth. In
Eva's view, the challenge of single parenthood then 'reintegrated' Ruth.
Despite her late academic start she became a noted philologist, a satisfying
though financially unrewarding career. Meanwhile her daughter – reared
as a stalwart atheist – had been absorbed into a way-out Kabbalistic sect
which disapproved of earning so she couldn't afford the bus-fare from
Safed and hadn't visited her mother for years. There were shocking
reasons for Ruth's impoverishment. The German government had
provided an insulting US$3,500 as 'compensation' for six years in
Czestochowa labour camp; and she had never received her annual
'Reparations' pension. This should have been paid through the US-based
Conference on Jewish Material Claims Against Germany, a coalition of
potent Zionist organisations. For decades it had been deflecting many
millions from the rehabilitation of individual victims to the rehabilitation
of 'communities' – i.e., the coalition's cronies. In 2000 the German
government admitted that scarcely 15% of the funding allocated to Nazi
victims through the Claims Conference had reached those victims.

Tel Aviv, with its population of over a million, sprawls and my search for Ruth's flatlet took me far from the garish seafront playground and the shop-till-you-drop department stores to a Bauhaus neighbourhood mainly occupied by Falashas (Ethiopian Jews), Moroccans and labourers from the Far East on temporary visas. In the 1960s the city's celebrated Bauhaus buildings – more than 4,000 of them – were dwarfed by 'developments'; most are now failing to age gracefully, looking shoddy rather than mellow. The coast's moist, salt-laden air has left a sad percentage of the distinctive rounded balconies and massive 'portholes' cracked or crumbling. To gain space some bedsit residents (including Ruth) enclose their balconies in plastic screens.

Ruth was a woman of great dignity and quiet charm, physically shrunken but mentally effervescent. While the percolator bubbled we small-talked. Then, as we sipped our coffee, my hostess began to recall her first impressions of Israel and I understood why Eva had assured me that with her oldest friend (they had sustained one another through Czestochowa) I needn't 'watch my words'.

To many survivors their supposed 'homeland' offered rather a cool welcome; in official circles their past ordeals and present problems aroused limited concern. Ruth remembered being shocked and bewildered by the contempt expressed for those who had 'allowed themselves' to be exterminated – a contempt that seemed to rub off on the numerous boatloads of destitute 'stateless persons' only arriving in Israel because unwanted elsewhere. As Hasan had remarked the day before, most were unwilling colonists, not fervent Zionists. Ruth's parents had been among the many German Jews who preferred not to 'relocate' to Palestine during the 1930s. Others, known as 'Yekkes', did take advantage of the Jewish Agency's resettlement scheme, designed to fortify the Yishuv with immigrants' money and brains. 'That's why they scorned us,' said Ruth, 'when we became stateless. Our families weren't interested in regaining the Promised Land.' As she saw it, Germany's Jews had become so complacently assimilated they were able to blind themselves to the Nazi threat, to regard it as just another test of Jewish endurance, a crisis they could live through.

'You look puzzled,' observed Ruth. 'Let me tell you a story. Once upon a time – in 1743 – a fourteen-year-old boy arrived alone in Berlin. He had walked for five days from his home town. He was a hunchback with a stammer and no money. He couldn't read or write German. He spoke only Judendeutsch – a mix of medieval German and Hebrew, cruder than Yiddish. Very few Jews – the *rich* rich! – could then live in Berlin. The rest could stay no more than two days. Jews and cattle had to use the Rosenthal Gate. One of the 1743 entries in that gate-keeper's register says, "Today passed six oxen, seven swine and a Jew." Jews had to pay the same commodity tax as Polish oxen. In Berlin, Moses Mendelssohn found his former Talmudic teacher who had become a rabbi. Less than twenty years later Mendelssohn was an internationally honoured German philosopher, philologist and literary critic. Without realising it he'd sown the seeds of our emancipation. I was brought up on his story. My father said Mendelssohn laid the "assimilationist" foundation stone. Others might not give him all the credit. We shouldn't forget Frederick the Great, the first European ruler to state, officially, "All religions must be tolerated". Two centuries after young Moses passed through the Rosenthal Gate we felt more at ease in Germany than anywhere else – even New York! And the Zionists hated us for seeming more German than Jewish.'

Looking at things from the Palestinians' point of view (as she often did), Ruth saw an obvious resemblance between Hitler's determination to give his dictatorship a veneer of legality and one of the Israeli governments' favourite devices – a 'respectable' statute book. (I remembered Hasan's noting 'there are loopholes . . .') It's too easy to design 'respectable' laws that give only minimal protection to a victim population. Within 45 years (1948–1993) the Knesset put in place thirty statutes giving the State ownership of land, previously privately owned by Palestinians, to which no refugee, as a result, may return.

A long hot walk took me to Echiel's roomy bachelor flat, reminiscent of my grandfather's house where one had to move cautiously between stacks of books for which – we were assured – shelving would soon be provided. In the professorial kitchen, those spaces normally occupied by culinary items held scores of files, clearly labelled in Arabic, Hebrew, English and French.

We sat with our beers on a seventh-floor corner balcony overlooking on one side Tel Aviv's umbrella-strewn beach and on the other a dull expanse of three-storey, detached residences set in small, arid gardens. My host was olive-skinned and grey-haired, short and sturdy but prematurely stooped with a faintly American accent. Leaning sideways in a cane rocking-chair, he peered down at the street. 'Here we see a few obvious tourists but mostly Israelis. If you saw them in New York, London or Vienna, could you identify them as Jews?'

I also peered down and replied, 'Probably not.'

'*Certainly* not!' said the Professor. 'Don't you know half of us are Turks?'

I conceded that many years ago Arthur Koestler's *The Thirteenth Tribe* had planted that suspicion.

Echiel scowled. 'Koestler – too unstable! Why did he dodge his own researches' logical conclusion? Remember the Appendix? Where he wrote about "a century of peaceful Jewish immigration" and backed Israel's "right to exist" regardless of chromosomes. Seems he'd been intimidated. But why did that book cause such controversy in '76? The Khazars' blood donation was interesting but changed nothing. Common sense tells everyone the Wandering Jews' progeny are hybrids – how could they be otherwise? The "typical nose" of the caricaturists makes me laugh. It isn't found among true Semites like pure-bred Bedouin. It's found more among Amerindians and Mediterranean peoples than among Eastern European Jews. And it dominates among various Asia Minor tribes – Armenians, Georgians, Ossets and so on.'

When Echiel paused to open my second beer I tried to push our conversation towards contemporary events but keen hobby-horse riders prefer not to be reined in. Happily the Professor galloped on. 'Thorough-bred Israelites never existed. Only mongrels were bred at this crossroads. Consider the mix: tall blond Amorites, dark-skinned Mongoloid Hittites, negroid Cushites and who knows how many minorities . . . And none into selective breeding or monogamy. Our Prophets' rules about not marrying daughters of a strange god didn't restrain Israelite leaders. We're told Daddy Abraham took an Egyptian beauty to bed. Joseph married the daughter of an Egyptian priest. Moses married a Midianite, the great Jewish hero Samson was really a Philistine. The champion lecher King Solomon was the son of a Moabite Hittite. And now we know Jehovah himself had a missus called Asherah, a Canaanite fertility goddess. That discovery enraged quite a few. Israelites and Canaanites weren't meant to be sharing the same pagan polytheistic mindsets in the eighth century BC! So when did monotheism come on the scene? We're still arguing!'

Echiel habitually ate out and on our way to a restaurant I again tried to advance into the twentieth century. But my companion preferred to speculate about rape in ancient times. Did the Israelites incidentally condone it? They were forbidden to marry gentiles, with the exception of women captured in battle. And how many victorious warriors, wondered Echiel, would have formally proposed marriage to their nubile captives? 'Yet now half-educated journalists treat raping soldiers like some shocking novelty! Troops' payment-in-kind always included the right to rape. Cossacks who regularly imprisoned hundreds of Jews for ransom repeatedly raped. In the seventeenth century Poland's Jewish Council held a special meeting about half-Cossack babies – and there wasn't the stigma you'd expect. To keep communities together they were well treated.'

We sat at Echiel's usual corner table in a cramped, smoke-browned, thoroughly unrenovated restaurant in the Yemenite Quarter. Taking advantage of a menu-reading pause, I asked when Echiel's family had moved to Israel. While answering, my companion changed in tiny but telling ways – his body language, the timbre of his voice, the set of his jaw. Perhaps dwelling on the remote past – with an oddly forced frivolity – was more than a scholar's engaging obsession. It might well be an escape from the recent past.

Echiel's family came from one of the world's oldest recorded Jewish communities, in Cairo, which enjoyed a particularly good relationship with the Fatimid caliphate. Since the tenth century some families had consistently maintained complex international trading networks. 'We were globalising pioneers!' said Echiel. 'Then after the Nakba we were targeted. An exodus began when bombs killed 76 of our neighbours and maimed hundreds. Jews were also being attacked in Baghdad, Damascus, Alexandria, Sa'na. Ben-Gurion's lot blamed it *all* on Muslims. Mostly the terrorists remained unidentified but a Zionist input was only half-concealed. Murdering a few hundred Jews made sense to political Zionists when that sent tens of thousands to Israel with their money and talents. Some Mizrahi were very rich and very smart. And the poor were needed, as labourers, to replace Palestinians. My family stayed on till '53. Then Nasser played the Zionists' game by squaring up to capitalists. The main props of Egypt's economy – Jews, Italians, Greeks – uprooted and took their assets with them. Later my father made big mistakes and lost a lot. I did my masters in Canada and thought about staying there. But really I'm an *Arab*, a Jewish Arab. Why can't you have those as well as Christian Arabs? I was homesick and came back to my mother – very old now, living in the flat below mine. We still talk in Arabic. She got a good education in Cairo and likes helping me. I'm writing now about the Kaifeng Jews – very challenging! Along the Silk Road they set up a trading post in the early twelfth century.'

Now the professor was looking happier, back in the past. Innocently I asked, 'BC or AD?' 'You mock me!' said Echiel.

Later, standing by my bus stop, the professor spoke of Matteo Ricci, the seventeenth-century Jesuit missionary who studied the Kaifeng and noted the tolerance of their Chinese neighbours. But in time Confucianism eroded Judaism and miscegenation had its way. 'By the nineteenth century,' said Echiel, 'no Kaifeng could read the holy scrolls so they sold them. I don't know to whom – there's a lot of research needed. In Shanghai, after the Boxer Rebellion, a remnant hoped European Jewry might offer cultural resuscitation. But they looked Chinese and were accused of fraud. It's said they've vanished without trace but I don't believe that. The original group was so small they must have proselytised – maybe leaving records, given the Mandarin bureaucracy. Jews aren't associated with missionaries but we did have them, especially between Jerusalem's fall and Constantine's taking up Christianity. From around then you can date Saharan Berber Jews, Yemenite Jews, Ethiopian Jews – who most likely got their Judaism lite from Yemenis.'

As the No. 22 appeared I mentioned my 1967 trek through the Falashas' native mountains – eighteen years before Operation Moses, the famous airlift to Israel. Echiel shouted after the bus – 'Come back to finish that story!'

Towards sundown, seeking access to the medical consultants' flat (at the other end of the spectrum from Ruth's bedsit) I fumbled the electronics and attracted the wrath of a security guard armed as though on a battlefield. That apartment block houses several prominent politicians.

Anna and David were spontaneously friendly, witty and well-travelled, eager to advise the newcomer, intrigued by my way of life, quick to notice an empty glass. They deplored the military occupation of the West Bank ('unfortunate' was Anna's word, making her sound like Hillary Clinton) and considered the settlements 'a grave miscalculation' (David's phrase, making him sound like a professional diplomat). Yet our conversation soon became stilted. Clearly it would have been impolite to discuss or enquire about any seriously organised active opposition (however non-violent) to either the occupation or the settlements. Here was theoretical liberalism in the old-fashioned sense of that word. This kindly, intelligent couple, who donate to Independent Jewish Voices, seemed unable to empathise with Palestinians as individuals. The daily suffering of millions of men, women and children was perceived as a purely political problem, its moral dimension evaded. Just so do Rich-World leaders regularly grieve in public over the starving, the homeless and the diseased, while ruthlessly protecting an economic system largely responsible for Poor-World statistics. I declined an invitation to stay for dinner.

The No. 10 took me to Jaffa's promenade. Below the sea-wall is a narrow strip of sandy beach, approached over sharp rough rocks – not tourist-friendly. There merry groups of young Muslim women and their small children were immersing themselves in the warm, starlit sea, splashing, laughing, squealing but not swimming. The mothers were fully clothed, of Islamic necessity, so presumably they lived nearby.

Later I wrote in my journal:

Ruth and Echiel could I suppose be described as impotent dissidents. Anna and David should be able to contribute to change but only if they rocked their own boat. They can admit the Nakba happened but can't allow themselves to react emotionally to its consequences. Is this a big part of Israel's problem? The 'moderates' keeping their heads down . . . Rather proud of their moderate image on the international stage but avoiding the front line . . . I should've stayed to dinner and probed more. But I'm not an evening person and Echiel's pedagoguish outpourings are exhausting – because worth concentrating on. Where does racism come into it all? Anna and David share Ruth's cultural background and made sure I was aware of their ancestral links with a distinguished 'assimilated' coterie in 1920s Berlin. Naturally they disdain both crude political Zionism and fanatical super orthodoxy – while personally prospering in this expansionist and increasingly 'observant' State of Israel. Does that ambiguity ever keep them awake? And how would they get on with Echiel, the self-described 'Arab Jew'? At the end of my third day in this fraught little country I'm more than slightly flummoxed and with no hope of becoming less so.

CHAPTER 2

On a Kibbutz in the Negev

In Tel Aviv's central station, early on a Sunday morning, hundreds of conscripts were returning to their Be'er Sheva base on the edge of the Negev desert after Sabbath with the family. Almost everyone was smoking. Several girls pulled sleek swanky suitcases that ill-matched their heavy weapons. Some rucksacks were expensively comfortable but most (made in China) must have been hell to carry. Skullcapped youths with bad teeth and acne dragged battered kitbags and one couldn't but note the connection between skin colour and luggage quality.

Every seat had been taken when I boarded the Be'er Sheva train and a standing granny moved none of these youngsters to pity. Then a slim, spectacled civilian, carrying a worn briefcase and an armful of books, squeezed through the strap-hangers and said, 'Please to my seat, it waits for you.' Of course it wasn't waiting but my knight shouted something that quickly shifted the occupant.

Israel built fast and cheap during its first few decades and, gazing out, I remembered Jakov Lind's 1970s comment on this same journey: 'Within the last fifty years alchemists have transformed ordinary stone and sand outside the train window into innumerable towns and suburbs. Some more attractive than others. All of them dull.'

Beyond Jaffa's orange groves ochre ploughland merges into the level grey-brown Judean desert – a startling transition, within a mile, from fertility to barrenness.

Be'er Sheva (population 185,000) is mentioned half a dozen times in the Old Testament – its only distinction. Long before the New Testament was penned it had sunk into an obscurity from which the Ottomans failed to rescue it until the end of the nineteenth century. Then, as their administrative centre for the Negev, it acquired one notable building, a splendid Governor's mansion. When General Allenby's cavalrymen arrived in October 1917 it was a large village, mainly Bedouin. In 1948 it was captured again, after an Israel versus Egypt battle. Since the 1960s it has become Israel's fourth-largest city, a dusty, dishevelled place raised in such a hurry no one could spare the time to tidy up. Many millions of dollars have bred an industrial park dominated by Intel. And development continues; on every side cranes swing across the hot blue sky, dangling their cargoes of prefab slabs. While waiting for the kibbutz bus I ambled aimlessly; there is nothing to aim for, apart from the Negev Palmach Brigade Memorial, celebrating that 1948 conquest.

Outside the railway station one immediately registers a multi-racial population. Tall, aloof Bedouin men, gracefully robed, are followed by veiled, black-gowned women. In the humdrum 'native' market flashes of gold bracelets may be glimpsed as a wife's hand emerges to receive a carrier-bag while husband pays. The handsome Falashas from highland Ethiopia couldn't possibly be mistaken for Africans from anywhere else. The Russians are no less numerous but to identify them one has to stand around, listening. The Moroccans are quite distinctive; newcomers find other Mizrahis indistinguishable.

En route to the kibbutz the only traffic signs said: 'Beware of Camels Near Road'. A needless warning: the few dejected specimens were picketed beside improvised hovels on those meagre patches of desert to which the Bedouin have long been restricted. Granted, camels never look jolly but they can look stately; it saddened me to see such pathetic last links with a tradition stretching back several thousand years. Then I recalled that the Sabatean traders' hundreds of camels, loaded with spices and silks, were tended by slaves – and that put a brake on my romanticising. Later, Mohammad's all-conquering army consisted mainly of warriors mounted on camels bred for speed.

Our bus had shed its silent Bedouin passengers before the kibbutz appeared, defiantly green amidst the Negev's monochrome aridity. The three kibbutzniks, youngish women occupying front seats, had snubbed me in a stony way unrelated to the language barrier – my first indication that members' guests, though tolerated, are rarely made to feel welcome. Most Kibbutzniks wish to live apart from 'ordinary' life, quietly doing their own thing.

Beside an electronic gate in a high, wire security fence stood an empty sentry-box. When the driver demanded 'ID!' I showed my passport and mentioned my hostess's name. He grunted and nodded, then watched until Irina had loaded my rucksack onto her bicycle. She led me along bougainvillaea-bright paths linking small villas and maisonettes, and low blocks of flats and roomy bungalows – all dispersed in a pleasingly unplanned way and surrounded by lawns and flower-beds. Schoolchildren were coming from every direction, walking or cycling home to lunch – lucky children, free of adult escorts. Irina shouted angrily at litter-droppers, ordering them to bin the offensive scraps. Most obeyed her, muttering and pouting but not disputing the elder's authority. When I remarked on the blissful lack of motor traffic Irina explained that private cars are *verboten*. In emergencies, or on special occasions, a few elderly self-drive vehicles are available for the cost of the petrol.

This was one of three illegal kibbutzim set up in the summer of 1943 to determine the region's potential for supporting an influx of penniless post-war immigrants. After the Warsaw Ghetto uprising, details of the Holocaust began to filter through and simultaneously it seemed Rommel's army might at any moment come rumbling across the Negev. To avoid British restrictions, the Jewish National Fund described such kibbutzim as 'climate survey bases' or 'agricultural research stations'. As a new member, in 1948 Irina had been thrilled by some of the pioneers' stirring tales.

We passed several communal buildings and, feigning naivety, I asked, 'Where's the synagogue?' My companion couldn't have bristled more if I'd asked, 'Where's the brothel?' For secular Zionists, making the desert bloom was exaltation enough. When I commented on the numerous *kipas*, Irina testily conceded that by now this kibbutz's secular ethos had been seriously eroded. Deviant members attend a synagogue in another place. That brought to mind Musa's assertion – 'Religion is not the problem. Land ownership is the problem.'

Irina's flat overlooked an expanse of arable land and miles of regimented olive trees. From my guest-room window I could see a low ridge where the standard 'tower and stockade', the original kibbutz building dating from 1943–44, is now listed as one of Israel's numerous 'Nostalgia Museums'.

Most kibbutz farms, explained Irina, are three-pronged: field crops, livestock, orchards. During the 1960s mini-industries were introduced in the larger kibbutzim but 'our factory closed last year, was too little to compete with the biggies'. Also, the more labour-intensive crops (peaches and soft fruit) had recently been given up because 'today's kids won't do boring jobs'. By now the hiring of imported labour (mainly Thai) has undermined kibbutzic principles.

At that point I felt sorry for my hostess. The daughter of 'survivors', she grew up in an English-speaking country, then backpacked around the world before making *aliyah* and choosing the kibbutz way of life. She agreed with Reuven Cohen who wrote, 'The formation of worker-based enterprises is a first stage in the take-over of the economy from private capital and its transfer to the working-class.' His movement, though averse to Soviet communism, had something in common with Cuba's Castroism, practising the communal ownership of assets and the equal distribution of profits. As always in Israel, there were tangled roots. The rich Diaspora Zionists (not enthusiastic socialists) sustained the Jewish National Fund which bought the kibbutzim lands. During the 1980s kibbutzic principles became an embarrassing anachronism to Israel's free-marketeering generations. But disappointment had not corroded Irina's integrity. In her personal life she remained a stalwart, old-fashioned anti-consumerist.

A kibbutz report, translated by Irina, listed the current population: 322 adult members, 195 children, 28 IDF security guards, 32 students being prepared for military service, 75 new immigrants (candidates for membership) and 16 hired Thai labourers living in dreary barracks built more than sixty years ago when the stockade was bombed. Newcomers are tested for a year before members vote, in a secret ballot, on their acceptability. A few of those elected subsequently fail to conform and, for lack of any ousting mechanism, this can generate dissension, usually muted. In such an isolated, introverted community open faction-fighting must at all costs be avoided.

When I began to fantasise about our politicians studying the technique for muting dissension Irina reminded me that 'democracies' need faction-fighting (aka 'party politics'). I listened with astonishment to her version of Israel's birth, having not yet realised that most Israelis never question Zionism's supremely skilful propaganda. However even on neutral ground I wouldn't have argued. Experience has taught me (in Northern Ireland, inner-city Bradford, Apartheid South Africa, post-genocide Rwanda) that when people are frightened, challenging their prejudices tends to limit rather than extend one's own understanding. The fearful cling to prejudices as to a life-raft and arguing with them can be unkind. For positive developments to occur, their leaders must change course.

Against Irina's advice, I planned to set off for the stockade early next morning. She begged me to keep far away from the fence and never to leave the kibbutz, even were I to come upon an open tractor gate – a most unlikely event. I asked, 'Are there dangerous animals out there?' Irina nodded. 'Yes – known as Bedouin!' On my return we would tour 'the amenities'; she was giving herself a day off though this meant she must work an extra hour a day for a week. Even elderly members are scrupulous about their labour input.

At dawn the desert silence was fractured only by military jets on their way to fly low over Gaza or the West Bank, terrorising children, shattering windows and damaging ear-drums. After sunrise two young men on antique tractors jolted along rough tracks and I noted evidence of decline all around: weedy fields, blocked irrigation channels, collapsed damlets, scour-afflicted calves and bony cows. A dairy herd is impractical when tons of hay must come from beyond the desert. Even the fence was being neglected; twice I came upon stretches where child-sized holes had been cut in dense rolls of razor-wire. As I climbed the rocky ridge there was no one in sight – until suddenly a man appeared some fifty yards away, pointing a rifle at me. Seconds later I identified him as an effigy of a Palmach fighter, wearing 1940s combat gear and defending a trench.

Faded, typed information sheets, in Hebrew and English, are nailed to each door of this carefully restored tower-and-stockade. The original groundbreakers, from the Yishuv's Labour Youth Movement, worked with Germans and Italians who had arrived in Palestine as children before September 1939. Naturally they knew nothing of the Negev and an academic agronomist, who couldn't tell a spade from a shovel, supervised the sowing of their first grain crop on unirrigated land. Its failure was instructive. Meanwhile the watchtower was being built, above a quadrangle of small rooms with firing-slits (trimly curtained) instead of windows. I had my own nostalgic moment in the kitchen/living-room where everything, from primus stove to double-boiler to hand-mincer, might have come from my childhood home. In the Heath Robinson shower room another effigy provided light relief; in the crucially important communications room telegraphic equipment, once cunningly hidden from British eyes, is now on display beside the essential carrier-pigeon bands. Everyone slept in tents until May 1948 when Egyptian strafing forced them into an elaborate Nabatean cave system below the tower. Some 2,000 years ago this was a water reservoir; the Nabateans knew more about water management than most twenty-first-century hydrologists. Another cave, the ammunition store, now holds a selection of weapons illegally acquired by the Pachmac when Israel's future leaders were being described as (and behaving like) terrorists. The study is furnished with ink bottles and steel pens. Here, in August 1948, Avraham Klasky wrote:

> At first the landscape was strange and the land seemed as if it had been asleep for thousands of years. It had the charm of creation. The Biblical stories about the wanderings of our patriarchs became illuminatingly clear . . . We had the feeling of satisfaction of people who are settling a new land but also the thought and awareness that in the Negev we will create vibrant Jewish life . . . The expression which best fits this feeling is the wonderful Biblical verse in its simple truth: 'Give me a blessing for you have given me the land of the Negev'. We have no doubt the Negev will one day be the bread basket of Israel.

Around the same time Ben-Gurion was having a vision:

> I can state that the pipeline which was placed in the Negev is not only one of our great projects for which we take great pride, but is also the single most basic thing for our ability to survive and defend the Negev . . . Its defence, however, is not similar to the defence of any other region. We will not be able to defend it if we do not give it what it now lacks – Jews, many Jews. Jews who are armed with machine guns, mortars, rifles, grenades, armoured vehicles, tanks – also ploughs, shovels and pruning hooks . . .

The average annual rainfall (100 mm) thwarted Ben-Gurion's agricultural ambitions but his military daydream has come true. The Negev is now a military zone extending over some 50% of Israel's land mass.

Standing on the tower's roof one can see the residential area, marked by immensely tall palms. And one can imagine the pioneers' adrenalin rush as they were challenged by the enigmatic Negev and threatened in turn by the British, the Germans and the Egyptians, while having to rely on carrier pigeons in crises and to acquire weapons furtively. Unsurprisingly, they never doubted their 'right to return'. No one had told them that the Negev then provided a homeland and a livelihood for 140,000 Bedouin.

In the late '60s and early '70s quite a few of my friends went kibbutzing, another way of dropping out for those uninterested in the hippy trail to Kathmandu. They returned tanned and happy, proud to have contributed to such an egalitarian enterprise, unaware of the kibbutzim militants' role before and during the Nakba. At the centenary celebrations for Deganie, the first kibbutz, President Shimon Peres (himself a former kibbutznik) recalled how much the movement had achieved in 'building the land, defining and defending its borders . . .'

Few of the almost half a million international volunteers noticed that only Jews can become kibbutz members, as distinct from temporary guest-workers. Even the most secular kibbutzim, stuffed with atheists, cannot accept non-Jews. The gentile wife of a kibbutznik might pass all tests and be elected – but that's not enough. She must attend one of the conversion schools maintained by the Israeli Chief Rabbinate and be formally converted – a long process which includes, for a woman, being viewed naked in a purifying bath by three rabbis. This ritual prompts some oblique ribaldry in the Hebrew media but was little known, internationally, until 1999. Then it was mentioned, as an example of the growing influence of Jewish fundamentalism, by Israel Shahak (a Bergen-Belsen survivor) and Norton Mezvinsky (a Jewish-American history professor). They added, 'We need not emphasise the wide discussion that would ensue if a British or American institution allowed Jews to become members only if they converted to Christianity.'

A minority of volunteers did see what was going on behind the jolly, egalitarian façade. On my return to Ireland I had a letter from one of Eva's nephews, the grandson of Russians who still spoke Yiddish thirty years after settling in Manchester. Joseph wrote:

In the early '60s I did a hitch-hiking holiday in Israel staying and working in Kibbutzim. Near the Gaza Strip I remember having to walk quite a way as it was Friday night and the buses had stopped running. I met an Italian chap who invited me to stay in his closer kibbutz. The lights were twinkling in the distance and as we approached the entrance the notes of a Chopin nocturne floated towards us on the warm breeze from the children's block. So this was my 'idealist' introduction which was to be somewhat shaken a few days later when, during an evening socialising in the house of a kibbutznik who had lost a leg in the '48 war, I was shown a map of

Palestine and it was pointed out that much of the West Bank would eventually be part of Israel. Insights such as this convinced me that Israel wasn't a country for me to settle in though I would have been assured a good career.

Below the stockade, café tables stood under date palms smuggled from Iraq and Iran when the pioneers were masquerading as climate surveyors. Those trees caused another disappointment; the Negev's cold nights rendered them fruitless. Here Irina joined me, pedalling staidly on her thirty-year-old bicycle, an admirably solid machine looking ready for the next thirty. She had borrowed the key of a small Visitors' Centre where we watched a video of the kibbutz's development. Nowadays few visitors appear, apart from schoolchildren on brainwashing excursions.

At the 'Children's Zoo Corner', at breakfast time, a squat, swarthy keeper, wearing overalls and wellies, was affectionately addressing individual animals while distributing lavish helpings of the appropriate sustenance. Here were donkeys, Shetland-type ponies, long-bearded goats, camels, warthogs, baboons, ibex (two of each). All looked healthy and as content as imprisonment allows. Inevitably I thought of the nearby Bedouin who never enjoy equivalent meals: a thought not shared with Irina.

Sweat was flowing (mine, not Irina's) during our herb-scented walk to the long, low, vine-draped school, now under-populated and not visited by us because foreigners, being so rare, allegedly over-stimulate the pupils. Further on, we relaxed in the three-roomed kindergarten, set in a large playground. The happy toddlers and babies, ranging from pink-cheeked Ashkenazis to extraordinarily beautiful Falashas, were being imaginatively entertained, and gently disciplined when necessary, by four cheerful young women – all kibbutz-born and uninterested in the world beyond Be'er Sheva. I commended the washable nappies and the sensibly few wooden toys. Irina tended to linger among the babies; a long-time widow, she was impatiently awaiting grandchildren.

This was not one of the kibbutzim recently shamed by revelations about child sex abuse, from which Judaism is no more immune than Christianity. That said, Israel has never – so far as is known – sunk to the level of depravity common for generations in Roman Catholic Ireland. There offenders were 'protected' from our police by order of the Vatican.

The privatisation of many kibbutzim has, notoriously, pauperised some elderly members. But here, in a new and thoughtfully designed Leisure Centre, retired kibbutzniks were playing chess and cards, brooding over crossword puzzles and jigsaws, sipping coffee and nibbling buns, exchanging knitting patterns and developing artistic talents hitherto unsuspected. Everyone looked Ashkenazi and Irina remarked that culturally disparate members sometimes find integration difficult.

In the circular, glass-walled dining-hall above the theatre, we lunched at a table for four overlooking a gable end of the immensely long cattle-shed. Our companions – arthritic sisters – at once reminded me that millions of 'displaced persons' were homeless at the end of what my generation still quaintly describes as 'the war'. Because Jews had suffered most 'we deserved to get a *nation* of our own'. In 1939 two of their relatives, having been refused immigration certificates to Palestine, secured a passage on the *St Louis*. For months those 937 refugees desperately sought asylum, being rejected by every country until Holland relented. As Jakov Lind observed thirty-five years later:

> While no one talks about it, everyone knows that 'Amerikke' did not want the Jews Hitler wanted to get rid of. When the world refused the Jews in 1939, Hitler had the world's silent majority of Gentiles on his side.

Some members choose to take away their evening meals and others habitually cook at home. The sisters remembered the old days when, at unifying communal meals, kibbutzniks discussed further development possibilities. Irina shrugged and said bleakly, 'So now we're *not* developing.' The menu seemed symbolic: varied but based on processed foods (apart from the excellent salads) and free of Arab influence.

Outside in the midday sun I began to fret about my beer supply. Obligingly, Irina led me to the simple grocery store which opens five days a week between 1.00 to 3.00 p.m. Alas! it was beerless; seemingly that potation is associated with an undignified way of life. But in a far, untidy corner I excavated two bottles of barely drinkable wine. Kibbutzniks tend to discourage, without actually forbidding, most forms of alcohol and the Moroccans are reviled for (among other things) their centuries-old addiction to *mahya*, a peculiarly potent Maghreb brandy.

Nearby, in a sweltering, hangar-like laundry, women of all ages, shapes and pigmentations were wrestling with industrial-sized washing-

machines, sweating over ironing-boards, patching and darning, striving
to reunite pairs of socks, sorting and folding garments to be stacked on
neatly name-labelled shelves. Irina assured me that all kibbutzniks take
on such unpopular jobs in rotation and for comparatively short periods.
Her turn was coming.

We strolled then through an olive plantation covering many acres
where new-style harvesting had begun, each tree being seized and shaken
by a nasty little petrol-fuelled machine. Showers of olives pattered onto
plastic sheets for transport in a low trailer to the kibbutz oil factory. The
foreman was a burly, blue-eyed, bearded member, the six hired labourers
were Gaza Palestinians whose lack of a work-permit went unnoticed
because it drastically lowered their wages. When I greeted them
with 'Salaam alaikum' they beamed but Irina wordlessly registered
disapproval.

Our tour ended on the southern border of the kibbutz in a secluded,
pine-enclosed cemetery, its symmetrical rows of gravestones unadorned.
In the oldest graves lie pioneers killed on the ridge in '48 and Palmach-
niks who, in Avrham Klasky's words, 'came to fight for the Negev and
signed a pact in blood'.

In Tel Aviv Ruth had given me an introduction to Daniel, a colleague of
hers now retired and living in Be'er Sheva. His grandson Amos met the
kibbutz bus – chubby-faced, mousy haired, rather serious. Against the
morning desert chill he wore a quilted jacket over a sweater and my T-
shirt and bare arms worried him. On our way to his little car, lovingly
polished but severely dented, he told me the recession had stymied his
plan to backpack around India, as thousands of Israelis do at the end
of their army stint. He couldn't decide what to read at Ben-Gurion
University. 'I need a break to get myself sorted after too long in Hebron.'
Months later I grasped the full significance of that remark.

Following a wide busy road we seemed to be leaving the city; then I
realised that it consists of a few tenuously linked towns separated by
patches of littered desert. The 1950s 'fast-housing' estates, first occupied
by immigrants from Displaced Persons camps, next sheltered Ethiopians
and now Russians have moved in. Approaching a more affluent district,
the Yitzhak Reger Boulevard, Amos said, 'This is a détour, you must see
something you can't see anywhere else in the world!'

Politely I didn't laugh at this colossal extravaganza of tin, glass and brownish Chinese granite – the last to match the adjacent desert. Salo Hershman designed Payis Performing Arts Centre more than twenty years ago as a 'psycho-architectural experiment' part-funded by Israel's national lottery. White-hot controversies slowed construction but when it was opened, a few weeks before my visit, the Municipality Manager assured a small crowd that 'the centre will underscore the city's place on the national and international cultural map and its success will spur momentum in other areas'.

Payis covers 9,000 square metres and has two 900-seat concert halls and a 420-seat theatre. The bill came to 145 million shekels (about 30 million euros) and 8 million shekels will be the minimum annual maintenance costs. (Be'er Sheva is not a rich city.) The cost far exceeded the original estimate and I could smell a nest of rats; my homeland is permanently overrun by similar rodents. Optical illusions promote the 'psycho' component. The main auditorium emulates the Tower of Pisa 'to create a reverse effect of a sloped stage' and already visitors were complaining that this illusion made them feel dizzy and nauseous. In the shiny-tiled foyer a looking-glass ceiling brought back to me another criminally wasteful development, Rostov's new railway station. Outside it, free-market-stricken Russian pensioners huddle in corners, begging for alms; not far from Payis, hungry Bedouin huddle in cardboard shacks. Amos however was immensely proud of his city's aberration. He had grown up during the long years of conflict and saw Hershman's victory as a triumph for Israeli originality.

In a red-roofed block encircled by date palms Daniel shared a ground-floor flat with Amos and his widowed mother. She worked as a physio-therapist at the nearby Soroka Centre; his army officer father had been killed during the second Intifada by a Palestinian sniper.

Immediately I took to Daniel, a vigorous Polish-born octogenarian with an Einstein hairstyle, lively blue eyes, a strong chin and a kind smile. To him Hebrew's revival as a spoken language was Zionism's greatest achievement; without it Israel would have lacked coherence and validity as a united nation. Being an Irishwoman I knew exactly what he meant. In fact, Daniel emphasised, Hebrew never died as a written language though it had ceased to be commonly spoken before Christ was born. From the tenth century AD to the 1490s the Iberian peninsula's Jews studied both Hebrew and Aramaic religious texts and spoke Arabic. But Hebrew remained their literary language, which probably accounted for the nineteenth-century Ashkenazi impulse to revive spoken Hebrew; it frustrated them that their pronunciation made it impossible to appreciate the rhythms of medieval Hebrew poetry. However, most revivalists came to accept the Sephardic pronunciation. When the infant Daniel arrived in Jaffa in 1926, less than 20% of settlers had learned Hebrew, yet a 1938 census showed 79% claiming it as their first language.

According to Maimonides, the illustrious twelfth-century philosopher and rabbi, 'Anyone who knows Hebrew, Aramaic and Arabic, knows they are only three branches of the same language.' Maimonides wrote his major works in Arabic, with one exception, and theologians of all three monotheistic faiths studied and debated those books. ('God be with the good days!' as we say in Ireland when reflecting on happier times.)

Back home, I re-read a relevant passage from Barnaby Rogerson's *The Prophet Muhammad*:

> We know from archaeology that there were at least four distinct lettered languages in existence in ancient southern Arabia and at least four in the north. Among the more famous of these northern languages are Aramaic and Hebrew. Both of these influential tongues seem to have been formed at about the same time, around 1200 BC, by nomadic tribes migrating out of the Arabian desert into the fertile crescent. In the Hellenistic period Aramaic had emerged as the language of the street throughout the Middle East . . . However, all of these tongues, despite centuries of official and literary use, would ultimately be eclipsed by the unwritten speech of the desert . . . By the fourth century AD Arabic was understood across the length and breadth of Arabia.

One of those lettered languages has bequeathed us the Gezer calendar, dating from the tenth century BC and proving, said Daniel, that for at least three millennia Jewish culture has been rooted in Hebrew and Aramaic religious texts. He went on to mourn the death of Yiddish, the *lingua franca* of most East European Jews – ultra-orthodox or secular, Kabbalistic or Communist, rich or poor. During the nineteenth century, a vivid, distinctive Yiddish culture had evolved – then been extinguished by the Holocaust. Its embers glowed briefly in what Daniel described as 'those shameful Displaced Persons camps' where a few newspapers were produced by the more resilient survivors. Sadly Yiddish was cruelly discouraged in Israel. Ben-Gurion ordered the newcomers to learn Hebrew at once and forget both their origins and their sufferings. Addressing an assembly of Labour Zionists, he voiced popular sentiments:

> Among the survivors of the German camps were people who would not have been alive were they not what they were – hard, mean and selfish – and what they have been through erased every remaining good quality from them.

Reviewing the new state's first decade, Dina Porat, an Israeli historian, wrote:

> In the absence of education, research, art forms, and human dialogue on the subject of the Holocaust, concern for the murdered European Jews seems to have been limited to formal state declarations tailored to fit the needs of Zionist ideology.

When Daniel asked if my travels had taken me to Poland I boasted of having attended, as an observer, the momentous 1981 Gdansk Solidarity congress. Moreover, I was privileged to meet Marek Edelman, one of the heroes of the Warsaw Ghetto uprising, and talk with him for an hour. The mention of that famous name transformed my host. Daniel, so civilised and endearing while discussing Hebrew's revival, was now glaring angrily at me – but why? Could it be because I admired a Jew who had stayed on and prospered in Poland? Gripping the arms of his chair, Daniel leant forward to rant, his old voice croaking and wavering with rage.

'In '39 we were nearly four million in Poland! By '45 most had been murdered and their murderers had Jewish collaborators!'

Not only had Edelman stayed on – in 2002 he publicly and powerfully protested against Israel's show trial of Marwan Barghouti, one of the Palestinians' few valuable leaders.

'He's a traitor,' continued Daniel. 'He wrote an open letter praising Arabs who're trying to finish the Nazis' job!'

The fanaticism fuelling Daniel's rage scared me and was totally unexpected, cancelling what had felt like a burgeoning friendship.

Amos appeared in the doorway, looking anxiously at his agitated granddad. I stood up, very ready to go, and offered a goodbye handshake. Daniel ignored my hand and in Hebrew said something short and sharp.

On our way back to the bus station Amos asked, 'What went wrong?' I tried to explain but he interrupted me on hearing Edelman's name. 'Why did you want to meet that snake? Mossad should have got him fifty years ago!'

We completed our journey in silence.

Later I reproved myself for not having argued quietly with Amos, presenting my version of Marek Edelman. I remember him as a singularly inspiring representative of humanist Judaism. As an adolescent he had joined the Jewish anti-Zionist Socialist Bund, as an octogenarian he proved his moral consistency by defending Marwan Barghouti. In the decades between, his skill as an innovative heart surgeon saved many lives and, when I met him, he was among Solidarity's most energetic and influential supporters. Ever since I've been grateful for that memorable hour; ordinary people need such encounters with extraordinary people.

CHAPTER 3

A View from Jerusalem

Leaving the dull coastal plain, intensively cultivated, a busy road coils up and up into the Judean hills. Jerusalem has been a pilgrim-magnet for some 1600 years, ever since its Christians nobbled a Roman emperor's mother, and on the bus I envied those millions who rode donkeys from Jaffa to the Holy Places, stopping off at Ramleh, Emmaus and Arimathea. One fifteenth-century Englishman, William Wey, wrote a guidebook urging pilgrims to dismount and walk beside their donkeys on the steepest stretches, through territory 'mountainous, rocky and very depressing'. Until the British took over from the Ottomans Jerusalem remained hard to reach. Even a century ago the Romans would have recognised these hills, now ravaged by a network of noisy highways on stilts and an urban sprawl that might be anywhere.

My seat companion was a slim, pale, long-skirted girl, her hair contained within a mob-cap; she never raised her eyes from a small, well-worn religious text. Across the aisle sat (I deduced) her bearded father and brother, their ear-locks shoulder length. The bus was crowded but silent; Israelis in transit are not gregarious. As the road climbed, large blue and white bilingual (Hebrew and English) signs proliferated, some names familiar because infamous: Ma'ale Adumim, Beitar Illit, Pisgot Zefay, Har Homa – all illegal settlements built on the sites of Palestinian villages razed during the Nakba, though most settlers are unaware of this.

As we approached West Jerusalem something baffling appeared in the distance – far higher than any visible building – semi-circular, strangely radiant, both massive and delicate. Five minutes later it was identifiable as a suspension bridge, without apparent purpose – not joining A to B though all around streams of vehicles sped hither and thither on a muddle of dual carriageways. Its sheer irrationality, dominating a main entrance to Jerusalem, seemed a useful allegory. Soon I learned that it is known as the Bridge of Strings or the Bridge to Nowhere and is Santiago Calatrava's contribution to Jerusalem's light rail project – but someone miscalculated and in fact the railway doesn't need it. During my stay in the city, Nir Barkat was elected mayor and decided to hold an all-

Jerusalem contest – who could give this construction a purpose in life? The inauguration ceremony (costing millions) was itself a test of ingenuity: how to inaugurate a bridge leading from nowhere to nowhere? That occasion proved a decisive factor in Mayor Barkat's election victory. The Municipality, then Haredim-run, outraged thousands of seculars and moderate-Orthodox by insisting on a troupe of teenage girl dancers covering their hair. This focused attention on an alarming statistic: one-third of Jerusalem's Jews are now fast-breeding Haredim. At once the secular Barkat, aged 49 and a self-made millionaire, began to overtake his Haredim rival, Meir Porush, in the opinion polls.

The light rail project is designed to reinforce Israel's version of apartheid by linking the settlements surrounding Jerusalem to the city centre. It will also, if fully developed, link those settlements with others yet to be built, illegally, in the Jordan Valley. In 2006, the Irish-Palestinian Solidarity group successfully blocked the training of Israeli drivers and engineers on the Dart, Dublin's light railway, as part of the Boycott, Divestment and Sanctions campaign.

From the central bus station, incorporated in a three-storey shopping mall, a No. 21 took me along the Jaffa Road, in times past Jerusalem's Main Street. At the first stop I watched white-hatted men in orange and yellow jackets standing around a giant digger loudly quarrelling and gesticulating. The nearby drilling made toddlers whimper and bury their faces in maternal bosoms. Gazing into a deep chasm, I fretted about possible damage to precious artefacts – perhaps even to traces of Jebusite walls? But no, anything Jebusite would be much further down.

At another stop, beyond stacked railway lines, a long, handsome stone arcade, once part of a thriving Ottoman market, was being renovated for sale to 'dual citizens' – US Zionists, many of whom fancy themselves as Israeli property-owners. A towering SAIDOFF billboard proclaimed 'Your Luxury residence in new Old Jerusalem'. Usually public inform-ation, including the destinations on bus and train tickets, comes in Hebrew only. Next morning, walking past at 6.30, I applauded the nocturnal protester who had spray-painted the billboard – FUCK THIS FASCIST SYSTEM. Two hours later the first word had been blotted out but the rest remained. All Jews, whatever their origin or circum-stances, are entitled to Israeli citizenship. Not one displaced Palestinian has been allowed to return to his/her ancestral homeland.

Where the Jaffa Road became impassable a short détour took us to Mamilla, one of the city's many contentious districts. Its new developments culminate in a glitzy shopping mall ('our Bond Street' said an Israeli acquaintance unfamiliar with London) that seems to insult the Old City walls, constructed under Suleyman the Magnificent between 1537 and 1542.

It's a mistake to first enter the Old City by the Jaffa Gate; at once one is exposed to mass tourism. But not for long: when I turned left at the end of David Street most of the 'guided tour' zone was behind me. The many pairs of heavily armed police or soldiers who stood or patrolled near the main junctions were unhelpful when asked for directions. Hasan had recommended a hostel in the Muslim Quarter and without his sketch map I could never have found its low, narrow, arched doorway – unmarked by any sign.

Sari greeted me in fluent English – a tall, white-robed elderly man, lean, handsome and short-bearded. His centuries-old hostel (there are Mamluk vestiges) is inconveniently attractive with few windows, domed moulded ceilings and awkwardly twisting steep stone stairs, foot-worn in the middle. To gain a licence, certain dissonant modernisations had been unavoidable, like tiling the shower-room. Above the 16-person mixed dorms, four single cubicles had been jerry-built on the wide roof, where laundry was done and guests could relax. We were requested to be nice to Sari's obese tabby tom who spent his days on the roof; at night he sought comfort in a dorm and quickly identified me as a willing bed-mate.

The low-ceilinged ground-floor cafeteria, furnished with three computers, offered chips and omelette or rice and omelette. During the day, while guests were out sightseeing, Sari's friends gathered here to drink coffee, smoke *narghiles*, play backgammon and talk with their host, evidently a man of some influence. My attempts to converse with the English-speakers among them at first aroused some suspicion. East Jerusalem's atmosphere is permanently tense; paid informers, native or foreign, abound. When Sari decided to probe me we had a long tête-à-tête in his family quarters and after that I was accepted.

Mixed dorms in the Muslim Quarter had surprised me but Sari was pragmatic. Born into an old Jerusalem family in 1958, he remembered the Six-Day War *feeling* longer than six days though his neighbourhood escaped the worst of it. 'Afterwards I wasn't traumatised, didn't notice

much difference between Jordanian rule and Israeli occupation.' But his
father had lost a well-paid government job and soon the nine-year-old,
who had four younger siblings, was being despatched every day after
school to sell his mother's home-made sweets outside the central bus
station. In 1980 he migrated and spent 13 years in Switzerland. When I
asked, 'Doing what?' he slid away to another subject – my political
attitude, of which he disapproved. In his view, when Jews returned to
their Promised Land – promised by Allah through Abraham – they were
only doing what Allah wanted them to do. 'All would be fine if they'd
treated us justly, given us fair shares, let us go on praying at places sacred
to both. And didn't try to destroy evidence that Jerusalem was mostly
Muslim for 1400 years.' Repeatedly Sari used the words 'justice' and
'dignity'. Quietly he insisted that for decades the Zionists had been
doing as much damage ('spiritual damage') to themselves as to the
Palestinians. 'I don't know much about history,' he added. 'I never read
books – only *the* Book! That's all we need, to read and heed the word of
Allah! By trusting him, everything will get to be OK even if it's getting
to look worse in our lifetime . . .'

I felt a spasm of impatience. In old age I'm increasingly exasperated
by those who pass the buck to God. Yet I was moved by Sari's summing
up: 'Jerusalem is where Heaven and Earth meet. Angels are here –
everybody's angels – Jews', Christians', Muslims'.' His sentiment
reminded me of a pathetic letter written in 1918 to Sir Ronald Storrs,
Palestine's Interim Military Governor. It was signed by more than a
hundred leaders of Jerusalem's Muslim and Christian communities,
representing thousands of ordinary citizens. In part it read:

We have noticed yesterday a large crowd of Jews carrying banners
and overrunning the streets . . . They pretend with open voice that
Palestine is now a national home for them. How do the Jews expect
Palestine to be a national home when the Muslims and Christians
never asked that it should be a national home for those of them
who are not inhabitants of Palestine? . . . We Arabs, Muslim and
Christian, have always sympathised profoundly with the persecuted
Jews and their misfortunes in other countries as much as we sympathised with the Armenians and other weaker nations. We hoped
for their deliverance and prosperity. But there is a wide difference
between this and accepting such a nation in our country ruling over

us and disposing of our affairs . . . We expect that a power like Great
Britain well known for justice and progress will put a stop to the
Zionists' cry . . . In conclusion, we Muslims and Christians desire to
live with our brothers, the Jews of Palestine, in peace and happiness
and with equal rights. Our privileges are theirs, and their duties ours.

If only Britain had taken this letter seriously, considering all
its implications. The Balfour Declaration, made only a few months
previously, wasn't written in indelible ink. Nor did its weasel words
guarantee British support for the displacement of 'existing non-Jewish
communities in Palestine'.

The Holy Land held no particular attraction for Theodor Herzl. Few
of the early political Zionists were religious and they took for granted the
separation of church (or synagogue) and state. Yet at the second Zionist
Congress, when Herzl proposed Uganda as a more promising land,
agriculturally, than Palestine, the delegates were outraged and he had
to forget alternatives or lose his leadership position. As an influential
journalist (Paris correspondent for a Viennese 'heavy') Herzl was so
comfortably assimilated that before the Dreyfus affair he had considered
going over to Christianity. Jerusalem he found tiresome, with its miasma
of religious connotations. Following a visit in 1898 he confided to his
diary: 'When I remember thee in days to come, O Jerusalem, it will not
be with pleasure.' He visualised the future Land of Israel as a 'bulwark
against Asia, serving as a guardian of culture against barbarism'. Semi-
Oriental Jerusalem blurred this vision and it disconcerted him to find
political Zionism regarded as near-blasphemy in the Jewish Quarter.
Decades later, when national-religious Zionism had evolved, many new
Yishuv rabbis preached that God had willed the State of Israel into
existence, thus signalling the start of the Jewish people's promised
redemption. The euphoric atmosphere after the Six-Day War conquest
of East Jerusalem nourished this illusion and soon it was clear that Israel's
'unified capital' would be a source of grief and conflict for the foreseeable
future. Both Diaspora Zionists and Israelis invest lavishly in 'renovation'
schemes which intrude on the Muslims' Holy Places, and those
desecrations provoke civil disorder and occasional suicide bombings.

Long before contemporary politics, Jerusalem's hallowed ground had
been notorious for bringing out the worst in human nature. Today six

Christian sects compete for control of their Holy Places – quite often coming to blows, needing to be separated by Israeli riot police. It's all peculiarly disedifying yet an expanding global tourist industry lures more and more ecstatic pilgrims to the Holy City – people who are swept along on a wave of religiosity that some observers find downright unhealthy. Usually I'm susceptible to ancient sacred places; their emanations can soothe and fortify, whatever the cultural background. But Zionism's physical and emotional violence has polluted Jerusalem, as once the Crusaders' rule must have done. To me the city now feels sick rather than sacred, its energies soured.

As an antidote to the fractious church of the Holy Sepulchre, where I witnessed Christian clergy of various denominations competing for the shekels of tourist groups, I recommend the Crusader-built Chapel/Mosque of the Ascension, on the Mount of Olives. Most tour operators ignore it so the door may be closed but a holy man (possibly Christian, possibly Muslim) will quickly respond to your ring. This small, octagonal sanctuary, dimly lit and pleasingly austere, originally formed part of a fortified monastery; the dome and mihrab were added after Saladin's liberation of Jerusalem. Muslims believe that from here Jesus ascended to heaven. A cheerful old man, wearing a snow-white beard and a trailing black turban, quoted the Koran – 'Behold! God said: O Jesus, I will take thee and raise thee to Myself . . .' He showed me a vaguely oval depression in the stone floor: Jesus's last earthly footprint. In this mosque, on three days every year, Mass is celebrated and over the past eight centuries there is no record of dissension between the two faiths.

As I was leaving, my guide pointed towards a small crypt hardly visible to passers-by and long predating the Crusades. Within lay the bones of (some say) a tenth-century Bedouin woman saint, Rabia al-Badayiya. In the fourteenth century Ibn Battuta became involved in a prolonged controversy about the true identity of these bones (or this dust). A Mesopotamian faction backed a Muslim woman mystic who died in Basra in 801AD. A Jewish faction backed the prophetess Huldah (see 2 Kings 22). Jerusalem's Christians backed St Pelagius, the sensible fifth-century monk who denied original sin and so got into big trouble and gave his name to a heresy. Now, said my guide, there are ominous rumours about DNA tests. He whispered this, as though speaking aloud might make the sacrilege more likely.

Throughout this whole area graveyard buffs can gorge themselves, beginning with three monumental tombs from Hellenistic and Roman times. Absolom's Pillar is none the less impressive for being a fake dating from the first century BC, hundreds of years after King David's disloyal son died. Nearby are two columns with Hebrew-inscribed Doric capitals, honouring a renowned family of Jewish priests, the Bene Hezir. And only yards away is the tomb of Zechariah (second century BC) with a remarkable pyramidal roof. Its survival in such good condition on such an over-used battlefield seems almost miraculous.

Since ancient times burial in the Kedron Valley has been desirable if you can somehow squeeze in. Many believe the upper part to be the Yehoshaphat Valley, where the Day of Judgement is to happen on a date not yet decided. The lower part provided my favourite bit of touristic Jerusalem: King Hezekiah's tunnel and the pool of Shiloah. As the Assyrians approached his fortress, the King of Judah ordered a 1700-foot tunnel to be hewn through solid rock to carry water from the Gihon spring to the pool of Shiloah – lest there might be a siege. As is usual in Israel, too much has been done to make this 'experience' tourist-friendly. Yet for half an hour or so you do have to slosh through water a foot deep and you can still stroke the original tunnel walls and feel in touch with Hezekiah's slaves. The Assyrians arrived as expected and surrounded Jerusalem. Then suddenly they retreated – because of Yahweh's intervention, said the Israelites. Historians assume a plague hit them; Assyrians didn't normally do retreats. My only subterranean companions – a bronzed Boston couple wearing wet-suits and headlamps – took the Israelite view.

I walked up the valley towards Silwan, through a much-vandalised Muslim cemetery where sheep grazed between the graves, tugging at minuscule weeds and sampling discarded milk cartons. A skinny little shepherd stared at me with mingled apprehension and hostility. On the motor road far above I counted 44 parked coaches; their contents were panting around the Mount of Olives which may fairly be described as a Biblical theme park. Higher still, a vast Jewish cemetery, dating from the first millennium BC, is too well protected to be vandalised. It had recently been made neat (Americanised) and the new road around its edges – of course closed to Palestinians – benefited nearby illegal settlements.

My faint sheep's path led to a broken concrete wall through which one could easily scramble. And then I was in a shameful slum, deliberately created by a rich government.

> Israel has failed properly to maintain Arab East Jerusalem . . . while nearby the government has built beautiful new Jewish neighbourhoods to encourage Jews from Israel and around the world to move onto land expropriated from Arabs . . . It has forced many of them from their homes, all the while lying to them and deceiving them and the world about its honourable intentions. And what makes all this so much more inexcusable is that there was no reason for it. Governing Jerusalem properly would not have jeopardised Israel's claim to the city. Indeed, it likely would have eased the growing conflict over Jerusalem's future.

Those words come from the final page of *Separate and Unequal: The Inside Story of Israeli Rule in East Jerusalem*. The authors are a retired Israeli army colonel, a journalist with the conservative *Jerusalem Post* and an Adviser on Arab Affairs to Ehud Olmert. Their book was published in 1999. Seven years later Meir Margalit's *Discrimination in the Heart of the Holy City* reported that Palestinians then made up 33% of the population and were allowed 12% of the welfare budget, 15% of the education budget, 1.2% of the culture and arts budget and 8% of engineering services.

Beyond the wall I was on a steep, narrow street of ramshackle two-storey houses. There was no one in sight. Slowly I walked uphill, with broken glass underfoot, passing smelly piles of household refuse. Around the first corner – a hairpin bend – half-a-dozen men were animatedly discussing an aged car missing one wheel. My arrival silenced them; their expressions showed more hostility than curiosity. Then a middle-aged woman appeared in her doorway and sharply questioned me. I apologised for speaking only English and hastily displayed my passport to avoid being mistaken for a compatriot of Tony Blair. Interestingly, that lessened the tension, though not enough for me to be welcomed. The woman retreated, slamming her door. The men turned back to the moribund car. As I walked on five small boys gathered at a corner, the sort who might be expected to beg from a tourist. Instead, as I drew near they took refuge amidst mounds of rubble.

It surprised me to meet so few people, given Silwan's population; then my ears registered an exciting televised soccer match. Perhaps that was fortunate. Near the site of three recently demolished homes several youths came running towards me, shouting angrily and making 'get lost!' gestures. Soon after I did get lost, briefly, amidst a maze of pathways between the clumsily built houses that perch on Silwan's rocky outcrop. From here one has a heart-stopping view, across the Kidron Valley, of the golden Dome of the Rock which for most people will always symbolise 'Jerusalem' – to the Zionists' fury. Political Zionism is chillingly consistent. In 1897 Herzl told the First Zionist Conference, 'If I ever take control of Jerusalem I will take away all the holy places except the Jewish ones.'

During both Intifadas Silwan's enraged residents bit off their noses to spite their faces, destroying anything associated with the hated municipality – water mains, sewage pipes, lamp posts, public buses, ambulances. Council employees arriving to unblock sewage manholes were stoned, likewise electricity repair teams. The police then chose Silwan to test new items of riot gear. Small wonder I was not made to feel welcome.

Next day I learned that in high-tension zones strangers need to wear some insignia identifying them with a pro-Palestinian group. Otherwise they may be suspected of mere vulgar curiosity or even of wishing to witness for themselves the Palestinians' humiliation.

On my way down I skirted the settlers' area where a towering block of flats, faced with golden stone, looks tauntingly affluent amidst the prevailing squalor. It is draped with an Israeli flag at least two yards long and five yards wide. By 2008 more than seventy settler families had forced their way into Silwan homes or demolished them and built on their sites. Long, drawn-out and hugely expensive court cases have established that most seizures were/are illegal, according to *Israeli* law. Yet the government arrogantly backs the settlers, making a nonsense of Israel's claim to be a Western-style democracy. In Silwan, Sheikh Jarrah and elsewhere, armed groups conducting preparatory nocturnal operations (e.g., terrorising families to reduce resistance) are protected by paramilitary Border Police, the most feared of all Israel's security forces.

In this district I was conscious of being on an academic battlefield where the main weapons are biblical interpretations and archaeological facts (or the lack of them). Allegedly Silwan is built over part of the City of David to which Zionism attaches particular significance. The well-endowed settler cabal which began to invade Silwan in the early

1990s is known as ELAD, the Hebrew acronym for the City of David. Shockingly, all responsibility for the local archaeological sites has been ceded to ELAD by the Israeli Antiquities Authority (IAA), despite anguished and sustained protests from several of Israel's most respected archaeologists. Perhaps (a charitable explanation) the IAA fears ELAD, whose potentially lethal thugs dominate both the new excavations and the Archaeological Garden's Visitor Centre.

In Jerusalem, professional archaeologists have found little or no trace of David's 'empire' despite a century of dogged digging. It seems the Israelites did not after all compete successfully with the Great Powers of their time. Stimulated by this, and by significant shifts in approaches to the text of the Hebrew Bible, certain brave scholars have recently been treating Palestinian history as something with its own validity rather than as an offshoot of biblical studies. The 'shifts' in question have provoked much hitting below the belt as every nuance of every word is debated. 'Politics is everywhere', as Edward Said dryly observed, yet most mainstream biblical scholars persistently deny the political element in their construction of Palestine's past. They do not like Keith W. Whitelam who wrote in the mid-1990s:

> The discourse of biblical studies has imagined an ancient Israelite state that is remarkably similar in many aspects to the modern state. What is striking are the recurrent themes, images and phrases which appear throughout this discourse from the 1920s to the present day: the Davidic monarchy as the defining moment in the history of the region, the existence of a Davidic empire to rival other imperial powers in the ancient world, the defensive nature of David's state, the paradox of the alien nature of the monarchy to Israel, and Israel as a nation set apart from surrounding nations . . . It is necessary to trace the discourse of biblical studies in relation to the invention of an Israelite 'empire' in the context of the Zionist agitation for and eventual realisation of a modern state of Israel.

The transition from the rest of the Old City to the subdued Jewish Quarter needs no street signs to mark it. Here the four-storey buildings are taller than the Old City norm, the trendy shop façades and interiors contrast pointedly with the souk's caverns, the narrow laneways and symmetrical cut-stone stairways are garbage-free, hanging flower-baskets replace sagging overhead cables and the residents are homogenous.

When the Company for the Development and Reconstruction of the Jewish Quarter expelled the Muslims and Christians after the Six-Day War they were forbidden to return: this 'Jews-only' development is an early example of Israeli-style apartheid. Originally it was intended to house an Ashkenazi elite but they soon moved out, not relishing the lack of parking space and the nearness of all those *muezzins* calling five times a day starting at 4.30 a.m. Their replacements represent a new breed, outwardly conventional ultra-Orthodox but including some alarming recent immigrants – fundamentalist Jews, their accents American, their mission to advance West Bank settlements. Such people have been gaining influence in Jerusalem's municipal council and also in the Knesset; Israel's parliamentary system leaves the main parties much too dependent on destabilising splinter groups. Significantly, I never saw tourists being led through the residential streets; they would be unwelcome beyond the areas excavated and rebuilt to attract them.

The neat, narrow, silent Street of the Chain overlooks the Western Wall esplanade. This wall, built by King Herod, is regarded as the last vestige of the Second Temple, destroyed by the Romans in 71 AD. In 1487 the Italian traveller, Obadiah da Bertinero, wrote of the 'large, thick stones such as I have never seen before in an old building, either in Rome or in any other city'. Yet it became of interest to Jews only when, during the construction of the present city walls in the 1530s, Suleyman issued an edict permitting them to make it a special place of prayer. Soon the centre of their religious life had been transferred from the Mount of Olives to what was known for many centuries thereafter as the Wailing Wall. When the irreligious Herzl first visited Jerusalem in 1898, he deplored 'the craven attitudes of worshippers clinging to stones and the superstitious custom of thrusting written prayers between those stones'. Tel Aviv, not Jerusalem, was to represent the Zionists' new Judaism.

Having passed through an airport-like security barrier, one descends on a wide, stone stairway shadowed by the dour bulk of the Yeshiva HaKotel. Old photographs show that this stairway obscures a high rock wall, a cliff the Romans (or Christ) might have looked upon. Here I remembered the night in 1967 when the 700-year-old Moroccan district's 150 families were given three hours to leave their homes. In darkness, Mayor Teddy Kollek supervised army bulldozers quickly clearing the space before the Western Wall for use as an open-air

synagogue (men this way, women that). Afterwards, Major-General
Chaim Herzog bragged, 'We hadn't been authorised by anyone and we
didn't seek authorisation.' As Jeremy Bowen noted, 'They were worried
that if they did not act decisively it would become politically impossible
to knock down the houses of so many civilians'.

About one third of the esplanade is cordoned off as a strictly segregated
prayer area, always a busy scene, and thronged at special times. Now it is
overlooked from two sides by aggressively opulent buildings, purpose-
fully out of tune with the Old City's heritage and funded by named
Diaspora Zionists (e.g., COLEL CHABAD – free kitchen for the needy
– sponsored by the Luxenmerg Family, NY). More painful still is the
area's militarisation – rows of armoured vehicles parked behind high,
angular steel barriers appropriate to an army camp in enemy territory
rather than to a place of prayer. Later, I was to discover that the Wailing
Wall's Zionist ambience grievously offends the sensibilities of those
visiting Jews who truly value Jerusalem's significance.

On the esplanade I observed a moment of wordless hostility between
a trio of *yeshiva* students in their early twenties (beards enable an age
estimate) and a pair of loutish on-duty conscripts. The latter were
lounging in a conspicuous spot, close to a 'No Smoking' notice, defiantly
lighting cigarettes. When they blew smoke towards the students, while
exchanging amused comments, one Haredi youth made an impulsive
move towards them but was restrained by his companions.

In 1952 Rabbi Avraham Yeshayahu Karelitz talked Ben-Gurion into
exempting *yeshiva* students from all military service and granting their
large families generous child allowances. At that date the Haredim were
an insignificant minority but by 2008 63,000 men didn't have to earn a
living. As Torah students they received a monthly stipend of NIS720,
plus child allowances, boosted by gifts from the Diaspora. Secular Israelis
condemn this anomaly and were pleased to see Diaspora subsidies shrivel
in the heat of the US credit crisis. Then they were displeased to hear
Haredim leaders insisting that 'Israel's survival needs Torah study, therefore tax-payers must make up for the Diaspora's betrayal'. It is frequently
and forcefully pointed out that those scholars could continue to study
the Torah in their spare time at the end of an honest day's work. But the
Haredim are represented in the Knesset by tiny but tough parties which
wield disproportionate influence when a big party needs support.

CHAPTER 4

Odd Laws in a Divided City

A small advertisement in *The Jerusalem Post* said 'Peace Now invites you to get to know what's happening behind the headlines! Meet at 9.00 a.m. tomorrow outside the Crown Plaza Hotel'. Clever wording, I thought, likely to lure curious outsiders who had never heard of Peace Now but felt 'peace' was a good idea.

The Crown Plaza, almost opposite the central bus station, is among Jerusalem's tallest buildings and has no nearby rival. But its planners disregarded walkers' needs and its entrance proved ridiculously difficult to find. Eventually I strayed into an empty car park giving access to a low-rise annex draped with blue and white banners emblazoned 'G.A.' The United Jewish Communities were holding their General Assembly – a great occasion, as 2,500 delegates gathered from all over North America. There wasn't a security guard in sight but no doubt electronic eyes were everywhere.

By 8.50 I was alone on a charmless concrete terrace outside the main entrance. Sitting under a gnarled, pollarded fig tree, I opened my *Jerusalem Post* and read that the GA meets annually 'to discuss Israeli-diaspora relations'. In his welcoming address Mayor Barkat had noted: 'Every Jew in the world is a shareholder of Jerusalem . . . We must not accept the fact that this is the poorest city in the country. We must work hard to make it rich in industry, culture and jobs.'

I remained alone until 9.15 when two elderly women arrived, heavily made-up and not well-disposed towards gentile tourists – delegates to the GA, I later gathered. Then the coach appeared and gradually filled up with an intriguing mix of limping, American *olim*, keenly pro-Palestinian Internationals, agency workers (mainly Scandinavian), journalists (German and Australian), a middle-aged Canadian and his young American colleague (both sociologists) and two serious-minded backpackers born in Egypt but carrying British passports. The Canadian, Rafi, sat beside me and didn't like what he was hearing from Monika, our guide. He was on his first visit to Israel and knew nothing of Peace Now's origin or ethos.

Monika was small and sinewy, ginger-haired and freckled, intense and humourless. She introduced herself by mentioning that when the Oslo Accords were signed her platoon had to watch the ceremony on TV and 'As kids we saw hope then – soon gone! After I'd served a bit more at checkpoints it looked like the settlements were bad for Israel. At university I joined Peace Now.' She was brave, I reckoned, to take on this busload of unknowns whose political predilections and prejudices might not easily coalesce. Carefully she chose her words, using 'non-Jewish Israeli' instead of Israeli Arab, avoiding Samaria and Judea and 'occupied territory', leaving political parties nameless, identifiable only by their policies and referring to the Apartheid Barrier as 'our most troublesome security idea'. For the numerous aborted 'peace processes' she blamed all leaders equally, which drew some muttered protests. Monika frowned at the mutterers: she had already made it plain that this was not to become a 'discussion group'. We were there to listen, our tour was an initiation into the mysteries of the settlement project.

The civilian occupation of the West Bank, based on the Allon Plan, began in the hot depths of the Jordan Valley immediately after the Six-Day War in 1967. Yigal Allon, then chairman of the Ministerial Committee on Settlements, had an ambition to strengthen Israel's defences by redrawing the border to include the Jordan Valley and Judean desert. His strategic plan, though never openly government-approved, determined settlement locations until 1977. Monika sketched its outlines without quoting its central message: 'Maximum security and maximum territory for Israel, with a minimum number of Arabs'. Allon saw the planting of 'a Jewish presence' as the first step towards annexation.

Only Israel-registered vehicles with yellow number plates may use the settlers' roads and our circular tour showed how effectively the settlements have cut East Jerusalem off from its natural hinterland while almost bisecting the West Bank. We didn't stop to stare, merely cruised around viewing the green lawns, swimming pools, shade trees, flowering shrubs – all made possible, Monika explained, by the diversion of most of the area's limited water supply away from Palestinian villages, fields and orchards. We avoided all 'outposts' where an unarmoured ('enemy') vehicle might well have been stoned or worse. Monika wanted to show us two industrial areas (Mishor Adumin and Binyamin) but we were refused entry at both checkpoints. Many secular/moderate settlers are unnerved by the ever-increasing tension which also reduces the value of their property. Monika believed that such people (her parents among them) would gladly return to Israel if adequately compensated. A generation ago government subsidies induced many non-observant Jews to exchange shabby homes in an overcrowded, under-resourced, dusty city for new houses on an airy, well-watered hilltop. Some well-off urban dwellers bought sites and built for themselves. Some ultra-Orthodox families claimed to have bought sites but the relevant documents proved to be forgeries. That however could not be held against them by the authorities – themselves responsible for the whole illegal project. Peace Now excoriated the government's complacent admission that it has been consistently contravening its own law, clearly established in a 1979 landmark case in the Israeli High Court of Justice. Monika emphasised that the territories conquered in '67 were never annexed (apart from East Jerusalem) but left with the 'spoils of war' status, a crucial fact easily overlooked. For more than forty years those 'spoils' have been ruled, in theory, through the laws of the State of Israel.

Here our guide again repeated that all Peace Now's information is obtained from the Israel Civil Administration, the government agency responsible for settlements. According to their own data, almost 40% of appropriated land is/was privately owned by Palestinians who collectively own the other 60%.

Monika corrected the current image of settlers as a uniform sub-culture of surly, racist, trigger-happy religious freaks. Those nurtured by Gush Emunim ('Bloc of Faithful', founded in 1974) do indeed blend messianistic maunderings with shrewdly calculated territorial expansionism. This bloc, self-described as a 'national-religious' organis-ation, has leant hard on successive governments to sponsor more and more settlements in the mountains, close to Palestinian cities and villages. Quite different are the seculars living just beyond the pre-'67 border known as the Green Line. Some of those 'community settle-ments' faintly resemble kibbutzim; would-be residents are vetted and their ideological leanings and degree of religious observance (if any) are regularly monitored. But there the resemblance ends. Such hard-working citizens are card-carrying members of the consumer society (often carrying several cards, which has led here as elsewhere to destabilising personal debts). Our tour was planned, said Monika, around these 'garden suburbs', designed to serve as dorm-towns for

Jerusalem and Tel Aviv. ('Dorm-town' has to be one of the twentieth century's dreariest innovations.)

A rough unpaved cul-de-sac led to our only stop, Nabi Samuel, on a barren 2,500-foot hilltop some four miles east of Jerusalem. Here, in the sixth century, the Emperor Justinian built a mini-monastery over the Prophet Samuel's putative tomb. Within a few centuries this monument was being equally revered by Jews and Muslims – until the Crusader tyrants forbade Jewish pilgrimages and erected a church. Saladin's regime encouraged the building of a synagogue and in the eighteenth century the church was converted to a mosque. Adjacent synagogues and mosques could cause prolonged petty squabbles, as when Muslims campaigned to have Jerusalem's very beautiful thirteenth-century Ramban Synagogue closed down because loud praying distracted worshippers in the next-door al-Umari Mosque. For decades, in that case, the *qadi*'s judgement favoured the Jews; but in 1587 the Ramban was permanently sealed, leaving its small congregation to store their scrolls at home and pray privately. Nabi Samuel provoked similar tensions with a different out-come. Although Jewish pilgrims tended to scorn gentile pilgrims, the local *qadi* always backed the Jews.

From this hilltop the Crusaders first saw Jerusalem and therefore named it 'Mount of Joy' before galloping down to slaughter Jerusalemites on an industrial scale. By 1192 the Europeans' luck had turned, to the great benefit of everybody else. Richard the Lionheart's Third Crusade waited a long time on the Mount of Joy for essential reinforcements that never turned up. The Crusaders were about to lose their state. As Karen Armstrong writes:

> There were Franks in Jerusalem who realised, like many Israelis today, that their kingdom could not survive as a Western ghetto in the Near East. They must establish normal relations with the surrounding Muslim world. But the Crusaders' religion of hatred was ingrained: on one occasion they attacked their sole ally in the Islamic world and also turned venomously on one another. The religion of hatred does not work; it so easily becomes self-destructive.

This hilltop's strategic relationship to Jerusalem made bloodshed inevitable during the First World War and again in '48 and '67. The Six-Day War sent most Palestinians fleeing into Jordan from dwellings that for generations had been clustered around the mosque. When the village's total demolition took place in 1971 those remaining (200 or so) were 'relocated' to a hamlet that at first sight seems abandoned. Then I noticed two new houses at the edge and associated them with the IDF's masts – gigantic constructions, visible from the Old City walls. Until 1986 this isolated community had to buy water from far away; both their springs had been requisitioned for the benefit of Ramot, a nearby settlement. All building is forbidden; Nabi Samuel is not even allowed to maintain its tracks and pathways. Nor may its inhabitants use personal cars; they must walk to the main road, then take a taxi. The Apartheid Barrier now cuts them off from 90% of their land and Monika told us the surrounding area (*part of the West Bank*) had just been set aside for development as a 'National Park' to be run by *Israel's* tourist authority.

Our bus parked beside the only other vehicle on the hilltop, a West Jerusalem taxi whose five Haredim passengers, wrapped in prayer-shawls, were ambling towards the tomb, quietly chanting. Despite contemporary animosities, it moved me in a strange way to see them here, linking us to beliefs and rituals predating both Jesus and Mohammad.

Soldiers with fingers on triggers flanked the turnstile through which we slowly shuffled, one by one, being checked by a policewoman with a long equine face and large clumsy hands. As on the Wailing Wall esplanade, I resented the 'spirit of place' being obliterated by militarism while slick security devices diminished the dignity of this half-ruined mosque. Within the fence, we loitered on a causeway overlooking recent excavations. In the 1990s, when archaeologists arrived to dig below the razed village, they found a second-century BC Hasmonean public building, a Byzantine winepress, a block of Crusader stables, a Mamluk iron foundry and much else. For reasons Monika wouldn't disclose, a stroll through these widespread treasures was not possible.

At one end of the ruin, close to Samuel's large white tomb, the Haredim were vigorously rocking to and fro, intoning fervent prayers. Monika led us away from them, up the minaret's steep spiral stairway of worn stone. From this height, on a clear day, much of the West Bank is visible, mile after undulating mile of brownish (in November) Occupied territory. Ramallah's expanding suburbs smudged the horizon and Monika drew our attention to the Apartheid Barrier 'protecting' various settlements. The extent to which Palestinian villages are entrapped and deprived of their farmland was so evident that involuntarily my fists clenched. Monika pointed west and south to Har Ha'dar and Giv'at Ze'ev, and to Ramot and Ramat Shlomo just beyond Jerusalem's municipal border. Much closer – almost within earshot – was the hi-tech industrial estate of Har Hotzvim, offering no jobs to Palestinian manual workers. More than 220,000 settlers now live on this confiscated land.

As I stood by the parapet, scribbling notes, a tall thin man, silver-haired and slightly stooped, paused beside me. He had noticed my passport and spoke with an agreeably soft Boston accent. 'Irish journalist? Learning a lot today? Hard to believe . . . We've a good mentor, well practised but a bit selective. Better she'd allow questions to liven things up.'

I opined that given a heterogeneous busload and a contentious theme, things could quickly get too lively. Jeff shrugged, then introduced himself as an opponent of AIPAC, the American Israel Public Affairs Committee, the most powerful pro-Israel lobbying group in the States, 'here to research the nutters'. He peered over the parapet – 'Like that bunch down there, never raising their eyes to acknowledge other sorts of humans. I figure Israel needs to recalibrate them – has to. And has to have a new government. Can't go on with a prime minister heading to jail for corruption – or so I hope. You wonder what the GA delegates use to dull their pain . . . since childhood cheering Israel on, now looking at a country whose President is charged with rape and a lot more besides and whose prime minister has sticky fingers in Diaspora purses . . .'

I found myself defending Israel. 'At least dirty linen is washed in public, discussed in the media, maybe even punished in the courts.'

'Sure, but the traces of democracy are getting fainter. And the courts are reliable like a torn mosquito net.'

At which point Monika summoned us back to the bus.

Our driver was an East Jerusalemite and at the checkpoint below Nabi Samuel an insolent young soldier chose to relieve his boredom at our expense. Slowly and suspiciously he examined the driver's ID card, before getting into a long argument with Monika who obviously had not wanted our tour to be so true to (Palestinian) life. We were made to pull over for twenty minutes while two adolescents, male and female, came on board to scrutinise everyone's papers. Meanwhile their officer sat in a hut beside the watchtower, ostensibly establishing the validity of the driver's blue card. Monika, her anger not quite concealed, tried to keep up an informative flow but was repeatedly interrupted by indignant objections to 'this stupid delay'. Even more up-scuttling, from her point of view, were pertinent questions from two Swedish Internationals.

'Why has Hillary Clinton called the PA "the Palestinians' only legitimate government"? Didn't Hamas win the democratic election in January '06?'

'Why did the Quartet call it "a terrorist organisation" after it won most votes?'

This is the sort of challenge Peace Now finds distasteful. One simply does not discuss Hamas.

Discipline was breaking down. On the way back Jeff questioned Monika about recent violence germane to her theme. In a Jabal al-Mukabber *yeshiva*, where young men train to become religious settlers, eight had been killed and thirty-five injured by a solo Palestinian gunman. Then ultra-Orthodox settlers attacked Palestinian homes and businesses; next day the police apologised for being 'unable to get there in time'. A few weeks later, as part-revenge for the *yeshiva* murders, a fifty-one-year-old father of nine was stabbed in the back on his way to work. Five other fatal stabbings followed. Monika admitted that Israeli police do not rush to protect Palestinians.

When we had left the bus Jeff commented, 'It's only amazing there isn't more killing. But there will be. What does it do to young men to see their homes and lands taken from them week after week, year after year – while they can only stand around, watching . . .'

I nodded, remembering my clenched fists on the mosque roof.

Next day, drinking beer with my new friend Jeff in the seclusion of the American Colony Hotel's refreshingly green garden, I learned much about Israel's US support groups. Best known are the GA, AIPAC, the United Jewish Communities, the Birthright Israel International and the Anti-Defamation League. When the Swiss government did a €20 billion energy deal with Iran the latter could afford a half-page advertisement in the *International Herald Tribune*:

> Hezbollah and Hamas may get tens of thousands of additional missiles. The Iranian regime will be able to accelerate and complete its nuclear program. Terrorist cells in Europe, the Middle East and around the world will have access to new weapons and support.

Said Jeff, 'As we speak, the Israel lobby will be weeding its few opponents out of Obama's new administration. This year Jews voted Democrat by about four to one and most of the lobbyists are funded by liberal Jews. But on big Israeli issues they'll always manoeuvre with Republicans. I want people to understand the lobbyists don't represent most American Jews. It only looks that way, they're so fast on their feet.'

'And so rich,' I said.

Jeff's face hardened. 'Annually, 600,000 individuals each donate anything from one hundred to five million dollars. Donors asking how their money's spent hear it's not earmarked but helps many needy projects. A big minority would kick against subsidising settlements – especially outposts, banned even by Israel. Gush Emunim defies official US policy so the Jewish Agency must work hard to keep donations tax-free. They've gone through a bureaucratic hell to shift their Settlement Department to the World Zionist Organisation (WZO). On paper this looks fine, on the ground the same individuals spend those dollars on the same projects – wearing another uniform!'

Jeff looked at his watch, then had to hurry away to keep an appointment with a Yiddish speaker in Mea She'arim, the ultra-Orthodox district of Jerusalem.

On the hostel roof, where I often talked with Sari's English-speaking friends, one young man provided a footnote to my Peace Now tour. 'Did you meet the spies?' he asked. 'Mossad's helpers live at Nabi Samuel, trying to get tourists to hire them for guiding.'

When I looked blank Mustapha explained; those new houses on the hamlet's edge belong to collaborators who dare not sleep in their homes. At night they move to a flat in Ramot, the nearest settlement. Puzzled, I asked, 'What's the point of spies if their job is known?'

Mustapha smiled sourly. 'It's a way of intimidation. People knowing someone is always watching have no calm. Israelis are wanting those people gone, trying to make every day so bad they go. For a Nature Park they want to bulldoze Nabi Samuel, al-Qubeibeh and al-Jib. My father's parents ran from Nabi Samuel in '67. They came to Jerusalem for medicines my grandmother couldn't get when the IDF made our village a prison.'

Conversations on the roof could be harrowing, all the more so for people's sufferings being understated. It bothered me that most men weren't outwardly angry, but seemed resigned to being bullied for the foreseeable future. Sari had indicated that in general East Jerusalemites chose to distance themselves from the OPT's resistance fighters. Seemingly the second Intifada – the merciless suicide bombing and Israel's over-reaction to it – had engendered a below-the-surface despair. In 2008 things were comparatively quiet again; the bombers had realised their murdering of civilians was counterproductive, the tourists were back. Yet the average East Jerusalemite remained exposed to a police-state routine of humiliating, relentless, low-key repression. Inevitably this erodes self-confidence, as it is meant to do. These harsh restrictions also affect OPT residents needing hospital treatment unavailable at home; they cannot visit Jerusalem without hard-to-get permits.

Palestinians born in East Jerusalem, of families rooted there for generations, are in an irrational category, one of many contrived by the Israelis. They are 'immigrants with permanent residence status'. (Immigrants from where?) Despite annexation, those persons are rendered stateless, denied the rights to citizenship, to a passport, to a vote in national elections. East Jerusalemites who need to work or study abroad lose their blue card if they cannot afford to return annually to renew it. Once lost, it's irretrievable and that individual can *never* return to his/her homeland. The government may then seize the 'absentee's' property, left unoccupied by the owner because he/she has not been allowed to return. Yet Zionism's 'Law of Return' gives all Jews from everywhere Israeli citizenship, with few questions asked about *how* Jewish they are. What percentage of the 1990s Russian influx was genuinely dedicated to either Judaism or Zionism? We do know that a high percentage were uncircumcised – to the vocal horror of various rabbis.

Zionists have nightmares about 'the demographics'; will Jews be in a minority in Israel by 2020? Hence the 2003 'Citizenship and Entry Act', preventing non-Jewish spouses from entering Israel – where one-fifth of the population is non-Jewish! If an 'immigrant' marries an OPT resident the couple must live apart, or the Jerusalemite must move and forfeit his/her blue card – or both must risk severe punishments.

The aptly named Educational Bookshop on Saladin Street is the scene of monthly literary 'events' and Arabic film showings. There I first met Shaul, a volunteer worker with B'Tselem, Israel's foremost human rights organisation. On the telephone he had described himself as 'skinny and bald', leading me to expect someone of mature years. In fact he was young and energetic, small and olive-skinned, with a receding hairline. His parents, who made *aliyah* from Miami before he was born, deplored his activism. After several coffees (Saladin Street is in a 'dry' zone), he proposed a tour of East Jerusalem on the morrow, ending in Sheikh Jarrah where friends of his ran a rudimentary medical centre provided in 1993 by the Jerusalem Foundation. This group's foreign donors usually fund only Jewish projects but Mayor Kollek had persuaded them to spare a little for Arabs – 'in Israel's interest'.

We met at the Damascus Gate and on the Nablus Road passed a long queue outside the dreaded Ministry of the Interior. There Palestinians of all ages and states of health must stand for many hours (or sit on the ground) while waiting to obtain residence cards, travel permits (necessary even for the twenty-minute journeys to Ramallah or Bethlehem) and those numerous other documents designed to make their personal and business lives a misery. Shaul hoped the system might soon be changed; a case against the East Jerusalem Ministry of the Interior was being taken to the High Court. This office was open for only four hours from 8.00 a.m., to serve a daily average of 200 people. Some had to queue for days. Shaul didn't doubt the under-staffing was deliberate.

In Obeida Street we paused to salute the fabled Orient House, the Husseini family's dignified mansion – now all shuttered and padlocked and drab. Built in 1897, it saw many historic meetings and occasions, starting with an Ottoman tea party for Kaiser Wilhelm II in 1898 and including conversion to a 'palace' when Haile Selassie held court here in 1936–37 during the Italian occupation of Ethiopia. Shaul was momentarily overawed when I recalled standing within ten yards of the minuscule emperor in 1967 (a few weeks before the Six-Day War) as he quelled a student riot in Addis Ababa – not by any display of weaponry but by his physical presence, unguarded, among the angry crowd.

'You *are* old!' exclaimed Shaul. 'And that's like a fairy story about some magic spell!'

After the Nakba, Orient House became a hotel run by the Husseinis and then – in Sari Nusseibeh's words – 'the powerhouse of Palestinian national politics'. Here the PLO held apparently important talks with foreign delegations and diplomatic missions – talks doomed to wither on the vine. In August 2001, when all Palestinian institutions were closed, Orient House was declared off-limits to East Jerusalemites – 'and that gate has been padlocked ever since', said Shaul. 'My parents cheered as the Arabs lost their recognised base. I was seventeen and that gloating switched me to activism. That was in the middle of the suicide bombings – we were scared to get on a bus or sit in a restaurant. But still I could see how the despair makes extremists.'

Beyond Obeida Street we were overlooking Wadi al-Joz (Walnut Valley, but walnut trees are rare nowadays). Here Jerusalem's nineteenth-century notables lived in stately homes; a few of the buildings remain, slummified, surrounded by two-man factories, junkyards and motor repair workshops. During the Mandate a prosperous middle-class moved in, built villas, cultivated gardens – then moved out to make way for the displaced thousands arriving and needing every sort of help.

On the valley floor we passed the unremarkable mud-coloured Tomb of Simon the Just, only noticed because several Haredim were praying nearby. Shaul dismissed Simon the Just as a figment of the collective imagination of certain nineteenth-century Mizrahim who acquired the tomb in 1890 and put it about that the bones within belonged to a fourth-century BC High Priest. (Which may be true; hereabouts nothing is impossibly ancient.) Since '67 throngs have prayed around the tomb every day and this suits ELAD, whose interests have always extended beyond the City of David.

For thirty years or more, this neighbourhood has been under threat of Judaisation. In the late '80s Ariel Sharon, the settlers' patron devil, planned to evict all Wadi al-Joz Palestinians but was thwarted by legal constraints. Here Shaul admitted to being a new-fledged lawyer, planning to specialise in land and property for the Palestinians' benefit. 'I don't need to earn,' he said simply. 'The Miami grandparents left me enough. In Sheikh Jarrah I'm learning as I go. Most Judaizers favour dodgy land deals, using shell companies on Pacific islands. Or intimidation, including murder. Or bent laws – but that's time-consuming. Bulldozers come only if the home is flimsy and the site is what counts. ELAD don't like TV images of women weeping beside bulldozers in action.'

As we walked slowly uphill, taking short-cuts through a smelly shack-land between the Mount Scopus and Ambassador hotels, it amused my companion to hear me complaining about the heat. To him, this autumn day felt pleasantly cool.

I asked, 'Why have the settlers so much power?'

Shaul replied, 'They only have as much as the government gives them. They couldn't do what they do without government support, available whichever party is in. Sharon, as Housing Minister in 1990, helped a lot. He ordered all East Jerusalem lands and homes controlled by the Custodian of Absentee Properties to be sold to three settler/development groups. One was ELAD. Then he told the Custodian to lower prices. Next his Ministry *gave* those groups the purchase price. Some settlers need pay only token rents, like NIS33 per month for a two-storey building on a busy shopping street. That's about ten dollars. It's all "Through-the-Looking-glass" stuff. But Zionists like their actions to have a legitimate gloss. Between 1949 and 1990 our Knesset made about thirty statutes transferring privately owned Palestinian land to the State. The Jewish National fund paid to make 95% of Israeli territory "State lands", to be held forever for the Jewish people. Non-Jews can't even lease land. Where does that remind you of? Both Nazi Germany and apartheid South Africa!'

As a prominent activist Shaul drew warm greetings on Sheikh Jarrah's streets and was affectionately embraced in the ill-equipped health centre. Its verandah and hallway were so crowded that his friends had no time to talk and we didn't linger. 'Let's visit the Khairiyas,' said Shaul. 'They're needing comfort.'

A littered track followed the hill's contour and Shaul pointed down to what he called 'the Frustration Zone'. In the '60s an urban renewal project, including a bus terminus, had been planned by the landowner, Rawhi Khatib, the last Palestinian mayor of East Jerusalem. But alas! a more profitable usage came up (of no benefit to the locals) and urban renewal was forgotten. Even more frustrating – the Municipality refused to sanction an urgently needed secondary school for 800 girls because the Hyatt Regency Hotel objected that it could become 'a point of confrontation'. A care centre for 200 handicapped youngsters was also stymied 'for security reasons' although backed by a cross-section of well-known Israelis. One member of the Knesset (MK), Yigal Bibi, pointed out, 'Those youngsters may be handicapped, but that doesn't mean they've no arms to throw stones.'

The Khairiyas lived on a slope officially labelled 'State land', not far from the Hebrew University – itself built on land confiscated during the Mandate from a Wadi al-Joz owner. Here four homes were awaiting demolition. The Khairiyas' crudely constructed three-storey house sheltering seventeen members of an extended family, had been built in 1990 without a permit. Said Shaul, 'Twenty years ago no permits were being granted to Palestinians – same as now. So what do you do? You have a family to shelter, you can't get a permit, you can't move to a location where you can get a permit. Therefore you build where you are, hoping for the best. Then you rear your family in suspense, always fearing the worst . . .' And here the worst is about to happen – 200 new housing units for settlers.

At 10.30-ish nine Khairiyas were at home: the sexagenarian grand-parents, two sons and their wives, an ailing teenage grandson (flu) and two toddlers. Those absent were either at school or working for a pittance if lucky enough to have found some odd job. The younger generations spoke Hebrew but out of respect for the elders Shaul insisted on practising his Arabic. Its imperfections served a useful purpose: occasional smiles and giggles broke the tension. We sat on blanket rolls in a neat, clean living-room where large photographs of Arafat and Mahmoud Darwish flanked something unexpected. This copy of the 1947 UN Partition map included Beersheba, Acre and Nahariya in the proposed Arab state, with Jaffa as an Arab enclave and Jerusalem as an international zone. As I stood studying it Shaul clicked his fingers and said sharply – 'Sit down! We all wonder "What if . . . ." But let's focus on the future.'

A tin kettle of tea appeared and two plates of shiny pink biscuits – a toddler-magnet but both were restrained until the guests had had their fill. My presence was ignored, not impolitely but because this family's crisis left them with nothing to spare for conventional social intercourse. Stress showed on all the adult faces. Unlike my hostel friends, the Khairiyas did not repress their anger while showing Shaul the latest round of correspondence with the Municipality. Voices trembled, eyes flashed, arms were waved and feet stamped. Shaul looked increasingly wretched. He couldn't honestly encourage hope, could only listen – which he did, for more than an hour. Stupidly I asked, 'When their home is gone, where will they live?' Impatiently Shaul replied, 'They'll separate and go to the already overcrowded homes of relatives and friends.' Earlier, he had told me that in '48 both grandparents' families had fled from a prosperous village near Jaffa.

The goodbyes were prolonged and painful. Then both sons escorted

The situation in 1946

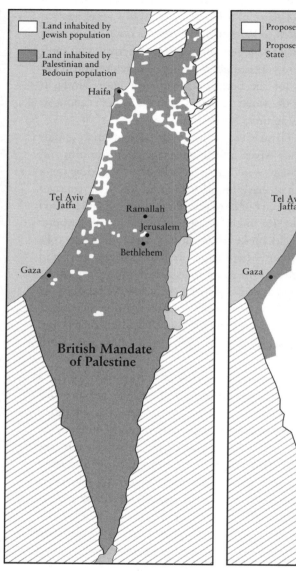

Land inhabited by
Jewish population

Land inhabited by
Palestinian and
Bedouin population

Haifa

Tel Aviv
Jaffa

Ramallah

Jerusalem

Bethlehem

Gaza

**British Mandate
of Palestine**

The UN partition plan of 1947

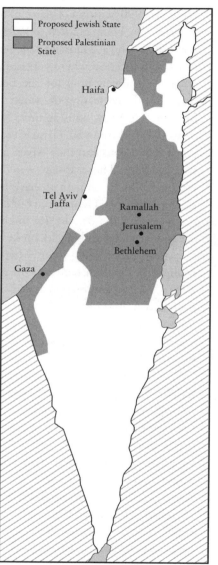

Proposed Jewish State

Proposed Palestinian
State

Haifa

Tel Aviv
Jaffa

Ramallah

Jerusalem

Bethlehem

Gaza

The situation in 1949

Changes between 1967 and 2000

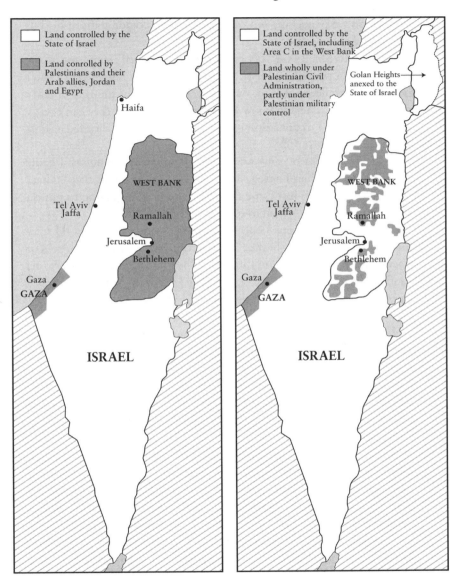

Land controlled by the State of Israel

Land conrolled by Palestinians and their Arab allies, Jordan and Egypt

Haifa

WEST BANK

Tel Aviv Jaffa

Ramallah

Jerusalem

Bethlehem

Gaza

GAZA

ISRAEL

Land controlled by the State of Israel, including Area C in the West Bank

Land wholly under Palestinian Civil Administration, partly under Palestinian military control

Golan Heights anexed to the State of Israel

WEST BANK

Tel Aviv Jaffa

Ramallah

Jerusalem

Bethlehem

Gaza

GAZA

ISRAEL

us down to a bus-stop on Wadi al-Joz Street, a major road. For one
disordered moment I fancied the fast sleek motor cars of the Occupying
population were mocking our companions who couldn't afford the bus
fare to al-Aqsa mosque.

On the bus Shaul said, 'It's a relief they can let off steam, too many
can't.' After a pause he added, 'As for me, I feel so *humiliated*! I can't
help and I should be able to. As an Israeli I'm part of the system that's
torturing them. They do know I care about them. But they can't really
understand *why* I'm not helping. Part of that anger was directed against
me – did you notice?'

I had noticed but by now was past making consoling noises. I badly
needed a beer. When I asked, 'How come they have that map?' Shaul
shrugged. 'Prob'ly it just came their way and was something to put on
the wall. They won't brood over it as you or I might.'

Back at the Damascus Gate I suggested R and R at my Old City
local – St George's café, in the Christian Quarter. Alcohol is not sold or
openly drunk in the Muslim Quarter. (The Hamas effect: on the hostel
roof my beer wore a Coca-Cola disguise.) Happily St George's was a
mere five-minute walk from the hostel – less if one were very thirsty –
and I had established a sound relationship with the proprietor.

We sat close to the wall, out of the tourist flow, and watched tour
groups being led to and fro along Muristan Road, the Old City's
widest street. 'Let's do a tally,' I said – and ten minutes later we
had identified Italians, Japanese, Russians, Nigerians, Indians, Poles,
Brazilians. I wondered, 'How many would be upset, even outraged, if
informed about life in Silwan and Sheikh Jarrah? Places they pass in
their coaches . . .'

'Not many,' said Shaul. 'They've paid for a nice holiday with much
praying to make them feel good. They don't want to be informed about
not nice things. At home, on computers and TV, maybe they see
demolitions and settler building and IDF aggression. But we're just
another distant problem – more suffering, and nowhere near as bad as
earthquakes, floods, hurricanes, famines. Of course to me, an Israeli, it
seems worse – so calculated! We're supposed to be a democracy, the only
one in the Middle East we're told every day. And our government gets
full support from the "international community" with just occasional
cautious little criticisms. But nothing sustained, no penalties, nothing
that hurts. It's like we're painted with a magic potion.'

Recently Shaul had met members of an EU Mission reporting on Israel's East Jerusalem policies. It puzzled him that such high-powered people had been expensively despatched to gather facts and figures known to thousands of Palestine's supporters on every continent. However, he faintly hoped the Mission's eyewitness evidence would change the EU's trading relationship with Israel.

By the time the report came out, in March 2009, I was living among refugees on the West Bank. Friends there teased me about my eagerness to find a copy. Said one, 'People have been writing reports about *us* for fifty-seven years – and we're still here!'

This report, dated 15 December 2008, recognises that Israel is 'actively pursuing the illegal annexation of East Jerusalem'. It continues:

New settlements, construction of the barrier, discriminatory housing policies, house demolitions, restrictive permit regime and continued closure of Palestinian institutions increase Jewish Israeli presence, weaken the Palestinian community in the city, impede Palestinian urban development and separate East Jerusalem from the rest of the West Bank . . . The fourth Geneva Convention prevents an occupying power from extending its jurisdiction to occupied territory . . . Demolitions are illegal under international law, serve no obvious purpose, have severe humanitarian effects, and fuel bitterness and extremism.

When I next met Shaul, in April 2009, we gloomed together over the EU's failure to change its trading relationship with Israel.

'The magic potion is still working,' said Shaul.

CHAPTER 5

From Ancient Acre to Newish Ashkelon

It's usual to 'do' Acre in a day; as my 2007 *Lonely Planet* noted, 'Accommodation is sadly lacking.' However, Sari knew of one hostel, within the Old Town ramparts, and he gave me the address of his only surviving uncle who in May '48 saw most of Acre's 15,000 Palestinians fleeing into Lebanon. Abu Jawad's family were among the 3,000 or so who stood fast within the Old Town where he still lives, surrounded by three younger generations.

On the bus to Haifa I shared a front seat with a heavily built English-speaking woman who wore a fake mink jacket until her brow began to glisten. Her 1950s perm had a coppery sheen, her nails were painted black, her chunky jewellery rattled with every move. By mobile she complained at length about a stupid car mechanic who had reduced her to bus travel. Two long chats in Hebrew followed. Then I sought information about onward transport to Akka (tactfully avoiding 'Acre') and got a curt reply – 'Train'. The *Lonely Planet* warns – 'Israelis themselves recognise their rather brusque (sic) mannerisms: a native-born Jew is known as a *Sabra* (a prickly pear).'

I should have taken a slow, indirect bus, the sort that wriggles across the landscape servicing small towns. This non-stop coach took the four-lane Yitzhak Rabin Highway, overlooking miles of plastic tunnels, brown ploughland, sparse conifer plantations, occasional expanses of scrub brightened by cascades of bougainvillaea and an ugly proliferation of long, straight roads, some on stilts. Suddenly I felt an aching sadness and recalled Uri Davis, the Israeli Human Rights Worker's, lament:

For the colonised, a joint revolutionary effort would involve basing the struggle for liberation on the awareness that the father land is . . . a destroyed fatherland, controlled by the occupier, dominated by the conqueror, colonised, violated. That effort must take as its point of departure the reality of achieved destruction: the ancestral villages being literally buried under the sprawling metropolis, the olive trees felled, the vineyards levelled down.

Haifa's 'sprawling metropolis' – below Mount Carmel, on the Gulf of Acre headland – had by 1930 become a considerable industrial port with rail links to Damascus (since 1905) and to Cairo (since 1919). From its railway station my destination was visible, beyond a dazzle of blue Mediterranean. Our train stopped at two stations serving crowded suburbs of apartment blocks, factories and car showrooms. Then it followed the shoreline, allowing glimpses of the Galilean hills and of globalisation in action – two colossal container ships approaching Haifa from different directions.

Shaul had warned me that Acre was 'going through a tense time'. A few weeks previously, on the wide street outside the railway station, a Palestinian and his small son drove by on the Sabbath, having taken a wrong turning, and were badly beaten up – ostensibly because they were driving on the Sabbath. Their Russian attackers came from a poor newish housing estate and were described by Sari as 'seculars' who hid their racism behind the ultra-Orthodox Sabbath obsession. According to his Uncle Jawad, gangs from the same estate had more than once been observed beating up black Jews. During two days of subsequent rioting the police didn't notice arsonists targeting Palestinian homes in the New Town.

Most of Acre's dull New Town (population 40,000) was built in Mandate times when Muslims outnumbered Palestinian Christians by two to one and Palestinian Jews came by the dozen. Now 7,000 Muslims live in the impoverished Old Town, whose drug dealers find the sensitive Lebanese border surprisingly porous and do a brisk trade with foreign day-trippers and Tel Aviv's rich young.

Beyond suburban streets (prim villas in shrubby gardens), Acre's famous walls come suddenly into view, massively following the coastline's curve. Here all buildings recede and between high embankments no traffic flows. Nor was there anyone in sight as I climbed a long stairway to the ramparts. Now I could see the Old Town – by regional standards not very old, structurally. Most of its notable buildings date from the eighteenth century. Within the wide, deep moat the smooth turf was unexpectedly green and the wild flowers abundant: red, blue, orange, yellow, pink. When a gusty breeze came off the sea those colours were replicated in a cloud of plastic bags swirling through the air.

One tours the ramparts following multilingual wall plaques, complete with diagrams, clearly explaining every detail of Napoleon's siege. I

wondered where he was (at sea or on land?) when giving advance support
to political Zionism:

> Israelites, unique nation, France offers you at this very time . . . Israel's
> patrimony! Take over what has been conquered and with that nation's
> warranty and support, maintain it against all comers!

Shortly after those words were written a ferocious Balkan sea captain,
Ahmed Pasha al-Jazzar (*jazzar* is Arabic for 'butcher') repulsed Napoleon's
army with British naval help.

Old Acre received a UNESCO World Heritage label in 2002 but had
not yet taken appropriate action. Magnificent cut-stone walls remained
defaced by obsolete air-conditioning units; some metal double doors,
replacing the original iron-studded oak ones, were painted a strident
blue; heaped litter from shops, offices and kitchens lay in corners; public
spaces were plastered with enormous, garish municipal election posters,
spray-painted or hanging in tatters. The souks were bustling but their
limited range of goods suggested a community with thin purses. Acre
(Old and New) ranks among Israel's poorest cities with a high rate of
migration to more prosperous areas.

I found the hostel's front entrance in the Souk-al-Abyad, opposite a
small mosque with a tall minaret. The firmly locked door looked unused:
shouting and knocking brought no response. Passers-by stared at me,
some laughing; I had already got the impression that not all Acre-ites
love tourists. Then, from a balcony across the street, a kind woman
indicated that I must go behind the building. And there, close to the
ramparts, a faded little notice ('Chambres') pointed to a shaky metal
ladder leading to the roof of a long-defunct restaurant annex. This roof
was the hostel's common room, some thirty feet by sixty, open on three
sides with a canvas awning. In the centre stood an antique oval table of
inlaid walnut surrounded by ten plastic garden chairs. There was no
other furniture apart from an electric kettle and fridge in a kitchen
corner. A step-ladder led to the main building, through a half-glass
door. My knock brought Zee hurrying from within – a within I was
never to see because the bedrooms led off the common room. Zee was
in her sixties, thin and haggard with dyed black hair and sharp watchful
eyes. I must pay immediately: there were no doors to prevent guests
slipping away undetected. My sheetless, grubby bunk bed was in a six-
person dorm – the wall shedding slivers of pale blue plaster – and

unsurprisingly I had the room to myself. Neither towel nor loo-paper was provided and I did not engage with the shower's dilatory drip. That evening my fellow-guest, a young Dutchman with peeling sunburn and a long pony-tail, had to pay for a sheet.

At first Zee viewed me uneasily, but hours spent writing at the oval table seemed to reassure her. Gradually she became communicative, in broken but graphic English. Of her nine children, eight had emigrated, to the US, the UK, Denmark, Austria. Not one of them has a good job, but they'll never come home – why should they? For what? No one wanted peace or by now they'd have it. Not one of the talking people at the top ever talked about the forgotten Israeli-Palestinians who in their own homeland are worse off than refugees. What difference would it make for them if the other Palestinians got independence? All the time life gets harder. Zee could be repetitive and at times incoherent but the gist of her monologue was clear. The IDF and Border Guards acted more cruel since a million racist Russians had arrived. The Borders were the worst. In Acre the tourism was never good and the second Intifada nearly killed it. It wasn't fair to blame Arab Israelis for suicide bombs and rockets. As a Christian, Zee didn't want Hamas telling her how to live her life. It was good that on the West Bank Abu Mazen's police were helping the IDF to catch them . . .

It seems unfair that in Acre 'tourism was never good'. The longer you spend dawdling around the Old Town, the more it fascinates as those layers preceding its eighteenth-century revival become apparent – such as the twelfth-century fortress area where the Knights Hospitaller have left many marks. Less agreeable is another fortress, the sinister citadel, used by both the Ottomans and the British as a prison and now a Haganah museum and memorial to terrorists – with special emphasis on Jabotinsky, whose Irgun gang bombed Jerusalem's King David Hotel and organised the Deir Yassin massacre.

Acre's roots rival Jaffa's, stretching back to an Egyptian reference in the nineteenth century BC. And the Old Testament records (Judges I) that 'Aser destroyed not the inhabitants of Acco . . . and he dwelt in the midst of the Canaanites the inhabitants of that land and did not slay them'. (In those days *not* slaying was something to write home about.) Alexander the Great, when choosing a site for his mint, preferred Acre to Tyre; a sound choice – that mint operated non-stop for six centuries.

The Crusaders made Acre their main port and when the Mamluks besieged the city for two months, outnumbering the occupiers by ten to one, both the Crusaders and the city were obliterated. (Happily without too much bloodshed; most residents had fled to Cyprus.) The Mamluk Sultan, Maybar, then established Safed as Galilee's new capital.

In its subsequent village incarnation, Acre enjoyed a few comparatively calm centuries until a freelancing Druze prince attempted restoration. But in 1635 he was decapitated before achieving much and his pickled head sent to Constantinople.

A Bedouin, Daher al-Omar al-Zaydani, took over in the mid-eighteenth century. Cotton was then northern Palestine's main source of wealth and soon Acre was attracting many merchants, especially from Venice, Genoa and Amalfi. Under Daher's protection they inspired and sponsored most of the Old Acre we now see. Daher may have started life as a camel driver but he died in battle, aged 85, as the uncrowned 'First King of Palestine'.

Finding Uncle was not easy though Sari had said 'Neighbours will show you his home.' Few neighbours were visible within Acre's Ottoman warren and those to whom I showed my slip of paper looked blank. Stone stairways led to enclosed corners where narrow, heavy doors lacked names or numbers and the high, round windows were securely barred. It was all romantically 'oriental' but frustrating for a visitor in search of a host. I was about to give up when a vegetable-laden young woman proved to be Abu Jawad's granddaughter-in-law. Smiling shyly, she beckoned me to follow her down an alley, twisting between windowless walls. These former family homes of rich merchants are now divided into flats, overlooking central courtyards where fountains no longer play.

Abu Jawad was my exact contemporary, aged sixteen when most of Acre's Palestinians fled. Sturdy and still vigorous, he carefully cultivated a rather comical beard, a brief white triangle. His blue eyes were, he assumed, a Crusader leftover. 'They didn't bring many women, they were around for a while, they weren't celibate – wouldn't you expect some blue eyes?'

This five-room flat had vaulted ceilings, curtained doorways, split-level stone floors and superb wrought-iron balconies. Abu Jawad shared it with his second son and his wife, their eldest son and his wife and four great-grandchildren. The three-storey building urgently needed restoration, for which all the residents had offered to pay – but no permits were being granted.

'They want us to go,' said Abu Jawad. 'They want to make old Acre into a smart place with holiday homes for American Zionists. You can see everything rotting away except what brings tourists.' He spoke calmly and when I looked into those blue eyes they were amused rather than angry. 'We're not going,' he continued. 'We don't like our homes falling down but we're staying in them. You know about *samoud*?'

I nodded. *Samoud* means endurance, steadfastness, perseverance. You have to know about it to understand the Palestinians' mindset. If Israel's leaders allowed themselves to recognise it, they might consider shifting some of their own attitudes.

In the 1930s Acre became a centre of resistance to Zionism's seizure of territory. Abu Jawad recalled Haganah's occupation of the town on 6 May '48. Together with his father, two uncles and two older brothers, he had been fighting for eight days despite almost hourly shelling. A sudden typhoid epidemic hastened the inevitable defeat, causing seventy deaths and widespread illness. All Acre's water came from the Kabri springs six miles to the north, via an eighteenth-century aqueduct, and that water was identified as the source of the epidemic. Fifty-five sick British soldiers were shipped to Port Said and Brigadier Beveridge of the army medical service stated that never before had such a thing happened in Palestine. The International Red Cross report specified 'outside agents' as the only possible explanation. Two weeks later, on 27 May, the Egyptians caught two Zionists, David Mizrachi and David Horin, as they were attempting to infect Gaza's wells with typhoid and dysentery viruses. When Ben-Gurion heard of this crime he briefly recorded it in his diary. Subsequently the Israel government pretended not to notice the execution, by the Egyptian authorities, of the two Davids.

This epidemic made continued resistance to the Haganah impossible and Abu Jawad said, 'I still hear, in my mind's ear, the megaphone threatening us – "Surrender or commit suicide! We'll destroy you to the last man!" Then the Haganah were told to loot to help the new arrivals. Coming from those camps in Europe, they needed everything. Our homes were stripped bare.' My host paused to pour more coffee, then added, 'Much later, some of us could sympathise with those immigrants. We'd learned that most wanted to settle in America, Britain, Australia, Canada. But they weren't welcome. Those government said, "Now you've got your own country." Like us, they'd been exploited by Zionists who needed Jews – any sort, from anywhere – to make their "homeland" work.'

After the Nakba came eighteen years of relentless military rule. No Palestinian could leave or enter his or her town or village without a permit from the Minister of Defence. This form of martial law, put in place by the British in 1945 to cope with Zionist terrorists, was now applied to 90% of Israel's Palestinian citizens. Certain clauses denied them access to civilian courts. Other clauses facilitated the confiscation of land and thousands of villagers were driven off their fields. Nobody listened when the Palestinians' few foreign friends protested that the Declaration of Independence, read out by Ben-Gurion on 14 May 1948, specifically guaranteed 'equal rights' to the Arab inhabitants of the State of Israel.

Meanwhile families such as Abu Jawad's, who had built homes in New Acre, were being forcibly 'relocated' to the Old Town. There Abu Jawad began work in the firm founded by his grandfather 'and I self-educated in my spare time'. That involved reading his father's cherished collection of English books and listening to the BBC World Service until the Shin Bet (Israel's internal security service) confiscated his battery-run wireless. Here was a nice little coincidence. Shortly before leaving home I had read Karl Sabbagh's moving memoir, *Palestine: A Personal History*, in which the author recalls Acre being mentioned in the BBC's first Arabic language broadcast, given by his father on 3 January 1938.

News from Palestine: Another Arab from Palestine was executed by hanging at Acre this morning by order of a military court. He was arrested during recent riots in the Hebron mountains and was found to possess a rifle and some ammunition.

In 1966 Abu Jawad, then a father of three, went alone to study in Beirut and returned with qualifications enabling him to teach in a Haifa academy to which he commuted daily by train. He also worked for two human rights groups, using his Beirut connections. 'But I gave up in 2000. Things have only got worse, behind the "peace talks" camouflage.'

While escorting me to Souk al-Abyad, Abu Jawad reflected on a sad paradox. The Nazi era influx of refugees had provoked much fear and some violence, yet he had no childhood memories of communal hostility. In Jerusalem this theme had become familiar to me: Zionism, not Jewishness, was the problem. Said Abu Jawad, 'An invasion of Muslims who acted like Israelis would be equally hated. It's what people *do* that counts.'

Israel's habitable area is very limited. At 6.35 a.m. I left Acre, ten miles from the Lebanese border, changed trains at Tel Aviv, then arrived in Ashkelon, eight miles from the Gazan border, at 9.00 a.m. precisely. And those weren't fast trains.

Ashkelon has replaced al-Majdal, a flourishing fishing town with a very deep harbour, renowned in biblical times as one of the Philistines' 'Five Cities'. By the time the IDF took over on 5 December 1948, after months of bombing and shelling, most Palestinians had been killed or had fled. The Israel National Plan named al-Majdal as the site for a 20,000-person urban centre and by December 1949, two thousand five hundred destitute immigrants had arrived from Morocco, Poland and Romania. The South African Zionist Federation was then drawing up plans for a 'garden city', Afridar, to which many South Africans migrated in the early '50s, followed by a smaller number of Anglo-Zionists. Meanwhile, on the site of a nearby 'requisitioned' village, al-Jura, Zvi Segal, one of the signatories of Israel's Declaration of Independence, was developing the exclusive Barnca neighbourhood.

In 1950 it was realised that many Palestinians were again living in or near al-Majdal – 'infiltrators'! Their return home criminalised them and between June and October most were dumped over the border in Gaza, which was then ruled by Egypt. According to Benny Morris, those were the lucky ones:

A large number of infiltrators were killed by mines and booby-traps. Hundreds of mines were laid each night along suspected infiltrator routes and anticipated targets, such as irrigation piping and water pumps, were booby-trapped. The office diary for the first half of 1950 of the secretary of Kibbutz Erez, on the Gaza border, gives an indication of the success of these measures: '8 Jan. Five Arabs killed by shrapnel mines laid by a kibbutz member Aharonik . . . 8 April: Successful ambush: two Arabs killed . . . 10 April: an Arab killed by a mine . . . 11 April: an Arab and donkey killed by mine . . . 13 April: an Arab killed by mine . . . 12 June: Two Arabs killed by a mine . . . 14

June: an Arab killed by a mine.' Mines were sometimes laid for infiltrators coming to retrieve the bodies of those killed the night before. In Kibbutz Yad Mordechai, also on the Gaza border, the settlers in May 1953 booby-trapped a water pump . . . killing a dozen or more . . . Israel's defensive measures resulted in the death of between 2,700 and 5,000 infiltrators, mostly unarmed, during 1949–56.

Outside Ashkelon station I rashly disdained a waiting bus, not realising that the city (population 111,000) is separated from the railway by miles of unshaded, sandy flatness. A mile later a dusty little car overtook me, then stopped and backed. 'Ashkelon?' asked a chubby young man with a crew cut and a kind smile. He put my rucksack in the boot (beehives filled the back seat) and his halting English had a familiar ring. Recently Jacob had made *aliyah* from Moscow to join parents who migrated in 2000. As a teenager he'd chosen to stay with aged grandparents averse to moving. On hearing about my journeys through Siberia he showed symptoms of homesickness. Always he'd longed to see Lake Baikal but it was too far from Moscow and now it was impossibly far, he could never afford to return to Russia . . .

As we drove into Ashkelon – its streets wide and clean, its palm trees and shrubs well tended – my companion pointed out the Israel Beer Brewery ('Coca-Cola own it'), the college where his wife taught English and the white globular Holiday Inn, resembling part of a nuclear power plant and dwarfing a thirteenth-century Muslim tomb. In the commercial centre Jacob drew my attention to a shopping mall. 'You remember? Six months ago a rocket from Gaza hit, big damage, fifteen with hurts – you heard?' His voice had changed, become shaky with rage. 'Last March we have 230 buildings hit and 30 cars. All day we must have fear . . .'

I asked, 'Was anyone killed or badly injured?' Jacob shrugged. 'No one killed but everyone made sick to have fear all days.' He slowed down and asked, 'Which hotel?' My plan to find a hostel made him laugh. 'Ashkelon have no tourists, no hostels, only big hotels for rich Israelis. You must go beach, is one cheap hotel – I show you.' And he generously drove me another few miles to Hotel Ha-hof, a two-minute walk from the Mediterranean.

I invited Jacob and his wife to a meal next evening. 'Yes, yes,' he said, 'please thank you! But first I help you tomorrow. Saturday, no work; my wife like talking English, you like see desert?' I replied, 'Yes, yes, please!' We arranged to meet at a little distance from the hotel, for reasons I later understood.

From road level the Ha-hof seemed long and one-storey; in fact its enormous empty foyer was the top floor of a three-storey building: one went down to the bedrooms. Thrice I banged on the counter loudly; the room keys all hung on their hooks, a tariff list was in Hebrew only. At last the receptionist appeared, buttoning her cardigan – a dumpy, sallow, middle-aged woman with frizzy hair, thick spectacles, permanently compressed lips and an oddly belligerent aura. Peering suspiciously at my passport she hesitated: momentarily I feared rejection. Then abruptly she said, '250 shekels' in English and beckoned me to follow her along two zig-zagging corridors, down two flights of stairs and along another corridor to a single room overlooking a cactus-hedged vegetable patch. When I proposed paying later she snapped 'Pay *now!*' Meekly I followed her up all the stairs, along all the corridors – the décor duck-egg blue and fawn. There was no register to be signed and I asked myself, 'Is this a record for succinctness?' The receptionist had used a total of four words.

Ashkelon's upmarket (sort of) marina was far away; the Ha-hof's environs included a pleasingly undeveloped beach (no chairs, umbrellas, cubicles), a few locked boat-huts, a cafeteria that would open at 5.00 p.m. – and no shop. I needed food but there was no one about of whom to seek guidance – until a car drove onto the sand and a fair-haired couple liberated an excited toddler. As I approached, their friendly smiles suggested they were newcomers to Israel. Soon we were strolling by the wavelets and I was hearing about their Swiss-Jewish background. Four years previously they'd indulged a romantic longing to marry in Jerusalem, then found Israel so stimulating they decided to make *aliyah*. Both sets of parents disapproved, reckoning the Zionist dream had already ended in tears. They however relished Ashkelon's multiculturalism and sheer 'newness'; to them (living in Barnca) the city felt like an affirmation of Jewish resilience and creativity. I listened in polite silence, wondering how much they knew about the transformation of al-Majdal into Ashkelon. Both spoke fluent English – and German, Hebrew and French. Israel's language barrier is higher than normal – they said – because Zionists interpret 'not bothering' to learn Hebrew as a mark of disrespect. They apologised for Ashkelon's irregular public transport; I would probably have to walk to the shops so a street map was drawn in the sand.

A few miles later, as I traversed a residential suburb, a young man, carrying his baby to its car-seat, offered me a lift to a supermarket. His American accent at first misled me; he had studied at a US college in St Petersburg before realising 'Putin's dragging Russia back into Soviet Darkness.' Concentrating on his potted autobiography, I paid no attention to our route as we rounded many corners.

I left the supermarket laden with bread, sardines and beer, then paused to show the Ha-hof card and seek directions. But I'd lost it, perhaps while fiddling with shekel notes at the checkout. This almost qualified as a crisis. I hadn't memorised the hotel's name and if you don't know where you are going you can't ask the way or identify an appropriate bus or hire a taxi. 'The beach' was too vague: Ashkelon's built-up seafront extends for miles. Now I urgently needed an English-speaker but in this rather run-down district all was Cyrillic – shop signs and advertisements, magazines and newspapers, even the bus-stop legends. Immigrant Russians are much criticised for 'not bothering' and obviously the ghettoised elders don't need to make an effort. Of course their offspring must learn Hebrew, yet one of the three buses I took was packed with high-spirited schoolchildren all talking Russian on their way home for their Sabbath supper, a family gathering important to most Israelis, secular though they may otherwise be. On that crowded bus, two small boys stood up simultaneously to offer me their seats.

By the end of my third ride (none went anywhere near the coast) it was 3.00 p.m. when all public transport ceases on a Friday and doesn't resume until the first two stars are visible on Saturday evening. Not everyone shares my appreciation of this quirky side effect of Judaism; in Jerusalem frustrated tourists may be heard muttering about 'bigoted rabbis'.

For the next two hours oil terminal chimneys served as my landmark; at least these were on the coast, though far from the Ha-hof. And it was perfect walking weather: hottish sun, cool breeze. Beyond a semi-derelict industrial estate I found myself amidst four-storey apartment blocks where the lavish litter bore Cyrillic lettering, everything looked chipped or frayed and the locals were friendly. A youth pushing his younger brother (or son?) in a rusty buggy pointed across an expanse of sand and grey-green scrub – 'That way to hotels.'

Beyond this scrubland I had to wriggle under barbed wire to reach a narrow track patrolled by two uniformed security guards and their dogs. Although most guide books ignore Ashkelon, it does cater for a certain echelon of rich Israelis and this track gave access to two very 'gated' hotels with private beaches. Approaching the Ha-hof I saw a full car-park and on the front steps a young father, in full ultra-Orthodox gear, changing a baby's nappy. This astonished me at the time; later, I observed that many such fathers excel at childcare, as well they might, given their procreative tendencies.

The vast foyer was crowded with families in holiday-mood. Some older men wore high black furry hats, several wore knee-length, black shiny belted coats. Others (their beards and ear-locks exceptionally long) wore gowns striped dark and pale grey and black ballet dancers' tights instead of trousers. All the women wore ankle-length skirts and tightly bound headscarves of which Hamas must approve. Even small boys wore *kipas* and ear-locks. All the little girls wore identical pale pink dresses and white tights. The children played happily but quietly as mothers and grannies sat chatting on long sofas while their menfolk stood around in monosyllabic groups. Most adults carried prayer-books, large or small, and many were reading from them *sotto voce*.

Moving slowly through the bustle to a self-service tea-urn I attempted to catch some female eye, hoping to begin a conversation or at least exchange greetings. But I was consistently ignored. Not snubbed, or viewed with suspicion or hostility, simply made to feel invisible – quite an eerie sensation. Many years ago I experienced something similar as my daughter and I trekked through the High Andes; although foreigners were, then, a rarity, the Quecha peasants failed to react to our sudden appearance. This introverted group (an excursion from Safed, Jacob told me next day) were equally determined not to see the stranger.

Opposite the main entrance was the synagogue room, its rear one-third cut off from the rest by a white plastic screen – the purdah quarter. In some ways, Judaism and Islam have much in common. When every-one had flocked into this prayer-room I remained in my corner to enjoy the ritual chanting. Through a glass wall, separating foyer from restaurant, I could see dozens of tables laid for the Sabbath meal with trays of candles ready to be lit by mothers and stacks of bread, covered with napkins, ready to be broken by fathers, and bottles of wine and miniature goblets as centrepieces. At Reception my four-word non-

friend had been replaced by a very tall young man with a seal-shaped
head and a disfiguringly prominent Adam's apple. He explained in
Russian English that I must not enter the restaurant, dinner could be
served in my room for an extra charge. 'No thanks,' said I. Why this
segregation? Elsewhere I was to share Sabbath meals with apparently
ultra-Orthodox friends who found my presence unpolluting.

Pollution of another sort deterred me from swimming off Ashkelon's
beach. Here the sea, according to Jacob, suffers from 'dirty Arab water'.
Apparently Arabs dirty the water as Israelis do not – which may well be
true when those Arabs' sewage systems have been wrecked by Israeli
bombs.

As I walked south along the beach before dawn, Gaza's lights shone
briefly. Already a few fishermen were scrambling down the sandy cliffs,
wearing winter jackets and woolly hats and in a hurry to set up their
lines. They didn't greet each other and none responded to my 'Shalom!'
A strong headwind blew. Then a low cloud bank above the horizon
took fire and soon my hands were thawing. The sand was agreeably
firm, the shells (being collected for granddaughters) were agreeably varied
and the waves' rhythms agreeably soothing. An hour later, within
shouting distance of Gaza, I had to turn back. The 'MINES' warnings
were in Hebrew, Arabic and English. It would be over two years before I
was finally able to visit Gaza myself, such is the control exerted by Israel
over reporting from the besieged Palestinian territory. I've told the story
of that visit in *A Month by the Sea*.

On 15 November 2008, exactly a week before my beach walk, Mark
Weiss reported in *The Irish Times*:

The five-month-old truce between Israel and Hamas in the Gaza
Strip appeared to be on the verge of collapse after another day of
violent exchanges yesterday. Palestinian militants pounded southern
Israel with rockets and mortar shells after Israeli aircraft targeted a
rocket-firing cell wounding two gunmen . . . Prime Minister Ehud
Olmert vowed that Israel would continue to exert pressure on Hamas
in Gaza until the rocket attacks stopped. He emphasised that violations
of the ceasefire would not be tolerated . . . Yesterday an Israeli was
wounded and four people suffered shock when eight rockets slammed
into Sderot, the closest town to Gaza. Longer-range Katyusha rockets

hit the town of Ashkelon. Residents in rocket-range of Gaza were told to stay indoors.

This report failed to remind readers that on 4 November IDF troops had ended the truce by surrounding a Hamas house near a tunnel entrance inside The Strip. When the residents refused to surrender, a gun-fight started. One Palestinian was killed, six Israelis were wounded, none seriously. Five other Palestinians died nearby when an IAF helicopter fired on their vehicle. Before returning to Israel the IDF blew up the Hamas house. A Defence Ministry spokesman explained: 'This was a surgical operation against a specific threat. Hamas planned to use that tunnel to abduct an Israeli soldier.' Next day, when Hamas fired 35 Qassams, one landed in central Ashkelon but no injuries were reported. Those home-made Qassams rarely do more than fray nerves. As Professor Avi Shlaim has written:

Israel's response to the pinpricks of primitive rocket attacks is totally disproportionate . . . The way to get calm on the southern border is through indirect talks with the political leaders of Hamas . . . They have a solid reputation for observing agreements, whereas Israel's leaders do not.

As arranged, I waited for Jacob and Ellie out of sight of the hotel. It transpired that Jacob, knowing the provenance of my fellow-guests, had felt nervous about being observed driving on the Sabbath. 'In Safed they're all crazy!' exclaimed Ellie with a scornful laugh. She was a buxom, square-faced woman, conspicuously taller than her husband, with a mane of tawny hair. When I proposed a tour of development towns she looked disgruntled, then Jacob said something to pacify her. On a quiet secondary road to Kiryat Gat Jacob drove slowly across the predictable plain – patches of desert, plastic tunnels, conifer and eucalyptus plantations.

Ellie took it for granted that I must admire Zionism's achievements – otherwise why spend a month in Israel? Gesturing expansively, she said, 'Look what happens with sixty years of hard work! In 1948 all was bare, humans couldn't live here!'

I smiled vacantly and said nothing. In fact the desert-wise Bedouin had grazed enormous herds of camels and goats on what looked barren to everyone else. We passed several kibbutz signposts; most of Israel's 27 development towns were intended to service the surrounding kibbutzim. However those already had their own long-established trading agreements so the new immigrants were reduced to labourer status – or unemployment. For a decade or so from the mid-'50s, as the jobless rate rose, the government tried industrialisation. After '67, most of its attention and funding was diverted to settling the OPT. When I asked about the kibbutzim/Russian relationship Ellie pretended not to hear – an answer of sorts.

Even Ellie couldn't present the dismal and mainly Mizrahim towns of Kiryat Gat, Rahat and Ofakim as a triumph for Zionism. I had visualised stopping in each, strolling around, drinking coffee in cafés, getting into conversations about local conditions. But Ellie said, 'We needn't stop, we can see how it is.' She had an explanation for how it is. 'These are lazy people, living off Ashkenazi who work hard. They came and got free everything, houses, subsidies, factories set up for them – and they didn't know how to work!' She nudged my arm and pointed to a huddle of abandoned warehouses and textile mills; drifts of red-brown sand lay against long-locked doors plastered with council election posters. 'Look!' said Ellie. 'All dirty and broken – they're like Arabs! They *are* Arabs, acting to be Israelis. Why did we let them in?'

Here my self-control weakened but I spoke very quietly; keeping one's voice low and slow is, I find, a useful anger-control mechanism. The Mizrahi, I remarked, had been encouraged to come when the Jewish Agency realised that most of Europe's Holocaust survivors were less than keen on settling in the Promised Land. The Agency chose the sites for the new towns, without consulting the immigrants who were not given free houses. Most lived for a few years in tents without running water or electricity, then had to build their own homes.

Jacob turned around, not having followed our conversation but sensing tension between the women. At that very moment a distraction got us over the hump. We were on the outskirts of straggling Ofakim (big for a development town, population 20,000) when three unkempt young men stepped close to the car, shouting for help – one apparently badly injured, being supported by his friends. Ellie screamed and Jacob accelerated. 'Drugs!' exclaimed Ellie. 'They fool you to stop, then rob!' It seems Ofakim is Israel's third poorest town, only beaten to the bottom of the pile by two 'Arab' villages.

'They just sit around complaining,' said Ellie. 'Depression and suicides, drink and drugs and crime – that's Ofakim! Sderot is better, we'll stop there to visit my friend Leah. She's always lived there, can tell you all about rockets! She works with Jacob – not at his level, she has a small job.'

Ellie wished they could have settled in Tel Aviv but Jacob had a well-paid job in Ashkelon's desalination research station – the biggest and most advanced in the world, according to Ellie. She herself felt over-qualified for her present job: 'I should be at Ben-Gurion. It would be easy to commute, but we're so new I must wait and be patient, getting to know some people . . .'

As Sderot's leafy suburbs came in view, Ellie began a long threnody about the town's bed-wetting, nail-biting, tranquilliser-dependent children. It seemed she had reacted to my controlled release of anger by deciding to re-educate me. I thought of the forty-plus Gazan children who had been killed in February 2008 during one of Israel's many air raids.

Sderot seemed less deprived than the other towns. Runty palm-trees lined its central streets and at one junction an insipid example of 'public art' topped a mound of earth on which litter replaced flowers. Bus stops, fortified to serve as rocket shelters, bore an unusual density of graffiti. Near the municipal offices Jacob suggested a picture of the 'famous' Irish writer looking at the Mayor's collection of genuinely famous rocket cases – thousands of them, forming a grim cliff. Most visiting dignitaries (including then-Senator Obama in July '08) are given this photo-opportunity, for global consumption. When I said, 'No thank you,' Jacob looked disappointed and Ellie scowled.

I asked, 'Population?' and Ellie replied, 'About 24,000 before the withdrawal from Gaza, now half that. Many find work in Ashkelon.' Later Leah corrected her; only a quarter had left and most planned to return because the Sderot-born wouldn't want to live anywhere else. Their parents and grandparents had built the town *from nothing* in the '50s. 'People living in old places,' said Leah, 'can't understand "the construction bond" with a new place. It *belongs* to residents in a different way, it's paid for in sweat instead of money.'

Leah wore rose-tinted spectacles, a useful accessory helping her to feel less North African and more Israeli. There are many heart-wrenching accounts of how her parents' generation were received – sprayed with disinfectant as they disembarked, loaded onto packed trucks without seats, transported by night to the chosen settlement sites. Always by night – then the truck hastened away and when sunrise revealed desolation all around no other vehicle was available.

Leah's parents had arrived from Tunisia in 1952 when she and her brother were toddlers. Brother worked for the municipality and was about to retire early because of rocket stress; two had landed on his street. Leah taught French and English and lived in half a small bungalow built (literally) by her father. The other half was let to an aged couple also unnerved by the Qassams and now living with a son in Be'er Sheva. Her hobbies were weaving and stamp-collecting and she was happily unmarried. ('She likes many men,' Ellie miaowed later.)

We didn't sit on the verandah amidst Leah's unusual collection of flowering cacti. Puzzled, I asked, 'Isn't inside more dangerous, if the roof's hit?'

Leah smiled and shook her head. 'They're usually not strong enough to come through a roof. Some do, but most victims get hurt outside.'

The living-room reeked of air-freshener and was brightened by an array of mass-produced ornaments acquired over the years; one sees their like on every continent, replacing indigenous handicrafts. When Ellie told our hostess 'Dervla wants to learn about Israel' it seemed re-education time had come – then suddenly I was pitched into an abyss of prejudice and hatred. My companions, starting from very different backgrounds, had arrived, as Israelis, at a shared space: by the feet of Avigdor Lieberman.

Leah's being so obviously Mizrahi gave an extra dimension of horror to my learning curve. She said, 'We want to finish with the Arabs, stop stupid talk about "peace" and "two states". Why do we bother with the scum in Ramallah? Why ask the PA to help our soldiers? Why pretend to trust Arabs?'

Jacob no longer looked like the kindly, cheery young man who had offered me a lift. His eyes narrowed as he said something vehement in Russian. Ellie translated. 'More settlements faster are our way forward. Forget Oslo, get back full control of Samaria and Judea.' She added, 'We've no room for Arabs, they've other places to go. Plenty places – Jordan, Egypt, Saudi Arabia. They're not so many and the Arab world is big.'

Leah said, 'They don't belong here, the British brought them in for cheap labour. Why do they want a separate state? They couldn't run it, they're illiterate! Best at thieving and corruption – how they run

Ramallah.' And she went on to explain why voting for Yisrael Beiteinu offered the shortest route to 'a land free of Arabs'.

The young Lieberman arrived from Moldova in 1978, long before the mass migration after the Fall of the Wall. That 'ingathering', which included many ethnic Central Asians, wanted to participate in Israeli life, politically and culturally, as a distinct group and they aroused much controversy. Judged by strict Halachic criteria, about 30% are not Jews and a startling 10% to 15% claimed to be practising Russian Orthodox Christians although Jewish by *race*. The controversy seethed around the official recognition of these hybrids as Jewish by *nationality*. To cater for their special needs, in 1999 Lieberman founded Yisrael Beiteinu ('Israel is our Home'). At least 90% of Israel's Russians now find comfort in Liebermanism, which advocates the expulsion of as many Palestinians as possible as soon as possible from both Israel and the OPT, by whatever political means are available or can be contrived. Other means, Jacob hinted, would also be acceptable to Yisrael Beiteinu; but this has only been mentioned in Russian, the language in which their leader addresses enthusiastic rallies.

The million or so Mizrahim who arrived in the 1950s were soon systematically de-Arabised, or induced to seem so, a process which – some say – has left many with disturbing identity problems. An equivalent process hasn't worked with the secular Russians who didn't imbibe either Judaisim or Zionism with their mother's milk and in general are not fixated on Abraham's legacy. They simply want to banish Palestinians as an inferior breed. In Romania and Siberia I had encountered a similar form of racism but here it shocked me in a new way, as though a fatal ingredient were being added to an already contaminated brew.

Although without thespian gifts I do excel at concealing my feelings during Sderot-type conversations. Some critics deplore this, seeing it as tantamount to hypocrisy – or as a sort of eavesdropping, my companions not knowing to whom, really, they are baring their souls. However, if one wants to find out what makes extremists tick it's counterproductive to attempt a reasoned debate for which they, by definition, would have no time. Also, in particularly delicate situations, such as I was to encounter later on the West Bank, I carefully conceal my interlocutors' identities. And I sit steadily on the fence, eschewing leading questions. But sitting on the fence is not a restful posture; that evening I invented a headache and retired early.

CHAPTER 6

The Crater of Makhtesh Ramon

I was beginning to feel caged; towns and cities are not my natural habitat. So I went south to ramble through the celebrated crater of Makhtesh Ramon.

The bus from Be'er Sheva was half-full of Uzi-laden conscripts, the girls noticeably more cheerful than the boys. For them we did a 20-mile détour on a narrow military road lined with 'DANGER!' signs. Throughout this area the Negev is grievously scarred by tank tracks, wired-off corridors and metal barriers. When the conscripts disembarked they paused to light cigarettes before trudging off across undulating sandiness to an invisible base. Then the other passengers, five Bedouin women, adjusted their burkahs to expose fine features and pallid complexions. Seemingly the bus driver, being out of sight, didn't count. They all got off together and followed a faint path into the desert.

Mitzpe Ramon (population 5,700), an early development town, was experimentally dispersed over different levels of its wide hilltop. The original Moroccans have long since drifted away to slummy crevices of Tel Aviv and been replaced by – mostly – unskilled Russians. Jobs are few and the local council, a Jewish National Fund (JNF) protégé, energetically promotes eco-tourism. Curiously, its literature overlooks the 'Alternative Quarter', a former industrial zone housing an enterprising colony of artists, soap-makers, potters, a contemporary dance company and several vaguely creative drop-outs holding interesting views about twenty-first-century Israel. Those last may explain the colony's being overlooked by the council.

I met nobody while following a car-free street between dingy apartment blocks, boarded-up shops, a closed cafeteria and some bright hedges of drought-resistant shrubs. Discreet signposts directed me to the fortress-like 'Youth Hostel and Guest House', complete with conference hall, indoor swimming pool, audiovisual systems, a self-service restaurant, many bedrooms and dorms. I shared a six-person dorm with two other persons, both congenial.

*

Makhtesh Ramon is 25 miles long, 5 miles wide, almost 1,000 feet deep and approximately 110 million years old. I first approached the crater's edge at an open spot. Below me, as far as could be seen in every direction, stretched a chaos of cliffs and *wadis*, mounds and clefts, peaks and boulders, an incomparable diversity of shapes, textures and hues – yellow, brown, red, black, gold, white, all changing dramatically in response to the sun's movement. A mega-hotel was being built close to the Visitors' Centre, also on the cliff edge. Still worse, in the Centre's bar I met Amos, a developer, who talked excitedly of a row of chalets along the crater's rim and a tarred road along the crater's floor. When I registered shock/horror he pointed to the benefits for Mitzpe Ramon's unemployed. But there is ample evidence that the construction of luxury accommodation in 'backward' places only temporarily alleviates local joblessness. Multi-starred hotels are not staffed by the simple labourers who build them.

The Visitors' Centre, self-described as 'ammonite-shaped', looked to me like a misshapen grain silo rather than a magnified snail. (On matters architectural, Prince Charles and I are soulmates; I don't care how many dodgy fellow-princes he colludes with in his efforts to protect London.) The Diaspora funded the centre's impressive introduction to Ramon's geological, zoological and human history. Unfortunately some crude *hasbara* mars the video, otherwise scholarly and entertaining. A male Boston voice explains that it took Nature 110 million years to create Makhtesh Ramon but Man quickly changed it: the Israelites, Nabateans, Romans, Byzantines. Then came the conquering Arabs and civilisation ceased. Primitive nomads (the Bedouin were not named) occupied the territory until, in 1948, another strong government replaced Rome and offered 'civilisation' to the nomads . . . In another, shorter video the same voice extols Man's ability to subdue Nature and we see drills and bulldozers wrenching our planet apart. At which point, since I was alone in the video theatre, I felt free to stamp my feet and yell, 'You bloody fool!'

My return to the hostel coincided with the arrival of two coachloads of teenagers on a three-day expedition to hone their appreciation of Eretz Israel. Each youngster was burdened with more luggage than I would pack for a three-month journey. Their four armed guards, wearing scarlet private security company uniforms, remained on duty throughout the evening: in the TV/video lounge, the cafeteria and

restaurant, the pool and disco. Even primary school children, on brief
outings to local parks, are similarly guarded. Most children take life as it
comes and won't register the significance of this abnormality. Yet some,
as they grow up, must recognise the irony that Jews are less safe in their
'homeland' than anywhere else on earth. I remember Mitzpe Ramon as
the place where I realised, for the first time, that the Zionist State of
Israel cannot survive. That was a revelatory and rather shocking moment,
the awareness sharp and clear, not speculative or hesitant or in any way
amorphous.

Most of the Negev (a rock desert, covering 60% of Israel's territory) is
reserved for military use and in Makhtesh Ramon there are firing zones
along its perimeter. It can take a week to obtain army approval to hike
there, which in any case didn't interest me. The Centre's director worried
about my walking alone, though the crater has been criss-crossed by paths
since Nabatean times. 'Ring me,' she urged, 'if you need help.' On
discovering my lack of a mobile, worry turned to near-panic. 'But in a
problem – something going wrong – what do you *do*?' Although a middle-
aged woman, she had already forgotten that until very recently human
beings functioned as self-sufficient individuals not dependent on instant
communication with everyone everywhere. Now and then a traveller
might perish in isolation but not often enough for the risk to be inhibiting.

By purist standards Makhtesh Ramon is tourism-tainted, furnished
with twee little green-on-white trail markers and a campsite where palm-
frond umbrellas shade picnic tables at a discreet distance from the
'restrooms'. (How did this ludicrous term come into use? In such rooms
people urinate, defecate, wash and comb themselves, change clothes and
nappies, consume or trade in drugs, occasionally fornicate or bugger
each other – the one thing they never do is *rest*.)

Tourism can't be blamed for the sonic booms and menacing screams
of an air force intent on reminding Palestinians of Israel's apparent
national motto – 'Might is Right!' Other violators of the precious desert
silence were snarling sand-buggies carrying pairs of tourists (mostly
young, I was shocked to observe) along level tracks which happily limited
their range.

My destination was Saharonim spring; it attracted me not as a Spice
Road station but as a place where one *might* see an onager or two. The
onager looks like a donkey, with slightly longer legs, but is in fact
the world's smallest horse. It is totally resistant to domestication and

vanished from the Negev long, long ago, perhaps because the Romans relished onager foal meat. In 1983 the Israeli Nature Protection Authority decided on an experiment, much derided at the time. They let fourteen onagers loose in Makhtesh Ramon and by now more than 100 are thriving throughout the Negev, forty or so in the crater. Soldiers who enjoy shooting the Bedouins' goats and donkeys do not shoot the onager, which might be said to enjoy Ashkenazi status.

At dawn I set off and for a few magical hours, as Ramon's contrasting colours changed swiftly and subtly, this crater seemed like some vast studio where an invisible artist was at work. 'Beauty' misses the mark – too bland, not inclusive enough. Here all is extreme – the elemental grandeur of the rock formations monstrous and delicate, rugged and sleek – the eccentric, minute patterns wrought by erosion on boulders and cliff-faces – the eerie sense of having shrunk (like Alice) as one stands looking around, in mid-crater. 'Unique' is a hard adjective to justify yet I've no quarrel with those who thus describe Makhtesh Ramon.

To avoid the sand-buggies I took two gravel-slippy paths across what had looked from above like hillocks. In the noon heat they felt like mountains. At Saharonim I rested, emptied my water-bottle and longed to see an onager. None obliged. Heat exhaustion threatened as I slowly climbed out of the depths on a path that ended, mercifully, within yards of the Centre's bar.

At sundown Rebecca and Ida, my dorm-mates, joined me by appointment. They chose juices and looked slightly shocked when the granny-figure fetched herself a second beer.

Rebecca had a tangled background – born in Germany in 1980 to a Russian Jewess and an atheist Istanbul-bred Armenian. Before she could remember, her mother had 'gone ultra-Orthodox' and insisted on making *aliyah*. Her physicist father disliked having to pretend to be a Jew and after a few years returned to Germany. She herself couldn't accept the ultra way of life – 'it strangles women's academic ambitions' – and had rarely contacted her mother since going to university. In secular Tel Aviv she was at ease. 'I know I'm half not Jewish but it's the mother that matters! I don't like the religion but I love the land, Israel feels it's *my* place! I've had fun with my father in Germany and relatives in New York and Vancouver and I could get a job in Hamburg. But it's Israel makes me feel at home.' Rebecca lectured in Haifa University and was in Mitzpe Ramon to organise a field trip for her geology students.

Ida had arrived from Moscow as a twelve-year-old, soon after the death of her parents and older sister in an air crash. She swotted at school ('to help me forget') and fourteen years later graduated from Jerusalem's Hebrew University as a 'political sociologist'. She had enjoyed her two years of army life, especially serving in Hebron where she felt 'really needed'. Then came a year at Bristol University – good for her English but the 'anti-Semitism' of a 'certain sort of activist' bothered her. On the previous evening, when I had challenged this perception of the motivation of the 'activists', Ida either couldn't or wouldn't make the distinction between anti-Semitism and anti-Zionism. Although an ardent supporter of Gush Emunim, the settlers' organis-ation, she condemned 'illegal outposts'. On my remarking that all settlements are illegal by international law, she scoffed at the UN.

Ida was now researching relationships between Mizrahim and 'the Russian underclass' in development towns. I mentioned my tour with Ellie and Jacob and asked, 'Have you a theory about the undevelopment?'

The response came quickly, with a brief smile. 'I don't need a theory, I've the facts. All done for Ashkenazi profit. They led the town councils but lived somewhere else, keeping away from the trash. They started industries, privately owned by their friends, and workers never got the average wage. All profits went to them, no share for the councils. They built factories on kibbutz land so the business taxes had to go to the kibbutzim, not the councils. Everything went underfunded. The schools had bad teachers and called themselves "vocationally guided" and focused on non-academic subjects – if they focused at all. That's why communities collapsed completely when government switched to high-tech industries. Uneducated workers couldn't compete and still can't. Today I interviewed five families of three generations who never had regular jobs.'

Likud's historic 1977 victory was achieved with Mizrahim support, gained by making many promises that soon were broken. Ida explained how that came about. Settlers from the Ashkenazi National-Religious party were desperate for funding and most of the national budget went to them. By 1995 twice as much was being spent on settlements as on development towns. Oslo made that necessary, to remind the world that Judea and Samaria are part of Israel and will stay that way whatever accords may be signed.

When Amos, the developer, emerged onto the verandah he asked if he might sit at our table. Pale, pudgy and forty-ish, he was struggling not to be one of the unsuccessful Russians. Rebecca and Ida, both on the way to success, were unwelcoming. But perhaps Amos didn't notice. He had had a good day; almost certainly the holiday homes project would get approval, despite gathering public opposition. My companions looked at their watches and reminded me that it was dinner-time at the hostel. I finished my beer and followed them, feeling slightly ashamed of myself, wishing our snubbing of Amos had been less direct.

Next morning I walked beyond the Camel's Head Hill on a tourist trail that morphs into a foot-wide unprotected path along an almost sheer slope overlooking Makhtesh Ramon. Then, rounding this mountain's shoulder, I was suddenly beside an IDF Field School, its dozens of prefab huts packed onto an artificial ledge. At 7.00 a.m. the sentry box was empty. My pathlet ran so close to the wire-mesh fence I could have touched noses with two startled girl conscripts, hanging out their washing. Three chained Alsatians gave hysterical displays of thwarted savagery and several youths came to doorways peering at me sleepily. I waved at them (no response) before the pathlet descended to a narrow road.

From here, said the map, a three-mile walk would take me to Mitzpe Ramon's most bizarre tourist attraction, a long-established alpaca farm belonging to a local politician. His flock, imported from Chile, provides wool for scarves and caps sold on the premises. Who, I wondered, wants to observe misfortunate exiles from the *puna* enduring life in the Negev? But Ida had urged me to talk to the staff – 'They have first-hand information about the Bedouin, stuff you won't get in the media.'

Beyond a shallow *wadi*, the road turned this way and that between long, low grey ridges scattered with prickly pear and an odd hedgehog-like plant. Here was an unmilitarised zone – not a building to be seen, not a vehicle to be heard.

The alpaca farm – a bungalow, huts, stables, barns – is tucked into a fold between the ridges, sheltered from one side by a high bluff. There was no security fence and an old wooden double gate stood wide open. Inside, alpacas and a few llamas were ambling around without restraint and might have liberated themselves had they not known on which side their hay was baled. I too ambled around, occasionally pausing to scratch the more sociable alpacas between the ears. Repeatedly I hallooed but no one appeared. The farm's appearance suggested a shiftless staff. I was about to leave when angry shouting summoned me back and a tall, bearded young man, wearing cowboy gear and speaking Strine, accused me of trying to sneak away without paying. He held out his hand: entrance 25 shekels. I hesitated; it's not easy to part me from my money. But given the vibes an argument seemed not worthwhile.

By 2.00 p.m. I was looking for the cafeteria in Mitzpe Ramon's one-storey shopping centre where the town's poverty goes naked. Kind Ida had invited me to join the party at the end of her lunchtime interview with two Black Hebrews.

Of Israel's variegated communities, none can be odder than these. In 1966, when racial tensions increasingly troubled the US, a black Israelite bus-driver (Ben Carter aka Ben Ammi ben Israel) got an urgent message from the Angel Gabriel: the black Israelites, defeated and exiled by the Romans, were the legitimate owners of the Holy Land and he should now lead them home. More than 400 were easily persuaded to accompany him to Liberia, where they 'purged themselves' for two years before moving on to their inheritance. Israel put out no flags; here was obvious development town material. The Chief Rabbinate deemed them non-Jewish and as two more batches arrived, in the early '70s, it seemed quite a few had criminal records. When the government gave them a choice – 'convert or leave!' – they refused to do either, accusing the Ashkenazi of being imposters and dictators. For the next twenty years they defiantly retained their own adaptation of Judaism while existing in a legal vacuum. At intervals, when threatened with expulsion, they went on hunger strike and were backed by some wacky US politicians. In 1990 they acquired tourist status, with renewable visas, but the real breakthrough came during the second Intifada, when a Palestinian murdered six Black Hebrews. This tragic event secured them residency though not citizenship. The majority still live in Dimona, a development town with a difference; nearby, Israel produces nuclear weapons while the 'international community' pretends not to notice. Since the '80s, a small group has been living in Mitzpe Ramon.

The drab cafeteria smelled of over-used cooking oil, hot dogs, instant coffee and fake ice-cream. But one corner was colourful; Ida's smiling companions, broad-shouldered and big-bellied, wore loose cotton tunics striped pink, orange, purple, scarlet. Uriahu and Ephraim were both middle-aged with rotten teeth, which surprised me; Black Hebrews are vegan and severely punished if they transgress. A jolly pair, they had soon sold me four DVDs of their famous choir, internationally acclaimed and the community's main source of income. Ida treated them almost deferentially; perhaps that was her professional style with all interviewees.

By now, in Dimona, there are some 2,500 Black Hebrews, including 700 or so primary school children for whose education US Congress had recently donated $1 million. 'I guess those Congressmen are proud of us,' said Uriahu. 'We weren't gonna be kep' down by no one!'

Ida noted, inter alia, that Black Hebrews are consciously maintaining their American accents.

Ephraim boasted that he had provided four of those 700 children, with some assistance from his third wife. His ten older children were past school age but couldn't find jobs. I enquired sympathetically about the fate of the other wives, then discovered that Black Hebrews are polygamous. 'Very polygamous!' chuckled Ida. 'Uriahu has five wives.'

Uriahu beamed at me, looking self-satisfied. 'It's because of menstruation,' he explained. 'For so long every month a woman can't touch food or come close, so we need many.'

I asked if young Black Hebrews, not being citizens, can escape conscription.

'They can serve or not,' said Ephraim. 'Most kids want it – boys, not many girls.' But there were complications because Black Hebrews must wear only cotton garments and never touch leather. However, the IDF had compromised, allowing canvas boots. And the Black Hebrews had compromised, allowing non-cotton uniforms. It seemed neither of these men had much use for militarism; they were allied, Ida later told me, with some equally ersatz Christians in a Peace & Reconciliation Centre. She also remarked on certain similarities between the Black Hebrews and the ultra-Orthodox: no contraception, women expected to lead dependent lives, complex taboos around cooking and eating. In Mitzpe Ramon she was hoping to visit homes, having failed to gain access in Dimona. 'Could be another taboo about that. I want to look at the power structure within the community – nothing to do with my current research, but they fascinate me!'

My next stop was Sde Boker, where generations of Israelis have communed with Ben-Gurion's ghost as part of their Zionist conditioning.

On the scattered campus I stayed in the guesthouse, run by London-born John – generously helpful, witty, intelligent. He had made *aliyah* in the '80s, labelled himself 'English Zionist, non-observant Jew' and couldn't understand why anybody should criticise Israel. 'Has to be all that anti-Semitic stuff, we hear it's growing everywhere around the world.'

Sde Boker comes in two parts. Haganah soldiers, newly released from British Mandate jails, founded the famous kibbutz where Ben-Gurion daydreamed about making the Negev bloom. The trees he so emotionally planted in May 1952 form an impressive oasis. Quite separate is the campus, an extension of Be'er Sheva University, housing hundreds of research workers and students who focus on solar energy, environmental protection, desert agriculture and kindred disciplines. One conspicuous block caters for research students, mainly African, from countries with severe desertification problems. This unit was established when Shimon Peres persuaded the German government to divert some of its own 'Aid for Africa' to the Israeli project. In the mid-'80s the Peres regime made strenuous efforts to repair relations with those African states which had been snubbing Israel.

John invited two of his English-speaking neighbours (Uzi a geologist, Yagil a solar physicist) to give me insights into Israel's peculiar difficulties. Together the four of us strolled through an attractive Ben-Gurion memorial parklet furnished with gazelles; Bedouin workers had built the handsome dry-stone wall and chosen a range of desert-compatible plants to ensure year-round flowering. Soon we came to the graves of Paula and David Ben-Gurion, simple sarcophagi overlooking the Zin Valley and Avdat plain. The cliff-top had been modified (desecrated) to allow excursions to pay homage and now two coachloads of children were approaching from the invisible car park. Uzi had been talking about the kibbutzim having their ideological roots in late nineteenth-century Germany, and he remarked that Zionism's insistence on showing children every region of their country had the same provenance. 'It's necessary,' he said, 'to strengthen nationalism, patriotism. You can't have a democracy without nationalism. It unites a mix of people as citizens, all equal under the law.'

I cautiously put one foot on thin ice. 'What happens if some in the mix are not equal under the law?'

Uzi laughed. 'The law must change!'

I took a risk with the other foot. 'When d'you think the Knesset will change it for Israel's Arabs?' Deliberately I had avoided the provocative word 'Palestinians' but still the ice broke.

'Their status is appropriate,' snapped Uzi. 'This is a Jewish state.'

John and Yagil had been walking a little ahead: now Yagil fell back to rescue me by reminding Uzi, 'Some visitors take time to get used to this country. Then they see why we must run it our way.' I quickened my pace to catch up with John.

Sde Boker was preparing for a ceremony held annually beside the Ben-Gurion graves and usually attended by both President and Prime Minister. On the wide campus streets trees and shrubs had been pruned, verges tidied and scores of small orange flags – about a foot square – attached to fence struts. When I asked about their significance everyone became evasive, muttering and mumbling incoherently. Later I learned that such displays affirm active support for Gush Emunim.

Kind John tried to plan my second Sde Boker day; much remained to be seen, like the Ben-Gurions' home, the Ben-Gurion archive, the kibbutz's winery, sculpture museum, reptile farm and craft shop . . . Then I revealed my own plan, to give myself a therapeutic seventy-seventh birthday present by walking up the Zin Valley, an area free of signposted paths, sand-buggies and restrooms. Like a good host John at once changed gear and offered to lend me an essential stout stick. His verbal directions were precise: how to go one way along the valley floor and return across a high *mesa*. And he didn't freak out at the prospect of my taking off without a cell phone. He may sound like an unreconstructed Zionist but he's also a common-sense Englishman.

The guesthouse stands where campus meets desert. As I walked through the soft dawn light a fox crossed my path, trotting briskly – then took fright, dropped his empty dog-meat tin and raced away. The Zin canyon remains invisible until it's *there* – an absent-minded walker could tumble over the edge into rocky depths. That edge is crumbly; but I soon found a safe way down, a pebble-slithery zigzagging goat trail. During my descent the sun rose, spotlighting the opposite cliff wall; its distinct layers of white, russet and gold were mathematically regular.

On the wide valley floor my path ran straight between low hills – some round, some pointed, all dwarfed by the gaunt cliffs. The hills' sandy surfaces, strewn with slivers of polished stone – black and brown

– glittered as the sun climbed. The southern cliff formed the edge of that *mesa* I would cross on my way back. Where it sloped slightly down, the path turned right to negotiate a jumble of rocky hillocks supporting glossy dark green bushes – the only vegetation in sight. The absence of birds was no surprise but the presence of snail shells was – thousands of them, all white. When the path vanished my way forward was obvious for lack of choice: through a narrow *wadi*, packed with smooth boulders to be scrambled over slowly and carefully. Here a nearby movement caught my eye – a herd of Nubian ibex, seeming to flow *up* an almost sheer precipice, their agile grace making mountain goats look clumsy.

John had mentioned a microclimate and soon tough little plants were growing from crevices in the underfoot rocks while tenuous creepers trailed from the cliff-tops. Then an extraordinary phenomenon appeared, a 'road' of smooth white gypsum slabs – each flawless, without a crack or a chip, measuring up to thirty feet by ten, their edges rounded. For half a mile or so these extended contiguously, providing the day's easiest walking. Then the *wadi* became a cleft between highish cliffs sprouting a lush variety of vines and grasses.

Ten minutes later I stopped, transfixed. The way ahead was blocked by my destination. This natural grotto, some thirty feet high and narrow in proportion, was apparently supported by a semi-circle of slender, soaring columns topped by symmetrical bulges – erosion's 'capitals'. Within lay a pool of spring water, now depleted and rather scummy; November had been alarmingly dry. On the surrounding mud, amidst many animal footprints, I fancied I saw a leopard's – not improbable. Nearby, proving the spring's subterranean vitality, stood a magnificent display of feathery reeds, twice my height, swaying slightly in a breeze I hadn't previously noticed.

For a long time I rested by the grotto, in a trance of delight. This birthday present felt very therapeutic.

The return journey might have been an anticlimax but wasn't. To climb out of the cleft – John had explained – one must find an iron ladder implanted halfway up a cliff where in times past the Nabateans, Romans and Byzantines had hewn steps in the rock and kept them free of vegetation. While seeking this 'facility' I slipped but fortunately (the lesser of two evils) fell into a retaining cactus – an amiable cactus, which didn't punish me too severely. Pulling myself onto level ground, I sat briefly, to recover from the fall and say farewell to the grotto – its mysterious symmetry even more arresting, seen from above.

On the far side of this wide, level plateau, my faint path (too narrow for a pack-animal) rounded a bulky mountain with a sheer 300-foot drop on one side. I've never had a good head for heights and old age affects one's balance; that 20-minute ordeal made me sweat with terror. Then the Zin Valley was again visible, far below, and the path was replaced by a tangle of old goat tracks, wriggling between outcrops and into clefts and over mounds of loose shale.

Suddenly I was amidst an erosion-exhibition such as I have never seen elsewhere – and I've seen many. All around stood an extraordinary array of squat gypsum pillars, weirdly akin to pedestals in a sculpture gallery, and on most of them rested a chunk of grey limestone grotesquely weather-worn to gargoyle faces or mythical monsters. Most were within touching distance and at eye-level, as though positioned for the benefit of passers-by. Was I hallucinating? For a moment I fancied human intervention but John later assured me these are *bona fide* works of Nature's art. As with real gargoyles, their ugliness was at once entertaining, repellent and enchanting. I lingered until lengthening shadows spurred me homewards across the *mesa*, which doesn't quite live up to its name; there were several gullies and hillocks. In one hollow, three wretched Bedouin children crouched beside an antiquated primus stove outside a patched tent. When I greeted them they looked scared so I quickly walked on, passing a bony donkey picketed beside a wooden crate containing two hens. These were the first fellow-beings I had seen in ten and a half hours.

To give myself a happy birthday I had been trying not to think about the Bedouin but in the middle of the Negev it's hard to filter them out. Without their homeland they are, as a people, doomed. Some individuals will thrive, given a chance, but such a distinctive culture cannot be transplanted. Desert nomads need their desert.

As I began the descent, two griffon vultures sailed into view just below me; they nest hereabouts on the highest ledges. My Negev souvenirs are six enormous snail shells and a fine selection of porcupine quills, now decorating the table on which I write this.

Sde Boker's Desert Research Institute is passionate about molluscs and John lent me a paper by Moshe Shachak and Yossi Steinberger, the fruit of twelve years' study. Most of it was beyond my comprehension but I gleaned that the Negev's snails and woodlice are survivors from before the last Ice Age. When the Big Melt came, and then evaporation brought about the Middle East's deserts, both hung in there and adapted to a two-inch annual rainfall. The snails are active for an average of twenty days a year. The other eleven months and ten days are spent in aestivation (hibernation during summer). Being hermaphroditic aids survival: everyone can lay eggs. They do however mate; their reproduction is not – as in my ignorance I had always supposed – a DIY job. When the rain comes they emerge, after a year-long fast, thinking only of sex. Not until mutual impregnation is completed, and all sex glands are producing eggs, do they set about gorging themselves on enough post-rain algae to get them through the next year. Each snail lays 30 to 40 eggs, incubation takes a month and the infant mortality rate is not far off 90%. They may well be around long after homo sapiens has engineered his own extinction.

The assertion 'He should be shot!' is common enough. We all know it isn't meant to be taken seriously, merely expresses angry frustration. But when it was used about a dear Israeli friend of mine in Sde Boker, I was shaken. Occasionally, in the Holy Land, people perceived as traitors are murdered and the murderer is not universally condemned. My friend, who has publicly scrutinised the murky origins of the State of Israel is, therefore, to some, a traitor.

There were five of us sitting around a table in the craft shop café. My companions were distinguished in their various fields, on campus for a conference. I had lit the fuse by referring to post-Zionism, a concept I assumed could be discussed calmly in such company. Neither of the two who affirmed 'He should be shot!' had studied (or even skimmed) my friend's work, yet both knew a lot about his family and personal history. Of course they themselves would never murder a political enemy but they would most probably condone his assassination. Abruptly I was jolted back to Northern Ireland in the 1970s. There I also met people who regarded the assassination of perceived traitors as reasonable and desirable. The difference was that those Northern Irish (Orange and Green) were not eminent academics. And the activities they perceived as 'traitorous' were not being conducted on an intellectual plane. What so disturbed me, around that table, was the antagonism to honest debate and the fear so palpably felt when Zionist myths were challenged.

I prefer not to name-drop but on this occasion I did, saying that I knew the hated scholar and defending him as a responsible Israeli citizen who loves his country. At that date, remember, I was a tyro in Israel, only half-aware of what I was up against. Reading over my journal record of that long argument, I mock my own naivety.

I was tightening my rucksack belt when John hurried in to say, 'Forget the No. 60! Menachem's going to Jerusalem – you'll enjoy him, he's an environmentalist, very Green.'

Ten minutes later Menachem collected me – a fit and bronzed fifty-year-old, a desert-lover who wished he didn't have to spend the next week in a city. I resolved to avoid matters environmental; already I had my doubts about Israeli Greens who can be useful to Gush Emunim in complex ways that needn't detain us here.

It startled Menachem to hear that I was staying in the Muslim Quarter. 'Aren't you afraid of them?'

'Afraid of what?' I asked.

'They're murdering dogs! And you're a woman alone in their place – they might think you're a Jew! At school they're all taught to kill Jews if they can!'

That common slander may well be part of the propaganda package in many Israeli schools. I referred Menachem to Professor Nathan Brown, an acknowledged authority on post-Nakba education. He has concluded:

> The vitriolic and often inaccurate criticisms of Palestinian textbooks should not obscure the fact that those books do treat Israel with a remarkable awkwardness and reticence. Jews are mentioned primarily in a religious context and not in a political context. However, the silence on such issues is more confused and embarrassed than it is hostile . . .

Menachem laughed. 'Are you with those ISM people? I've no ideology or ideals. I don't feel like I'm a Zionist but I say "yes" to settlements. We've 20% Arabs here. If they can live in Israel, why can't we live in Judea and Samaria?'

Menachem's unresentful acceptance of my textbook stance emboldened me. 'Isn't this oranges and apples? The Arabs belong in Israel. The settlers don't belong in Samaria and Judea.'

'Sure they do!' said Menachem. 'You know they do, it's all part of our inheritance. *Every* Jew's inheritance!'

I couldn't resist deploying the most dog-eared argument which does have the merit of making political Zionism look silly. 'How would our world be if everyone said they were entitled to settle on land inhabited by their ancestors 2,000 years ago?'

'You're provoking me!' complained Menachem. 'Jews are different and everyone knows why. No Holocaust if we'd our own land then – six million lives saved!'

I continued to provoke. 'How many of the comfortably assimilated Jews would have come in the '30s even if they could?'

'My grandparents came from Prague,' said Menachem. 'And they were very comfortably assimilated. Millions more would have settled here if the British hadn't kept them out.'

We came just then to a 'viewpoint' and Menachem stopped, suggesting a stroll through pine trees to an artificial lake. Then he noticed two Bedouin sitting nearby in a rusty little van and changed his mind. 'You go down, it's worth seeing the water lilies. I'll stay here with the car.'

On the road again, Menachem said, 'Let's have some music to relax.' We listened to Bartok, Liszt and Smetana all the way to Jerusalem, where magnanimous Menachem went far out of his way to leave me at the Jaffa Gate.

CHAPTER 7

Finding Balata

Balata is the West Bank's most populous refugee camp; 24,000 Palestinians are confined to one square kilometre. In 1948, when thousands fled from Jaffa to Gaza, thousands more camped near Tel Balata (the biblical Shechem) on a stony slope at the foot of Mount Jerzim. For four years six thousand lived in tents, provided by a special UN agency, without running water, electricity, sanitation or adequate food.

In Jaffa Hassan had recommended Balata as my West Bank base. He said, 'If you want our problem condensed, at its most heroic, most degraded and most harrowing, go to Balata. It's a tough place. They're proud of their reputation as a centre of anti-IDF excellence. They say the babies are born knowing about resistance and can aim stones before they can talk. I get news from my cousins there and now it's quiet. There's a lull, the PA are supposed to be half in charge. People welcome foreign supporters. If you go to the Yaffa Centre its Director will help you find lodgings.'

During the second Intifada (2000–5) many Balatans fought against the paratroopers' bombing and shelling, shooting at water tanks, bull-dozing of clinics and shops, looting of homes and storehouses. In March 2002 the commander of an IDF paratroop brigade brought ridicule upon himself (in certain circles) by announcing on TV 'Balata has surrendered!' The camp's defenders were untrained in combat, armed only with home-made hand-grenades and AK47s. No wonder they surrendered to a brigade of the world's fourth strongest army. However, the commander's audience were no doubt comforted to hear that their daring paratroopers had vanquished hordes of vicious terrorists.

By now Balata is a big town on the edge of the big city of Nablus. From East Jerusalem one takes a No. 18 minibus to Ramallah, another to the Huwwara walk-across checkpoint, then a shared taxi to the Jacob's Well junction where Balata begins.

On a clear crisp morning – the eastern horizon faintly pink – I secured a front seat: important for my first visit to the West Bank. An odd phrase, 'the West Bank'. In conversation with myself I always use Samaria and Judea, only politically incorrect because hijacked by Zionism. To me those names have the value of an ancient coinage that should not be exchanged for transient paper currency. Mourid Barghouti, one of Palestine's most esteemed living poets, objects to 'West Bank' for more trenchant reasons:

> If you open the map of historic Palestine, you will find it located between the Mediterranean Sea on the west and the River Jordan on the east. The Zionist gangs occupied western Palestine, the country's Mediterranean coast, and most of its inhabitants took refuge in eastern Palestine, which extends to the River Jordan. Since the aim was to wipe the name 'Palestine' from the map, from history, and from memory, this area was attached to the River Jordan and called, in Arabic and every other language, 'the West Bank'. With this, the name 'Palestine' finally disappeared from the maps of the world. If the west of the country is now called 'Israel' and the east is called 'the West Bank', where is Palestine? For Palestine to be lost as a land, it had to be lost as a word too. Every time I hear the term 'West Bank', I think of the enormous and deliberate pollution of language that has led to the assassination of the word 'Palestine'.

Somehow 'the Bank' doesn't quite work but I've tried to use 'Palestine' as often as possible.

At the back sat four workmen, scarved and gloved as though the Ice Age had returned, on their way to Atarot industrial estate. Most of the other passengers were students whose hard-won passes allowed them to attend Birzeit University near Ramallah.

Beside me sat Hanna, wearing the *hijab*, and blue jeans under an ankle-length black coat, and carrying a briefcase too fat to be closed. She lived in Silwan, had to rise on lecture days at 5.30 a.m., didn't get home until after dark and couldn't join in any of the university's evening activities. If Jerusalemite students were to do the normal thing and move to live near Birzeit they would permanently forfeit their blue ID cards.

Hanna, in her third year, hoped an economics degree would open the way to a job in a PA ministry. 'Except you know it's not a real government,' she said, looking sad. 'It's an *administration*. A real government fully controls. The PA only controls bits Israel doesn't want.'

If, as a graduate, Hanna filed to get a security pass to work in the OPT, she would have to choose between employment and family. 'This makes me worry. My parents are brave, saying I must take any job. Then I lose my blue card because I'm living outside Jerusalem. After that I can't visit them and they have no pass to visit me. People say it used to be like this in South Africa.'

Hanna's eyebrows went up when I revealed my destination. 'Why Balata? It's a place with too many problems and very rough people – be careful!'

As grimy Atarot appeared, my companion told me that Ezri Levi, of the Jerusalem Development Authority, had lied about its purpose. It would give employment, he claimed, to West Bank Palestinians who could get passes (not easily done). But the real advantage goes to Israeli firms who can compete with Palestinian firms for cut-price labour – while Palestinian firms are forbidden to compete for Israeli customers.

Approaching Qalandiya checkpoint, in the emotional shadow of the Wall, Hanna asked, 'You've seen it before?'

I nodded. 'Several times – but always I have an equally strong reaction.' I paused, unable to find words to describe that reaction: a searing mix of horror, rage, grief and despair. Also revulsion, its ugliness is so overwhelming; and its environs have been brutalised by gigantic machines and defaced by builders' left-overs – hillocks of litter-strewn rubble, cottage-sized chunks of jagged concrete, rusty twisted girders. However many photographs and films one has seen, to be in this menacing presence is profoundly distressing – and frightening. It symbolises (amongst so much else) an over-armed regime that has lost the plot.

In any OPT context, to say 'the Wall' is enough. But we need something more precise because much of this barrier is a fence. One has a wide choice. The verbosely titled (and disposable) UN Special Rapporteur on the Situation of Human Rights in the Occupied Palestinian Territories uses 'Annexation Wall'. So does Al-Haq, the Palestinians' leading human rights NGO. Other options are – Separation Barrier, Security Fence, Apartheid Wall. I've chosen to pick 'n' mix and use Apartheid Barrier. However named, we should remember that civilised Israelis, many of whom have been injured on anti-Barrier demos, abhor this malignant construction.

I never got used to Qalandiya's electronic, war-zone checkpoint, which highlights the humiliating reality of military rule. This was a routine crossing, on an average day, so why was there a 20-minute delay before two conscripts came on board to check our IDs? They moved provocatively slowly, stopping twice to exchange amused comments about certain IDs – shades of my Peace Now bus tour. As I swore *sotto voce* Hanna said, 'They're not all like this. Some are tougher, some better. Coming back is much worse.'

Beyond Qalandiya high-quality graffiti decorated the Apartheid Barrier on our left. A varied exhibition: poignant, defiant, comical, threatening, bland, sarcastic – all of it cheering.

Immediately we were in a built-up area where the newish (sixteenth century) village of Ramallah and the ancient (Canaanite) village of al-Bireh have merged into a city of 60,000. As the PA capital, Ramallah is growing fast and untidily. Post-Oslo, billions were donated by the EU, US, Japan and others. Several ministerial office blocks, as pretentious as they are superfluous, illustrate the abuse of that funding. As Hanna had indicated, Oslo was a con-trick, giving the Palestinians an illusory authority that suited Israel's plan to retain control of the West Bank with Fatah collaboration. In theory the Accords, signed in 1993, marked a stage on the way to Palestinian independence. Yet shrewd observers like Edward Said and Raja Shehadeh at once diagnosed another Israeli device to placate the 'international community' while settlements expanded to ensure that the two-state solution could never amount to more than a set of bantustans. Ariel Sharon, the settlers' most powerful patron, himself used that loaded word in conversation with the then prime minister of Italy, Massimo D'Alema. Said Sharon: 'The only possibility for a solution for the Palestinians would be the establishment of bantustans.' Tellingly, the Oslo Accords set up three administrations within the Occupied Palestinian Territories. Area A (less than 3%) is fully controlled by the PA; Area B (25%) is under PA civil control and Israeli security control; Area C (72%) is under full Israeli control, exercised through Military Orders.

Hanna gave me her Silwan address before getting off at the entrance to Ramallah's bus station and hurrying away to the distant Birzeit taxi stand.

Within the station – disorganised, ill-lit, stinking of spilt petrol – scores of canary-yellow minibuses were parked haphazardly with open sliding doors and no labels. Both passengers and drivers' touts moved around shouting destinations. Here I felt myself relaxing, both emotionally and physically – being at ease as I could never be in Israel. This admission does nothing for my reputation as an 'objective reporter' but I had long since abandoned that role. Amidst the Palestinian/Israeli turmoil, not taking sides is immoral.

I sauntered to and fro shouting 'Nablus!' and soon was directed to the last seat in a vehicle near retirement age. Tickets are not required; one pays en route, people passing their 15 shekels (3 euros) to the driver at no particular stage. Change can be a problem but during many bus- and taxi-rides on the West Bank I never once heard a dispute about money.

Beyond the first army checkpoint we were in the hills, some topped by red-roofed settlements. Limestone boulders flecked wide slopes, grey-brown in winter, their terraces pre-dating Jesus. Spontaneously I thought of myself as being at last in Samaria but that was politically very incorrect. One fiercely resents the Zionists' hijacking of Judea and Samaria, those resonant names we should all be able to use instead of 'south West Bank and 'north West Bank'. Signposts benefiting Israelis only pointed to Ma'ale Adumim, Shiloh, Ofra and other smaller settlements. Palestinian cars cannot use apartheid roads; that's part of the bantustan project.

Beside me sat a slim dapper man with the sort of features cartoonists once conferred on Jews. Mr Ishaq had recently returned to Nablus after working for twenty-five years as a hotel manager in Toronto. 'Exile is hard,' he said. 'Every day I lived away I felt sad for these hills.' As we passed a crossroads he pointed to the signposts. 'Those names celebrate victories, the theft of our land and water. Successful theft, never to be punished.'

This road once linked Damascus to Jaffa and Mr Ishaq drew my attention to interesting villages. He knew exactly where to find the ruins of four Ottoman caravanserais and advised me to visit Sinjil; its mosque is a converted Crusader church. 'But don't try to enter. A few people have become prickly since the settlers fire-bombed some mosques and made dirt on the Holy Koran.' Most villages stand on the hills' lower slopes and are approached by rough tracks.

The dejected little town of Huwwara lines the road not far south of Nablus. Here, in 1974, a vanguard group of settlers arrived, led by the infamous Rabbi Zvi Yehuda Kook, then aged eighty-four. Among their supporters was General Ariel Sharon, on his way from military glory to political prominence. When confronted by Major-General Yona Efrat, the regional military ruler, Rabbi Kook said, 'Bring a machine gun and shoot me.' Instead, the Major-General ordered his men to remove the settlers because they lacked government approval. This temporary setback became a valuable recruiting device. Enlarged press photographs of soldiers manhandling unarmed, *kipa*-wearing youths significantly increased support for the embryonic Gush Emunim. When I asked Mr Ishaq if he remembered any of this he replied, 'I remember how soon they came back and stayed.'

And there they were, around the next corner, where an apartheid road joins the main road near Huwwara checkpoint. Every day settlers – usually women and children – wait here for a lift to Jerusalem or elsewhere. They feel safe because nowadays the IDF are always on their side. I never got used to this tragic juxtaposition of Palestinian throngs being processed at the checkpoint and little groups of settlers standing by the roadside – the Israelis forbidden to enter Nablus city in Area A, the Palestinians forbidden to set foot or tyre on the settlers' road. Is this any way for human beings to live in a twenty-first-century democracy?

At Huwwara minibuses and serveece taxis park on a stony acre close to the IDF base (complete with prison). Here enough troops were encamped to enforce martial law in Balata and Nablus should that seem appropriate. For arrivals there are no ID or luggage checks; departing is a very different experience. Mr Ishaq escorted me through heavy turnstiles and along a wired-in walkway that made me feel zooified. He warned, 'Be careful of Nablus taximen. They're mixed. Some like to give foreigners free rides. Others try to cheat. We've no tourists. Most foreigners they see work for NGOs, earning big. It's natural some try to cheat.'

Only serveece taxis awaited us beyond the walkway; for some neurotic 'security' reason minibuses were then excluded from Nablus. While our taxi was filling up Mr Ishaq gave me his card and invited me to meet his wife in January. Then, during a five-minute drive through a moribund industrial zone, he advised, 'Don't walk alone after dark in Balata. Remember it's abnormal. All refugee camps are. But Balata even more – so many people, so little space!' As he spoke, the taxi stopped to let me off at the Jacob's Well junction.

Opposite the Greek Orthodox church built around Jacob's Well I turned into a narrow laneway. No sign indicated that here is Balata Refugee Camp, rather than an impoverished suburb of Nablus.

Hammering noises came from a handsome new Saudi-sponsored mosque going up amidst the ramshackle squalor. Half a dozen small boys, playing on a pile of builders' sand, paused to stare. Then they yelled jeeringly and threw sand. I stood still to shake it out of my hair and asked, 'Yaffa Centre?' At once the mood changed. The boys moved closer, smiling, and the smallest, aged sixish, beckoned me to follow him. That said a lot about the benign influence of the Yaffa Cultural Centre and its remarkable Director, Mahmoud Subuh. As Hasan had predicted, Mahmoud was welcoming and helpful. Yes, in January I could rent a room from the family of one of his assistants, at 350 shekels per week (about 70 euros). The Centre hoped soon to set up a children's library so I gratefully promised to donate as many books as could be transported from Ireland by one person.

Back at Huwwara I entered an enormous foot-passengers' wired-in shed. Motorists queue at a road barrier flying outsize Israeli flags; they place their IDs in hands emerging from sandbagged sentry-boxes. Some car searches take a very long time, inciting angry outbursts which can lead to arrests.

In mid-afternoon the segregated shed queues were short; 26 men, 17 women. Iron bars formed corridors suitable for herding cattle at vaccination time. We showed our IDs and every bag, box, carton, sack, bucket and pocket was slowly probed. Looking at the young conscripts' expressionless faces, I wondered how they felt. Although the Palestinians' faces were equally expressionless, their feelings were easily imagined. One has to rage against the cruel absurdity of it all, the calculated dehumanising of people, categorising them into oppressed and oppressors, depriving ordinary Palestinians and Israelis of the right to relate to one another as individuals.

My passport caused a brief extra delay. The young woman looked suspiciously from photo to face and back again before asking, 'You come here why?'

'On pilgrimage,' I replied, giving her a pious old lady's vague smile. 'I've been to Jacob's Well.' She hesitated, then called a colleague. They conferred and he scrutinised all my passport pages before waving me through without a bag search. On occupied territory the IDF cannot legally hinder foreigners but this delicate matter was then and still is under consideration. Some Knesset factions long to legislate so that foreigners who visit the West Bank cannot return to Israel. So far the

tourist industry has blocked this extension of Israel's apartheid laws.
Bethlehem is on the West Bank.

In the parking space a row of barrows appears daily, selling the sort of
snacks, baubles, men's socks and baby garments found in poor corners
the world over. There is also a fresh fruit drinks stall and as I waited
for orange juice a middle-aged woman stopped beside me and spoke
Scottish English. Fathiyyah had studied medicine in Edinburgh before
returning to practice in her home city. Standing behind me in the shed,
she had recognised my Irish English and now fondly recalled a holiday
on the Dingle Peninsula where everybody sympathised with her as a
victim of occupying troops. We sat together on the way to Ramallah
and I asked, 'Why so much security hassle here? Most of these cars can't
get into Israel, they're confined to the West Bank.'

Fathiyyah patted my arm and said, 'You're forgetting something very
important! They might drive out of Nablus with a bomb for settlers.'
The young man sitting to my left said, 'Wouldn't that bomb make
sense? Who started this war?'

Nawaf, a geography student at Nablus's An-Najah University, offered
me a guided tour of the new Saudi-sponsored campus. 'I will look for
you in January, but not in Balata! That is a place too dirty and dangerous.
On our tour please don't talk about Palestine's politics, An-Najah has
tensions. International politics is OK.'

Fathiyyah said something in Arabic that hugely amused Nawaf. To
me she apologised – 'Sorry not to translate but Palestine's politics are
too complicated.'

Three more checkpoints delayed us; what should have been a
fifty-minute journey took almost two hours. Nawaf got off at Birzeit
University and Fathiyyah soon after, leaving me with another card for
my promising West Bank file. In the bus station a youth tried to pick
my pocket, an obvious amateur who looked scared when reproved. The
No. 18s were filling quickly and at Qalandiya mine joined a half-mile
queue.

From my back seat I surveyed this eclectic vanload: two svelte young
women carrying outsize nylon bags of fruits and vegetables, a few office
clerks (I guessed) with perfumed hair oil and plastic briefcases, workmen
in dusty dungarees, yawning students (probably up before dawn), three
mothers with numerous amalgamated offspring so mobile you couldn't
tell who belonged to whom, two senior citizens with walking-aids and

an aloof imam – aloof until a child spilled something fizzy on his gown. Then he snapped at her nastily, causing tears.

I timed our crawl towards the checkpoint: 43 minutes. One of the clerks sitting beside me said, 'Waiting is normal.' The other asked, 'Do you have it like this at home with the British army?' That gave me something to talk about; regarding Northern Ireland's conflict I was to find many Palestinians tendentiously misinformed. The general air of calm resignation worried me – yet made sense. If this is your daily collective punishment, you either accept it without wasting psychic energy on futile resentment or you participate in an Intifada. (The children did become fractious, but only slightly so.)

Beyond Qalandiya's sentry boxes, flanking a pole barrier, our driver parked facing a high blank wall and switched off the engine. Here everyone had to disembark, except me. I was forbidden to move. The disabled men pleaded to be allowed to stay on board but were sharply ordered to follow the rest and be electronically processed while traversing a long corridor past one-way windows; passengers can't see through them but the invisible IDF (or Shin Bet?) can. I had this *1984*-ish experience at a later date when crossing as a pedestrian.

Our driver stood at a little distance, smoking, while two soldiers with sniffer dog and a hand-held bomb detector (which probably has a more scientific name) came on board to check the vehicle – inside, outside, on top, underneath. Eventually we drove on to pick up the passengers from a hyper-secure doorway where the ancients were just then hobbling out. Both clerks were upset and very puzzled; documents to do with hydrology on the West Bank had been confiscated from their briefcases.

We stopped often in East Jerusalem; few remained on board all the way to the Nablus Road terminus. Walking towards the Damascus Gate, it seemed a good omen that on my first visit to the OPT four fellow-passengers had spoken with me. In Israel one misses this sort of public transport sociability.

That evening I wrote in my journal:

The name Balata Refugee Camp is inaccurate on two counts. The residents are not, strictly speaking, 'refugees' but displaced persons within their own country. And what began as a camp has become an urban slum. Yet they make a point of keeping 'camp' in their address –

not that they need an address, there's no postal service. 'Camp' is important to signal they don't accept this urban slum as their permanent home. They cling to their 'Right of Return', granted in 1948 by UN Resolution 194. Some observers see that clinging as pathetic, to others it's gallant. At present it looks even less realistic than it did sixty years ago.

Qalandiya reminded me of Mourid Barghouti's lament, in his memoir, about how the Palestinians' lives have come to be dominated by politics 'ever since the Zionist project started knocking on the glass of our windows with its sharp nails and then on the doors which it kicked down to enter all the rooms of the house and throw us out into the desert'.

I also remembered General Moshe Ya'alon's exhortation to his troops during the second Intifada. Said the IDF's Chief of Staff – 'The Palestinians must be made to understand, in the deepest recesses of their consciousness, that they are a defeated people.' Tzipi Livni, then foreign minister, was more succinct. 'We're going to keep our finger on the trigger.'

Throughout November the media had been preparing people for what the world came to know as Operation Cast Lead. On 2 December, in *Ha'aretz*, Mohammad Naim Farhat, lecturer in sociology in Bethlehem University, wrote presciently about the approaching assault:

... Let us assume the worst from the point of view of us Palestinians: Israel invades Gaza and eliminates the infrastructure of Hamas, Islamic Jihad, and others, gaining complete control over Gaza. It thus ends the rocket fire, all without the Israeli army losing even one soldier. But when the task has been completed, Israel's political and military leaders will face the question of what happens next. What do they expect – in light of experience – will grow from under the rubble as a result of tightened Israeli control?

Shaul saw me off at Ben-Gurion airport with a gloomy warning. 'Things could be a bit tense when you get back. Don't carry anything showing an interest in Palestinians. And don't tell them where you're going. They call Nablus "the capital of terrorism".' Two years previously, he recalled, a nineteen-year-old-girl (US passport, Iranian name) was held for a week in the airport jail before deportation – held under brutal conditions, not allowed to contact family or friends. She had asked for a tourist visa but carried leaflets about voluntary jobs available in Nablus.

Friends were baffled by my flying home on 7 December and returning to Balata on 3 January. I explained that whereas some people consult astrologers before planning a journey, I have to consult my animal-sitters. Who can come when to replace me? Obviously these stand-ins are a carefully chosen elite. It's much easier to qualify for a seat in the Lords than to be accepted as the humble servant of my four bouncy terriers, who need long daily walks in rough terrain where their hunting instincts can be gratified. Then there's Herbie, a vain and idiosyncratic cat who will only eat with a human being sitting beside him making admiring noises. And so it came about that I was at home in Ireland on 27 December 2008 as the Israeli offensive began.

PART TWO

CHAPTER 8

The Friendliness of Nablus

Because of my load of books for Balata's Yaffa Centre, Sari had recruited a friend to meet me at Ben-Gurion airport with his taxi; Salim's vehicle enjoyed a special permit, allowing it to be used on both sides of the Apartheid Barrier. We sped through the harsh brightness of nocturnal Israel, then, beyond Rosh Ha'ayin, approached the hills on a less well-maintained 'Palestinian' road. Salim spoke adequate English but didn't want to talk about Gaza. A few weeks later, when I had taken the West Bank's political temperature, I linked this puzzling silence to his vehicle's special permit. Injudicious remarks could endanger it.

Huwwara was almost deserted as Salim escorted me through the walkway and heaved the books into a serveece; his permit did not cover Area A. My immediate destination was the al-Yasmeen hotel in Nablus; I had booked in for two nights while Ismail prepared my Balata squat, just vacated by relatives visiting from Abu Dhabi. The 30-room al-Yasmeen, semi-attached to the Kasbah, is a hotel with a personality, imaginatively adapted from a fifteenth-century ruin. It opened in 2000, was hard hit by the second Intifada, then became the NGO workers' favourite rendezvous. There were then 74 foreigners resident in Nablus, the majority involved with university-run projects or international NGOs.

In midwinter, enchanting Ottoman relics were needed to warm the public rooms. These waist-high, mobile metal boxes – deep, long, narrow, full of glowing charcoal – stood on spindly legs beside occupied tables in the restaurant. Solitary customers were provided with a few embers placed on a little pewter tray near their feet. Let's hope central heating never replaces a system that seems so right in a region settled by Canaanites 6,000 years ago.

In the L-shaped foyer-cum-cafeteria, with seating for scores, a giant TV showed al-Jazeera's bloodily detailed Gaza pictures – hour after hour, day after day. On my first evening the dozen or so viewers watched in silence with set faces and angry eyes. This was to be the pattern for the next dreadful fortnight. Al-Jazeera kept the public informed, all over Nablus and Balata, but in my presence few commented openly.

In 70AD a well-known developer named Titus chose a site at the foot of Mount Jarzim for his 'new city', Flavia Neapolis, so called to celebrate his father the Emperor Flavius Vespasian. Recently the Palestinians renamed Nablus 'the Mountain of Fire' to celebrate its role as the West Bank's centre of resistance to the Occupation.

Before breakfast next morning I strolled through the Kasbah, quiet at dawn though soon to be crowded. Between 3 and 21 April 2002, after a months-long siege, the IDF invaded this precious place, using tanks, bulldozers, helicopters and F-16 fighter jets to destroy or deface many structures of immense historic and aesthetic value. These included the tomb of Sheikh Badr ed-Din, the St Demitrios Greek Orthodox church, the esh-Shifa Hammam, the Mamluk al-Khdra mosque – its façade vandalised by a bulldozer – and two thirteenth-century soap factories which had been in production to the day of their bombing. (In the twelfth century Nablus soap was already prized by rich Europeans.) It made my heart ache to gaze upon those shattered structures revered by so many generations – now deliberately smashed, within moments, by our era's military technology. This pulverised Kasbah exposes the Zionists' vindictive hatred for a past that ill accords with their own claims on Samaria.

Extra bombs fell on the labyrinthine alleys where 'terrorists' might be lurking in inaccessible first-century cellars. Scores died and hundreds of wounded were denied access to hospitals. More than 500 buildings were struck – 60 obliterated, 221 left too unsafe to enter – and the infamous curfew prevented salvage work. From 1 April to mid-October this curfew – a punishment imposed on the entire population – was lifted for precisely 79 hours. Thus it was hoped 'to make the Palestinians understand in the deepest recesses of their consciousness that they are a defeated people'.

My exit from the Kasbah took me onto Martyrs' Square, dominated by an inexcusable multi-storey shopping centre. Here, on a raised circular bandstand, Cast Lead had generated a token 'protest tent' where small crowds gathered daily at noon to make impassioned speeches, sing defiant songs, march around the square, display harrowing photographs of the most recent atrocities and hang supportive handwritten messages on nearby railings. During the coming fortnight I was to learn a lot in the environs of Martyrs' Square.

After breakfast I set off on foot for Balata, a brisk 30-minute walk. Nablus fills an east-to-west gorge, perhaps half-a-mile wide, between the long ridges of Mount Jarzim (about 2,600 feet) and Mount Ebal (about 2,800 feet). In 2009 the locals could assume their foreigner visitors to be actively pro-Palestinian and I appreciated the big friendly smiles, vigorous handshakes and shouts of 'Welcome!' from across a street or within a shop. Within half-an-hour I had been invited to a village ('Come for tasting our nice food!') and to a wedding on 21 January. But Nablus's dire poverty soon diminished my exhilaration. Since 2000, seven army checkpoints had been controlling the movements of 134,000 Nablusis. All Palestinian centres of population were economically handicapped by closures but none suffered as much as Nablus. Then there was the bomb damage, visible on both sides of the dual carriageway linking the city centre to Balata. Previously this waste-land was an area of light industry and administrative offices. At each road junction quartets of dour PA police stood by their vehicles nursing Uzis and observing Nablus's trickle (by urban standards) of traffic. Wordlessly they checked my ID, eyeing me uneasily. Foreigners – especially aged females – don't *walk* . . . They never again asked to see my passport and in time I overcame my distaste for what they represent and occasionally made them even more uneasy by attempting a conversation.

I was to meet Hasan's cousin Karim outside the Greek Orthodox (Jacob's Well) church and so close was the family resemblance I could have recognised him in a crowd. As an UNRWA school teacher he might be considered prosperous, yet when we had become friends, he admitted to feeling envious of Hasan's Irish opportunity.

As usual, I wanted to be alone on my first Balata walkabout but Karim insisted on a conducted tour. Balata is not Nablus, foreigners *qua* foreigners are suspect. He tried to explain the psychological frame-work within which people live when for 60 years their community has been thinking of itself as entitled to return to comparatively nearby homes. All OPT refugee camps are essentially artificial, not only because the residents are really 'displaced persons' but also because of the time factor. However tragic the circumstances of their dispossession, genuine refugees usually manage to reroot themselves within a couple of generations. In the Palestinians' case, a fourth generation is being born into an environment in which the majority must grow up without hope of ever rerooting and leading a 'normal' life. True, all over the Poor World millions are being born into equally hopeless urban slums and are materially even worse off, without UNRWA support. But these Palestinians are painfully aware of being the victims of an anachronistic Zionist colonialism sustained by the 'international community'. Therefore they have a hard-edged motive for hating their ever-present oppressors. The younger generations hear their grandparents and great-grandparents recalling a time when they lived in villages or towns where survival may not have been easy but where self-respect could flourish because hard work had its traditional rewards. To have been driven into camps that became slums, and to have an awareness of that defeat kept fresh in the collective memory, is surely a disadvantage peculiar to Palestinian 'refugees'.

One square kilometre, 25,000 people – need I say more?

A 1950 photograph of Balata shows neat rows of small white tents against a background of low mountains; in the foreground a caravan of loaded camels heads towards Nablus. UNRWA then calculated that a square kilometre would be space enough – just – for 5 to 6,000 displaced persons. By 1960 there were more than 9,000 and structures had replaced tents: one 3 x 3m cement block room per family. In the 1970s a sewage system was provided, and running water, and each family got a bathroom. In the 1980s electricity arrived. Meanwhile families were growing and the occupying power forbade building beyond the one square kilometre – so the Balatans built *up*. And up and up, on foundations that were dodgy to begin with, using the cheapest possible materials.

As Karim led me down one of the main streets – a rough track, car-wide – swarming children stared at us; a few seemed hostile, several were predatory, seizing my forearm and demanding, 'Shekel, shekel, give shekel!' Karim delivered stern reprimands, describing me as 'a friend of Yaffa'. I asked him to make it very plain that I had no shekels, and never would have, so hassling me could achieve nothing. It seemed prudent at once to clarify that fundamental point: 70% of Balatans are children.

We spent half-an-hour strolling between four-storey houses through narrow lanes and even narrower alleys where anyone broader than I am would have to walk sideways. Vitamin D deficiency is a big problem, remarked Karim: sunlight cannot reach most of Balata. He pointed to evidence of regular military incursions and we paused respectfully beside elaborate shrines to 'martyrs' – some murderers (suicide bombers), others murdered (IDF victims). Twice Karim shouted outside a house and a woman's face appeared at an upper window. Thus was I introduced to Noha and Th'aer, English-speakers who soon became pivotal to my Balata social scene.

Karim told me that as the population increased, UNRWA's funding dwindled and once-regular rations had become sporadic and meagre. Since the second intifada most of the 60% of men employed in Israel or on settlement building sites had been punished by extra closures, curfews and ever harsher permit restrictions. Only 5% had permits and unemployment was reckoned to be at least 70%. What little cash circulated came from skilled workers in the Gulf States (Ismail's father among them) and from relatives and friends settled in Jordan where the majority population is Palestinian. Nablus offered few job opportunities; in 2008 its own unemployment rate was 50%.

Karim's paternal grandfather (murdered by the Haganah in 1947) owned a large restaurant and three flats overlooking the sea in Haifa. But for Zionism, his family would be rich – or at least, not *poor* . . . As for the Arab states, 'They treat us like something you sweep up and throw away. Never we had anyone to help, our own leaders care most for themselves. Oslo gave us our first chance to run things and we made big mistakes. Like South Africa's blacks, after Affirmative Action put them in management jobs. The Israelis use the Fatah–Hamas fighting, and all the PA corruption, to divide and separate Gaza from us. That, with the settlements, makes two states impossible. Israel never wanted two states. So why do those Quartet people and the Yanks keep on pretending it's the solution?'

'Possibly,' said I, 'they haven't time to study the details. Or it could be they're happy to play the Zionist game. Blair leads the Quartet and recently accepted a prize from Tel Aviv University for "exceptional intelligence, foresight and demonstrated moral courage and leadership". That prize was one million US dollars. People play games for less.'

In the early afternoon we parted. At the Yaffa Centre Ismail said firmly, 'You can't see your room today. It's not nice before it's clean.'

A serveece took me back to Martyrs' Square to join the vigil around
the tent: a few score Nablusis. Since morning a bigger display board had
been erected to take enlarged photographs of 'Yesterday in Gaza'. The
new messages on the railings included a few in English. 'Free Gaza!'
'Baby killers Go Home!' 'Thank You Shaveez!' 'Hoo wil hep us?' 'Fuck
Boms!' 'We need Food Water Medicine Peace!' A young woman teacher,
bareheaded and intense, urged me to support the next day's demo,
being organised by the Union of Palestinian Teachers. I promised to be
there before noon.

Every vigil had uninvolved spectators, jobless males of all ages sitting
on benches or lounging against the railings. Two peripatetic coffee-sellers
competed, their tiny polystyrene mugs of hot liquid (only remotely
related to coffee) in great demand as the cold penetrated threadbare
garments. One was a jolly old man whose quips made his customers
smile; he would never accept money from me. The other was a stunted
eleven-year-old – equally jolly – who reckoned going to school was a
waste of time. Those mugs contributed significantly to the West Bank's
litter problems; for lack of bins, mine were pocketed – to everyone's
puzzled amusement.

Next morning a message came from Ismail. My room wasn't yet ready,
I must postpone moving in. A neighbour had accidentally shot himself
in the head while cleaning his gun and funeral rituals would take up the
rest of Ismail's day.

If possible, Muslims are buried before sunset on the day of death: I
knew that. There was however a faint aura of implausibility about this
story. But I asked no questions; in Balata one doesn't expect formalities
like inquests or gun licences. Weeks later, when I was on gossiping terms
with my new friends, it was suggested that that 'accident' may have been
the execution of a collaborator. Balata gossip can be too spicy for comfort.

The teachers' demo flopped, attracting not many more than the daily
vigil, plus a small contingent from the surrounding area. Central Nablus
is thronged at noon and Union officials appealed to the passing crowds
– 'Join us! Show your feelings!' In vain: most Nablusis were choosing to
keep their feelings to themselves. That evening, in the privacy of my
hotel room I benefited from a long conversation with the intense young
woman; she had identified me as a kindred spirit, in the Palestinian
context.

Leila, who had come home from England to help, was not as young as she looked. She asked, 'Do you understand we're in a civil war?' This wasn't a rhetorical question; she wanted an answer. Readily I revealed my confusion. How could an outsider make sense of the odd ambience of Nablus's tent and the West Bank's generally ambiguous reaction to Gaza's tragedy?

Leila said, 'People are afraid. Over the past week 23 teachers lost their jobs for sympathising with Gaza when the attack started. If the Education Minister in Ramallah could hear me now I'd be fired. Before Cast Lead, more than 400 Hamas supporters were arrested on the West Bank. Arrested for supporting the party that won a democratic election three years ago! Here in Nablus in the past five days more than 200 were arrested, mostly university students. Our own journalists and cameramen are being beaten up in Ramallah, Hebron, Bethlehem by *our own* police – for reporting anti-IDF protests! Not pro-Hamas, *anti*-IDF! Other journalists are being threatened every day, one told he'd have broken arms and legs if he reported pro-Hamas demos. Yesterday a Bethlehem journalist had his nose broken and his camera confiscated. And you can imagine the much worse happenings in prisons. The PA's Preventive Security Force and General Intelligence Service, while working with the IDF and Shin Bet, are supervised by US security experts. They must report to Fayyad – an unelected Prime Minister, the US prop – not to President Abbas. In Area C, around villages, the IDF has arrested dozens suspected of being pro-Hamas. Abbas has banned pro-Hamas placards, flags, slogans, banners – and demos can't move towards checkpoints or settlements. He got public praise from the Israelis for "using an iron fist"! We're angry with Israel for all the slaughtering but even angrier with Abbas for blaming it on Hamas. Last Friday, for the first time, Palestinians used tear gas against Palestinians. Isn't all that civil war?'

'Sort of,' I said. 'Or you could call it another stage in the colonisation of Palestine. Now with the assistance of native troops and a pliant Maharaja.'

Suddenly Leila was weeping, her face in her hands. A moment later she apologised. 'I'm being not sensible, it's the frustration, we feel so much and we can *do* nothing! You're right, it is more colonisation. That's why if we don't resist the Occupation we'll no longer exist as Palestinians. Fatah have become the native troops, only Hamas still resists. You can see at least four Hamases if you look hard. The one the West Bank mostly supports is our resistance movement – until with the Gaza attack on, we support them all. Why are Americans so hysterical about Islam? For them Hamas is only an *Islamic* threat. They don't see it's firstly and mostly our liberation movement. They want a secular, free-market colony – Fayyad admits this. He offers low-paid jobs for Palestinians glad to get any job. That's good for Americans and Israelis – they've been scheming for years to divide us. United, we could kill their colony plan. We're not stupid. We watch what goes on. We know why they're making a civil war here, now – same as in Gaza in '07.'

Leila was referring to a heinous US crime. Soon after Hamas's election win, George Bush warned Abbas that were he to hold unity talks with the 'terrorists', Fatah would lose all its US funding. Saudi Arabia then intervened and in March 2007, in Mecca, King Abdullah witnessed the Fatah and Hamas leaders agreeing to form a coalition government. As Mark Perry, Director of the Conflicts Forum has recorded, Bush then 'directed' the CIA to remove coalition-inclined Hamas leaders from Gaza. Millions were spent on arming and training Fatah's security forces and encouraging them to attack Hamas through-out the Strip. Observing manoeuvrings, Hamas moved first. This 'Hamas coup' was widely used, as Leila bitterly recalled, to 'prove' that extremist Islamists had overthrown moderate Fatah to gain total control of the Strip.

'Never mind,' said Leila, standing up to go. 'The truth is known all over the Arab world. Obama won't ever be able to undo the damage Bush did.'

Much had changed since January 2005 when Mahmoud Abbas, then running for President after Yasser Arafat's death, vowed 'never to take up arms' against militants whose elimination was then being demanded by President Bush's infamous 'Road Map to Peace'. Mr Abbas asserted, 'They are freedom fighters and should live a dignified and safe life.' During the same election campaign Jibril Rajoub, a Fatah security official, said, 'This election will be a turning point in Palestinian political life, and the minority must accept the choice of the majority.' He didn't repeat that when Hamas won the parliamentary election a year later after a contest universally acknowledged, even by the Israelis, to have been 'free and fair'.

In November one of my hostel friends had told me that his Balata cousin Taher Hiraz (an unknown cousin, without a permit to visit Jerusalem) had just been captured by 'special forces' – code for a joint IDF–Shin Bet operation. Hiraz, a senior Hamas official, was accused of involvement in several 'terrorist' attacks which may or may not have deserved that adjective. Hearing of my Balata plan, my friend asked me to enquire about his cousin's fate. 'What evidence? Which prison?' Innocently I obliged and thus began my Balata learning curve. One does not casually ask such a question in a community where informers abound and trust is in correspondingly short supply.

Next morning Ismail led me to his home along a deeply rutted lane, past a terrace of tall houses (no two alike) ingeniously built against the sheer cliff-face marking the camp's western border. This was Balata's most salubrious district yet its squalor surpassed that of any other area in which I have lived. (I make a distinction between 'squalid' and 'primitive' or 'impoverished'.) Below my room was the original dwelling (no longer usable) to which Ismail's grandparents had moved from the tented camp. Eventually his engineer father – helped by relatives settled in Jordan – found a secure job in a Gulf state. The house then gradually grew upwards and, from outside my squat's entrance, unsteady stairs led to three upper storeys. At the head of this stairway, a hall door opened directly onto the main road to Huwwara. From 'my' hall door, broken concrete steps led down to a patch of weedy rubble (handy for clothes drying). From there the way to the lane was through a wooden door, never locked, in a six-foot breeze block wall. Turning right, one was in an alley between sheds and lean-tos where men – assisted by platoons of small boys – did post-mortems on abandoned cars hauled in, by hand, from Allah knows where. Above this alley rose another cliff-clinging house with unstable-looking balconies on which, when I appeared, small girls gathered to practise their English. (Goodbye! What is your name? Thank you! Are you well? Where is your house? This is my house!)

Ismail seemed surprised by my first reaction to the accommodation on offer – a strong twinge of guilt. In Balata eight or ten people commonly share two small rooms yet I was being allocated a salon 25 x 10 feet with two big security-barred windows facing an enormous new girls' primary school recently built by UNRWA. Beyond and slightly below lay the 'real' Balata, sunless and sullen, while I could look out at a wide sky. Behind a partition were the loo, a mini-hand basin and what might one day be a shower; that depended on Nablus municipality's water supply and other mysterious variables. A second partitioned corner held a plywood cupboard and a large earthenware sink but no cooking appliance. This bothered Ismail but I assured him it didn't matter as I never cook for myself when living alone. Furniture comprised a camp bed, one warm blanket, a small table and chair below a wall socket. There was also a central ceiling bulb but one had to remember never to touch its loose switch with wet fingers. Apart from being accessible to sunlight, these cliff-face Balata houses enjoy an important advantage over the rest; two entrances make it less difficult (though never easy) to elude invading IDF troops.

Left alone in my new home, I made a shopping list. One reading lamp, one electric kettle, one double plug, two mugs, one bowl, one spoon, one knife, one plate. The expensive items had to be bought in Nablus, the rest were available in one of Balata's front-room shops, most of their shelves empty. 'Were they ever full?' I was to ask Noha. 'Yes,' she replied, 'before the first Gulf War.' In 1990, following Arafat's loudly voiced support for Saddam Hussein, 350,000 Palestinian workers – many of them Balatans – were expelled from Kuwait.

In Nablus it took time to find a kettle and even longer to find a lamp and nobody stocked double plugs: I should try Ramallah. Al-Jazeera was on in every shop and office and many passers-by paused at doorways or windows to view the Gazan carnage. Pairs of PA police stood at most street corners, within earshot of the TV commentary, and I wondered about their private reactions to what Uri Avnery has described as Ehud Barak's 'moral insanity, a sociopathic disorder'. They were now being ordered by Abbas to prevent anti-IDF demos while the IDF were massacring their own kith and kin.

I raised this question with Moussa. 'Yes,' he agreed, 'it's hard for such men to be Yankee stooges. But what to do? They need jobs to feed families.' We were sitting on a bench near the Protest Tent in Martyrs' Square, daily looking more bedraggled and futile. Moussa had spent exactly one-third of his forty-five years in Israeli prisons. He had also graduated from Birzeit University and had recently been appointed to a lectureship at Nablus's An-Najah University, a job now at risk. 'They think I've Hamas sympathies! Truth is, I'm anti-Fatah rather than pro-Hamas, like many who voted Hamas.' Moussa had stayed well away from the occasionally lethal whirlpool of university politics, about which Nawaf had warned me on the bus from Ramallah. But (shifting metaphors) An-Najah prefers its staff and students to be off the fence, standing upright on Fatah's side.

To Moussa's amusement I sought his advice about my mobile problem in which he found it hard to believe – 'Even the pygmies in the Congo can cope with cell phones!' I didn't dispute this disturbing fact but pointed out that my simple social life allows me to ignore the gadget. However, for my West Bank residency – given the lack of land lines – I had spent £14 in London on the cheapest possible model with the fewest complications. Then one unavoidable complication arose, called a SIM card, incorporating powers that not long ago would have been condemned as demonic. (When I was middle-aged a Congo cell-phone operator might well have been burned as a witch.) My new complication was an Israeli SIM's refusal to function on the West Bank. Moussa nodded. 'It's another trick to hamper our communications. Have you been warned not to use Nablus post office? Give letters to Internationals on their way home.'

In a cubby-hole shop an appropriate SIM was inserted by a charming old man who moved sinuously around his overcrowded premises and had sea-green eyes and a white goatee beard. He volunteered to weld a new plug onto mine, British plugs and West Bank sockets being incompatible. ('This I do as my gift to you.') Moussa instructed me to change cards before returning to Israel and to hide the West Bank SIM lest it be of interest to Shin Bet.

My friends apprehensively foretold a big demo after Friday prayers on 9 January. That was a cold morning, after a night of heavy rain, with clouds lingering along the mountain crests as I walked in from Balata. Most shops were shut; a little later the Kasbah merchants would display their goods, in preparation for brisk post-prayers trading. Already the PA police presence was formidable throughout central Nablus and by 10.00 a.m. hundreds had been deployed around the main mosque and Martyrs' Square. Some of my friends condemned this provocative show of force.

As I sat under the ragged awning, breathing on numb fingers, a trio of scruffy youths – the sort you see on TV stoning soldiers – insisted on buying me coffees. Then Jamal arrived (he whose wedding I was to

attend) and spread his good news: a family row had been settled. His
spirited fiancée refused to move into her in-laws' home, where she
could never uncover her head in the presence of father-in-law and two
brothers-in-law. Crisis! The family budget did not allow for Jamal's
paying rent. Threats were shouted, tears were shed, tension rose daily –
until a widowed aunt intervened, offering the couple rent-free
accommodation. Her sons had left home (two to work in an Emirate,
one to languish in 'administrative detention') and she would appreciate
young company. 'We all now are happy!' beamed Jamal.

This demo's leaders were an elderly rotund man, wearing a long old-
fashioned trench coat and a black-and-white *keffiyeh*, and a Western-
dressed middle-aged woman – the most eloquent of the half-dozen
speakers. Between speeches new Gaza-related lyrics came blaring out of
an antique amplifier, its decibels painfully high. By now many faces in
the regular vigil group were familiar to me but around noon several
newcomers appeared, Internationals from An-Najah University. Then
someone produced felt pens: please would we all send messages to Gaza
on strips of cardboard hanging from the railings. I wrote: 'In Ireland We
Are Sad With You' while wondering if that were true. Probably not.
The Irish were then feeling obsessively sad about the death of the Celtic
Tiger, a creature which should never have been born.

Beside me sat an unusually outspoken fortyish couple, the husband a
hospital lab technician. 'I'm secular, don't want any Sharia law. Today
we're here to resist the IDF murders in Gaza. It's bad so few come.
On al-Jazeera we see millions protesting – in Jordan, Malaya, Oslo, all
over – showing more anger than anyone here.'

His wife said quietly, 'We've used up all our anger. Now we're left
with grief.'

'And hate,' said a junior doctor who had joined us. 'Every day we
watch – can't act – feel hate swelling like a tumour.'

By 12.50 prayers were over. As the mosque emptied into the square
Leila divined, 'It's OK, there won't be trouble.' Many men at once
hurried away and among those who stood nearby, listening, several held
placards depicting Abbas. The speakers addressed this oddly passive
assembly at some length, their denunciations of the IDF drawing little
response. It was all decidedly anticlimactic, the police outnumbering
civilians. It was also undemocratic, as Moussa observed when we had
retired to al-Yasmeen for coffee.

A certain sort of Nablusi (addicted to 'free speech') felt more at ease in this hotel – where everyone seemed to know everyone else – than in city-centre or kasbah coffee-houses, where any stranger might be an informer. Israel's 'security system', so dependent on informing, spreads virulent mistrust throughout society – another threat, said Moussa, to any future Palestinian state. The machinery of democratic government needs the oil of mutual trust.

When I commented on the prevailing public mood Moussa sat silent for a moment before replying, 'We haven't recovered yet from five years of punishment. Some would hit me for admitting that but it's true. We'll recover, always we do. Now most of us are still worn out. Emotionally and physically. Especially the curfew did so much damage, parents under stress for not trying to find food for crying children, knowing if seen outside they'd be shot dead. Do people like you understand about IDF conscripts being conditioned to enjoy killing "Arabs"? At the start of our punishment [Lieutenant-General] Moshe Ya'alan told soldiers he didn't care if the army "looked like lunatics" – a straight translation from his Hebrew! At public meetings he said all members of Islamic organisations should be killed *en masse*. Israel doesn't train a normal army. In '03 the D9 tank driver who'd attacked Jenin [refugee camp] said, "The moment I drove into the camp, something switched in my head. I went mad, I wanted to destroy everything." Why didn't people round the world hear about our punishment and try to help us? Or did they hear and not care?'

I said, 'We heard much more about the suicide bombings. Such as 99 civilians being blown to bits in the month of March '02. Those murders stick in the mind, well-crafted headlines convey the horror of it. We can easily imagine ourselves the victims – sitting in our commuter bus, eating our evening meal, dancing in a disco. That's real terrorism, unnerving a population through criminal attacks on defenceless civilians. And we were told 74% on the West Bank supported the bombers. And Israel said the closures and curfews were to stop them. We know collective punishments are also criminal attacks on defenceless civilians but they're much harder to describe. We *can't* easily imagine whole populations being confined to their homes month after month on pain of death. Always hungry, family incomes cut off, insomnia rampant, electricity failing, illness and injuries untreated, nerves at snapping point, no schooling, children traumatised – it's hard for headlines or soundbites to convey all that. Or to explain why, in the OPT, killing Israeli soldiers is legitimate.'

Moussa asked, 'Who told you so much about our punishments?'

I explained, 'A new friend, a woman doctor met last month on the way to Ramallah. Yesterday afternoon she gave me a graphic account of life under curfew for a family of seven, including grandparents.'

Moussa fetched more coffee, then said, 'Be careful where you talk about killing soldiers. Israelis and Yanks say Oslo changed things, Arafat signed away our right to resist.'

I demanded, 'And who gave him the right to sign the Accords on behalf of you all?'

Moussa knew the answer, plainly stated in Mazin Qumsiyeh's *Sharing the Land of Canaan*:

> The agreements were entered into following the resignation of countless Palestine National Congress members in protest at the unilateral decision by Arafat to enter into capitulation agreements that would not protect human rights or be based on basic principles of international law . . . None of the agreements was to be subjected to a referendum of the occupied Palestinians. Oslo II was not even published in Arabic lest the public saw the capitulation it entailed. The biggest hurdle for acceptance by the Palestinian people was that the Oslo agreements provide Israel with a legal basis to occupy parts of the West Bank.

During the demo, Moussa had pointed to one senior police officer and identified him as a former commander of al-Aqsa Martyrs' Brigades, a Fatah resistance movement founded in Balata. Now he said, 'After Hamas won the '06 election and the Yanks banned them, you wouldn't want to live in Nablus and you wouldn't dare to live in Balata. We had real civil war, robbery, kidnapping, torture, killing. Al-Aqsa were supposed to fight the Occupation but then some militants were paid to hate Hamas more. You could stop a bullet on your way to the Kasbah to buy rice. And if you got to buy it your bag could be stolen on the way home. That's why people accept all those police. Even if we despise them they've made ordinary life safer.'

Among al-Yasmeen's quirky features is a wide, glass-walled 'bridge' connecting foyer and bedrooms; it gives a fine view of Mount Ebal, overlooks a corner of the Kasbah far below and is furnished with café tables for two. Moussa described it as a favourite spot among Nablusis wishing to exchange confidences. And there, that afternoon he talked freely about himself.

'I like reading quiet books about where life is always ordinary. We don't know how that must be – your own government, no army, no factions . . . Even my student time was scary when I followed Husam Khader, a Fatah activist. He represented Nablus when we had a Palestinian parliament and hated Fatah corruption as much as Islamic fanaticism. Before Hamas started in '87, the Islamist Movement tried to intimidate PLO students and take over their Councils. We were mostly secular, hating being bullied by "principles of the Koran". But Israel backed them in those days and jailed me for fighting them. They suited Israel's plan, to get rid of Arafat and have "Arab" conflicts blocking any united nationalism. In '91 the Yanks got the PLO "peace talking" with Israel in Madrid – while the Oslo plotting went on in secret. Hamas called people to continue the armed struggle, said the talks were "a heresy that will lead to the surrender of Muslim lands to Jews". Now we know they were right. Then, I wanted the peaceful way. In jail it upset me hearing about the Hamas anti-Madrid rally in Nablus being bigger than the Fatah pro-Madrid rally in Ramallah. All over Nablus gangs fought in the streets, some using guns. A Fatah man was killed, starting a general strike with more killed and many wounded. In the prisons we fought too – until Fatah recognised Hamas as a genuine political party, not only a religious militia making trouble. You can have this story for your book. I was a teenage Fatah atheist wanting to stop the religious ranters. Now I'm a middle-aged Hamas atheist wanting the ranters to save me from the Occupation. No one else is even trying . . . That's how the Palestinian pendulum can swing – not reliably!'

At sunset, as Moussa escorted me to the serveece rank near the Abdul Hamid bell-tower, we noticed an agitated group of men beside a mobile kebab stand. When one of them called my name and beckoned I recognised Jamal – half-crying, shaking with rage and fear. News had just come of his brother's arrest at a construction site in East Jerusalem. A month previously, this eighteen-year-old had paid NIS100 to be smuggled out of the West Bank. Israeli foremen on building sites favour 'illegals' who can be paid even less than Filipinos with temporary work permits. Said Jamal, 'The same law, employers break it – why only us to prison?'

Once more, frustration: nothing to be done, no legal safeguards for the accused, no reliable line of communication between family and security forces. Another measure of Israeli contempt for Palestinian rights.

The touchingly dogged vigils continued during the following week losing what little momentum they ever had as Gaza's death toll rose. A 'Women's Protest Against Killing Children' was to start at noon on Saturday but only a few hundred of us straggled around two blocks, brandishing placards depicting small corpses. Our rather timid chanting had an obvious theme – 'Stop Bombing!' The passers-by ignored us.

Monday was 'Children's Day' and that morning Leila looked haggard. For days she had been striving to enlist junior musicians and activate her fellow-teachers: to no avail. This was the dampest squib of all. Photographs of children killed or maimed festooned the Tent but few pupils appeared. A pipe and drum band from one co-ed primary school played martial airs whilst a hundred or so children trotted once around the square – and then went home.

Among the spectators was Shahdi, whose grandson had led the drummers. He introduced himself to me: 'I'm Moussa's friend, he told me about you.' In al-Yasmeen we drank coffee and Shahdi smoked a *narghile*. He blamed the demos' lack of fire and enthusiasm on organisational in-fighting behind the scenes. 'Individuals waste energy competing for publicity. Like Palestine itself, we've no focused leadership.'

Shahdi decried demos in general – 'stirring emotionalism that can do harm, rousing feelings when there's no constructive outlet'. He conceded their safety-valve utility in certain circumstances and perhaps the international demos being seen daily on al-Jazeera might boost Palestinian morale. 'But is that good? Or a false comfort? We know those crowds can't help us – or push their governments into helping.'

Shahdi, a retired teacher, ran a one-man humanitarian enterprise 'to help the poorest women and children who suffer most from Occupation. We talk too much about martyrs and heroes, not enough about survivors. It can be bad luck to survive if desperately damaged in body and mind and with no one left to care for you.'

Anonymous (to the general public) individual donors in the Gulf funded Shahdi. 'I'm told I should expand, raise more dollars, get an office, hire staff, buy an SUV! That way I could help more, they say. But extra dollars might be spent on becoming an NGO! I feel better staying myself . . .'

Good news had come that morning from Ramallah. Mustafa Barghouti, then leader of the Palestinian Medical Relief Committees and independent member of the Palestinian Legislative Council, had persuaded the Council to condemn the PA for using Palestinians to repress popular demos. All the Council's diverse factions, including Fatah, had signed the statement which also urged national unity in relation to Gaza. 'This is very, very important,' pronounced Shahdi. 'Next Friday you won't see many police. That statement is a loaded gun pointed at Salaam Fayyid's head.'

Sure enough, on 16 January the few visible police were tactfully tucked away in corners, their weapons inconspicuous. Fewer men turned toward the Tent after prayers and all the speakers sounded wary. Two Christian dignitaries were welcomed politely but not enthusiastically by the organisers. They sat stiffly under the awning for a token twenty minutes, side by side but ignoring each other with traditional clerical Christian charity. The Roman Catholic may have been a bishop; his scarf concealed the colour of his buttons. The Greek Orthodox was an archimandrite attached to the Jacob's Well church. His wide grey beard was absurdly long, his hat absurdly high and he kept the skirt of his black robe gathered in his left hand out of dust's way. Both clerics looked as though they would much prefer to be elsewhere but Leila judged their presence a good omen. 'By next Friday,' she accurately predicted, 'the attack will have stopped – before Obama's inauguration.'

Meanwhile a controversy had been simmering around Joshua Rifkin's visit to Nablus planned a few months previously when he was invited to conduct three concerts in Israel. As one of the US's most illustrious pro-Palestinians, it was unsurprising that he wished to give a piano recital in Nablus and encourage the city's most musically talented youngsters. However, many now thought his visit inappropriate. Its organiser, Sami Hammad, wrote to him explaining that his audience-to-be felt they couldn't enjoy a concert while nearby hundreds were being killed, thousands maimed and the Strip's infrastructure destroyed. Mr Rifkin was asked to reconsider his visit 'in solidarity with Gaza and so that it will not be interpreted as support for Israel'. Sami Hammad, a jobless engineer and founder of Nablus's music school, is a thoughtful man of

great integrity. When Joshua Rifkin insisted on coming – though there
would be no recital, only a meeting with young musicians – his reluctant
host received him courteously (on the eve of the ceasefire) and explained
his stance in more detail.

Although low key, this controversy inevitably bred factions. Leila
traced its roots to Sami's rift with Daniel Barenboim who in 1999 –
inspired by Edward Said – created the now famous Diwan orchestra in
which young Palestinians and Israelis play together. Barenboim sponsors
musical education throughout the West Bank and for a time his project's
teachers visited Nablus – though not often enough or regularly enough
for the steady advancement of scores of gifted pupils studying a variety
of instruments. Barenboim, wishing to recruit Nablus's most outstanding youngsters for the Diwan, was stricken when Sami refused to
co-operate. Thus ended their partnership. At the time of Joshua Rifkin's
visit, Nablus's music school had been closed for two months; Sami
couldn't find a new partner and there was no money to pay teachers.

In 2004 Avi Shlaim wrote about the Diwan orchestra:

> Culture is a huge resource for power and Barenboim and Said used
> this resource towards a positive end: peaceful co-existence between
> Jews and Arabs in Palestine . . . . Raised in enmity, the exceptionally
> talented young men and women set an example by their devotion to
> the demands of their common craft . . . . When looking at the
> orchestra, it is utterly impossible to tell the Israelis from the Arabs or
> Palestinians. This is a brilliantly successful experiment in breaking
> down national stereotypes and . . . a beacon of hope on the dismal
> political landscape of the Middle Est. The challenge lies in translating
> this imaginative artistic concept into the realm of politics. No one
> underestimated the magnitude of the challenge . . . yet Barenboim
> infected many of us with his confidence that the impossible is easier to
> achieve than the difficult.

Leila listened attentively as I paraphrased this; then she had a lot to say,
her hands tightly clenched on her lap. 'Sami disagrees with all that. He
says the orchestra only gives "an illusion of harmony" – his own words.
Its fame on the world stage blurs the main problem, our lack of every sort
of freedom. If you invite me to a concert in Jerusalem I can't go – no
permit! If my brother needs a spare part from Kefar Sava for his electric
drill he can't fetch it – no permit! If my father wants to sell his vegetables

in Natanya he can't – no permit! If any of us wants to swim in the sea we can't – no permits! If my niece falls in love with a Nazareth man she can't live in his home. If my mother needs urgent medical care she may die at a checkpoint. We're prisoners and the Diwan orchestra doesn't have a key. Since Shlaim wrote that, how many more kilometres of Apartheid roads have been built over our best land? How many more kilometres added to the Wall? How many more of our wells poisoned by settlers' toxic waste? Having 0.1% of brilliant youngsters playing nicely with their Israeli friends doesn't even *begin* to help the rest of us! It's fine for individuals and their families who get privileges but it's not a step forward, not "a beacon of hope". From where we are, we can't see that light. Sami founded our music school with a strong ideal. Not focusing on a few who can excel but giving all our talented kids equally good tuition.'

This debate, coming to my attention in Ireland, would have made me feel uneasy. True, Israelis do deploy such phenomena as the Diwan orchestra to 'prove' that 'Arabs' get a fair deal. But I would also have judged Sami too inflexible – even monomaniacal in his sacrificing of talented youngsters' chances to uphold his own 'strong ideal'. In Balata I felt less decisive. For a fortnight I had been witnessing, every day, a community's normal activities being paralysed by lack of freedom. This had alerted me to the feebleness of statistics. My head was full of percentages to do with Israeli violations of Palestinian human rights, yet pre-Balata the implications of those figures were only half-realised. Now, while continuing to feel grateful for the Barenboim/Said innovation, I did wonder if it could have any positive political relevance. Didn't the Sami/Leila hard-line make sense?

I said, 'Isn't it too soon to measure the Diwan effect? Think twenty years ahead – some of those playing together today may be able to influence things in ways we can't imagine. Because of this experiment.'

Leila shook her head. 'That's sentimental! Legal reform is our first and greatest need – not beautiful music! If you want to change how *most* people behave, you don't play them Beethoven quartets. You legislate for every citizen to be treated equally and for all laws to be enforced. Should we wait twenty years, suffering multiple injustices, while Barenboim's kids are gaining influence? As the Yanks say, get real!'

We arranged then to walk together to Jamal's wedding. Unlike most Palestinian women, Leila enjoyed hiking.

*

The Yaffa Cultural Centre (YCC), a non-profit-making NGO, was formed in 1996 by the Committee for the Defence of Palestinian Refugee Rights. Mahmoud, its Director, is among the most memorable people I met on the West Bank. Born in the Balata 'prison', his remarkable talents allowed him to escape and benefit from a sponsored education in the US where he could have continued to dwell in a profitable ivory tower. Instead, he returned to use his talents for Balata's benefit – as Leila had returned from England. A heartening number of Palestinians do this: escape, prosper, reject prosperity and come home to help.

The YCC's three-storey Centre, built in 2004, is of incalculable value to the minority who can participate in its programme. Its atmosphere is cheerful and busy in a purposeful way that starkly emphasises the lethargic hopelessness too common beyond its walls. Mahmoud achieves much with limited resources. Unlike the average Western 'humanitarian' NGO, YCC is a model of frugality and creative recycling. But Balata needs at least one hundred YCCs.

I should have written 'almost always' cheerful. The adults, throughout Cast Lead, showed their grief and anger – though here, too, comments were muted. Meanwhile the teenagers and children hurried from one absorbing project to the next, ignoring the ghastliness being transmitted by al-Jazeera. When three little boys crossed the hallway wearing violin cases Mahmoud exclaimed, '*That's* what we want to achieve! Those kids used to spend all day playing with toy weapons and dreaming about real ones. Then we coaxed them into a music class. Then they started saving cash gifts from relatives in the Gulf – to buy violins! Sometimes we feel we're winning. A delusion – but we need those to keep us going.'

Mahmoud found it hard to talk about Operation Defensive Shield. That military over-reaction in 2002 to the indiscriminate suicide bombing of the second Intifada had driven so many Oslo-disappointed, despairing young Palestinians to promote and glorify violence. The whole of the West Bank, and the refugee camps in particular, continue to suffer from the fall-out. 'You can't compare infernos,' said Mahmoud. 'Ours and Gaza's – equal but different . . .'

In a student restaurant opposite the new university campus, on the eve of Jamal's wedding day, Leila met me looking tight-lipped and red-eyed. Jamal had been arrested hours before, charged with hoisting a green Hamas flag at the Huwwara checkpoint to celebrate the Gaza ceasefire. He and four friends were now in an IDF prison.

When we visited Jamal's village a few days later (Leila my interpreter) his mother didn't doubt her son's 'guilt' but couldn't blame him for defying the ban on Hamas emblems. 'We're democratic,' she said. 'Three years ago most of us voted for Hamas – why not fly their flag?' She admitted that some elders, including herself, condoned certain forms of defiance as a safety-valve for an anger that might inspire suicide bombing if too repressed. 'Now he's detained,' she said, 'and maybe being tortured. But he's still *alive* . . .'

On the walk home I marvelled at the extraordinary stoicism (if that's what it is) of mothers like Jamal's. She now had two sons in custody and a marriage had had to be indefinitely postponed hours before the ceremony. Her eighteen-year-old would certainly get a jail sentence and Jamal's 'administrative detention' could be renewed every six months – yet she remained calm while I, an outsider, was tense with rage.

'I know how you feel,' said Leila. 'Coming home from England I felt the same. It all seemed so unjust, so cruel, I couldn't accept *doing nothing*. But when the oppressor is so powerful you've got to adapt. As a child I knew that, in England I forgot it. Now I've learned it again. Mothers like Jamal's must accept having no power. She has younger kids who need her staying calm.'

Since 1967 more than 700,000 Palestinians have been detained, which puts them among the world's most imprisoned peoples. Such detentions in Israel are illegal, according to the Fourth Geneva Convention: 'Protected persons accused of offences shall be detained in the occupied country, and if convicted they shall serve their sentences therein.' In cases of administrative detention, Military Order 1229 decrees that neither the detainees nor their lawyers may see the evidence against them or know the reason for their detention. In IDF courts, children as young as 12 are charged and may be sentenced to six months in an adult prison. There are no juvenile courts or prisons. Over the age of 14, children are tried as adults. Between September 2000 and August 2008, approximately 6,700 children were detained. B'Tselem, the leading Israeli human rights group, reports that 86% of Palestinian detainees are tortured.

Military Orders – which ban, among other things, 'political expression' – partly explain these shocking statistics from which the 'international community' keeps its eyes averted at all times. On the West Bank some 1,500 such orders are in force and specific Orders may be issued for particular districts but not publicised. Therefore many are detained for breaking rules they'd never heard of until finding themselves handcuffed and blindfolded on the floor of a vehicle. Military Order 938 defines as 'a hostile action' supporting 'a hostile organisation by holding a flag or listening to a nationalist song'.

At Huwwara that evening several Israeli flags flew high above the queuing Palestinians. As I went to and fro (to Ramallah, Bethlehem, Qalqiya) my Irish passport prompted different reactions. Occasionally a soldier disputed my visa and I cringed as those behind me were delayed while a radio check established that indeed Irish citizens need only three-month tourist visas. A few conscripts were interested in a friendly way – why on earth should this old woman be living in hard-line Nablus? (They didn't have to know I was based in even harder-line Balata.) Probably the amiable ones, future refuseniks, would have preferred not to be part of a hated occupying force.

CHAPTER 9

Surrounded by Settlements

My Balata routine was designed to fortify me for whatever harrowing encounters the day might hold. Weather permitting (as it usually did), I enjoyed an early hill walk, following goat paths or donkey tracks through olive groves enhanced by pink-tinged boulders, diversely eroded. I rarely met anybody; the locals fear the settlers. As a newcomer, I made a fool of myself by asking Mahmoud, 'Why don't the children play on the hills? They've such a superb space only ten minutes away!' Someone less gentlemanly would have laughed at my dumbness. Mahmoud quietly replied, 'Certain settlers attack first and ask questions later. You too must take care. Walk far from their fences.' During the olive-picking season villagers need protection – not provided by the IDF – and the presence of brave Internationals, picking with them, does reduce violence. From Mount Jarzim's crest eight settlements are visible, their red-tiled roofs clustered on hilltops. The apartheid roads and IDF checkpoints and security barriers left Nablus a city besieged.

The Nablus and Hebron areas share the grim distinction of being Gush Emunim's seedbed. It is no coincidence that Operation Defensive Shield began soon after a Hamas militant killed three El Moreh settlers. El Moreh, not far from Balata, is among the most extreme of several settlements established in 1978 by Ariel Sharon, then Minister of Agriculture. His 'redemption of the land' project had just won a five-year struggle in the courts, at that date less settler-friendly than now.

My confrontations with the IDF were unavoidable. One morning, having visited Awwara village, I chose another route home and found it blocked at a junction by a four-man checkpoint. Here a trilingual sign, marking Area A's border, warned Israeli civilians to go no further. A tall youth with a Russian accent scowled at my passport, pointed to Huwwara and ordered – 'Back that way!' I smiled sweetly and said, 'I'm going to Balata, on *this* road!' – pointing beyond the Area A sign. He shouted, 'No walk, no! Tourist drive car, *must* drive!'

I stopped smiling and matched his scowl. 'As a foreign tourist, I can go from here to Balata however I please – walking, cycling, riding a donkey or an elephant.' No doubt many of these young conscripts are so unpleasant because so scared, doing a job which *ipso facto* provokes hostility. When defied by Palestinians they tend to become vicious, when challenged by an exasperated foreign granny they tend to lose their nerve. This youth hastily returned my passport and waved me past the barrier. On the other side, five Nablus truck-drivers, who had witnessed our argument, leant out of their cabs to give me the V-sign. At such rural checkpoints, many soldiers tauntingly ignore lengthening vehicle queues while chatting among themselves. Twice I observed all drivers being ordered to leave their vehicles some twenty yards from the checkpoint, remove their shirts and walk slowly towards the barrier. For some Muslim men, this public exposure of bare torsos is deeply distressing.

My occasional walks within Nablus were less relaxing. Away from the centre, packs of angry small boys roamed aimlessly, swearing and stone-throwing. Several times they tried to grab my walking-stick, twice they tried to pull a small knapsack off my back. They all looked hungry, most suffered from rotten teeth and face sores. Oddly, such lads seem not to mutate into teenage gangs; I was never harassed by anyone above the age of twelve or so. Someone in the YCC office theorised that around puberty boys become more susceptible to benign mosque influences – a reassuring notion, but someone else scoffed at it.

Balata's ghosts make Nablus feel newish; 2,000 years before Titus, the Canaanites had built their city of Shechem where Balata now stands. While living on a site of such consequence I had to have a Bible to hand, heavy though my edition is. When such places remain unexploited (not many do) one doesn't have to be a believer to appreciate them.

By the nineteenth century BC Shechem led the confederation of Canaanite city-states and was considered worth capturing by Pharaoh Sesostris III. Subsequently its territory stretched from the Jezreel Valley to Jerusalem – until Ahmosis I led more Egyptians onto the scene, *c*.1540 BC, and destroyed Shechem's fortress, the region's strongest.

I always visited Tel Balata at dawn, to avoid possible juvenile harassment. Its colossal stone blocks, long known as 'the Cyclopean wall', overlook the fertile plain of Ashkar – described in Genesis as 'the noble vale', where Abraham and his tribe relaxed after their long journey from Ur of the Chaldees. If the archaeologists have it right, other massive stones formed the foundation of the Canaanite temple of Ba'al-Berith, an important centre from *c.*1500–1200BC. Given foundation stones so mighty, this must have been an awesome edifice when –

> Abimelech the son of Jerobaal went to Shechem to his mother's brethren and spoke to them and to all the kindred of his mother's father, saying: Speak to all the men of Shechem, whether it is better for you that seventy men all the sons of Jerobaal should rule over you, or that one man should rule over you? And withal consider that I am your bone, and your flesh – And his mother's brethren spoke of him to all the men of Shechem and they inclined their hearts after Abimelech, saying: he is our brother. – And they gave him seventy weight of silver out of the temple of Ba'al-Berith: wherewith he hired to himself men that were needy, and vagabonds, and they followed him – And he came to his father's house in Ephra, and slew his brethren the sons of Jerobaal, seventy men, upon one stone . . . And all the men of Shechem were gathered together and they went and made Abimelech king, by the oak that stood in Shechem. – This being told to Joatham, he went and stood on the top of Mount Jarzim: and lifting up his voice he cried, and said: Hear me, ye men of Shechem, so may God hear you. (Judges: 9)

But of course Genesis is more relevant to our contemporary problems:

> And Jacob having called together all his household said: Cast away the strange gods that are among you, and be cleansed and change your garments . . . So they gave him all the strange gods they had, and the earrings which were in their ears: and he buried them under the turpentine tree, that is behind the city of Shechem . . . And God appeared again to Jacob, saying: Thou shalt not be called any more Jacob, but Israel shall be thy name. And he called him Israel – And said to him: I am God Almighty, increase thou and be multiplied. Nations and peoples of nations shall be from thee, and kings shall come out of thy loins. – And the land which I gave to Abraham and Isaac, I will give to thee, and to thy seed after thee. (Genesis: 35)

And then there's Joshua: 24 –

> And Joshua gathered together all the tribes of Israel in Shechem, and called for the ancients, and the princes, and the judges, and the

masters: and they stood in the sight of the Lord: – And he spoke thus
to the people: thus saith the Lord the God of Israel . . . And I took
your father Abraham from the borders of Mesopotamia: and brought
him into the land of Canaan: and I multiplied his seed . . . And the
bones of Joseph, which the children of Israel had taken out of Egypt,
they buried in Shechem, in that part of the field which Jacob had
bought of the sons of Hemor the father of Shechem, for a hundred
young ewes, and it was in the possession of the sons of Joseph.

From Tel Balata a short walk takes one to Joseph's Tomb, a shrine
with (until recently) a white cupola, restored in the nineteenth century.
It may or may not be the plot that Jacob bought; for unreckoned
hundreds of years a Muslim *maqam* has stood here. In the 1980s
national-religious settlers occupied the building, with IDF help, and
even after Nablus and Balata became part of Area A in 1995 the settlers
retained control of the shrine. The army used it as a base during the
second Intifada and this provoked gatherings of infuriated protesters,
seventeen of whom had been shot dead within a month. After
the army's withdrawal other protesters attacked the desecrated shrine,
destroying its roof and cupola. An elderly relative of one of those killed
told me he witnessed the destruction and saw it as a symptom of
collective rage erupting out of decades of repression. The building,
intact when the IDF left, could easily have been cleansed of their litter
and crude graffiti. On the opposite wall, across a laneway, Palestinian
graffiti included one weeping eye, drawn with delicate precision – a
plump dove of peace poised to take flight – and a strong fist and
forearm clutching a dagger.

Genesis records Abraham's arrival in Shechem where God appeared
to him and said, 'To thy seed will I give this land.' There's nothing
remarkable about someone seeing and hearing God; such hallucinations
are common enough, especially after prolonged exertion like riding a
camel from Ur to Shechem. (We can assume Abraham didn't walk.)
What is remarkable – in fact utterly mind-boggling – is the complex
political fall-out, in our own day, of a tribal chief's hallucinations a few
thousand years ago.

When Nablus/Balata/Shechem became an Israeli-free zone in 1995
(another vile symptom of Apartheid) the national-religious settlers
went berserk. One can see their point without condoning their violent

reactions. If an atheist like me can be moved by the fragmentary remains of Shechem, with its ancient resonances, the place must be of over-whelming, inexpressible importance to Gush Emunim fanatics. Sadness fills me when I think of how things might have been in the Holy Land. Holy to the three Peoples of the Book – the Book I held in my hand as I circled those Cyclopean stones. If only the colonial, secular, political Zionists had not created a space in which obsessives could 'redeem the land' at the expense of everyone else – before finding themselves excluded, by the Oslo machinations, from one of their most sacred places (a ghastly paradox replicated in Hebron). At least the Islamic *dhimmis* system, while never pretending to promote equality, fostered the peaceful sharing, by Jews, Christians and Muslims, of sites revered in common. The inevitable ruler *v.* ruled friction never replicated the Crusaders' massacres of all non-Christians – or the Zionists' discrimin-ation against Palestinian Christians and Muslims. Although only 20% of Israeli Jews are 'religious', this minority packs a powerful punch. Whether aided or opposed by various political and military leaders, it has done more than its share to promote ethnic cleansing.

Around Nablus, one's perception of time changes. This must be to do with what has been verbally recorded, or can reliably be deduced from archaeological evidence, about the Land of Canaan. While standing by Jacob's Well (five minutes' walk from Joseph's Tomb), one can picture the weary, thirsty Jesus sitting on this well while his disciples went into the city to buy meats (the city now beneath Balata). And he seems quite close in time – just halfway between today and the founding of Shechem. Also the dialogue between Jesus and the Samaritan woman has a curiously modern ring – 'Jesus saith to her: Give me to drink. – Then that Samaritan woman saith to him: How dost thou, being a Jew, ask of me to drink, who am a Samaritan woman? For the Jews do not communicate with the Samaritans.' (John 4:9)

In Jerusalem and Bethlehem the 'Jesus and Mary' sites seem problem-atic, having been pilgrim/tourist magnets for so long. In contrast, Jacob's Well seems credible. A well is a well is a well – it has a simplicity and authenticity setting it apart from those if/maybe sites of birth, cross-carrying, crucifixion, burial and so on. The Samaritan woman accepted this as the well where Jacob watered his sheep (John 4:12) and I could accept it as the well where Jesus got involved with her disreputable community, accepted their offer of hospitality and stayed two nights

before continuing to Galilee. One wonders, did he walk or ride a
donkey? Hereabouts donkeys are still numerous. However, for a vigorous
young man walking would make more sense in a region short of fodder.

A Greek Orthodox church is built above the well on the ruins of a
church wrecked in 529 during the Samaritan rebellion against Byzantine
rule. Recently it has been pleasingly restored – so recently that it still
smelled of fresh paint. In 1979, after the settlers' initial seizure of Joseph's
Tomb, they also claimed Jacob's Well and in an assault on the church
hacked to death, with 35 axe-strokes, the Archimandrite Philoumenos
Khassapis. An outraged international reaction quickly subdued them;
thirty years later, they are less controllable.

Contemporary Jews do communicate with Samaritans – have co-
opted them, as 'the remnant of an ancient people, descended from the
Kingdom of Israel, whose attempts to achieve peace among the people
of Israel was rejected by the leaders of the descendants of the Kingdom
of Judah'. Today 300 of the 700 or so Samaritans live on Mount Jarzim's
flattish summit as their ancestors have done for a very long time –
perhaps since the first half of the second millennium BC. The other 400
have migrated to Holon, near Tel Aviv. In the fifth and fourth centuries
BC they numbered over a million and wielded considerable power in
Samaria. Now most are bilingual (Arabic their first language) and DNA
tests show how closely they are related to the local Palestinians. Their
Pentateuch-based religious rules have remained inflexible. For seven days
a month women are excluded from all domestic activities; likewise for
41 days after the birth of a boy and 80 days after the birth of a
girl. Women may not 'marry out' but men may, if they organise
their betrothed's conversion. This requires a six-month study period,
supervised by the High Priest who will decide on her suitability. Their
mountain-top being outside Area A, Samaritans at present need permits
to work or shop in Nablus, where once there was a Samaritan district in
the Old City.

My interest in the village was mundane; there one can buy alcohol,
unavailable in Hamas-influenced Nablus. Some outsiders resent this
prohibition but as a resident of Balata I applauded it. One prefers not to
imagine the consequences if so many angry, stressed-out (and often
armed) men could drown their problems. When I told Ismail of my
plan to cross the main road to Huwwara and zigzag up Mount Jarzim
he looked worried. The IDF would not approve, from al-Dawwar I

must take a serveece to the At-Tur checkpoint. But I chose to walk up; on my loaded way down transport would be essential.

The wide flanks of both Jarzim and Ebal provide many natural ledges, Ebal's mostly built on, Jarzim's being 'developed'. Inhabited ledges are linked by steep flights of scores of steps (sometimes hundreds), now in a dangerous state of disrepair. The Jarzim road, overlooked by newish but already dingy apartment blocks, is a series of very tight hairpin bends. I rested on a shattered pillar within Nablus's Roman amphitheatre (second century AD) This was among Palestine's largest, seating 7,000, but since its unearthing in 1979 it has been shamefully vandalised. Instead of excavating with t.l.c., the authorities used part of Hadrian's bequest as a quarry and bulldozed a road through another part to serve the nearby rash of post-Oslo villas. These tell us something about the funding (mostly from the EU and US) that has been flowing into Area A since 1995. It is not trickling down; it is spurting up.

On the summit the IDF has made its mark: towering metal masts, concrete observation posts, bleak barracks behind rolls of razor wire. From the nearby Bracha army post, directly above Nablus, soldiers often amuse themselves at night by firing downhill towards the residential suburb where Fattiyeh lives. When she confronted their commander he replied blandly that shots were frequently heard in her area, his men were simply defending themselves. Shots are of course a nightly event (often heard in Balata) but it was inconceivable that those soldiers, within their fortifications, could have been injured. This persistent random firing kept a whole neighbourhood on edge for months – as it was meant to do.

Outside of commuter hours, At-Tur is little used and must be an unpopular posting with so few to hassle. The pair at the barrier-pole viewed my approach with mingled incredulity and suspicion. One was lanky, blond and blue-eyed, his accent strongly Brooklyn; perhaps he had made *aliyah* quite recently (or taken up temporary residence to serve in the IDF: some do). His Mizrahi comrade – small, dark, silent, surly – stood staring at me, finger on trigger, while my passport was being radio-checked in a sandbagged sentry box. Then Blondie raised the barrier without speaking to me or looking at me.

For half a mile the road runs between high hedges to the unexciting, nineteenth-century village built when the Samaritans, after a long period of restriction, were again allowed to practise their rites on Mount Jarzim.

The small temple, called a synagogue since the reconciliation, is said to contain a complete list of High Priests, extending over 130 generations. The museum was closed on each of my four visits. The 'Peace Centre', a forbidding, angular edifice, looked (appropriately) unused. The few residents in sight were unwelcoming. 'Hostile' would be imprecise: it suggests animation and I had the impression of a community passive, introverted. Even in the shop – large, with many bare shelves – the stranger drew no greeting from a grumpy, unshaven settler with a concave chest, sitting hunched over a little table doing accounts. He spoke huskily in Hebrew and only reluctantly sold me six tins of beer, stored far away in a back room where wine was stacked to the ceiling. Over the shop door a faded sign described it as a 'restaurant' but the second Intifada had put a stop to tourists eating out on Mount Jarzim.

Beyond and slightly above the village stands Tel er-Ras, an expanse of ancient ruins. Inaccessible, according to Ismail – a fenced-off military zone. But in the rusty wire fence, hung with 'STOP!' signs, I noticed two interesting weak sections. And there were no 'MINE' signs. And the site was not overlooked by the nearby settlement or the army post. Below lay Balata; I could gaze directly down at my squat's roof. From this height there seemed to be no space for even a cat to slink between the camp's tall, jerry-built houses. A small boy on a donkey was cautiously descending that steep, boulder-strewn slope. Anyone ascending at dawn would be through the fence before anyone else was likely to observe them. And even were one caught in the act, septuagenarians can suffer from Alzheimer's and wander away from their minders.

Back at At-Tur, I tried chatting to the comrades while awaiting transport. They gestured dismissively: I should move on, wait some-where else.

Ten minutes later a serveece left two Samaritans at the barrier. The jovial white-haired taximan was an unusual Nablusi, a fluent English-speaker who had spent thirty years driving long-distance trucks in Europe and the US, before returning to enjoy his six grandchildren. Living mainly in trucks ('to save money to send home') Tayeb had read widely in both English and Arabic. Unlike most Nablusis, he had no inhibitions about speaking his mind. He said, as we parted in al-Dawwar, 'Forget two states. My grandchildren need one state. Equal rights for all, no Gush Emunim, no Hamas, no religion. We won't see it, our grandchildren must. What's the alternative?'

I assured Tayeb that I had already forgotten two states and we arranged an al-Yasmeen meeting. He wanted to introduce me to his daughter: 'She's a dangerous revolutionary!'

Two days later, as a rising sun glowed golden on a mesmerising complexity of Tel er-Ras ruins, I was breakfasting beside the clearly defined octagonal foundations of a Byzantine church. Before me rose mighty pillars (some fallen), broken balustrades, the sturdy remnants of Justinian's fortifications, the soaring walls of roofless churches or temples, isolated archways, stairs leading nowhere and an immense flight of half-exposed semi-circular steps – all Roman, Byzantine or early Ottoman. At a little distance, around a hillock, were the half-sunken remains of a later village or town; a few millstones remained in some of the tiny rooms and what might have been a wine and/or oil press was hewn out of the rock. The archaeologists who worked here before the Occupation had provided short plank bridges over awkward spaces. A Tel Aviv University research paper notes sadly, 'There are multi-seasonal excavations at Mount Gerizim, Nablus, that have produced only limited topical reports.' In general, Palestinians have been indifferent to their archaeological wonderland. During the 1930s 266 main sites were listed in the Nablus district; most have since been destroyed.

What may best be described as 'subsistence looting' is becoming ever more widespread. The second Intifada closures prevented Palestinians from working in Israel and a year later the antiquity authorities reported a spectacular rise in detected looting incidents. Around Nablus, Hebron and Jerusalem, teams of four to ten jobless men dress in black, work by night and are well equipped and knowledgeable. In Balata most looters can distinguish between their Bronze Age, Byzantine and Islamic finds and are proud of their dating being routinely confirmed by dealers. They justly complain of being paid scarcely 1% of the market value of their finds. (Deborah Sontag has estimated that in 2000 Israel's 80 licensed dealers had a turnover of US$5 million.) My looter friends regarded all professional archaeologists as allies of the occupying power and didn't see why Palestinians should not benefit from whatever they could locate, after much exertion, on their own land. They only regretted that feeding their families had to involve collaboration with Israeli dealers. My worried murmurs about possible damage being done by amateurs brought understandable responses. 'If foreigners didn't pay for what we find, would we look for it?' And, 'What's more important, an ancient scarab or a hungry baby?' In a sane world, those men would be academically trained and earning an adequate livelihood by revealing and then protecting what they must now 'steal'.

All day the sun shone warm, the breeze blew cool, the white clouds sailed high and enchanting families of marmots bounced to and fro over a soft carpet of vivid new grass. I wandered and sat looking – and wrote a few notes and wandered again – and sometimes gazed over the plain beyond Balata where a lot went on after Ahmosis's rampage *c*.1550 BC. At intervals various unremembered outsiders ruled Samaria and in 724 BC the Assyrians made their fearsome mark. A colony of Alexander's veterans settled here and Shechem last experienced wealth and power as a pagan Hellenistic city. It never recovered from its conquest in 117 BC by the Hasmonean king John Hyrcanus. His first move was to level the temple to YHWH (Yahweh) on Mount Jarzim; evidently the Samaritans were still of some consequence. Finally Titus obliterated Shechem (and no doubt looted many of its stones) as he was developing Nablus.

If any traces remain of YHWH's temple I couldn't identify them – or see any vestige of its replacement, desecrated by the Emperor Zeno (74–91) when he put an end to the Samaritans' uprising with an Old Testament-style massacre. He then built a victory church dedicated to Mary Theotokos; this was renovated by Emperor Justinian (527–65), an upholder of Chalcedonian Orthodoxy which advocated the total destruction of Judaism. No wonder the surrender of Jerusalem to the Caliph 'Umar, in 638, caused rejoicing amongst diverse communities: Jews and Samaritans, Nestorian and Monophysite Christians – all persecuted by the Byzantines. The Emperor Heraklius had been about to have every Jew forcibly baptised when 'Umar rode to the rescue. As Karen Armstrong notes:

> He presided over the most peaceful and bloodless conquest that the city had yet seen in its long and often tragic history. Once the Christians had surrendered, there was no killing, no destruction of property, no burning of rival religious symbols . . . and no attempt to force the inhabitants to embrace Islam. If respect for the previous occupants of the city is a sign of the integrity of a monotheistic power, Islam began its long tenure in Jerusalem very well indeed.

One side of Tel er-Ras had to be avoided; beyond lay an IDF shooting range. Nobody noticed my intrusion until I was leaving when a distant figure shouted something and agitatedly waved its arms. I waved back gaily before hastening down to the village where a friendly young man was minding the shop. Having bought twelve tins I sat on the verandah to drink one, apparently looking as exhausted as I felt: this good Samaritan offered a lift to At-Tur in his battered little car. Fortune beamed on me that day; a taxi was turning at the barrier.

Because settlers have seized so much grazing land, there are displaced animals on the West Bank as well as displaced persons. Almost opposite Joseph's Tomb, three misfortunate black-and-white cows, and a July-born bull calf, were stabled in a pitch-dark car-repair workshop built into the cliff face. From within, even when the double doors were closed, came the stinging reek of ammonia plus motor-oil. At dawn Yakob released his beloved 'herd', one by one, and milked them on the verge, his stool an old tyre. Meanwhile his grandsons, aged fourteen and ten, were wrestling with a long hose-pipe running from their home high above the 'stable' into a huge wooden tub – the sort people washed clothes in when I was young. (All this a hundred yards from where Jacob watered his sheep, if the Samaritan woman is to be believed.) The cows were picketed all day on a barren bomb site, their fodder occasional armfuls of mouldy hay and maize stalks, and barrow-loads of banana skins and other less identifiable vegetable matter donated by kind Balatans. The calf was short-tethered on rubble at the base of the cliff; he rarely stood up, was caked in his own dung and had permanent sores on his hindquarters. He still enjoyed finger-sucking and though he was a little old for that indulgence I felt his special circumstances justified it. He was much loved by the family and his elders' milk yield proved their successful adaptation to refugee life. By mid-February their diet was improving; within the bomb crater heavy showers had brought up an abundance of nettles and other greenery. I often saw grannies there as well, teaching granddaughters which weeds were edible.

My neighbours' goats (the nannies with udders securely bagged) grazed on another bomb site. One morning I chanced to pass as they evaded little Ali (who usually had an older helper) and went bounding up a long stairway devouring everyone's potted plants en route. (The lucky few Balatans within reach of even an hour's sunshine assiduously cultivate pots of herbs, flowers and beans.) Poor Ali felt mortified and I gave evidence that evening when he was being unfairly scolded. There was nothing an eight-year-old could do once the goats had twigged the absence of his older brother.

I once met a flock of about sixty sheep and a dozen goats being driven past Joseph's Tomb to the main road. Their weather-beaten shepherd wore a clumsily home-made sheepskin jacket, threadbare jeans and broken boots. When he yelled something brief and rude I fell behind and followed at a little distance. Where could he find pasturage for so many? The sheep were in pitiably poor condition, many limping, all their fleeces dirty and matted. The goats, as usual, were doing much better.

We passed industrial zone bomb sites and the enormous UNRWA BALATA WAREHOUSE with a large, fraying blue and white UN flag flying high above its blue iron gate. Hereabouts were two large, time-stained notices – each decorated with national crests and corporate logos and promising rehabilitation and development. There were as yet no signs of any rehabilitation or development. Talking with Tayeb and his daughter Razan in al-Yasmeen, I heard some acid criticisms of the international donors who hasten to repair the damage done by Israeli aggression. Instead, argued Razan, those donors should compel Israel to make reparations for the wanton destruction wrought by her over-armed forces.

On the main Jenin–Jerusalem road the shepherd led his flock north, away from a checkpoint, then turned east into a cleft between low hills. I followed along a narrow path, literally holding my nose. In this hidden valley were dumped animal corpses (sheep, dogs, cats, a pony) at various stages of decomposition, and much post-bombing rubble – broken furniture, fragments of carpets and mattresses, lengths of charred timber. Soon I saw the shepherd sitting on a boulder lighting a cigarette; his flock had dispersed to graze where a wiry scrub grew between stones. Noticing me, he beckoned urgently, shouting a warning. He had disliked me on first sight yet now felt obliged to protect me from the settlers whose nearness restricted his flock's movements.

By the time I returned from my morning walks Balata was bustling – children going to school, taxis bringing farmers' produce from nearby villages (if the checkpoints had let them through), women hanging bedding over window sills, stalls being set up along the main street. This runs from Balata's largest mosque (a dark dismal building) to the by-now overcrowded cemetery. It passes UNRWA's shabby headquarters, two schools and many rickety DIY buildings. Being truck-wide, it also serves as the children's main play area.

I often breakfasted at an open-fronted eating-house where Ahmad – long-bearded, slightly bent, wearing a red-and-white *keffiyeh* – was helped by a jolly fifteen-year-old grandson who had dropped out of school when his father was jailed in 2003. Ahmad managed his tar-barrel charcoal stove ingeniously, getting the most out of each glowing basin. For 7 shekels (just over a euro) he served a substantial meal of mixed salad, hummus and hot flat bread. At first it surprised me to see so many Balatans 'eating out' but of course that made sense, given their cramped living conditions, shortage of water and expensive fuel. 'Take-aways' are popular, the washed plates and bowls soon returned. (It's always a relief to escape from our ludicrous EU rules about food hygiene.) Bowls are needed for Ahmad's excellent soups, made from bits of animals contemporary Westerners have never heard of (though Mrs Beeton promoted them) and raised to *haute cuisine* by clever blendings of spices and herbs. I only avoided the improvised kebabs, chunks of gristle and fat discarded by Nablus butchers.

Despite my age, no male or group of males would visit me in my room and the Balata lifestyle does not include sessions in al-Yasmeen. This limited me; noisy overcrowded rooms don't allow one-to-one conversations about crucial matters. In such public places as Ahmad's, some men gladly sat with me, sipping tea and practising their English – but not baring their political souls. Therefore I was overdependent on my women visitors and their 'take' on past events and current affairs.

It intrigued me to meet elders of both sexes – many educated in pro-British, Jordan-run schools – who held Britain chiefly responsible for their having spent most (or all) of their lives in a refugee camp. My villager friends, too, had resentful memories of British troops standing by, during the last year of the Mandate, watching the Nakba gaining momentum, too concerned for their own safety to defend the Palestinians. At some stage some (PLO?) polemicist must have used extracts from Lloyd George's *Memoirs*; I several times heard a certain contentious passage being paraphrased – always accurately. According to Lloyd George, in 1917 the British government 'had informed King Hussein of its plans to recreate a Jewish Homeland in the Holy Land'.

'*Its plans*', mark you – not the Zionists' plans. Ben-Gurion scorned this version of events. Yet it's true that in 1913 scarcely 1% of the world's 11.5 million Jews had registered support for Zionism by buying the shekel. Younger Balatans, focused on day-to-day events, were more aware of the US and its unscrupulous Israeli Lobby. All age groups understood that the State of Israel could never have happened without Great Power patronage. The twenty-first-century Palestinians may not know where they are going but they do know where they have come from – and how and why.

A macabre rivalry was apparent between Balata and Jenin, the main centres of resistance during Operation Defensive Shield in 2002. It irked Balata that Jenin stole the limelight by killing 23 soldiers and injuring more than 100, at a cost of 52 Palestinian lives. In Nablus/Balata, between 2–21 April, 80 Palestinians were killed and over 300 wounded but Israeli casualties were few so media attention was minimal. Balata's status as a major centre of resistance boosted its communal self-respect, but at a very high cost. From here the al-Aqsa Brigades emerged to fight so pervaciously that the IDF took a special pleasure in wrecking pathetic homes and beating up the occupants of both sexes and all ages; the nightly Defensive Shield attacks were random and sadistic.

On 22 January I wrote in my diary:

What are the Balatans' options? Go on resisting and take the consequences. Or stop resisting and continue to live under intolerable conditions, without hope. All who know them predict 'sustained resistance'. Nor will the Gazans give in, despite a press conference report from Washington quoting the President (with Hillary Clinton at his elbow) – 'We are determined to prevent Hamas from rearming.' As Moussa commented, 'Those two should spend a weekend in Gaza and another in Balata, meeting people like Mrs Kasab.'

I bought my goat-cheese from Mrs Kasab, a sixty-year-old born in a tent soon after her family were driven off their land near Ashkelon. Her five sons were killed in action, during IDF incursions. In 2004 her captured husband was sentenced to twenty years, having already been in 'administrative detention' for varying periods. By some mysterious process, utterly beyond my comprehension, Mrs Kasab's pride in her sons' valour ('They knew nothing about guns but they wouldn't give in!') seemed to hold her maternal grief in equilibrium. A two-room flat, full of small squealing grandchildren, had become a picture gallery commemorating the martyrs and featuring many sketches – drawn by a sister – of those guns of which 'they knew nothing'. This was in fact a three-room flat but at night goats occupied the third room, their muskiness pervading the whole building but being tolerated by the neighbours in exchange for cut-price cheese.

My antennae are sensitive to propaganda exaggerations, whatever their source, but in Balata the evidence of damage, both emotional and structural, was there to be seen in home after home. The IDF treated the entire population as terrorists by association. Repeatedly I was told that their actions and attitudes have turned many families – naturally disposed to avoid trouble – into vengeful supporters of the al-Aqsa Brigades.

CHAPTER 10

The Griefs of Occupation

Since early childhood, graveyards have attracted me; where others might hasten towards the local beauty spot, I hasten towards the cemetery. (There must be a name – probably Greek – for this condition.) Balata's cemetery, two minutes' walk from my room, is by now as crowded and unlovely as the 'camp'. From its few raggedy palm trees hang colourful 'martyrs' memorials', large wooden boards depicting one or more young men. Their expressions vary (determined, sad, scared, defiant, sulky); several bear arms, one wears academic robes – tragic role models for Balata's children.

The cemetery was rarely visited but one morning I met Nasr beside his maternal grandmother's grave. He had come for her funeral from his home village near Ramallah where he worked as a freelance journalist and stringer. At once he identified me as possible raw material and didn't share the Balatans' inhibition about visiting my room.

As I made tea, Nasr explained his fluent English, learned from an extraordinary great-uncle. This man, as a ten-year-old, had taken a bullet in the spine while his village was being 'cleansed'. His devastated parents, who had lost everything (house, land, animals) looked at their paralysed son and advised him to use his brain since he could no longer use his body. That advice would have been hard to follow but for the intervention of an orthopaedic surgeon, a 1930s immigrant from Germany. Anton Goldstein was so appalled by the Nakba that he unofficially adopted several of his Palestinian patients, subsidising their education. Eight years later Nasr's great-uncle was translating for a Jordanian businessman based in East Jerusalem; his mother pushed his wheelchair to and from the office. Then came '67 . . . Again this family, like thousands of others, was displaced, driven out of the shack they had contrived to build in Silwan. Happily, great-uncle's employer stood by him and soon he and his younger brother (Nasr's grandfather) were working in Ramallah, their wages minimal but their jobs secure.

'There are many good Jews,' said Nasr, 'but their government never hears them.' He told me then about the novel he was writing, based on 'the worst experience of my life'.

It happened the day Nasr overslept, was late for an important appointment, tried to avoid a checkpoint delay and was arrested. The handcuffs went on but no blindfold. 'Later I wished I'd been blindfolded.' As the soldiers locked him in a sentry-box-type cell beside the gate he noticed that one of them was a newcomer; later it transpired that this was the youngster's very first day on checkpoint duty. His three mates were well known to the locals.

Soon, through his cell's tiny window, Nasr could see a friend approaching: twenty-seven-year-old Ali, accompanied as usual by his seven-year-old son, on their way to the family fields. Ali had passed through the gate, exchanging polite greetings with the soldiers, when one shouted a request for 'a light'. In response Ali turned, fumbling in a pocket – whereupon the newcomer panicked and shot him in the stomach. As he fell his son fled towards home, screaming. Nasr could see and hear the shooter becoming hysterical, as he realised his mistake, and being hugged and comforted by his mates. A helicopter would soon have arrived to rescue a wounded soldier but Ali lay unattended for four hours. On this side road no vehicle passed for the first hour. When a crowded taxi did appear, the soldiers dragged Ali onto the verge, opened the gate and ordered the driver not to stop. Now Nasr could see that his friend, only a few yards away, was still alive. 'I saw his chest rising and falling. I shouted again and again for an ambulance. They wouldn't listen, they wanted him to die first. When he stopped breathing they called the ambulance and it came in twenty minutes.'

Subsequently, a doctor noted Ali's body's sinister yellow hue; this was a corpse drained of blood and the wound need not have been fatal. An inquiry heard evidence that Ali was about to attack, was carrying a long, sharp knife. 'True,' said Nasr, 'he carried that knife to cut cauliflowers to sell in Ramallah.' Nasr's evidence was not required and he spent the next six months in 'administrative detention' (Israel-speak for imprisonment without trial). The inquiry concluded that Ali's death was accidental. Nasr was given to understand that if he disputed this verdict he would spend much longer in detention.

Three years later Nasr's nightmares persisted. 'What stays most in my head is the boy's screams. He's ten now and he'll soon be an activist.' (I didn't ask what form his activism might take.) 'Asleep or awake I remember the blood running into the ground and me shouting and they didn't care – he's only an Arab, I'm only an Arab.'

I asked why the villagers hadn't come to Ali's aid and Nasr replied bluntly, 'We're always afraid of the army. If soldiers say Ali was a terrorist, people helping him would have their homes demolished. That's how Israeli terrorism works.'

This was my second eyewitness account of an IDF victim being deliberately left to bleed to death. The first was even more distressing because a group of settlers from Homesh stood with the soldiers, at Tapuah West junction, watching it happen.

Nasr opposed my plan to visit Homesh on foot, pretending to be a keen tourist hiker. When my morning walks took me up Mount Ebal, this illegal outpost was visible, within easy distance. 'No!' exclaimed Nasr. 'They are very mad! They could kill you!'

I tried then to explain my increasing personal frustration, my resentment of the restrictive, ominous tensions generated by the proximity of so many aggressive settlements. Farmers afraid to weed their fields, shepherds afraid to graze their flocks, wives afraid to fetch water, children afraid to collect kindling or play on the hillsides . . .

Nasr – hitherto so quiet-spoken – suddenly clenched his fists, struck his knees and yelled, 'I would kill them!' Then abruptly he stood up. 'My aunt waits for me. Don't, please, go near Homesh!'

Next day I consulted Moussa who echoed Nasr's warning; a mine, rather than a settler, might kill me. The IDF had recently laid anti-settler mines which were not deterring a group who could afford (all those US Zionists' dollars!) to buy the latest in mine-detectors. Reluctantly I abandoned my plan. There are nicer ways of dying . . .

In 2005 Ariel Sharon's cunning disengagement manoeuvre (withdrawing settlers and the IDF from Gaza) deceived many outsiders. Homesh was one of the four small West-Bank outposts from which Israelis also withdrew – pro tem. The settlers reacted to the bulldozing of their homes by rebuilding – and they rebuilt again and again. 'Same as we do when the Caterpillars go,' said Moussa, half-admiringly. 'Except we rebuild on our own land and *they* rebuild on *our* land! They go wild about Abraham. They reckon he made this sacred land Jewish for ever. The IDF shifts them, they're back, opening a *yeshiva*, advertising pilgrimages, threatening to take over Joseph's Tomb. Every year they get bolder as the army gets more religious. If ordered to uproot their buddies, some battalions might mutiny. That's all the Holy Land needs – an Israeli civil war!'

A rabble of settler rabbis regularly reminds recruits that 'The holy Torah prohibits taking part in any act of uprooting Jews from any part of our sacred land'. Another rabble, calling itself 'SOS Israel', awards cash prizes of 20,000 shekels (around 4,000 euros) to soldiers who promote this message. Certain brigades' ceremonies have had to be modified because religious-national soldiers consider it sinful to listen to women singing. According to Amos Harel, such men have come 'to see themselves as leading the army'. In November 2008, he reported in *Ha'aretz* that the IDF's Chief Rabbi, Avichai Rontzski, had been accused by a senior officer of 'religious brainwashing and, indirectly, also political brainwashing'. Rontzski had been chosen in 2006 to placate increasingly vocal national-religious elements. Three years later the International Crisis Group quoted an unnamed but evidently unhappy General, 'Today, over a quarter of young officers wear skullcaps. In the combat units, their presence is two or three times their demographic weight. In the Special Forces it's even higher.'

When the General was young, most IDF officers came from the Ashkenazi secular middle class and a military career conferred status. By now, free-market Israel offers a wide choice of lucrative careers and in elite front-line units Ashkenazis have been replaced by upwardly mobile recent immigrants. Also the religious-national element has been strengthened by government-funded Hesder *yeshivas*, where for five years young men can combine Torah studies and army service. These academies attract recruits from ultra-Orthodox families previously allergic to military training and the International Crisis Group learned that 'In a few years, religious soldiers will make up the majority of brigade commanders in all areas'.

In Balata I got to know six 'human shields', young men and boys abused by the IDF in a procedure outlawed by Article 28 of the Fourth Geneva Convention. Two seemed undamaged, or at least were able to conceal any damage by bragging about their ordeals. The others, according to their parents, had reacted variously. A fourteen-year-old, aged eleven when tied to the front of an armoured vehicle for three hours while it patrolled Balata's periphery, couldn't concentrate at school and was still having nightmares. Two others, said to be obsessively planning revenge, kept their mothers' anxiety levels at 'High'. The sixth, now aged twenty, had become 'always sad, never talking', as his father put it. Everyone was indignant because in 2007 a TV crew (Associated

Press) filmed a human shield 'episode' in Nablus – why hadn't the cameras focused on Balata where the abuse was much more common? My suggestion that their insurance might not cover Balata caused some gratified amusement.

When the Refusenik movement began some thirty years ago, it was unpopular in Balata. One sixty-year-old woman, responsible for nine orphaned grandchildren, described 'Soldiers of Conscience' as 'selfish kids'. They were 'the best Israelis' and should have 'stayed on our territory to help us. Every year we have worse oppressors, like the ones who killed Zarmina's baby. They are friends of the settlers, always they let Homesh people go back to build again.'

Even now, recalling the loss of Zarmina's baby makes me feel queasy with horror and anger. I won't fill in any details. This is how I recorded it in my journal that evening:

> West Bank residents can't enter Jerusalem without a special permit – very hard to get. Not long ago a young mother was having a difficult labour: her first. A doctor gave her a letter in Hebrew and Arabic saying she MUST be rushed to a Jerusalem hospital. At Huwwara the IDF wouldn't let her hurry through, made a great thing of radioing here and there to get permits for the couple. The journey, if unimpeded, would have taken one and a quarter hours. Three and a half hours later the baby was born dead. At once the soldier who had insisted on the delay grabbed the tiny corpse, stuffed it into a cardboard carton, held it aloft for the queues to see, laughed loudly and yelled, 'I've killed an Arab!' He was arrested soon after and held for 24 hours in the army post's detention centre – in an IDF cell complete with TV and an electric heater. Then he was transferred to checkpoint duty near Hebron. And today, to my friends' inexpressible rage, he was back on duty at Huwwara where the baby's family will have to confront him regularly. In December the IDF lied, said he'd be punished. Very many locals, of both sexes, must be strongly tempted to attack him. The army's arrogant irresponsibility, in returning him to Huwwara, is past belief.

In fact disbelief was my first reaction to the whole story; it seemed impossible that any soldier, however religious-national, could be so depraved. Yet no Palestinian found the tragedy at all surprising: very shocking, but not surprising. Then the post-Cast Lead media debate began and I realised that that young man was not, as one would have hoped, exceptional. Several newspapers, including the London *Observer*, showed photographs of T-shirts designed for the Givati Brigade to commemorate their achievements in Gaza. These depicted mothers mourning over their children's graves, a gun aimed at a child, dead babies in grotesquely distorted positions, a weeping mother holding a dead toddler, a teddy-bear beside the inscription 'Better use Durex' – and a pregnant woman with a bull's-eye superimposed on her bulge. The English slogan read '1 shot, 2 kills'. That last photograph is in my IDF file, tangible proof that the greatest threat to Israel's survival comes from within rather than without. The damage done to the Palestinians is obvious. But what of the damage done to the Israelis by the convergence of brutalising militarism and manic Judaism?

In Tel Aviv Ruth had advised me to read *Jewish Fundamentalism in Israel* by Israel Shahak and Norton Mezvinsky, which turned out to be the most relevant of all the relevant volumes on my shelves. As its authors note, Israeli fundamentalism is 'especially significant in regard to the principles of Israeli state policies'.

Israel Shahak, a Bergen-Belsen survivor reared in the Warsaw Ghetto, died in 2001 after a long life dedicated to scholarship in the service of human rights. His US-Jewish friend and co-author wrote of him in a Preface to the new (2004) edition:

> . . . He felt a great responsibility to criticise what he considered to be negative aspects of the state of Israel . . . which he loved and in which he lived . . . Too many people outside the state are fearful of being critical of any aspect of Judaism, lest they be accused of being anti-Semitic. The situation within the state is different. Negative criticism of Judaism is abundant in the Israeli Hebrew press. If published in translation outside of Israel, most of this criticism would most likely be considered anti-Semitic . . . As Jews we understand that our own grandparents or great-grandparents probably believed in at least some of the views described in our book. We believe that a critique of Jewish fundamentalism, which entails a critique of the Jewish past, can help Jews acquire more understanding and improve their behaviour towards Palestinians, especially in the territories conquered in and occupied since 1967.

Israel's secular aspect prompts us to underestimate the political importance of Jewish fundamentalism. But the National Religious

Party (NRP) alliance is underpinned by the teachings of many way-out quasi-mystical Rabbis like the late 'Lubavitcher Rebbe', Menachem Mendel Schneerson. He founded the Chabad movement in the US, and in 1965 compiled a book of messages for his followers in the Holy Land, which deeply influenced too many Israelis, including the Hebron mass-murderer, Baruch Goldstein, and Rabbi Yitzhak Ginsburgh who contributed a chapter to a book in praise of Goldstein's crime. 'Jewish bodies and non-Jewish bodies' – he pointed out – 'only seem to be similar . . . The difference of the inner quality, however, is so great that the bodies should be considered as completely different species . . . An even greater difference exists in regard to the soul. Two contrary types of soul exist, a non-Jewish soul comes from the satanic spheres, while the Jewish soul stems from holiness.' In a 1996 interview with the *Jewish Week* (New York), Rabbi Ginsburgh said, 'If a Jew needs a liver, can you take the liver of an innocent non-Jew passing by to save him? The Torah would probably permit that. Jewish life has an infinite value.' Commenting on this, the Professors note:

> Changing the words 'Jewish' to 'German' and 'non-Jewish' to 'Jewish' turns the Ginsburgh position into the doctrine that made Auschwitz possible. To a considerable extent the German Nazi success depended upon that ideology and upon its implications not being widely known early. Disregarding the potential effects of messianic, Lubavitch and similar ideologies could prove to be calamitous.

Rabbi Yehuda Amital proclaimed that the Yom Kippur War (1973) was against all non-Jews, including Gentile citizens of the US – without whose emergency military aid that war would have been lost. Shockingly, Amital was appointed Minister without portfolio in Shimon Peres's government. Before Israel's 1982 invasion of the Lebanon, the military rabbinate distributed a new map; Lebanese place names had been changed to Book of Joshua names and the troops were urged to replicate Joshua's conquests which eliminated all Gentiles.

The two messianic Rabbis Kook (father and son, founders of Gush Emunim) saw the seizure of Palestinian land as an act of sanctification. Their twenty-first-century successors also see themselves as redeeming the land by transferring it from the satanic to the divine sphere. All Gush Emunim members believe their sect is divinely guided, therefore cannot err. (Of whom does that remind you?) This conviction, shared with the NRP, amply justifies the Professors' apprehension about Jewish fundamentalism substantially affecting Israel's nuclear policies.

The illusion that Jewish blood is special ('the blood concept') has numerous consequences now plain to be seen. The security forces' freedom to ill-treat and torture 'the enemy', and the disappearance of so many Palestinians into indefinite detention, are but two examples. Also collective punishments seem entirely appropriate if non-Jewish blood is comparatively worthless. (Just occasionally the 'concept' works in the Palestinians' favour, as when 1,027 of their prisoners were released in exchange for one IDF captive.) This illusion also conditions the thoughts and deeds of many secular Israelis. Some 'seculars' do worry about the incompatibility between fundamentalist-pleasing policies and democracy – as when courts fail to treat alike Palestinians who have killed gentiles and Palestinians who have killed Jews. They recognise that the discrimination practised against Israel's Palestinian voters would be condemned as 'racist' if used by any Western government. Yet – 'In the voluminous descriptions in English of Israel, this phenomenon, though known in Israel, is almost never mentioned.' The Professors liken the majority of English-language books on Judaism and Israel to totalitarian state literature which may provide much accurate information while lying by omission – a flaw less often found in Israel's Hebrew publications.

On the medical stage, fundamentalism plays weird parts. Some rabbis permit Jews to receive non-Jewish organs in life-or-death crises. But non-Jews should never receive Jewish organs and Rabbi Sheinberger emphasises – 'Obviously it is prohibited under any circumstances to transplant Jewish organs into Arabs, all of whom hate Jews.' Pious Jews may accept blood transfusions only from other pious Jews – or perhaps from secular Jews (depending on your rabbi), but never from non-Jews. What would be the reaction if Christian leaders forbade their followers to accept Jewish blood? As for mother's milk – a Talmudic prohibition sees to it that no pious Jewish baby will be allowed anywhere near a contaminated non-Jewish breast.

For many years, the Professors tell us, 'books in Hebrew detailing instructions for spells and witchcraft recipes have been best sellers in Israel'. So, on the one hand we have advanced technology Israel, amply supplied with nuclear bombs (by courtesy of France), its scientists collaborating with the Pentagon's in the production of killer-drones

which expose their users to no risk. And, on the other hand, we
have kabbalistic, quasi-mystical Israel where rival politicians and rabbis
conduct interminable feuds with the aid of magic. I mean real, old-
fashioned magic, dating back to at least the second century AD and also
common in certain districts of Paris, London and New York. Individuals
who habitually use magic find it easier to win political contests: or so
many believe. According to some serious political analysts, Netanyahu's
1996 victory over Peres was linked to the exclusive blessings bestowed
on him by the cabbalist Rabbi Kaduri and to the boycotting of Peres by
most magicians. Today this aspect of Judaism has enormous political
and social significance and as the professors note, 'The misguided attempt
to hide this past and present tendency, which is widespread in Israel, has
infested the English-language histories of the Jews.'

The religious settlers who so menacingly surround Nablus and Hebron
are 'theologically motivated and a manifestation of fundamentalism'
only loosely connected to the Bible. They look back to Abraham and
the Promised Land mainly in media interviews. Otherwise, they are
eagerly looking forward. They know the messiah is on the way, the
world is already in the messianic age, therefore they need to be rooted in
Samaria and Judea. We hear strangely little about this, as a political
problem, from our 'expert' commentators. Yet when political waters are
being muddied by Muslim fundamentalists, their religious motivation is
heavily underlined.

Gush Emunim is supported by about 50% of Israel's Jewish population,
plus financially important Diaspora adherents. The *Jewish Press*, the most
widely read US-Jewish weekly paper, vigorously promotes Gush Emunim,
regularly gives its spokesmen op-ed space and has praised Yitzhak Rabin's
'religious' murderer, Yigal Amir. Speaking of Rabin's murder, which
delighted millions, the professors emphasise:

> The historic features of Jewish fundamentalism during the past 800
> years were manifest in the Rabin assassination and in the reactions to
> it . . . It should not be forgotten that democracy and the rule of law
> were brought into Judaism from the outside. Before the advent of the
> modern state, Jewish communities were mostly ruled by rabbis who
> employed arbitrary and cruel methods as bad as those employed by
> totalitarian regimes. The dearest wish of the current fundamentalists
> is to restore this state of affairs.

For decades, most outside observers have been confused by various 'Peace Processes', as have many Palestinians and Israelis. *Jewish Fundamentalism in Israel* reveals *why* there never was any such thing. It shows us a two-tier structure. The elaborate top tier involves Zionist leaders at home and abroad, AIPAC-controlled/funded US Presidents, Secretaries of State and envoys, permanently frustrated teams of backroom negotiators, the impotent UN, the vile Quartet and occasional myopic EU Observer Missions fostering Free Trade Zone agreements. The lower tier is reality: Israel's fundamentalists, resolved never to permit 'peace' on any terms acceptable to the Palestinians. To what extent is the refusal to recognise that reality a form of culpable ignorance?

CHAPTER 11

Bethlehem Besieged

Not many Nablusis visit the Holy Land's second most popular tourist destination and I had a long cold wait while the Bethlehem serveece filled up. At sunrise business was brisk for Huwwara's many vendors of hot pseudo-coffee, oven-warm crisp bread and the grilled legs of fowls whose chickhood (judging by muscle development) was long past. As I sat in the front seat gnawing on a leg Mahdi recognised me – one of Karim's many cousins. He worked in Bethlehem as a freelance guide dependent on unpackaged tourists and soon was telling me, 'I've a Birzeit degree – economics – no use on the West Bank if you've no friend in Ramallah!' (By 'Ramallah' he meant the PA.) 'I'm lucky,' he continued. 'I like foreigners and using English. In Jerusalem people get warned not to hire people like me but that's OK, independent travellers want to talk to Palestinians.'

Every few minutes a youth thumped this serveece's roof while yelling. 'Bethlehem! Bethlehem!' By 7.30 we were on our way, jolting over a rough twisting track. The driver apologised; a friend had just cell-phoned to advise him to avoid the Tappuah junction on the main road. An extra-nasty IDF unit was causing a long tailback with some arrests and much ransacking of car boots. Checkpoints so easily evaded make a nonsense of their 'security' function; they are maintained as part of the Arabs' punishment.

Our roundabout route, via Wadi Nar, avoided Jerusalem (barred to most 'Bank' residents) but the city is visible for much of the way, as are many settlements. Their signposts grate: Ariel – Ma'ale Adumim – Ofra – Beitar Illit – Nokdim – Ikola – Efrata – Gilo – Har Homa – Giv'at Hamatos – each name representing multiple gross injustices. Ma'ale Adumim covers fifty square kilometres and houses 32,000 Israelis; Balata covers one square kilometre and houses 24,000 Palestinians. In the first post-Oslo decade, settlement numbers more than doubled, urged on by Ariel Sharon's 1998 war-cry: 'Grab the hilltops!' Travelling through Palestine can no longer be enjoyed. In Kenneth Frampton's words:

. . . one can observe the paradox of suburban hilltop fortresses, totally and utterly inimical to the culture of an ancient landscape . . . No future resolution of the conflict will ever be able to heal the scar inflicted by this tragic combination of political and topographical violence.

A midwinter aridity prevailed across Judea where long slabs of limestone lay amidst a fuzz of grey-brown scrub and the villages were litter-fringed. Some gradients are so steep that vehicles seen from across a narrow valley seem to be climbing the opposite near-precipice on their hind legs, as it were. Occasionally a cloaked shepherd appears on a faraway skyline, or a woman is glimpsed riding side-saddle on a donkey, balancing a sack behind her, followed by children carrying jerry-cans. A few shaggy black tents and tethered goats marked a Bedouin camp beside a *wadi*. A car dump, usually buzzing with scavengers, despoils one valley floor. Yawning gravel quarries, machine-noisy and exhaling mile-wide clouds of fine white dust, prove how deep the exploitation of Palestine's land goes.

Israelis operate nine quarries in Area C, which covers approximately 72% of the 'Bank' and is controlled by the misnamed army-run Civil Administration. Most such quarries have been in use for over 40 years and the Civil Administration lets them off the 'competitive tender' hook because Israel's mandatory tender law of 1992 does not apply on the Bank. At least 94% of their output goes to Israel, supplying 25% of its gravel needs; according to Shimon Giller, a quarry industry geologist, transport costs determine the price. For 'security reasons', Palestinian quarry-owners are prevented from using the shortest route to a building site and this gives their Israeli competitors a huge advantage – being able to charge 30 instead of 60 shekels per ton.

Yesh Din, an Israeli human rights group focused on the OPT, identifies quarrying as yet another violation of International Law – that Fourth Geneva Convention again! 'An occupying power cannot legally extract natural resources for its own benefit.'

As Har Homa's ever-expanding complex appeared, Mahdi recalled his father and two uncles working on the dominant condo-tower; the land had been confiscated, post-Oslo, from the villagers of Beit Sahour and Umm Tuba. On 12 July 1999 an extraordinary first meeting took place, between Yasser Arafat as PA President and Ehud Barak as Prime Minister of Israel. It was no coincidence, Mahdi believed, that on the same day one of the few remaining local forests was burned to make space for Har Homa – despite an energetic 'Save the Forest!' international campaign. Har Homa completes a chain of settlements, complemented by the Apartheid Barrier, separating Bethlehem from Jerusalem. The Israelis impose land control through a wide range of 'legal' tricks. Over the years numerous 'Green Areas' have been listed, Jabal Abu Ghneim forest among them, ostensibly for environmental reasons – then Palestinians are forbidden to build on their own land.

Har Homa is to accommodate 30,000 and will include tourist hotels, already numerous in Bethlehem but the Israelis advise foreigners to avoid those. Nearby two more new settlements were growing, one on An-Nu'man land – what little is left of it, post-Barrier. This small Bedouin village, on a hilltop between Bethlehem and Jerusalem, has long been the victim of an Apartheid-flavoured error. In 1967, when Jerusalem illegally expanded its municipal boundary, An-Nu'man was placed within East Jerusalem – but another set of bureaucrats gave the villagers West Bank ID cards. Ergo: they couldn't enter Jerusalem though the municipality said they lived in Jerusalem. Oddly enough, this anomaly went unnoticed until the 1991 closure policy exposed these villagers as 'illegal residents' in their birthplace. This made life very difficult and it became even more so during the second Intifada when the IDF blocked the roads from An-Nu'man to Umm Tuba and Sur Baher. The Jerusalem authorities then cut off the Bethlehem to An-Nu'man water and telephone connections because an Area A municipality was not entitled to service a Jerusalem village. In 2004 life became almost intolerable: the Barrier – with no gateway accessible to walkers – enclosed An-Nu'man, cutting it off from the West Bank and caging people unable legally to enter Jerusalem. An-Nu'man has no school or health services; the villagers were totally dependent on Umm Tuba, now beyond reach. In 2008 they took their case to the High Court – and lost. B'Tselem foresees: 'In these circumstances it is likely that, sooner or later, the residents will be left with no option but to leave the village.' The Israelis covet that hilltop for yet another outrageous development, as outlined in the Jerusalem Municipality Draft Master Plan. As Gideon Levy puts it:

> An immense degree of wickedness is required to take away from the Palestinians their last piece of land, to occupy it so crudely and to say: everything, absolutely everything is ours, because we are stronger, because we have the power to take it.

For at least 1,000 years a certain Beit Sahour field, east of Bethlehem, has been revered by Latin Christians as the place where angels told shepherds about the birth, a mile away, of Mary's special baby. Here the Byzantines founded a monastery in around 454 – soon demolished by the Samaritans. In the 1950s an Italian architect designed a tent-shaped church in which the filtered lighting effects are quite beautiful. Other fields on other slopes are of course identified by other Churches as the *real* field. Surely a superfluous squabble: angels, being immaterial, could have delivered the glad tidings simultaneously to all the shepherds on all the hills around Bethlehem.

Even a century ago, Jesus's contemporaries might have recognised the small stonemasons' village of Beit Sahour – but not now. It has become an important industrial centre, by Palestinian standards, producing plastics, noodles and textiles. Its present population (15,000 or so) is said to have the highest percentage of university graduates in the Arab world. Many have come home to live permanently in Beit Sahour, after studying and/or working abroad. During the first Intifada they distinguished themselves by organising a campaign of non-violent resistance that infuriated the Israelis. In 1987 the first Intifada's executive committee had advised people to withhold all taxes as a major part of their non-violent resistance to military rule. The idea appealed but was acted upon in a desultory and disorganised way, and only in Beit Sahour did everyone, together, withhold all taxes for a prolonged period. A handbill, delivered to each home, pointed out that Israel's tax-collecting in occupied territory flouts the Geneva and Hague conventions. Moreover, in twenty-two years the authorities had never accounted for West Bank tax distributions. And they had introduced several new taxes, including VAT, while providing no free education or medical care or social services of any kind. Instead, they had taken control, by force, of all the OPT's water resources, diverting them to the settlements and charging Palestinians very high prices for inadequate rations. This handbill ended:

> For these reasons – and as a consequence of our conviction that the money taken in by the high taxes we pay is spent on ammunition and tear gas used to kill our children – we have decided not to pay taxes any more.

Punishment came in the autumn of 1989. The IDF surrounded Beit

Sahour, blocked all the exit streets, cut the telephone lines and imposed a strict house curfew for 39 days. The town was declared a military restricted zone and no one was allowed in: not the Palestinian MKs, not religious leaders from Jerusalem (Beit Sahour is 80% Christian), not European consuls representing foreign factory owners. Yitzhak Rabin, then Defence Minister, boasted of 'teaching the Beit Sahour inhabitants a lesson'. To sharpen this 'lesson', looting was permitted during the curfew. An elderly Lutheran pastor told me that shopkeepers' and families' possessions, worth more than US$1,800,000, were 'confiscated' and protesting victims were jailed. As my Lutheran friend sadly observed, 'Here you see a big bit of our problem. If *all* tax-payers did like us, the government could not have punished them like us.'

Bethlehem's abundance of spring water, on the edge of the Judean desert, gave it considerable importance from time immemorial. Canaanite princes communicated with Egyptian pharaohs about the king of Jerusalem's entitlement to rule over an aspiring city-state named after its protective goddess, Beit Lahmu.

Fast forward to 313AD when the Emperor Constantine legalised Christianity and Jesus's birthplace began to attract pilgrims. Churches and monasteries proliferated until by the sixth century Bethlehem was a thriving, strongly fortified city. Yet the Caliph 'Umar conquered it almost effortlessly, in 638, and then signed a treaty with Patriarch Sophronius guaranteeing the Christians' human rights, as we would say.

Very fast forward to certain mid-nineteenth-century events which have directly affected twenty-first-century Bethlehem. As the Ottoman Empire went into a coma, Europe's colonial powers encouraged their missionaries to work in Palestine's major cities where they were soon joined by zealous colleagues (or rivals) from the US. Various denominations competed for influence, founding schools and hospitals which rapidly improved education and health care, especially among the Roman Catholic and Greek Orthodox communities. Missionaries also sponsored the emigration of their more talented students to Europe or the US. In our own time Palestine's Christians, given their links with Western mother churches, have been best placed to escape from military rule. This, not Islamic hostility, explains why Bethlehem now has a two-thirds Muslim majority.

Here, some of Palestinian nationalism's first buds unfolded. During the Mandate years, seeing the menace implicit in Britain's alliance with the Zionists, the Palestinians of Bethlehem and Beit Jala repeatedly organised public protests against a law withdrawing citizenship from most Palestinian emigrants while granting it to Jewish immigrants a mere two years after their arrival. The mayor of Bethlehem, Issa Bandak, who led that and other protests, was deported in 1938. Ten years later, in a Bethlehem suburb, Palestinian guerrillas defeated the Haganah – such a very rare event that it is still celebrated. Twenty-five Haganah fighters were killed and 22 of their vehicles destroyed while British troops rescued 149 Zionists.

Bethlehem is in the OPT only because Israelis feared the wrath of all the Christian Churches if they seized Jesus's birthplace when they were seizing other towns *not* allocated to Israel by UN Resolution 181. Greater Bethlehem's present population, including villages and three refugee camps, comes to around 180,000; 30,000 or so live in the Old City. On its periphery are an increasing number of utilitarian apartment blocks housing thousands of villagers driven off confiscated lands.

In the late 1990s the PA allocated more than US$200 million to the 'Bethlehem 2000' project, disrupted by the second Intifada. Throughout much of December 2000, Bethlehem was under siege, being attacked daily by F-16s and Apache helicopters. As the Rev. Mitri Raheb has written in his sad little book, *Bethlehem Besieged*:

> While Christians all over the world sing 'O Little Town of Bethlehem', Israel makes sure that this town stays as little as possible, as little as two square miles, surrounded with thirty-mile-long walls, fences, trenches, with no future expansion possibilities whatsoever.

The serveece put me down a few miles short of Bethlehem, in Beit Sahour, where I had an appointment to meet George, a Christian Palestinian who runs the awkwardly named but quietly constructive Palestinian Centre for Rapprochement between People. The PCRP inaccurately describes itself as 'non-governmental and non-political'. It is obviously non-governmental but its three purposes are political: to empower youth to be advocates for the Palestinian Cause, to resist the Occupation non-violently and to disseminate reliable information to the media. Palestinians are as prone as anyone else to exaggerate but in general their support organisations, whether Israeli, international or

Palestinian, are not tempted to distort. The facts of Palestinian life need no embellishment to arouse sympathy for the cause.

George is a man of immense compassion, with what I think of as a Quaker-like strength. He was just back at his desk after a week's sick leave. 'My heart was sick, not my body. For twenty years we've been working here – then Gaza felt like the end of all hope of rapprochement.' I could empathise; those weeks of insane violence had lacerated everyone who cared. Happily, later meetings showed me George back on form, believing again in the younger generation's capacity to think and feel and act in new ways.

We both derived comfort from something indisputable that official Israel strives to conceal. Beginning with the Nakba's 60th anniversary (2008), there has been a global surge of support for Palestinians' rights, including the Right to Return. And this quickening of concern *preceded* Cast Lead which doubled the membership of many support groups.

A trio of PCRP workers were discussing the role of the media – why not show the reality of conflict? Why show only the wonders of military technology, deleting what those wonders do when they hit the spot? Millions remember al-Jazeera's pictures of white phosphorus victims – and bits of bodies here and there – and child corpses, including a baby with a chubby ivory face recalling the marble effigies of infants on tombstones. One father had been filmed as he entered his bombed home, found five dead children, shuddered for a moment, his sobs soundless – then howled and choked with grief. Temperamentally I'm a reserved person yet were I bereaved in such circumstances I would certainly want the world to know exactly how I felt. Our western preciosity stimulates debate about the ethics of intruding on personal tragedies, failing to respect the dead and so on. In Palestine the debate is about the ethics of indiscriminate bombing and shelling. Halfway through Cast Lead al-Jazeera juxtaposed two contrasting videos. One showed mangled corpses, screaming victims of shrapnel, smoking ruins and wailing relatives. The other showed a conference of sleek political leaders sitting in opulent surroundings exchanging platitudes. Then one senior US official came to the point and stated flatly, 'It's too soon for a truce!' Another agreed – 'Israel's gotta clean all terrorists outa Gaza!'

I asked, 'Had those decision-makers watched what we'd been seeing, how d'you think they'd have reacted?'

After a long moment one young man replied, 'Probably not the way we do. To them dead Palestinians are dead terrorists.'

This didn't entirely convince me. If forced to look and listen for hours – as distinct from glimpsing a two-second shot of a bloody burden being shoved into an ambulance – might not a few of our leaders feel a twinge of remorse? Even an impulse to *stop it*, rather than discouraging a ceasefire? Another point – most of Israel's weaponry is subsidised by US taxpayers. Are they not entitled to see, close up, what their dollars make possible?

Faisal arrived then, one of Moussa's activist friends who worked at Deheishe, the largest of Bethlehem's refugee camps. Like so many of the Palestinian men I met, he was respected for having 'done time' – 10 years in his case. I understood that respect; in Ireland many of my generation grew up boasting about those relatives who had done time in British jails (3 years, in my father's case).

Faisal was keen to show me aspects of the city not burnished by the Millennium Fund. We hired a serveece for an hour and drove through Bethlehem's most desolate districts where the dark grey Apartheid Barrier, 24 feet high, coils around neighbourhoods like some sinister mythical monster, strangling them, leaving rows of boarded-up shops and abandoned homes on silent streets. From here, we could see Rachel's Tomb, embedded in the Barrier, but could not approach it. Faisal explained why one handsome three-storey house was standing alone in the Barrier's shadow; its rich owner could afford lawyers clever enough to defeat the demolition order.

I shook my head, bewildered. 'But who'd want to live enclosed by *that* on three sides?'

Faisal reminded me, 'Those are the sort of choices we must make. It's a loved house, with very old wood carvings inside. The family couldn't see it bulldozed, their spirit would've died.'

Our driver complained about taking us down a rough laneway within range of an army observation post built into the Barrier. Along here, during the second Intifada, the IDF regularly fired 'warning shots' at refugee children who could take no other route to school. The nearby Aida camp lost ground to the Barrier which now looms mere yards away from numerous permanently twilit homes. Aida residents live under extra surveillance and, said Faisal, had recently been compelled to give up boy-scouting activities mistaken as a smoke screen for 'terrorist' training. In 2000 a group of Aida youngsters set up the notably successful Laje'oon Centre to provide their contemporaries with educational opportunities wider than anything UNRWA could organise. Some of their projects are now funded by the EU which made Faisal a little uneasy for reasons I could well understand.

Turning away from the Barrier, our track bordered a large cemetery, another IDF 'playground'. So many mourners were shot-to-wound during funerals that most local families now go elsewhere to bury their dead – for them a deeply distressing spatial separation.

'The UN meant it to be so different!' said Faisal. 'Remember 181?'

Of course I remembered. In 1947 the intention was to give Bethlehem the same status as Jerusalem, an internationally supervised Corpus Separatum, guaranteeing equal access to Jewish, Christian and Muslim Holy Places – often sites revered by all three Peoples of the Book.

'This you may not know,' said Faisal. 'The Barrier violates Israel's commitments under the International Covenant of Civil and Political Rights. So the Middle East's only democracy is not much better than Saudi Arabia where Christians can't build churches.'

When Faisal asked, 'Manger Square next?' I said 'No thanks.' A month previously, while Bethlehem's tourist supply was cut off by Cast Lead, I had done a half-day trip, finding the Basilica of the Nativity empty at 9.00 a.m. – apart from a few pottering priests representing mutually hostile denominations. While sympathising with the closed souvenir shops and cafés, it was gratifying to have a major tourist centre available for my exclusive enjoyment. Not that Manger Square is very enjoyable: all those PA Millennium dollars reduced it to banality. But within the silent vastness of the Basilica it was good to stand alone amidst the colossal red limestone colonnades erected soon after 326, as Helena Augusta oversaw construction on her son's behalf. In 529 the Samaritans did much damage – but not to those columns. This claims to be the world's oldest continuously operated church. Most experts seem to agree that – despite so many restorations, renovations and additions – the colonnades are the originals, quarried nearby. How many individually skilled men spent how long shifting them from quarry to hilltop? One marvels at the skill and strength required to cut, transport, polish and then symmetrically place such columns. Now we depend on the ingenuity of a few very clever inventors who enable small teams of rather dumb and flabby workers to erect fifty-storey buildings in a matter of months.

Back in George's office, Mazin Qumsiyeh awaited me. We'd first met in January when he invited me to stay on my next visit to Bethlehem. George described his old friend (since schooldays) as 'multi-purpose'. When not running Yale University's genetics department, and writing learned tomes comprehensible only to fellow-geneticists, Mazin lives in his Beit Sahour family home and helps to run the Middle East Genetics Association, the Holy Land Conservation Foundation and Academics for Justice. The Palestinians see him as an uncommonly effective activist who organises many protests at home and abroad and e-mails graphic accounts of Zionist outrages to his contacts all over the world. Recently I had read *Sharing the Land of Canaan*, in which he uses simple English to untangle convoluted controversies for the average reader.

Mazin relishes being an unbeliever with a Greek Orthodox mother, a Lutheran sister, a Buddhist wife and two Muslim uncles. His 1930s home in an affluent suburb is imaginatively designed to make the most of a cliff backdrop. It overlooks a deep, half-developed valley, with Har Homa on the far side, and its neat, high-hedged front garden is guarded by a small, furry, vocal dog.

Mazin helped his wife Jessie to prepare lunch at one end of a bright US-style kitchen-cum-living-room while I read – in obedience to my host – *al-Majdal*, the quarterly magazine of the BADIL Resource Centre for Palestinian Residency and Refugee Rights. We spent most of the afternoon discussing that issue's theme, the promising BDS (Boycott, Divestment, Sanctions) campaign. In its present form this began as the second Intifada erupted but its roots are deep; a boycott of Zionist enterprises accompanied the 1936–39 uprising. After 1948, the League of Arab States launched a boycott in an attempt to thwart Israel's burgeoning financial and commercial international relationships. But those Arab rulers felt no real concern for the Palestinians and soon gave in to US pressure. 'Economic normalisation' with Israel was and remains a condition of any Arab–US bilateral trade agreement; without it the US ambition to set up a Middle East Free Trade Agreement (MEFTA) could not be fulfilled. BDS activists use 'anti-normalisation' to explain their opposition to treating Israel as a normal state. As they logically argue, it has delegitimised itself through the illegal occupation of the OPT and the imposition of Apartheid laws both within the territories and within Israel, where certain communities have been authorised to exclude non-Jews.

By 2005 the BDS campaign had devised a coherent strategy, now being internationally deployed, with varying degrees of success, by Palestinian support groups. One day BDS could prove a sharp – even decisive – weapon in the non-violent armoury. But it's not irrelevant that the ANC won in South Africa *after* the US ended its support for the Apartheid regime.

Before reading Mazin's *Sharing the Land of Canaan*, I had reluctantly accepted that to campaign for the Right to Return, six decades after the Nakba, was wildly impractical, however morally and legally justified. I saw the problem as logistical rather than psychological. But in fact, as Mazin plausibly argues, the available space would allow a return. The Nakba sent Gaza's population from 80,000 to 240,000 and by now it is an almost intolerable 1.6 million. Yet few Israelis would be affected if Gaza's refugees returned to southern Israel/Palestine and there – with appropriate financial assistance, as compensation for stolen property – created for themselves new homesteads. Similarly a return from Lebanon's camps to Galilee would affect only 1% of that region's Israelis. When almost a million Russian immigrants arrived during the 1990s no Israeli official said, 'No room!' And none questioned their often fraudulent Jewishness (though several rabbis did). As Mazin makes clear, this asymmetry is 'to do with racist and apartheid Israeli laws'.

Given Zionism's travel restrictions, it's easy to forget what a small area encloses the Palestinians' tragedy – 'the ongoing Nakba', as Mazin calls it. Most refugees, whether based in the West Bank, the Gaza Strip, Jordan, Syria or Lebanon, live close to their ancestral homes. Mrs Qumsiyeh's memories of childhood motoring day-trips puts those distances in perspective. An early start from Bethlehem, lunch with cousins in Beirut, a coffee break in Damascus where one bought a supply of the incomparable Syrian sweetmeats, dinner with in-laws in Amman, then late home to Bethlehem. Now it can take two or three hours – depending on the IDF mood at checkpoint Container – to cover the eight miles to Jerusalem.

That evening a birthday party provided light relief. Mazin opted out (his polymathic involvements leave no time for light relief) but the rest of us squeezed into an elderly saloon – Jessie the driver, Mazin's mother beside her, in the back Mazin's thirty-five-year-old unmarried sister (the youngest of eight siblings), myself and two small nephews, excited but charmingly well-behaved. Our destination was the top flat in a six-storey apartment block overlooking a dramatic decline towards the Dead Sea. The eldest nephew informed me that Bethlehem is only 14 miles from the Dead Sea but 3,842 feet above it. His brother informed me that Aunty's flat was not 'luxury' because it had no lift. A large wooden cross above the living-room door and icons on every wall proclaimed this family's Greek Orthodoxy but one got the impression religion wasn't taken too seriously, at least by the younger generation.

'Aunty', the twenty-four-year-old birthday girl, was Mrs Qumsiyeh's eldest grandchild and the mother of her first great-grandchild, aged three months. Although this was a large party, overcrowding a three-bedroom flat, I seemed to be the only non-relative present. Four generations of Qumsiyehs and their in-laws made for a happy occasion. Even the baby appeared to enjoy being passed from lap to lap and, when offered unsuitable 'treats', she spat them out without fussing. Most guests contributed home-made dishes to the lavish buffet supper and the multicoloured cake was repeatedly photographed while ablaze with candles. Segregation happened spontaneously, the men sitting at one end of a long, over-furnished room while their womenfolk busied themselves in the kitchen or hovered around the birthday girl (whose name escaped me) as she opened her gifts – expensive garments, also much photographed for transmission by computer to relatives in the US. Most people drank fruit juice or Coca-Cola though the fridge held an ample supply of Teybeh beer and the sideboard was laden with wines and spirits. Two white-haired men chose weak whiskey and the white-haired woman's intake of Teybeh caused some amused surprise. When the music started (country & western, much too loud) great-grandmamma and I exchanged glances; it felt like bedtime for the Oldies and Jessie seemed happy to oblige.

I wouldn't want to live in Greater Bethlehem; the whole area – dominated by the Barrier and by settlements always poised to grab more land – has an unquiet aura accentuated by coachloads of tourists whose Israeli guides want them to leave 'enemy territory' as soon as possible. (In compensation, most little grocery stores sell beer.) Given my notoriously defective sense of direction and the Old Town's twisting streets, I was almost bound to get lost on the way to the bus station. As so often happens, this enriched the day; people should give themselves more time to get lost.

At noon I rested on the doorstep of a half-ruined house, my Taybeh discreetly wrapped in the *International Herald Tribune*. Below me lay a deep *wadi* with a derelict factory at one end. Then, on noticing the Paradise Hotel in the distance, I realised I'd been walking *away* from the bus station . . . At which point Jibril appeared, asking if I needed any help, offering to lead me to a taxi rank, then inviting me to lunch. He was slim and handsome with a narrow face, a Hitler moustache, small bright eyes. His home stood across the road, on the edge of the *wadi*, a cramped, DIY breeze-block bungalow replacing the half-ruin – shelled by the IDF in 2002. 'We wanted to repair,' said Jibril, 'but to make a small house took less money.'

The twenty-nine-year-old Jibril was a trainee nurse; five years in jail, after the second Intifada, had slowed his education. Only his father, Mustafa, was at home. His new wife, a qualified nurse, worked twelve-hour shifts. In 2004 his mother had died of breast cancer. 'They wouldn't give her a Jerusalem permit for treatment. They said I was in jail, meaning she came from a bad family. Then it spread and she died.'

Of Jibril's four younger brothers, two were still at school; their education, too, had been disrupted by the second Intifada. The others were now working on a Har Homa extension, digging drains for the settlers on land where their forefathers grazed sheep. One of them used to risk working without a permit in East Jerusalem but in 2006 he was caught and jailed for a year. Jibril asserted that a big enough bribe could get anyone a day-permit but his father disputed this. 'It's all luck,' said Mustafa. 'The quota decides, lucky people get permits before it's full.'

In the early 1980s Mustafa had worked on London building sites until deported as an illegal immigrant. In the early 1990s closures ended his next job as personnel manager in a small East Jerusalem factory. He was a dignified, thoughtful man, aged 68 but looking older. This was a drab, impoverished home brightened only by Koranic texts and London picture postcards pinned to the walls. As we lunched (flat bread, tomato salad, hard-boiled eggs) Mustafa gazed across the road at the semi-ruin and said, 'All our old carpets and weavings were burned.' A moment later he added – as though reproving himself – 'We must control our anger.'

Jibril frowned and muttered, 'What changes before we *use* it?'

Quietly Mustafa pointed out that using it, in the second Intifada, had made things incomparably worse. His son retorted, 'OK, we didn't use it enough! Use it more and for longer, all using together – then change comes!'

I made no comment though agreeing with Jibril in my heart (if not in my mind).

Both men escorted me to the bus station, complaining all the way about Bethlehem's Multi-disciplinary Industrial Park. I had heard something of this in Nablus, though most Nablusis directed their resentment towards the al-Jalama industrial zone near Jenin. There farmers were refusing to sell their exceptionally fertile Jezreel Valley land to a consortium of PA, Israeli and German-Turkish developers.

Mustafa couldn't foresee any benefit deriving to ordinary Palestinians from the Bethlehem project, recently 'fixed' between President Shimon Peres, President Nicolas Sarkozy and Valerie Hoffenberg, the American Jewish Committee's Paris director. What chiefly enraged Jibril was the PA's issuing of title to 125 acres of Palestinian public property for the creation of this 'industrial free zone'. 'The PA is not a government!' he fumed. 'It's not elected, how it gives away our land? Mahmoud Abbas on 9 January stopped being President. He has no rights for ruling before getting elected again! Why no one talks about this? Why all like him so much? We know why! To Israel's foreign friends he gives our land! His sons – you know about his sons? From USAID both got contracts worth millions of dollars!' (Later I investigated what might have been mere rumour and found it to be true. Moreover, one of those contracts was 'to improve America's image in the Palestinian territories'.)

On the way home I thought about the term 'Occupied Palestinian Territories'. At the birthday party, one of the venerable whiskey-drinkers had argued that it is tendentious. 'Occupied' implies a temporary expedient, a state of affairs due to be ended by some political agreement. To use it is to play the Israeli game: 'Let's pretend our goal is a two-state peace while we extend the settlements.' Yet the Israelis themselves avoid 'occupied' – prefer 'administered'. The fact that the West Bank has in practice been annexed must never be admitted; annexation involves taking total responsibility for the residents of the annexed territory. Oslo made it possible for the US and EU to intervene in its administration by building a police state in which Fayyad's Free Trade Industrial Zones can safely operate and be slotted neatly into the Middle East Free Trade Agreement when the time comes.

CHAPTER 12

Too Many Prisoners

Razan was to visit me one evening, to discuss her work as an undercover agent for contraceptives, a topic she judged best avoided while talking with her father and myself in al-Yasmeen. Then at 7.40 she cell-phoned; her taxi couldn't get through, Balata had been sealed off by a score of IDF vehicles, which explained why silence had suddenly fallen. Normally the space outside my room was noisy until about 10.00 p.m. – boys romping, men talking, laughing and shouting as they tinkered with dead cars or sat huddled around a bonfire playing cards. Even in midwinter, males tended to spend as much time as possible outside their cramped homes. The night before, Razan told me, the IDF had invaded the Kasbah: much shooting, 17 arrests, a bomb set off on the wasteland where three seventeenth-century dwellings were demolished by the Israeli Air Force in 2002. Massive explosions in confined areas are a favourite IDF terrorisation ploy.

Moments later, I heard youths gathering in the laneway, chanting defiantly and hand-clapping rhythmically. From my doorway I could see frightened women leaning out of windows, yelling angrily, telling the young to go home. I wished they would; to me they seemed to be playing the IDF's game. And quite soon they had been dispersed by clouds of tear-gas; as Balata incursions go, this was a non-event.

Next day, when I visited Gabby, an unusually outspoken neighbour, he seemed slightly ruffled by my hinting that the energy expended on stone-throwing, throughout the OPT, might be used more constructively. 'What right have we to say "Stop!" – how else for them to resist? They've seen fathers and brothers killed and tortured, mothers and sisters insulted, homes robbed and vandalised, ways of earning destroyed, every day more land going, soldiers watching settlers destroy crops and attack olive-pickers . . . Why should they stand quiet or run away when the IDF come patrolling and jeering? They must feel free to show anger and hate. They're the third or fourth imprisoned generation – bred to resist. What to do but throw stones? They're not stupid. Even little ones know they can't hurt soldiers in armoured vehicles. But they need to show they want to hurt them. And don't fear them, though since 2000 they've killed 108 boys and 5 girls.'

I had nothing to say. The quiet-spoken Gabby never once raised his voice but it trembled with vehemence. Then I wondered – did he and many other adult males see the stone-throwers as their surrogates? How can outsiders possibly understand the Palestinians' desperation, as manifested in those youngsters' lack of fear? And in Gabby's inability to see the (by our irrelevant standards) counter-productive nature, for their own communities, of such token violence.

Gabby's parents had fled from Haifa in 1948 carrying 'a bit in the rag', enough eventually to build an atypical three-room home; its tiny yard, behind a six-foot wall, ensured a degree of privacy rare in Balata. As a seven-year-old Gabby was taken by an uncle to Amman, educated in an 'English' school, then employed by UNRWA. The second Intifada badly affected his ageing parents whose six other children by then lived far away. So Gabby transplanted most of his family to Balata, a remarkable move at that date. His wife Sireen, a strong-minded woman also of Haifa stock, had insisted on the two older sons remaining in Amman with their great-uncle – out of reach of the al-Aqsa Brigades. Both were now employed as car mechanics. An endearing twelve-year-old boy and two small daughters were making the best of Balata's schools and getting extra tuition from their parents. I became very fond of this cheerful, affectionate family, who were more relaxed with outsiders than most Balatans.

That evening Razan arrived in high spirits, bringing two tins of beer to celebrate the jailing of a rapist. (She reckoned she was the only 'drinking' Muslim woman in Nablus; later I met two others but they were Jerusalem-born and of notable families.) The harrowing rape case was not, alas, rare. In 2007 the IDF had lifted a twenty-year-old bridegroom and held him in administrative detention for six months. His father repeatedly raped the seventeen-year-old bride and when pregnancy happened, at a date precluding her husband's sperm, she was charged in a 'customary' court with 'destroying the family name'. Because an 'honour killing' loomed, two brothers-in-law sought help from a Women's Rights group with the human and financial resources to bring about the event we were celebrating. But their struggle had been long and arduous; twice their advocate was threatened. The rapist had in fact been found guilty of 'grievous bodily harm', rape not being recognised as a crime. 'We're campaigning to change that,' said Razan, squaring her jaw.

'And the baby?' I asked. Grudgingly Razan explained that her *bête noire*, Hamas, ran orphanages where such babies were labelled 'orphan' and reasonably well cared for to the age of sixteen. The young parents had smuggled themselves out of the OPT, having borrowed the bribe money, and were going hungry in a Jordan limbo – unable as illegal immigrants to register with UNRWA and unable to seek work for the same reason. But now Gabby, who had many connections in Amman, was trying to help.

The evening had turned cold enough for me to unzip my flea-bag so that we could both snuggle under it. In Razan's view, I was being overcharged for this unheated squat but what to expect at ten euros a night?

To promote contraception in Nablus-Balata, however covertly, took considerable courage at a time of increasing Islamist (as distinct from Islamic) influence. Razan was fiercely anti-Hamas. 'I'm a feminist first, then a Palestinian. They say Hamas are the only ones left fighting for our rights but do women want *their* sort of rights?' A huge question, which I felt unqualified to consider.

'I'm a good Muslim,' continued Razan. 'I believe, pray, keep Ramadan – that's why our men-serving misinterpretations of the Koran make me puke. Women to be subservient about everything, children taught to respect Father which they won't do if he can't or won't dominate the household. All this is behind our shameful record of domestic violence.' Then hastily Razan added, 'You understand I'm talking about *peasants*.' She looked very taken aback when I observed that in Ireland violence against women is found throughout society.

When Razan left she chose not to take the laneway past the Yaffa Centre and the new mosque but to ascend to the main Huwwara road via the long stairs up from my squat. 'In Balata after dark,' said she, 'there's too many kids with nowhere to go and nothing to do.'

I was rarely out late and always used the laneway, relying on old age as my talisman. However, by day it bothered me to see so much childhood aggression in the alleyways – more than horseplay or vigorous wrestling. This was fighting to hurt, the little faces of the protagonists twisted with animosity. As Moussa saw it, 'Too many are sick kids, born into violence, warped minds in stunted bodies.'

Personally I was never seriously hassled in Balata. And only once in Nablus, in a bombed and deserted corner of the Kasbah, where a small boy with a flick-knife threatened me when I ignored 'Give shekels!' He was so small that by swinging my knapsack in self-defence I accidentally knocked him to the ground.

That night and all next day it rained non-stop while thunder crashed and reverberated between Ebal and Jerzim – a suitable elemental accompaniment to the general election which brought Benjamin Netanyahu back to power. I stayed in my room reading and writing, seeing no one for thirty-six hours: a restorative dose of solitude.

My Balatan and Nablusi friends were supremely uninterested in Israeli domestic politics and, as the new government evolved, I gave up trying to understand a voting system that looks like an extension of the national madness. How could rational administrations be expected to emerge from this welter of conflicting minority interests in which most parties seem ready most of the time to compromise whatever it is they use instead of principles. And this is a government in control of more than 200 nuclear weapons and a wide range of other WMDs!

Around this time I was puzzled by the appearance in all local markets (even Balata's) of hand-barrows heaped with luscious strawberries, gleaming and glowing – a luxury fruit on the West Bank's cold heights. Noha recounted one rumour: EU countries had rejected most of this crop having detected an illegal pesticide. Th'aeir had heard another version: some legal pesticide had been over-used. 'So they dump them on us!' said Noha. Whatever the explanation, most Palestinians relished this exotic treat and scorned all my health-hazard warnings. Pesticides apart, BADIL activists were trying to persuade Nablusis to boycott all Israeli goods and buy only Arab imports. A flaccid campaign, so far. Said Noha, 'Israeli stuff is better quality, better value. And what did Arab countries ever do for us?'

One morning I watched an UNRWA food delivery from a giant truck parked at the camp's edge. Boys and young (mostly) men presented the family ration card, loaded porters' trolleys with rice, noodles, flour, beans, lentils, sunflower oil, then pushed or pulled their meagre supplies along rough steep lanes. 'Special Cases' – the handicapped, single mothers – get extra rations. Deaths go unregistered for as long as possible, so that the living may benefit from the deceased's share. Funding is not proportionally increased as camp numbers rise and Gabby – among others – encouraged some of the young to 'marry out', thus losing their refugee status. That was a hypersensitive issue, intertwined with the Right of Return and several other nuanced controversies. UNRWA is the second biggest employer of Palestinians, after the PA. Among the proud oldest generation quite a few expressed to me (as a new witness to this humiliating dependence) their unquenchably angry resentment of 'charity'.

Returning one morning from a walk along Mount Ebal, I heard several gun shots, very close – seemingly fired between the girls' new school and the cemetery. Rather scary: I've never fancied being a war correspondent. The shots came in two bursts with a short pause and were not from the IDF or PA police weapons; their presence – and the reaction to it – would have been obvious. Hundreds of pupils were chanting their morning prayer (a happy melody) and for a moment they faltered – then continued no less happily. I scuttled into my room, only emerging a silent hour later.

In the nearby market I greeted my English-speaking fruit-seller friend, a dignified old man with a long white beard and loose turban. While surveying his display I asked casually, 'Did you hear shots earlier?' Ali's face closed and he made no reply but drew my attention to browning bananas going at half-price; by then he knew all about my preferences. I bought a kilo, insisting on paying full price (€.50) and also indulged in a kilo of avocados (€.80) – my favourite laxative. Then on to Ajeeb the yoghurt-merchant, a chatty young man whose mother made the best yoghurt I have ever eaten. His English was limited; Balata's older, Jordan-educated generation were much more fluent. But he understood my question about those shots and his face, too, closed up. Soon after, I was in the Yaffa Centre where everyone seemed slightly tense. One man said, 'You didn't hear anything this morning, just remember you heard nothing.'

That afternoon, at a grim gathering near the university (all about student prisoners and PA police torture techniques) I chanced to meet Karim. At once he asked, 'Did you hear the execution? Will he be buried today?' I must have looked nonplussed because he added hastily, 'Don't worry, don't be scared – it's OK, we knew he worked for the IDF. Guys like that have to be killed.'

I could see his point – then was shocked by my ability to see it. Life on the West Bank can be very morally confusing. But why had he imagined I might know anything about the burial time? At first that intrigued me – then, on further reflection, seemed vaguely disquieting.

Karim had been advising a 'Students Against Torture' meeting, as he was well qualified to do. While he told me about his qualifications we sat in a shiny crowded café – its décor aping McDonald's or KFC – opposite the main gate of the new university campus. In the 1970s, at the age of nine, Karim and three contemporaries were arrested and held for some thirty hours beyond reach of their families. Once, having been arrested in a cousin's house high on Mount Ebal, he was interrogated while being repeatedly kicked and beaten for forty minutes by four soldiers. They then dragged him by the legs down 162 concrete steps, flung him into an APC and sat on him, fracturing three ribs. (I knew those steps, linking two residential streets.) In a cold, damp detention centre he was left lying on the floor overnight with about thirty others. Every hour or so a pair of soldiers strolled between the prone bodies, kicking them. Eight days later, Karim was released without charge.

As a twenty-year-old, in 1987, he found himself in a military court. When his woman lawyer was given only fifteen minutes to study the case against him he demanded the right to cross-question the soldier on whose evidence he might be convicted. This was granted. The judge then admitted he could not be convicted on such evidence – but within five hours had changed his mind and offered a three-month sentence if Karim would 'collaborate with the court'. Because Karim wouldn't he spent 25 months in a semi-autonomous Negev prison-camp. Many Negev prisoners choose not to have visits; a costly 12-hour journey earns relatives only 30 minutes without physical contact.

Undoubtedly, said Karim, severe ill-treatment and torture could extract quite a lot of information (not all accurate or useful) from simple, frightened youths without the resources to endure pain. Especially, he added, after mental torture has broken them, like seeing shit stamped onto the Koran or hearing conscripts threatening to rape mothers, sisters, wives, daughters – 'on that table, where you can see it'. Being a non-believer helped when the Koran was desecrated though it enraged Karim to see any religion's holy book 'disrespected'. 'But I'm only angered,' he said. 'Believers are demoralised and traumatised.'

*

between river and sea

IDF brutality is most graphically recorded not by its traumatised victims
but by refuseniks. These soldiers are also the people who have least
difficulty understanding a phenomenon that repels and baffles most of
us: suicide bombing.

Sergio Yahni, who served three jail terms for refusing, wrote to the
then Defence Minister, Benyamin Ben Eliezer, on 19 March 2002:

> . . . Tanks in Ramallah cannot stop your most monstrous creations:
> the desperation which explodes in coffee shops. You, and the military
> officers under your command, have created human beings whose
> humanity disappears out of desperation and humiliation. You have
> created this despair and you cannot stop it . . . Your army that calls
> itself the 'Israel Defense Forces' is nothing more than the armed wing
> of the settlement movement. This army exists to guarantee the con-
> tinuation of the theft of Palestinian land . . . It is both my Jewish and
> human duty to resolutely refuse to take any part in this army . . .

From Military Jail 4 David Haham-Herson wrote to his parents:

> . . . I am a God-fearing Jew, and as such forbidden to take part in
> denying freedom and serving in occupied territory . . . I am concerned
> for those whose homes have been demolished and their fruit groves
> devastated. I am concerned because I know that the terrible hatred
> towards me is justified. This hatred has led to horrifying and perverted
> manifestations, like the young suicide bombers, but we create the
> conditions that lead to this monstrosity . . .

In April 2002 Itamar Shahar (Military ID 7015540) asked himself:

> . . . how could I be in the ranks of a body, a considerable portion of
> whose present actions constitute terrorism against innocent civilians?
> . . . My act of refusal is not entirely altruistic: I am not refusing merely
> over the rights of the people of the West Bank and Gaza – even
> though in my view those are perfectly adequate grounds – but also
> for the benefit of Israeli society. The destinies of the two people are
> interconnected, and the harm inflicted upon the Palestinians prompts
> some of them to adopt non-legitimate measures of harming innocent
> civilians of Israel, so that fear has become a central component of our
> routine existence. Thirty-five years of occupation have made Israeli

society violent and racist, a society wherein many live in poverty and ignorance . . .

Idan Kaspari, a 1st sergeant with the Golani Brigade, signed the Courage to Refuse Declaration and wrote:

> Terrorism is the weapon of those who have lost hope, who are humiliated and powerless. Of those who have lost faith in this world and place it in the next world to come. Occupation feeds and sustains terrorism . . . Israel of recent years has defined itself by means of the occupation, by domination and humiliation of another people, and by a futile war against the terrorism generated by that hopelessness and humiliation.

Ro'i Kozlovsky, a lieutenant in the reserves, was sentenced to 18 days for refusing to guard settlements and on his release wrote:

> The settlements constitute theft of land that isn't ours . . . They exist on the army's bayonets . . . Collaboration with the policy of the Israeli government makes me a criminal, for the responsibility for committing immoral acts is not merely with those who give the orders; it lies with all those ready to carry them out even though they do not agree with them.

Omry Yeshurun, a lieutenant with an armoured unit, served in the OPT and one night several years later had a dream:

> . . . About the kid I dragged from his parents' home in the middle of the night; he pissed his pants and wept all the way to the Para's prison. In the morning, I wondered what that kid was doing now. And deep down inside, there was the answer, the answer I should have known long ago: that kid is now shooting at IDF roadblocks, or maybe has blown himself up with an explosive charge. Did I have a hand in that? . . . Israel, the strongest state in the Middle East, is scared that a bunch of stone-throwing kids will destroy it; and the fear is so strong we no longer look at ourselves in the mirror . . . We are beginning to resemble the most benighted regimes in human history: a state that sends its soldiers to break into the homes of the innocent and takes loyal care of the settlers who spit in its face . . . I will no longer take part in these crimes. I will not take part in destroying the state in which I live. Enough of the occupation.

Yigal Bronner, famed for his campaigning on behalf of South
Hebron's cave-dwelling shepherds, quotes Brecht:

> General, man is very useful
> He can fly, and he can kill.
> But he has one defect.
> He can think.

The disturbing question remains: why so few refuseniks? Why so few
thinking Israelis? Is it because of all that fear, relentlessly instilled into
every Israeli citizen from age zero – because without it the Zionist state
might dissolve into something more normal and civilised and less
amenable to indirect military rule.

Karim noted that Balata's reputation as an heroic centre of resistance
had been bought at a high price – as even I, a non-Arabic-speaking
newcomer, could see for myself. Most of the disturbing scenes I had
witnessed or heard about were directly related to the Occupation. Even
under the best conditions, men released after a long sentence have
problems adjusting to normal life, and fathers, unseen for 4/6/8 or
more years, are strangers to children who can find it hard to reconnect.
Then there is a startling new phenomenon, young grass-widows who
encourage one another to defy custom by going out in unescorted groups
to Nablus cafés where they may be identified by neighbours or in-laws.
Some of those pioneers are beaten up badly when their husbands return.
Chronic joblessness is another notorious wrecker of families; before the
second Intifada 60% worked in Israel or the settlements, in 2009 only
5% had permits. And of course the Balatans, in common with most
OPT residents, live in fear of the increasingly aggressive settlers whose
crimes the IDF either ignore or expedite. Moreover, heightened tension
is maintained by the camp's proximity to Joseph's Tomb, which Holy
Place inflames the Kooks' most menacing followers.

One of Karim's innumerable cousins was sentenced to nineteen years
for killing a soldier who had looked on, laughing, while two settlers
poisoned the family well near Elon Moreh. After Sharif's recent release,
Karim found him in a bad way, pleading to be returned to jail – 'It
often happens, specially when there's family worries.' Not long after
Sharif's arrest his beautiful wife had run away with a handsome French
IRC employee whose connections enabled him to smuggle her to an

unknown destination.

Almost everyone I met in Balata, and many of my Nablusi friends, had either been imprisoned or spoke of prisoner relatives. The majority of jailed Palestinians are male but several years ago one of Hana's grand-daughters, the mother of three small children, got a two-year sentence for carrying a weaving knife. Her husband then acquired a second wife and she returned to child-related problems and sought a divorce. Hana also knew three eighteen-year-old mothers who were found, by a bored eighteen-year-old female conscript, to be 'armed' with fruit knives. All were put away for two and a half years. And at Huwwara a fifteen-year-old youth had recently been arrested for carrying a three-inch pen-knife, the sort every small boy of my generation regarded as essential equipment.

To be young in the OPT is not very bliss . . . My teacher friend, Hussniya, complained about two of her fifteen-year-old star pupils having been taken out of school to marry, thus missing an important exam by a few months. If they ever had the freedom to complete their education they would have to repeat the whole course. Even more upsetting, a thirty-four-year-old construction worker with a job in Ramallah asked for the hand of an eighteen-year-old who disliked him so intensely that her father said, 'We'll give you Bab instead' – Bab being a fifteen-year-old who looked and behaved like a twelve-year-old.

Hussniya commented that the uncertainty of daily life makes many parents unduly anxious to get daughters married; their safety then becomes a husband's responsibility. And most mothers long to see sons married young; they hope family ties will counter militant tendencies. Hussniya added, sadly, that the traditional mutual support provided by neighbourhood communities has dwindled because of the Occupation – a judgement other Balatans echoed. Then, as an antidote, she introduced me to Nablus's inspiring Women's Study Group (WSG). This NGO was founded in 1989 by a woman of vigour and vision who, as a twenty-year-old, was jailed for eight years and made the most of that time to read for two degrees.

The WSG occupies one floor of a three-storey former mansion in the suburb of Rafidia – once a prosperous Christian village, now boringly modernised and striving to regain prosperity. (Here one finds Palestine's only stock exchange.) 'Study' is the key word in this NGO's title. All rooms vibrate with creative energy as severely traumatised and/or crippled IDF victims are gently encouraged to develop or discover their personal skills and talents. In groups or singly, they act, sing, dance, draw, paint, embroider, weave and contribute to a journal covering many topics with special emphasis on women's rights. The group also compiles an annual report on those who need special care (often the families of executed informers) and it collects evidence on behalf of certain victims of IDF looting and destruction of property – people determined to publicise those crimes though they have scant hope of redress. Most importantly, a unit of members who have themselves been bereaved, or maimed, or seen their homes vandalised remains on stand-by to rally round households in the immediate aftermath of military incursions. Four Balata families told me that these units, who 'knew what it felt like', were able to sustain them 'the morning after' as professional counsellors could not.

Another unit attempts to sow liberal seeds in arid soil, urging young mothers to treat girls and boys as equals from the moment of birth and to oppose forced marriages. (I mean liberal in the OED sense of 'not bound by authority or traditional orthodoxy'.) A delegation including two lawyers had recently presented 'President' Abbas with a demand to outlaw rape and under-eighteen marriages. A 1951 Jordanian Family Law lays down the minimum marriage ages for women (seventeen) and men (eighteen). But this does not apply in the OPT where fifteen-year-olds may wed if a *qadi* (Sharia judge) finds them 'at a fit stage for marriage'. In extreme cases birth certificates are forged and *qadis* not consulted before a child marriage is registered.

Half the WSG staff are paid a modest salary, the rest are volunteers. Palestinian women seemed to me notably less affected than their men-folk by Zionism's psychological torturing of the entire population. The imams were alarmed – said Karim – by the numbers of powerful women who came to the fore after the second Intifada, rejecting any man's assumed right to control – or to thwart – community projects emphasising gender equality.

I attended my only expat gathering in the WSG director's home, also in Rafidia. My fellow-guests were an affable Englishman, in Nablus to advise the local PA on 'political organisation', a forceful young German woman of right-wing tendencies who was advising on foreign invest-ments and a fat, chucklesome Belgian musicologist seeking apprentices keen to repair musical instruments. Also present was a fiery young

Palestinian woman economist with scant regard for the 'free' market. Her duel with the German made this luncheon memorable; she had just served a six-month sentence for distributing Hamas leaflets. (Hamas, lest you might have forgotten, was democratically elected in January 2006 to govern all the OPT. Incidentally, I have slighted Mahmoud Abbas' title because he had not been President since 9 January 2009 when his term of office expired. The US and Israeli administrations were continuing to refer to him as *President* for their own reasons. They also appointed the unelected Salam Fayyad as 'Prime Minster'.)

Time spent in the WSG centre, and in its director's ever-welcoming home, always lifted my spirits – as visits to INGO offices did not. To me those seemed uneasily remote from the surrounding realities. I sympathised with some of their local staff who admitted they often felt conflicted. To sound too 'Westernised' could be misinterpreted as disloyalty to the 'cause' so they hesitated to discuss customs perceived as 'backward', though realising such discussions could be helpful to their employers. Many Human Rights INGOs achieve little, being perversely addicted to political neutrality. Justice can't be won in a fenced-off space with active politics happening elsewhere. To talk of 'operating within a human rights framework' makes no sense when the available 'framework' is ignored by the other parties – Israel, the US, Fatah and Hamas included.

No one can become an effective human rights advocate without openly attacking the foundations of the systems that routinely disregard them. There is a tendency to treat the Occupation as an Act of God rather than a long-term political ploy to banish the Palestinians from their homeland. As one prominent Zionist (who wished to remain anonymous) said to me in Jerusalem, 'We waited 2,000 years to come home, we can wait one more century for the Arabs to leave.' Calmly he pointed out – smiling at me – that the settlements are not illegal under international law because there is no such thing as international law. Said he, 'You can't have a law without an enforcement agency. The UN has no power to stop Jews returning to Judea and Samaria.' He actually boasted that ultra-Orthodox 'outpost' settlements are sponsored by US Zionists *and* Christian Zionists. Those 'Friends of Israel' also fund secular, bottom-of-the-pile Israelis who join the settler movement for economic reasons. Of itself this fact proves that in Palestine/Israel 'advocates for justice' have to get their hands dirty with politics, even up to the elbow.

Before returning home, I sent my collection of printed matter ahead

by DHL, to avoid its confiscation at Ben-Gurion airport. It weighed
more than 10 kg and was mostly Human Rights Reports, all professionally compiled and expensively produced, complete with maps,
graphs, tables of statistics and excellent photographs. Add countless tapes
and videos, and such novelties as blogs and Twitter, and you realise how
over-monitored is this scene. But where and when does 'enforcement'
happen? Very, very rarely, and then in exceptional circumstances. On
the West Bank, and later in Gaza, and again in 2010 when I lived
among the justice-deprived Palestinian 20% of Israel's population, I
heard people mocking the 'Human Rights Industry' with its well-paid
staffs, comfortably furnished offices, fleets of vehicles (most forbidden
to give lifts to 'natives') and regular 5-star international conferences.
Occasionally I observed the statistics-collectors at work, their gleaming
4 x 4s parked outside two-room shacks housing families of fourteen or
sixteen. Understandable irritation is provoked by detailed lists of what's
wrong and a 99% failure to put anything right. If 'humanitarians'
tangled with the Occupation in ways which improved the lot of the
most repressed, their INGO might well become persona non grata. Yet
another horribly neat vicious circle . . . Talking to my mocking friends,
and trying to think positive, I argued that even impotent monitors are
better than no monitors. Possibly all those futile reports may be of
some use when the scene shifts – as eventually it must. But the longer I
spent among the Palestinians the more persuasive became their counter-
argument. The conspicuous presence, throughout the West Bank,
of INGOs dedicated to the Palestinians' welfare must buttress the
Occupation by indicating to outsiders that Israel is not really anti-
Palestinian – only anti-'terrorist'.

Too many indigenous local NGOs now emulate the foreigners, jargon
and all. According to the Palestinian Counseling Centre, 'A preliminary
study of wall-related symptoms in the Qalqilya area found a high
prevalence of depressive factors apparent in sleeping and eating disorders
as well as psychosomatic symptoms among adults and children.' In
2004 Save the Children UK and Save the Children Sweden presented a
typical paper to the UN Commission on Human Rights: 'There was an
alarming rise in children's sense of insecurity and risk from violence, and
a growing feeling of injustice to which they have increasingly violent
responses . . . Children were asked to write down words that describe
the wall. The most common word they used was "a prison".' Predictably,

no institution suggested any effective action (such as trade sanctions) to STOP barrier construction.

Advocates for justice can't rely on a theoretical framework to defeat Zionism's well-oiled international anti-human-rights machine. When millions of US and EU dollars are being spent annually on 'equipping and training' one lot of Palestinians to 'protect' Israel by repressing another lot (the victors in a free and fair election), then it's time to concentrate on direct political action. Like nurturing the BDS campaign; to increase its momentum we need to agitate for it *now*, and I mean *agitate*, going beyond the hoisting of placards and the chanting of slogans. One day BDS could make a crucial difference if it took off like the South African model. Most youngsters are astonished to hear that for decades Washington (echoed by Mrs Thatcher) condemned Nelson Mandela and the ANC as 'terrorists'.

In September 2013 Gideon Levy noted the influence of economic sanctions on Iran's nuclear policy. He added:

> We've seen that diplomatic and economic pressure on a state that flouts the international community's decisions can yield results. Perhaps we'll be hearing an analogy to another state that has also been blatantly flouting UN resolutions for decades. Why shouldn't we impose economic sanctions on Israel if they solve problems? This prospect is now frightening Israel . . .

Among the human rights activists who do help, and are valued and loved, one must count the brave olive-harvest support groups (frequently attacked by settlers), the checkpoint monitors (Israeli and International), the ISM volunteers (two of whom were murdered in Gaza by the IDF in 2003) and those self-funding freelancers who avoid all publicity while donating their time and skills to the most needy.

In Ramallah I met one such – Ruth, a well-connected Jewish-American physiotherapist, tall and slender, fluent in Hebrew and Arabic, who since 2004 had been regularly visiting the OPT to work with IDF-disabled children. In 2007 she became engaged to Khaled, a Palestinian doctor-cum-activist. Soon after, he was arrested and had been held for two terms of Administrative Detention in a remote prison where only his mother was allowed a monthly 30-minute visit. He had never been charged with even a minor infringement of a trivial regulation. Nor was he ill-treated – 'perhaps,' speculated Ruth, 'because of me in the background?' The day she and I first met, Khaled's case was being considered for the third time. Would he now be charged, or released, or held for another six months? His detention was extended and when next we met Ruth's triumphant air surprised me; Khaled had arranged a power of attorney to enable his brother to marry on his behalf. This stunned the relevant *qadi* but on recovering he was helpful – though he did ask the bride-to-be if she was 'a girl' (i.e., a virgin) which he had no right to do. The bridegroom's family then caused some confusion by arguing about the statutory divorce agreement; US$5,000 eventually became acceptable. Ruth and her obliging brother-in-law-to-be had to spend many days presenting sheaves of documents to various Ramallah offices. But the reward was rich. After the proxy marriage Ruth hastened south to Khaled who told her of his lawyer's constructive suggestion. As a married man, if he agreed to leave Palestine/Israel for three years he could be released. There was no moment of hesitation; Khaled carried a Jordanian passport and had several relatives in Dubai. And he planned, Ruth assured me, to continue his activism by remote control.

Not all such stories have happy endings. One of my closest Balata friends, Th'aer, told me in whispers about a niece who fell in love with a Swedish photographer. They planned to marry and live in Sweden but Th'aer's brother, the girl's father, vowed to kill them both if they didn't at once separate. This brother had migrated to the Emirates, where he prospered. Yet he became notoriously tight-fisted (an uncommon Palestinian fault) and contributed little to the family purse after his asthmatic wife's early death in a cloud of tear gas. The widowed Th'aer then brought his two daughters up with her own octet and so was blamed by their father for allowing such an unsuitable relationship to develop. When he asserted that he could afford to hire a Swedish killer the photographer very sensibly backed off; one can't assume such threats to be mere bluff. Another of Th'aer's brothers ordered his eldest son to kill an unmarried seventeen-year-old pregnant sister. Obediently the nineteen-year-old strangled her, then broke down, confessed to the police and was given an 'open sentence'. Nobody knew what that meant.

In Nablus I got to know one foreign wife, a German married to a junior academic at An-Najah University. They had met when Cosima, a freelance speech therapist, was helping Mohammad's nine-year-old sister, shocked into silence by a Defensive Shield bomb. Their enchanting trilingual son was regularly exercised in the optimistically named 'Childhood Happiness Center: Established in 1998'. After the second Intifada, the municipality restored this pleasant space where mature trees shade wooden tables and benches, shrubs are neatly pruned, litter-bins are emptied and toddlers frolic around a fountain of spring water with mugs attached. Directly above, Mount Ebal slopes towards the plain and a suburb of white residential blocks shows few Defensive Shield scars though the nearby factories and government offices were obliterated. Here I sometimes sat in the sun, writing my notes until interrupted by curious mothers, grandmothers or older sisters. Most were friendly Nablusi women; Balatans on the whole avoided the park despite their lack of play-space. When I asked 'Why?' people were evasive.

On first seeing Cosima in the distance, wearing a hijab and an ankle-length, close-fitting black coat (jilbab), I deduced her foreignness from her carriage; she moved like a woman who had grown up otherwise attired and enjoying physical activity. Soon we were wringing our hands over the local aversion to walking; both sexes habitually use taxis though they have so little money and so much spare time. Cosima had found that many of her middle-class contemporaries longed to cycle and to swim but cycling was totally verboten and swimming only allowed in segregated pools 'and Nablus has none'. She admitted that twice a year she needed to visit her parents in Hamburg 'for conversation and bookshops'.

Although An-Najah University (founded in 1977) is the West Bank's largest, with sixteen faculties and almost 20,000 students, Cosima repeated oft-heard criticisms of its low standards, especially in engineering – a popular choice of OPT youths who dream of jobs on Emirate building sites. (An exception is the IT department, run in collaboration with the Korean government.) Cosima rarely visited either campus, finding the vibes uncongenial. In May 2008 when a student (a Hamas 'suspect') was shot dead in mid-afternoon by a Fatah security guard, no inquiry was allowed. Nor is the university's human rights unit encouraged; the authorities prefer to keep aloof from students who are being harassed by the IDF or their PA accomplices. During Cast Lead the An-Najah president expressed sympathy with the Gazan people but ordered the students and staff to show no support for Hamas.

Karim was less scornful of An-Najah's academic standards and thought foreigners should be more tolerant of disorganisation and unco-

ordination, should make allowances for the Occupation's handicaps. All
West Bank universities were closed by the IDF from 1988–91 when An-
Najah's staff taught their students as best they could off campus, without
the normal resources. Both campuses (two miles apart) were almost
deserted by 4.00 p.m. because of checkpoint delays and the fear of
travelling after dark. Many students had to rise at 3.00 a.m. to be in time
for early lectures. Nor was the staff spared; Jerusalemites had a four-hour
commute though the normal driving time would be ninety minutes.
One couldn't wander in and out of An-Najah's campuses; security was
rigid and foreigners unattached to the university were not made to feel
welcome. The PA police had recently begun closely to watch certain
faculty members suspected of fundraising for Hamas' social services.

Cell phones now enable students of both sexes to be kept under
parental surveillance. 'A double surveillance,' noted Karim. 'Partly to
protect them from messing with each other, partly to protect them from
getting into dangerous "resistance".' If late, girls are ordered home *now*,
boys encouraged to return *soon*. However, some lads must find a doss
in Nablus and work their way to graduation; fees are high, at least
US$2,000 per annum. As girls may not work outside the home, many
do very beautiful weaving or embroidery in their spare time, for sale in
the Kasbah. I talked with one exceptionally attractive but quietly
unhappy weaver, a Balatan student who had fallen in love with a scion
of a notable and snobbishly anti-Balata Nablus family. For centuries the
city was controlled by a few strong families, now less rich but, because of
antique 'connections', scarcely less powerful. According to Karim, clan
loyalties have always been more important than newfangled political
alliances and the offspring of Fatah parents wouldn't normally switch to
Hamas. Yet whole families did switch in January 2006, to register
support for Hamas as a resistance movement while protesting against
Fatah/PA corruption, incompetence and laziness.

Leila invited me to accompany her to a 'Public Relations Workshop'
designed to prepare English-speaking students for interviews with the
media and debates with Internationals. At noon we crossed the wide
new campus, dominated by colossal, brilliantly white stone buildings
including two theatres. Leila quoted her father, who deplored so many
of the old campus buildings being wasted. Could all those oil millions
not have been put to better, job-creating use? What good are highfalutin
degrees to young people doomed to years of idleness? Leila only disagreed

with her Abu when he ranted against the high percentage of women on the academic staff.

Most students sauntered to and from their canteens in segregated groups but a few couples were daringly linked. 'They're married,' explained Leila. Not all girls wore the jilbab but the occasional bare-headed girl looked conspicuous. In Nablus, grumbled Leila, the hijab had become *almost* compulsory; why risk incurring Salafist wrath? Even progressive young husbands, eager to show off their wives' beautiful hair, allowed them to do so only when visiting Ramallah or Bethlehem. Several girls had been withdrawn from university when spies informed their families about hijab removal on campus. But, added Leila, here as elsewhere a significant number of militant females chose to cover their hair as a political statement.

This PR workshop reeked of unsubtle propaganda. One tutor argued that Palestinians never kill innocent Israelis because there's no such thing: all Israelis serve in the IDF. ('Not entirely true!' muttered Leila.) Another tutor asserted that 'martyrs' try to avoid targeting women and children. ('A lie!' muttered Leila.) When the third speaker likened Cast Lead to the Holocaust Leila gripped my elbow and hissed, 'Let's go!' Our move emboldened the only other International to follow us.

Emma was an exhausted-looking young woman, a Swiss human rights lawyer who had been working in the Nablus area for the previous two months – her second such stint. She now joined us for coffee and admitted that her close-up view of the IDF in action had left her averse to spending time in Israel on the way home. However, it cheered her to have found the regional tension much reduced since 2008 and she was amazed by the speed of construction in Ramallah – and, to a lesser extent, in Nablus.

Suddenly Gamal appeared beside our table, seized my hand and exclaimed, 'I'm sorry, I'm sorry!' An INGO co-ordinator, he had been 'in the field' at the times of my last two appointments with him. This didn't bother me; in the OPT one must be flexible. But I knew that some fast-moving foreign 'experts', with only two hours to spare for Nablus, give off toxic fumes if the representatives of generously funded INGOs are not in situ at the prearranged time.

Leila regarded Gamal as an unsung hero. Whenever he might be able to deter a 'martyr' he opposed suicide bombing, yet after the event he didn't oppose its glorification if that was indicated to ease the bomber's family's grief. He had bravely confronted one of Balata's imams whose

Friday sermons, audible all over the camp, too often condoned or even
suggested acts of vengeance. Listening from my squat, close to the biggest
mosque, one didn't need Arabic to discern the anger in that voice.

At our first meeting the middle-aged Gamal had said, 'It's hard for us
to watch the kids going sour. All twisted up inside with anger, hate,
sorrow, frustration – desperate for revenge. Revenge is instead of being
able to get justice, or even being able to fight for it without "collective
punishment". Kids know we can't win. Maybe we've worldwide support
but it's not from the governments that keep Israel safe.'

In the second Intifada Gamal lost two sons and a third was left
paralysed from the waist down. Palestinians endure such tragedies with
extraordinary courage and resilience though not necessarily with stiff
upper lips. Strong men are unashamed to weep when recalling their
children's or grandchildren's deaths.

Now Gamal suggested that we accompany him to a BDS meeting to
be addressed by Karim. This took place in the home of a lecturer, whose
job would have been at risk were it known that he fostered 'open
discussion' between students committed to neither Fatah nor Hamas.
It's the sort of discussion urgently needed if the Palestinians are ever to
escape into an arena of fresh thinking.

A year later Cosima telephoned Ireland from Hamburg with the news
that six An-Najah students had been arrested. And a professor of political
science, Abdel Sattar Qassem, had criticised the university administration
for not following a court order cancelling the expulsion of another four
students. The professor was at once condemned by An-Najah's president,
who also put pressure on the Student Union to cancel 'twinning' with
Essex and Manchester Student Unions unless they denounced Hamas
'terrorism', which they very properly voted *not* to do.

The PA's collaboration with Zionism had long since been noted in an
Amnesty International report (*Palestinian Authority: Silencing Dissent*,
2000): 'In the six years since its establishment, the PA has detained
dozens of human rights defenders, journalists, religious figures, writers,
government officials, trade unionists and academics solely for exercising
their legitimate rights to freedom of expression.'

Cosima's other news was more cheerful. Mohammad's academic
achievements had so impressed a German university that they would
soon be moving house.

CHAPTER 13

Ramallah: A Substitute Capital

At irregular intervals I visited Ramallah to buy *Ha'aretz*, a newspaper of which Israel should be proud. And there it was my privilege to meet Raja Shehadeh, the Palestinians' best known English-language writer whose five (so far) volumes of personal memoirs are dual purpose: as literature exhilarating, as aids to understanding The Problem indispensable. In time I became quite reliant on Raja's stabilising blend of humour, imagination, courage, shrewdness, common sense and sympathy. Sometimes we were joined by his American wife Penny, who radiates her own sort of calming cheerfulness. As an academic activist, she came to the West Bank for a year in 1982, met Raja and is still on the West Bank. Few foreigners have shared in the Palestinians' sufferings for so long.

Raja's office in the town centre, where he works as a lawyer, is soothingly predictable: a mellow Persian carpet, dark glossy furniture, shelves of sober tomes. He sits at his father's and grandfather's desk – a small, slim, soft-spoken man, diffident yet steely. At our first meeting, when I commented on Ramallah's death-dealing traffic chaos, he assured me that it was much reduced: not a trivial achievement, it went with a general restoration of civic order. Also, the PA was trying to lay the foundations for an honest justice system, without which no society can enjoy good health. He went on to explain one of the ways in which the settlements 'have damaged Israel as a viable state'. For any state to endure, its legal system, whether good or bad, must be generally accepted by the majority of citizens. They may complain and protest about its defects but if they get away with consistently breaking the law, in open defiance of court rulings, the validity of the state itself is brought into question. All the more so when the armed forces, and many politicians and some judges, collude with the lawbreakers in various ways, directly and indirectly. Not long before, several judges had pronounced certain settlements to be illegal according to *Israeli* law: then they blatantly advised the settlers on how to evade the relevant laws by using obscure loopholes. In the OPT five legal systems coexist: Ottoman, British,

Mandatory, Jordanian, Israeli Military Rule and Israeli Administrative law. To lay ears this sounds like a stray dog's dinner. When I said as much, Raja rang his aged uncle, internationally recognised as the leading authority on this issue, to clarify certain points. Then he assured me that in practice confusion rarely arises. To those with the knowledge and skill to wriggle around, over, under or through the various layers, it's all quite clear-cut. The Ottoman component remains extremely important and is routinely manipulated to the Palestinians' disadvantage.

Raja was a sixteen-year-old in 1967 when the Occupation began with a distribution, throughout the Territories, of notices in Arabic and Hebrew: 'The Israel Defense Forces are entering the area today and taking over control and the maintenance of security and civil order'. Soon Zionist politicians and army chiefs were talking about 'the administration of liberated territories'; 'occupation' and 'conquest' had the wrong flavour for the international menu. Long before the Six-Day War, in 1961, Judge Advocate Meir Shamgar, the IDF's highest legal authority – and soon to be the strongest legal champion of Gush Emunim – had begun to plan 'the operation of the IDF in neighbouring countries as a result of war'. To train future operatives, special courses were held, based on the experience gained during the period of military rule (October 1948–December 1966) over the Palestinians still resident in Israel.

By the time Raja returned from his studies in London to devil in his father's office, countless military orders had been promulgated on the West Bank. He was asked to prepare a subject index of those orders and immediately realised with what cunning skill the IDF legal unit had contrived to maintain an aggressive occupation while evading the duties of an occupying power – including the obligation to protect private property, an obligation scrupulously fulfilled on the West Bank when Jordan was sovereign.

The 1949 Armistice agreements, between Israel, Jordan, Syria and Lebanon, had left the West Bank (including East Jerusalem) under King Abdullah's rule. When His Majesty unilaterally annexed it in April 1950 only Britain and Pakistan recognised this move and Jordan passed no new legislation relating to the Palestinians' territory. For Israel to recognise Jordanian law (rooted in Ottoman law) on the West Bank, despite that unilateral annexation, was illogical but politically expedient. The ignoring of Article 2 of the Fourth Geneva Convention (deplored by several Israeli legal scholars) was justified on the grounds that to accept the applicability of the Convention would be to concede that the West Bank and Gaza Strip belonged to Jordan and Egypt – though the OPT, before the Zionist occupation, had *not* been under the sovereignty of a side to the Convention. Israel also denied the applicability of the 1907 Hague Regulations which deal with military rule over the land of 'an enemy state'. In the late 1980s Israel's Supreme Court went through a series of mind-boggling contortions to exclude the sovereignty issue from future legal deliberations.

As a newly registered lawyer, Raja attended the shabby Nablus court and remembered being called by an ancient who, in Mandatory times, had served with his grandfather, Saleem Shehadeh, for many years a district court judge. He was now seeing, close up, the sufferings being relentlessly inflicted on most Palestinians by the Occupation. Yet no one was protesting . . . So he set about founding Al-Haq, a non-profit-making organisation originally known as Law in the Service of Man. Modelled on 'Justice', the British section of the International Commission of Jurists, it monitors legal conditions under Occupation and tries to promote the rule of law. Raja's co-founders were two lawyer friends, a Lebanese-American Yale graduate and an American Jew, both keen to donate their knowledge and skills to the Palestinian cause.

That was in 1979. Thirty years later Raja and I were agreed on the futility of much contemporary human rights campaigning. In his most recent book, *Occupation Diaries*, the founder of Al-Haq sadly admits:

> These days I am not so excited about institutional human rights work. Our institutions are falling hostage to the funders, who keep asking for 'deliverables', as if human rights are an industry. Anyway, some of the same countries funding this work are creating the instruments of its violation, the security forces and the organs of the security state.

We also agreed that sick Israel cannot survive as at present constituted, a reality that is becoming apparent to an increasing number of thinking Israelis. For all concerned, the reincarnation process will be slow and painful but the end result has to be an improvement on the Holy Land as we now know it. While I daydreamed about the one-state solution, Raja looked ahead to a twenty-second-century federation of Palestine, Israel, Jordan, Syria and Lebanon, an entity bearing some family resemblance to the second-century AD Roman province of Syria-

Palaestina. To me this was a new idea and immediately I liked it
(though not as much as Palrael). Such a federation would certainly be
less artificial than the imperialists' imposition of 'statehood' on Iraq,
Syria, Kuwait, Lebanon, Transjordan and Libya.

As the weeks passed I benefited from Raja's sensitivity to the OPT's
political and social undercurrents, those minuscule changes happening
in the depths when it seemed on the surface nothing was changing – or
ever could. Since the Shehadehs' enforced departure from Jaffa in '48
they have been an inconspicuous but important part of OPT life,
as lawyers rather than politicians. Raja's father, Aziz, was among the
notables who in 1967 advocated a version of the two-state solution. A
day before the ceasefire, he met with David Kimche of Mossad to argue
for an autonomous Palestine with East Jerusalem as its capital, in
federation with either Jordan or Israel. Kimche then took the political
temperature on the West Bank and found wide support for an agreement
with Israel rather than a return to Jordanian rule. At once he urged his
government to declare a Palestinian state, before the conquered territories
had time to organise resistance to their occupier. But the moderate
nationalists' insistence on East Jerusalem being under Palestinian
sovereignty, and recognised as the new state's capital, was adroitly used
by those who meant to keep their grip on Eretz Israel. A few notables,
led by Aziz Shehadeh and Anwar Nussiebeh, continued doggedly to
campaign for independence but already a militant movement, soon to
be known as the PLO (Palestine Liberation Organisation), was evolving.
In February 1968 the Israelis arrested a Palestinian who had been sent
from Jordan by Arafat to assassinate Aziz as a traitor prepared to give
Palestinian land to the Zionists. Yet a mere six years later Arafat implicitly
accepted partition in his speech to the 1974 UN General Assembly.

On 2 December 1985 – a dark, cold, foggy evening – Aziz was
murdered, with a sharp knife, on his own doorstep by a Palestinian
never formally identified but known to be a collaborator who could rely
on immunity. It was presumed that a personal grievance had motivated
the murder. So much for law and order under military rule.

In October 1991 the Madrid Conference opened. 'A historic breakthrough!' exclaimed the international media, putty as always in Zionist
hands. Raja, as the Palestinian team's legal adviser, quickly became
disillusioned and went home. Unwittingly the Palestinians were playing
the Zionist game: prolonging the talks to prolong the Occupation to

prolong the settlers' expansion time. Soon the Madrid talks were moved to Washington where, over the next two years, nine sessions achieved nothing.

Meanwhile, in Oslo, the Accords were being secretly brewed. The Palestinian delegation, led by Ahmed Qurei'a (aka Abu Ala, later a PA prime minister) and Mahmoud Abbas (aka Abu Mazen), lacked any appropriately qualified legal adviser, much less an international contract lawyer of Raja's calibre, under whose aegis the Accords would not have happened. Raja describes them as 'the most shameful and damaging agreements the Palestinians could possibly have made with Israel'.

To compound the Accords' other inequities, they cleared the way for a Palestinian/Qatari consortium to destroy Raja's beloved hills north of Ramallah. As we spoke, ancient terraced olive groves were being acquired, cut-price, as the site of a new city (Rawabi) to house 25,000 Palestinians. If farmers refused to sell their land it was confiscated by the PA who were, in Raja's words, 'competing with the Israelis to see who could do most damage in the shortest time'. Two other housing projects, visually replicating the hated settlements, were being built on valuable *public* land *presented* by Arafat to a few of his cronies. Also, a Palestine Investment Fund project had made available, at public expense, leisure amenities for the enjoyment of the elite. The housing shortage is of course artificial. Area C offers ample space if only people were allowed to build around its villages instead of being condemned to live in Rawabi's high-rise blocks. Apologists for Oslo (a shrinking minority) often refer to Northern Ireland's 'Development and Investment for Peace'. Why not copy that on the West Bank? Create jobs and exports, create 'growth' by offering bank loans . . . It doesn't take long to silence those apologists. The reasons 'why not' are numerous and cogent.

Raja sees his parents as belonging to the Nakba generation, himself to the Naksah generation and present-day youngsters to the Oslo generation 'with its heavy toll of defeat disguised as victory and its measure of false glamour'.

That 'false glamour' was not yet polluting Nablus but in Ramallah it has long since taken over. On 27 December 1995, when the IDF handed Area A over to the PA, this town became the Palestinians' de facto capital as a result of Arafat's signing 'the worst surrender document in Palestinian history'. (Raja's words.) Then international aid flooded in, accompanied by foreign diplomats, INGOs and UN agencies needing luxury hotels, pricey restaurants, cocktail bars, nightclubs and cinemas. I was at once reminded of all those Third World (archaic phrase!) capitals where overpaid expats live in affluent ghettoes, and superfluous buildings absorb funding urgently needed for schools, clinics, housing. The PA's ostentatious multi-storey Ministry of Finance (a stage for unquantifiable dirty deeds) is only one of Ramallah's many shameless architectural excesses.

Sometimes I took the 7.00 a.m. bus to Ramallah, a vehicle noted for its wheezy engine, torn seats, filthy windows and friendly passengers. Twice, I sat with a Balata neighbour, a young PA civil servant who didn't foresee a third Intifada. 'People are too tired and hopeless, only wanting survival.' Before 2000, 40% of Balatan men worked in Israel; a trickle were now being allowed back but only seven or eight per cent of those who applied for permits received them. The rest had to evade the Barrier and so were paid even less than before; often that evasion was organised by their Israeli employers. On the bus this near neighbour chatted happily, yet within the camp, if our paths were about to cross, he went the other way. On his home ground it doubtless seemed wise for a PA employee to avoid an International who mixed with all sorts. At that time the tensions were such that Balatans who conversed casually with outsiders could be mistaken for collaborators and I had been warned that a minority of hardliners distrusted me. My claim to be a writer gathering material did not reassure; to them a writer is a journalist and journalists don't *live* in Balata. I might well be a spy and the friends I made, those who in time came to confide in me, were probably put on a 'to be watched' list.

   To some of my neighbours Hamas seemed a major threat, likely to bring more misery on them as the Border Police and IDF hunted those suspected of being Hamas supporters. In fact most camp militants were in al-Aqsa Martyrs' Brigade, Fatah's undercover militia. During the peak suicide-bombing period – the first two years of the second Intifada – Palestinians despatched 145 killers: 52 from Hamas, 40 from Fatah, 35 from Islamic Jihad, the rest freelancers.

   At first I remained on the fence between Fatah and Hamas, feeling uneasy about the latter's roots in radical/fundamentalist Islam. My Hamas friends in Nablus professed to abhor the sinister, perverted versions of Islam promoted by Al-Qaeda and the Taliban. However, those friends did point out that the international reaction to Hamas' 2006 election victory had made it much easier for 'mad mullahs' to recruit from among the hopeless, humiliated youngsters imprisoned – apparently for life – in the OPT. Having seen a 'free and fair' election being rubbished by the most vocal purveyors of democracy, and heard their party being discredited as 'terrorists' with whom 'we' cannot talk, many reacted to their 'criminalisation' by turning away from the ballot box and dwelling on alternatives.

I never cease to marvel at the sheer obtuseness of the Rich World's leaders.

Towards the end of my 'camp experience' I came off the fence, acknowledging that the Fatah-dominated PA had done nothing to earn my neutrality. Money talks as loudly in the Holy Land as elsewhere and Fatah had listened attentively. If they went along with the occupiers, lavish funding would continue to flow in their direction while Hamas was deprived of all support. It is too easy to bring to heel people demoralised by decades of poverty, military repression and thwarted hopes. Hence the horrible spectacle of armed Palestinian security forces collaborating with Zionists to eliminate Hamas – or anyone else out of favour with 'the international community'.

I spent one Friday afternoon in Ramallah drinking mint tea with three Palestinian Authority Security Force (PASF) recruits, young men newly uneasy about their role. (One spoke fluent English, courtesy of the Dayton Mission, the US-funded training centre.) Having visualised themselves serving in the army of an independent Palestine they now suspected PASF of morphing into a mere IDF-support paramilitary force. And 'independence' seemed to be receding . . . The mutual friend behind our meeting had vouched for my discretion so they spoke openly. Having grown up together in a militant community where Dayton dollars were not an acceptable excuse for joining PASF, they were now outcasts and finding their PASF comrades inadequate substitutes for family. Listening to all this, I heard echoes from the Irish past when a young man who joined the Royal Irish Constabulary (a colonial police service) might arouse the occasionally lethal hatred of his nationalist neighbours. I could think of nothing comforting to say to my politically naïve companions, now so angry with themselves for having been deceived by the vague but exciting promise of army service in an independent Palestine. I asked, 'Do many share your disillusionment?' The reply – 'We don't talk about it.' Plainly they felt trapped. IDF refuseniks may be scorned by their communities and serve short jail sentences; Palestinians who have second thoughts could be in a far more dangerous situation, equally mistrusted by the Israelis and by unforgiving elements within their own communities.

In Balata (and it would be the same in those young men's home town) Dayton was blamed for training Palestinians to use peculiarly vicious torture techniques. None of my neighbours understood that the PA's CIA-trained intelligence agencies and the newer Dayton-trained PASF were separate enterprises, both undesirable but the former demonstrably more so than the latter. The CIA's apparently limitless funding empowers it to corrupt a wide range of people in any population. As Professor Yezid Sayig records in a Carnegie Paper ('Fixing Broken Windows'):

> The CIA has made regular cash payments to the two [PA intelligence] agencies since 1996, which were not reported to the Ministry of Interior, the PA's General Accounts Office, or the Palestinian parliament. Part of this aid has reportedly been transferred to the Ministry of Finance since 2007, to be spent under the oversight of the Minister of Interior, but high-ranking intelligence officers and donor officials confirm that the 'black bag' persists, with 'tens of millions of dollars' being provided by the CIA and, more modestly, MI6 directly to the two agencies . . . Pursuing counter-terrorism in the absence of the rule of law perpetuates the undemocratic governance of the security sector and undermines state-building and post-conflict reconstruction.

Condoleezza Rice, when Secretary of State, proclaimed – 'In relation to Israel-Palestine, democratic development is at the centre of our approach.' But you don't promote democracy – or security or prosperity – by equipping and training men to spy on and kill one another. By now this fake zeal for 'democratic development' is past its sell-by date. Everywhere, younger generations are noting the contradiction when Pentagon spokespersons announce yet again their determination to dominate the world by military means.

As President Bush (Jnr) sat in the White House surrounded by Zionist advisers, devising his foredoomed Road Map, how aware was he of the nature and extent of Gush Emunim/NRP power? The ensuing

shambles suggests total unawareness. In 2004 he accepted the perman-
ence of the major illegal settlements, then made irrelevant demands for a
'ten-month freeze' – irrelevant because what he had already condoned
has left the West Bank so fractured there cannot be a viable, independent
Palestinian state. Yet few mainstream media commentators made this
obvious point – had they got lost in a *hasbara*-manufactured fog? Would
Israeli public opinion, if not itself disorientated by the same fog, have
allowed the extremists' alliance to gain so much power?

In a ramshackle, four-table eating-house near Ramallah's taxi terminus
I enjoyed hummus and falafel breakfasts and some interesting conversations. One young Christian Palestinian sociologist said his family
'have lived forever' in Ramallah but now he longed to emigrate – if only
some foreigner would sponsor him! He asserted, 'Israel has to collapse,
it's founded on a fantasy. But that won't happen soon and I need a job!'
He saw Cast Lead as having marked a stage in the 'collapse'. The demos
it inspired internationally were, he believed, 'a sign millions are rejecting
Israeli propaganda. They see Zionists taking everything and giving
nothing, then expecting support for war crimes because they're Jews!
Friends in Europe tell me everyone's tired of this Holocaust guilt-trip,
won't go on it any more. It's history, no part of their emotional scene,
not their baggage. Israel is flogging a dead camel.'

On another visit, Ramallah showed its positive aspect when I entered
a wood-panelled coffee-shop before realising it was male territory. As I
hesitated, the young man behind the gently gurgling coffee-pots smiled
and extended a hand and in English invited me to be seated. A dozen
not young men were relaxing in deep horsehair armchairs, contentedly
sipping coffee and bubbling their variously flavoured *narghiles*. A few
were playing cards or *shesh-besh* (backgammon) by the golden glow of
wall-lamps. Everyone wore conventional business suits and highly
polished shoes. There was no background muzak, no TV and no
conversation until a long-legged man with an aquiline nose courteously
asked me, 'Where from? What purpose?'

When I had told him, Dr Natsheh introduced himself. He was a
medical doctor, a Christian, educated at Ramallah's famous Quaker
school, a life-long pacifist and one of those easy people who don't feel an
hors d'oeuvre of small talk is necessary before strangers get down to the
main course. He was troubled by the thought that only violence keeps

the OPT on the international agenda. Like many Palestinians, he looked
back on the first Intifada as an opportunity missed – by the Zionists.
Had they not responded violently to a well-thought-out, non-violent
strategy, some compromise would have been possible then – the sort no
longer possible, given so many more festering grievances.

Dr Natsheh recalled that 'in the '70s the Hamas leadership concentrated on preaching and social work. One day Allah would make
everything OK, if Muslims didn't modernise or use violence. That
changed after 1980, when Military Order 854 made the military
governor a tyrant and we saw more IDF cruelty with more impunity.
The order was meant to block the growth of an autonomous civil
society, but in fact resisting it was good training for the first Intifada.
Then our resistance gained international support and the military
governor's power was lessened.'

Dr Natsheh brought out the latest Palestine Monitor Factbook:

> On many documented occasions the IDF have employed live
> ammunition, and most recently have begun showering protesters with
> a mixture of sewage water and chemicals from nearby settlements . . .
> Protesters being literally showered in sewage, beaten and sometimes
> killed in the daily or weekly events, reaffirms the notion amongst those
> most sceptical of a peaceful strategy that Israel only responds to violence.

Then he said what I have so often thought. 'It's hard to be a pacifist
on the West Bank. For over sixty years Zionists have been murdering
unarmed Palestinian civilians like some people shoot pigeons. Two
wrongs can't make a right but one wrong can *seem* to justify another.'

I mentioned a recent argument with a middle-aged Balatan who
couldn't accept that there was such a thing as an innocent Israeli victim.
Did I not know that all Jewish citizens of the State of Israel condone, to
some degree, the dispossession of the Palestinians? Could I not see that
Zionism's US-funded military machine leaves guerrilla tactics as the
only show of power available to Palestinians? This man (a Nakba baby,
born in July 1948) wouldn't concede that expertly indoctrinated Israelis
cannot be held fully responsible for crimes committed by their government. Nor did he want to hear about the many Israelis who have
jeopardised their careers in defence of Palestinian rights. He held fast to
his central point. The *Zionists* have decreed that violence should be the
name of the game.

Dr Natsheh nodded. 'True – if things go too calm provocateurs are paid to stir it. The Zionists know nothing else. They had to establish their state through violence – how else secure a "homeland" on others' territory? Fudging this is a major obstacle, now, to peacemaking.'

Walking along Rukab Street, our minds revolved, like hamsters on a wheel, round and round the question that has been puzzling millions for decades. How has it been possible so thoroughly to indoctrinate the majority of Israelis?

'Surely,' said Dr Natsheh, 'they *need* to submit to the process, *need* to believe in their creation myth to cancel out everything that's gone wrong – yes?'

'Maybe,' I replied, feeling the answer must be more complicated.

In a small smoke-filled café in neighbouring al-Bireh, near the meagre twelfth-century Ayyubid Khan ruins, I waited for Karim's friend Hassan – an ex-prisoner, like 40% of the present OPT male population.

In the week after the Cast Lead ceasefire more than 120 Hamas sympathisers were detained on the West Bank. Among them was Hassan, a thirty-year-old journalist who had suffered two periods of administrative detention during the second Intifada. His recent arrest was a typical IDF operation. After midnight a squad fired a few shots at his village home, smashed the front door, vandalised two rooms, made him strip naked on the public street, then removed him to one of Israel's five detention centres, leaving his family not knowing where he was or for how long. Within the 1967 borders there are also 21 prisons, 4 interrogation centres and one secret interrogation facility said to be furnished with state-of-the-art 'enhancement tools' donated by the CIA. In February 2009 there were 9,493 prisoners, 349 aged eighteen or less, 75 women.

This time Hassan was lucky. Having been charged with making a pro-Hamas comment on a local radio station, he was held for 55 hours in a cell without chair or bed. No food was provided, only three cups of tea per diem. But nobody beat him up – and suddenly he found himself free. Later I heard rumours that an entrepreneurial uncle of his, and a senior PA official and a junior IDF officer, formed a triumvirate associated with car smuggling, the sale of permits and the 'fixing' of land sales. Ramallah reverberates with such rumours, some no doubt based on fact.

After his release, while sitting in the back of a jeep awaiting transport to Qalandia, Hassan observed a four-man EU delegation being given permission to photograph a ragged, dirty, long-bearded man, shackled and blindfolded outside his cell; to some urban eyes he could seem quite menacing. The visitors were told this terrorist had been caught trying to bring explosives through the Barrier. When they had departed with their photographs the 'terrorist' was freed to join Hassan in the jeep. He had been arrested the day before and beaten up for having allowed his sheep to stray onto settlers' land – land grazed by Palestinians' flocks since before the Turks left Central Asia. Hassan had the impression the Europeans were not naive enough to boast about their encounter with a captured terrorist.

It's hard for those unacquainted with the OPT fully to appreciate what military occupation means. Outsiders glimpse it in action only when violence becomes 'news'. Having to live every day in the permanent yet arbitrary shadow of 1500 military orders is a special sort of living hell and not newsworthy. Most foreign residents assemble a checkpoint anthology and some pages of my diary resemble an INGO 'Report on IDF Abuses' – horrifying yet monotonous. Below I offer a representative selection.

Before the present permit system was introduced in 1987, followed in 1993 by the checkpoint system, it took forty minutes to drive from Hebron to Ramallah. Now, the settlement-avoiding Hebron–Bethlehem–Ramallah route can take two hours and ten minutes.

One afternoon, at the main checkpoint between Bethlehem and Ramallah, collecteeves (minibuses) were being stopped for their seven passengers' ID cards and permits to be slowly scrutinised. One university student was extracted from each of the six vehicles in our queue. For half-an-hour these young men had to stand, with arms outstretched, facing a high wire-mesh fence overlooking the austerely beautiful Judean Hills. As the IDF made much of checking their documents most passengers got out and stood around observing the scene impassively – while I loudly expressed my rage. Then, studying the others' expressions and body-language, I recognised in some a rage exceeding my own but rigorously controlled.

Our vehicle's victim was Jamal, an engineering student, son of a surgeon at a Hebron hospital, well known to a fellow-passenger who angrily told me, 'He's no sort of activist!' The six students were made to stand immobile, arms raised and extended; anyone who moved was shouted at abusively. When the documents were returned Jamal was ordered to present himself to the Big Man of the regional police, near Hebron, within seven days. As he rejoined us I asked what would happen if he didn't present himself.

'They'd come to get him,' replied a professor. 'And probably vandalise his home as punishment and perhaps give him six months in administrative detention. Don't you wonder – if someone is seen as a security threat, why let him go on his way?'

Think on't – six taxis, each delayed for 50 minutes while these students were being humiliated. Again I felt sickened by the young soldiers' enjoyment of such rituals. Also I felt frightened, not personally but at a deep collective level. We know to where such institutionalised inhumanity can lead. Avigdor Lieberman, when Israel's Deputy Prime Minister, referred to the release of Palestinian detainees and said, 'It would be better to drown these prisoners, in the Dead Sea if possible, since that's the lowest point in the world.'

How could this abuse, occurring throughout the OPT six days a week (most conscripts go home for the Sabbath), not provoke a third Intifada? And while these exposures of young Palestinian men's impotence fester within another generation, the courageous IDF men who 'break the silence' are ignored or reviled.

In Area B, under Palestinian civil control, seat-belts are optional and most passengers mark the transition from IDF-controlled Area C by unclipping. This wordless action might seem insignificant but feels quite powerful when all a vehicle's passengers simultaneously unclip. The prudence of doing so is another matter. Most of the OPT's super-skilful drivers are speed-addicted and competitive (few have access to sports grounds) and narrow escapes are frequent. However, while loyally unclipping I reckoned a belt wouldn't make much difference in a head-on collision at 70 mph.

On re-entering Area C, drivers usually remind passengers not to risk an unreasonable penalty. In al-Yasmeen I met an indignant elderly returnee from Canada whose daughter commuted by collecteeve to Birzeit University. When charged with being unbelted she refused to pay the 90 shekel fine, arguing that one can't wear a broken belt. She was then blacklisted and during the previous year had been unable to cross the Allenby Bridge because of her 'criminal record'.

The early serveeces to Ramallah were always packed with men due on their work sites by 8.00 a.m. One morning at Tappuah checkpoint, where an Apartheid road begins, we were ordered out and delayed for 35 minutes while a dog-handler trained her explosive-seeking Alsatian. Tappuah, one of the most rabidly lawless settlements, has its own road-block, CCTV, high electronic fence and heavily armed private security guards in sentry-boxes. It doesn't need a protective IDF road-block. As we stood silently by the roadside a soldier strolled to and fro, smirking, relishing the frustration of workers worrying about being late. Beside me stood a Nablusi teacher of English who couldn't find affordable lodgings in aid-rich Ramallah. He said, 'We're used to this treatment. It's better to stay calm, they think it's funny if we get angry.' Like many other forces, the IDF often use dogs to terrorise and everywhere it enrages me to see dogs or horses being abused to complement human nastiness. (Drug-squad spaniels employed at sea- or airports are another matter, always looking eager and happy, tails wagging as they sniff hopefully.)

That afternoon, on my way home, I saw two youths being arrested at Huwwara: handcuffed, blindfolded, flung roughly into a jeep and driven off to the nearby prison hut. Witnesses told me a few youths had stoned soldiers during the 1.00 p.m. 'changing of the guard', when conscripts walk from a jeep to their sentry-boxes. As the stoners merged into scores of passengers, toing and froing amidst taxis and minibuses, the off-duty unit arrested two other youths who had nothing whatever to do with the attack. It's unfortunate that this whole region, like much of the Holy Land, is strewn with large, sharp stones as though Nature, aeons ago, had foreseen the Palestinians' liking for such missiles. On hearing of this incident one of my neighbours gloomily diagnosed the start of another feud: stoners' family versus innocents' family.

Mid-morning was a quiet time at Huwwara. One cold foggy queue-free day two youths stood ahead of me, each carrying a large sealed cardboard carton displaying a colourful picture of the contents – biscuits. A black girl soldier ordered them to open the cartons, peered in, then ripped them up with a bayonet she happened to have handy, scattering the contents on the ground. As the boys struggled to gather dozens of small slippery packets, and secure them in the damaged cartons, their tricky task caused the conscript much amusement. Giggling, she called her Russian mate to come and watch. Luckily my capacious waterproof jacket served as a sack which the boys carried to their granny's huxter stall not far down the road, in Huwwara village.

I was, at that time, on my way to Birzeit University, a long sharp thorn in Zionist flesh ever since its foundation in 1972 by Musa Nasir, a Palestinian Christian notable and former Jordanian Foreign Minister. He dreamed of a mini-American University of Beirut but his dream couldn't come true; the occupiers disapproved. 'It is good for us if the Arabs are hewers of wood and drawers of water' – so said the official then in charge of OPT education.

Between 1979 and 1992, the IDF kept Birzeit closed 75% of the time, a collective punishment damaging the academic careers of thousands. During that period two faculty members, Sameer Shehadeh and Izzat Ghazzawi, were tortured by Zionist interrogators. Another, of whom I had first heard from my amateur archaeologist friends in Balata, was assassinated. Dr Albert Glock, a US archaeologist, began life as a Christian fundamentalist missionary but at Birzeit was converted to Palestinian nationalism and realised how adroitly Zionism had been misrepresenting archaeological evidence for *hasbara*'s sake. He was killed by a gunman near Birzeit in 1992, while writing a book about the more than 400 Palestinian villages depopulated and then bull-dozed in 1948. His researches, if published, would have reinforced the refugees' legal case against the State of Israel. The Glock family and their Palestinian friends thought they knew who had paid the assassin.

The university is in Area A, ostensibly an autonomous zone, yet the military still control all access roads. As our collecteeve crossed a high, cloud-wrapped ridge the driver's phone rang. If Arabic has four-letter words he then used them; ahead lay a flying checkpoint, a temporary road-block set up at random for an unspecified time and therefore extra-disruptive. Soon we were descending from the busy little town of Birzeit, about a mile north of the campus, and could see the IDF deployed where the university's private road meets the highway. The students were on strike, protesting against a steep rise in fees. At the checkpoint our driver consulted with his passengers. I opted to get out, the rest chose to continue to Ramallah – a few miles further on – via some détour that would add half an hour to their journey.

The university stands alone overlooking a landscape reverently described by Raja in *Palestinian Walks* but changed beyond recognition since his early hikes in the 1970s. One can't recommend Palestine/

Israel as a holiday destination; the Palestinians' sufferings and the landscape's despoliation complement each other.

I pulled up my jacket hood and walked slowly towards the Birzeit pole-barrier and sentry boxes. There was no demo, only a score of angry-looking young men – all muffled up, hands in pockets – hanging around beyond the barrier glaring at a half-dozen PA police who glared back. When I sought an English-speaker everyone glared at me – silently. I showed my academic friend's card but it was impatiently waved away. A policeman snapped something in Arabic which made his mates laugh. I scanned the students' faces and, seeing no smile, turned back to the main road just as two ill-advised English tourists were getting into trouble at the checkpoint. Their self-drive car had a yellow Israeli number plate and a GPS security gadget which signalled 'Stolen Vehicle!' when they entered Area C. I watched them showing their passports and pleading ignorance of Military Orders. One conscript barked at them in Hebrew, another radioed for instructions before ordering them to leave the car, load their luggage into a taxi, return to Jerusalem and report to the car-hire office. When I tried to talk to them a tall blond soldier with a French accent told me to get lost, then added that I shouldn't be wandering around on foot. I told him to get lost before strolling away through the fog towards Birzeit town.

I did have one agreeable Huwwara experience. Going through at a quiet time (10-ish), I realised that I had forgotten my passport. To a beautiful raven-haired girl soldier I whispered, 'Will you *please* let me through? Promise I'll be back by sunset!' At once she smiled, winked and nodded. I wished we could have talked and relaxed together, but it wouldn't do for a Balata resident to be seen fraternising with the IDF. Meanwhile, on the men's side, a boy was being vigorously searched by two yelling soldiers. I had seen him walking ahead of me, carrying nothing. Now he was being made to stand facing a sentry-box wall with arms extended. Normally I would have lingered to observe developments but on that occasion I was in no position to annoy our military masters.

CHAPTER 14

A Minor Injury

My Balata neighbours worried about the changing weather pattern. For two winters they had seen no snow, normally a foot deep on the high ground around Nablus, and the seasonal rains had been scant. Then abruptly, in February, unnatural warmth brought lizards out of hibernation a month early and butterflies that shouldn't appear before mid-March fluttered by and the bees acted strangely – a major concern. Honey is a reliable earner for families whose fresh fruits and vegetables are so often spoiled on the way to market by sadistic restrictions at checkpoints.

On the night of 17–18 February heavy rain delighted everyone – and undid me. Walking home next afternoon, via a short cut through an olive grove on a steep slope, I heard shrill, terrified screams. Some way below the path two boys, aged nine or ten, were frenziedly beating a third with heavy sticks – an extreme case of a sadly usual Balata phenomenon. Shouting angrily, I rushed downhill – there was no one else around – then slipped on the red-brown mud. By grabbing an olive branch I avoided falling flat but my legs splayed awkwardly and my left hip went funny-peculiar. Stumbling on, I continued to shout 'Stop it!' (as though they could understand English!) yet they didn't register my presence until I seized their sticks, one in each hand, and made as if to strike them. For a moment we stood in confrontation, both boys staring at me with an almost intimidating animosity. I played an old trick – crossing my eyes – which in disparate situations on three continents has served to cow potentially troublesome children. Here too it worked. Racing away, the pair shouted 'Fuck you!' over their shoulders: that much English they had learned from the IDF. Meanwhile their victim lay face down in the mud, his hands over his head, still sobbing in hoarse gasps and bleeding from a deep cut on his brow. As I helped him to his feet more blood could be seen oozing from his mouth. I tried to comfort him but he seemed terrified of me and went staggering away down the slope.

Slowly I limped home, each step more painful than the last. Later, getting to the loo involved an agonising journey and for three days I had to lie immobile on my bed, being fussed over by friends which made me feel ungratefully irritated. When ill or injured I much prefer to be left alone – like a cat. My own diagnosis was a pulled thigh muscle or groin tendon, for which time would provide the only cure. But my visitors became increasingly agitated, muttering about a fractured or displaced hip and other dismal possibilities. On the fourth day two of them conspired to hire a taxi, kidnap me and present me at the Hamas clinic for an x-ray.

This impressive modern building, well-equipped and efficiently staffed, is attached to a new mosque in the city centre, one of whose imams had just been imprisoned by the PA police. The Nablus government hospitals, run by the PA since 1995, are notably less impressive. I could see at a glance that my fellow-patients were not the sort one expects to meet in a 'private clinic'. This enterprise is one of Hamas' non-profit-making contributions to the public welfare, probably funded by oily money but one doesn't refer to that.

In the x-ray cubicle an elderly male radiographer briefly left me alone while fetching plates. Automatically I removed my boots, jacket and trousers and lay ready on the couch. Returning, the poor man yelped like a trodden-on puppy, then retreated, slamming the door and shouting 'Get covered!'

In due course a tall doctor with a silver goatee beard studied the x-ray and made no diagnosis but prescribed ointment and ten capsules. He advised that after a few days I could resume walking – slowly, over short distances – without hindering the healing process. My all-in bill came to €14. In the clinic pharmacy medications cost one-third the prices charged in Nablus's free-market pharmacies.

Back on my bed, reluctantly relaxing, I reflected that this minor injury was a small price to pay for having possibly saved a child's life. To my visitors – bearing bowls of soup and plates of salad – I merely explained that I had slipped on the muddy slope. It would have been unkind to report that grim scene of juvenile violence. No doubt there was a back-story and the less said the better.

That evening, long after sunset, there was a brief gun-battle nearby. Twenty-seven men were arrested, six wounded – a commonplace incident, ignored by the media.

When Leila arrived, laden with desperately needed books, she told me of a Nablus collaborator who had persuaded a sixteen-year-old mentally handicapped dwarf to wear a mock suicide belt and approach Huwwara. There a European journalist, on his way back to Ramallah, witnessed the 'terrorist' being caught and was expected to write about Palestinians trying to use child suicide bombers – with photos to 'prove' it. Later an IDF jeep dumped the dwarf halfway down the Jordan Valley, far from his home. Said Leila, 'That should help you understand why collaborators are executed.'

For non-Arabic speakers, disentangling Palestinian families can be quite a challenge, especially when polygamy, cousin marriages and over-lapping generations converge. Typical were the consanguineous con-volutions discussed by Amira and Maha, English-speaking widowed sisters who every day brought me sustenance. Both were in their mid-thirties and held strong views about male selfishness. Amira had two sons, Maha two daughters; their al-Aqsa Brigade husbands had died together in 2003. They were the youngest of a family of ten, plus numerous half-siblings; their father had enjoyed three wives simultaneously. In 2007 their adored mother's death increased their vulnerability as widows. She had protected them from Basem, a bullying eldest brother (eldest by which wife?) who appropriated most of the meagre wages they earned by spooling wool for a kasbah carpet-weaver. Basem's first wife had prudently left him before bearing a child. She was soon remarried, to a cousin of one of Basem's maternal uncles – a man of her own choice. For this she was much admired and no doubt envied by Amira and Maha. Basem's second and third wives bore him fourteen children, some of whom were married to some of the nine children of a half-sister (but whose half-sister?) living in a Jordan refugee camp. Another brother, trapped in Gaza since 2007, had 'six of each' by three (consecutive) wives, two of whom died in childbirth.

Repeatedly women assured me that Palestinians enjoy bearing and rearing all the children Allah sends and of many this is obviously true, difficult though it may be for twenty-first-century Western women to believe. Equally obviously, there are numerous exceptions, for various reasons. Strangely some of my friends became quite huffy when I referred to this. Th'aer's daughter Habsa was an example, very unwillingly carrying her third baby, suffering night and day from misnamed 'morning' sickness and fearful of death. During her last accouchement doctors had twice summoned the family to her bedside to say farewell. Home in Ireland, I was relieved to hear that she had been safely delivered of a third son. And Leila, in collusion with a humane doctor, had covertly talked her into tube-tying.

Another visitor, Ryn, from Askar refugee camp a few miles away, brought me four new-laid eggs and asked if I would like to meet her one-eyed nephew who was waiting outside, holding a shouted conversation with my neighbours on the third-floor balcony. Ahmed was a small, slight twenty-five-year-old; he wore a Dayan-style eye-patch and a wide smile showing broken teeth. He had been lucky to survive the rioting that followed the assassinations, in Askar, of two Hamas leaders, Faiz al-Sadar and Hamis Abu Salam, by a unit of naval commandos. Unlike his aunt, he spoke no English but was eager to communicate with the Irish granny – though disappointed to hear that I had never met Bobby Sands.

That Askar incursion took place on 9 August 2003 when the IDF were under orders to goad Palestinians into breaking a three-month ceasefire announced on 29 June. On 12 August two maverick suicide-bombers from Askar (cousins of Ahmed) killed two Israelis though at that date all Palestinian organisations were under orders to keep the ceasefire. On 14 August the IDF killed Mohammad Sidr, an Islamic Jihad leader in Hebron; assassinations are a favourite 'stone on the line' when Israelis wish to derail Palestinian moves towards a just peace (as distinct from 'peace' on Zionist terms). Sidr's death provoked a Hebron suicide-bomber to blow up a Jerusalem bus on 19 August, killing 20 Israelis, 6 of them children, and seriously wounding more than 100. End of ceasefire. Two days later five Israeli missiles eliminated Ismail Abu Shanab in Gaza City. Abu Shanab was among Hamas' most thoughtful and widely respected leaders, therefore detested and feared by Sharon. He had been hoping to negotiate a fifteen-year *hudna* (truce); his followers were encouraged to believe that by the end of that calm period a permanent peace might be within reach.

I thought I knew my visitor well enough to ask how she felt about her two suicide-bomber nephews. And about the Hebron suicide-bomber's victims – six children and fourteen defenceless civilians. Ryn's usually expressive face went stony as she looked down at her suddenly clenched fists and said, 'They weren't always civilians.' Ahmed, sensing the drop in temperature, looked anxiously from me to his aunt. A moment later she continued – 'You know how many children *they*'ve killed? Hundreds! Not by accident . . .'

Ahmed, who had been sitting on the one chair, stood up and muttered something and hurried away. Having ventured so far, I tiptoed on across this minefield, skirting the moral issue and quietly suggesting that suicide bombings do the Palestinians' cause no good. I used as an example Israel Shahak, born in the Warsaw Ghetto, a Bergen-Belsen survivor, who all his long life advocated coexistence without ever condemning Palestinian attacks on the IDF within the OPT. But suicide-bombing within Israel so sickened him that a few weeks before his death, in July 2001, he sadly concluded, 'Coexistence can never work. Separation is the only option.'

Ryn looked up, made a small dismissive gesture and said, 'You can't understand!'

I nodded. 'You're right, I can't – though I do try . . .'

We were interrupted by Ahmed calling from the alleyway where an octogenarian cauliflower-seller was slowly dragging a hand cart over the rough surface, offering his wilting wares at a reduced cost. (Wilting because he had been made to wait so long at the Deir al-Habab check-point.) Ryn stood up, tightened her hijab and promised to send me an esoteric ointment to be rubbed on the affected parts twice a day.

I lay back on my bed and continued trying to understand. I recalled some of the accounts I'd heard in Nablus about life under military rule. These were personal accounts, not mere anecdotes. The IDF had not allowed ambulances to take sick children to hospital during the curfew; two had died for lack of basic medical care. A week previously I'd lunched with a son of Mrs Shaden abu Hijleh, a vigorous peace activist whose death made world headlines via the *Christian Science Monitor*. In August 2002, during the 24-hour curfew period, she was sitting one morning with her husband on the verandah of their home in a secluded district – embroidering a cushion cover, her son recalled. When two IDF jeeps stopped nearby, on the deserted street, he was indoors and his mother called a warning – 'Wait! Don't come out!' As she spoke a soldier fired from the back of his jeep and killed her.

As usual, the IDF quickly fabricated a plausible (to outsider ears) defence; unluckily for them a senior British intelligence officer chanced to be around and promptly gathered evidence at the scene. All four abu Hijleh children had graduated with distinction from US universities; now they made sure their mother's murder was raised in the UN Security Council and brought by President Bush Jnr to Prime

Minister Sharon's attention. There the buck stopped. Nobody was to blame. Small wonder Israeli soldiers are so trigger-happy, cocooned in Occupiers' Immunity. B'Tselem's first Intifada files record 1,162 Palestinians killed by Israelis between December 1987 and September 1993. Of that number 250 were children. During the same period, five children were among the 160 Israelis killed by Palestinians. Come the second Intifada, between September 2000 and December 2003 the IDF reported 2,253 Palestinians killed (the majority civilians) and uncounted thousands injured.

Six months before Mrs abu Hijleh's murder, on 28 February 2002, a twenty-one-year-old Balata resident blew herself up at Huwwara four weeks after Israelis killed her brother and one week after they killed her betrothed. As the IDF were imposing collective punishment on Balata (and Jenin camp, thirty miles to the north), Nahum Barnea of *Yediot Ahronoth*, Israel's most popular newspaper, reminded his readers – 'The terrorism of suicide bombings is born of despair and there is no military solution to despair.'

Ryn has lived all her life in Askar camp, not far from Elon Moreh and other smaller but even more aggressive settlements. For decades she has been witnessing armed settlers attacking Palestinians and their property, knowing they can get away with it. Yet if Palestinians defend their crops, wells and flocks they and their extended families must endure savage retaliation from an army that doesn't notice settler crimes. Remembering all that, I spoke severely to myself. If suicide bombing is indeed born of despair we *should* be able to understand it.

Incidentally, Leila advised me to avoid the term 'martyr' which suggests to western ears an exclusively religious motivation. *Shadids* may have a mainly religious or an entirely nationalistic motivation – or a mixture of both.

On Day Five I wondered – 'Is it evident to my visitors that I've joined the Great Unwashed?' Normally I sweated the dirt off on Sunday mornings, when the As-Shifa hammam opened for women. Said to be the oldest functioning public baths in Palestine, it has changed little (apart from electric lighting and invisible solar panels) since the Tuqan family built it in 1634. Its fort-like walls were only superficially damaged in 2002 when an Apache helicopter aimed three rockets at this cherished feature of Nablusi life. Yakob, the seventy-year-old in charge, had befriended me on my first visit. We had much in common, including an aversion to television with which As-Shifa's soothing hush was now being threatened because of a discontented clientele. In an oddly named 'summer room' – a high, wide space with a stained glass dome – divans line the walls for post-bath cooling off and an ornate desk stands in one corner. Pointing to it, Yakob invited me to 'write in peace' any day of the week until men arrive. This I occasionally did, when my squat was extra-chilly. On the Sunday of my immobility it greatly cheered me when Yakob anxiously telephoned – 'Why no washing? Are you OK?'

Among my most regular visitors was eighty-four-year-old Hana, who spoke unusually fluent English and often lamented the second Intifada's emotional consequences for her great-grandchildren's generation. They had witnessed many IDF atrocities while Balata was burnishing its reputation as an heroic centre of resistance. Hana's anguished comparison of the two Intifadas made my heart ache. The first was community based and largely non-violent, a movement of ordinary people who had shown that Palestinians could effectively unite. Everyone participated: men, women and children, Muslims, Christians and agnostics, young and old, athletes and cripples. The traditional friction points – between clans, classes, sects, generations, political factions – were rarely allowed to stifle local initiatives. After a spontaneous beginning, creative committees and councils took charge in villages, towns, urban districts. Hana referred me to Walid Salem, of Jerusalem's Panorama Centre, who has written about the crucially important role of *bayans*. 'Those leaflets, distributed almost daily, called upon the people to join the movement of civic resistance activities, and did not call them to use arms because armed resistance would provoke devastating retribution by the Israelis.'

This movement aimed not only to boycott the occupying power's institutions but to lay the foundations for Palestinian counterparts; thus it engendered new professional organisations concerned with health, education, economic research and human rights law. It also hoped to demonstrate that without Palestinian cooperation the fourth strongest army in the world could not indefinitely dominate the OPT – or could do so only through Stalinist repressions not feasible under the global spotlight. Support came from small groups of brave Israelis whose participation modified IDF brutality. This initiative, sustained for some five years despite the extreme hardships involved, aroused considerable international sympathy – much of it lost when the second Intifada sent suicide bombers into Israel.

By unnerving the Occupiers, the first Intifada set the Oslo ball rolling. When Israel recognised the PLO in 1993 and allowed Arafat to return from Tunisia to 'lead his people towards a better future', a will-o'-the-wisp light was seen at the end of the Palestinians' tunnel. Given Arafat's status as the celebrated leader of all Palestinians – in exile and at home – Zionism's accommodation with him did briefly look like progress. Yet many of my Balata (and other) friends saw him and his militant followers – a generation bred in exile, knowing nothing of life under Occupation – as a negative influence, wrecking the cohesion of the first Intifada. And then failing to avert or modify the second, which broke out when people realised that Oslo had undermined their fragile peace plan. Ariel Sharon's vote-seeking Temple Mount walkabout (with a police guard of hundreds) on 28 September 2000 was like throwing a lighted match into an open oil-tank. He was then successfully competing with Netanyahu for the Likud leadership and out to please every sort of hardliner.

But no one I met accused Arafat of having provoked the second Intifada; that theory was the personal creation of Prime Minister Ehud Barak. He had begun to position himself as the leader who had done everything possible to reach a 'final-status agreement' with the PA and he needed to cast Arafat as the anti-peace villain – though all his intelligence sources saw the second Intifada as a spontaneous eruption of rage and frustration, unplanned by anyone. With mass media help, Barak's lie swiftly obscured the truth and ever since most Israelis have been condemning 'that demon Arafat'.

Among Palestinians the 'demon' is much praised for having kept their cause in view when the world would have preferred to forget it. Also, he did a lot to preserve the refugees' joint identity, when they might well have grown apart in the camps of Palestine, Jordan, Syria and Lebanon. Hana, however, was fixated on the damage he and his pampered cohorts had done on their return from exile. If only they had kept off the scene! If only the first Intifada could have continued, being recognised by the outside world as a victory for non-violence, then the Zionists' suppression of it would have exposed their long-term aim . . . Only Arafat's acceptance of Oslo's false promises, and the PLO's compliance with Israeli guidelines, had sustained the Camp David façade of 'seeking a solution'.

My simplistic outsider's gut reaction was to regard Arafat as yet another of the Zionists' victims. Consider Edward Said's verdict on Oslo:

> The PLO has transformed itself from a national liberation movement into a kind of small-town government, with the same handful of people still in command . . . All secret deals between a very strong and a very weak partner necessarily involve concessions hidden in embarrassment by the latter. The deal before us smacks of the PLO leadership's exhaustion and isolation, and of Israel's shrewdness.

One day on the bus from Ramallah my seat companion, a middle-aged man, mentioned Mahmoud Abbas's visit to Arafat shortly before the latter's death in 2004. As Abbas was leaving Arafat said, 'Goodbye, Karsai!' In my diary I noted, 'Possibly apocryphal but nonetheless significant.'

Hana may have been looking back on the first Intifada rather selectively, excising some negative aspects, but all agree that the second Intifada initiated a new sort of IDF campaign with disquieting implications for the State of Israel as a wannabe democracy. Chief-of-Staff Shaul Mofaz and his deputy Moshe Ya'alon ignored Prime Minister Barak's order to 'contain' the over-reacting IDF. Alarmed by an army gone berserk, Amnon Lipkin-Shahak, a former Chief-of-Staff, then tried hard, as Barak's go-between, to achieve a ceasefire. He publicly accused the IDF of 'waging a war on the ground different from the one the government had instructed it to conduct'. Soon after he resigned as go-between, in protest at the continued indiscriminate killing and bombing, the consequences of which were all around me in Nablus/Balata. The Prime Minister next delegated Ephraim Sneh to attempt to lessen the impact of collective punishments on civilians. Before long Mr Sneh was reporting – 'From the Chief of Staff to the last of the sergeants at the road-blocks, no one is implementing your policy.'

Repeatedly, after that, the Barak government's edgings towards negotiations were thwarted by the Generals' obdurate opposition to a ceasefire. Mofaz and Ya'alon and their merry men were thoroughly enjoying themselves. Something very like a temporary military coup was in place. When Yasser Arafat and Shimon Peres met in Gaza, towards the end of 2000, and came to a tension-easing agreement, the IDF at once rejected it. Said Ya'alon, 'To talk about a truce during the course of shooting is harmful and superfluous.' This delighted the settlers who were all the time shouting, 'Let the army win!'

The Generals then directly addressed 'the people of Israel', snubbing the government and attacking the media who, having dared to criticise IDF atrocities, deserved to be silenced. By this stage the more intelligent Israelis were predicting, 'Our democracy can't recover!' A few years later, Cast Lead sharpened their fears. As did Netanyahu's return to power in February 2009. An Israeli friend wrote to me from Jerusalem (his courier an INGO worker) – 'Could the right wing's lusting after Eretz Yisrael prove so incompatible with political Zionism's core ideology that territorial expansion will end in tears like an overblown balloon at a children's party?'

I replied 'Hope so!' and changed the metaphor. An earth-tremor won't help the Palestinians: they need an earthquake. Few on the West Bank, I noticed, could see much incompatibility between secular political Zionist groupings and God-struck millennialists. The former, though less physically aggressive (unless in uniform) showed cruel skill when devising and enforcing a corrupt legal system: one law for Jews, another for 'Arabs'. Such laws are a major resource for officials determined to deny Palestinians the right to work, to travel, to build a home, to access education and medication without undue stress. Fully to comprehend Israel's apartheid system it's not enough to visit the OPT for a few hours, VIP-wise, driving fast on 'Settlers Only' roads, being deferentially waved through army checkpoints. One needs the worm's eye view.

CHAPTER 15

The Malevolent Barrier

Towards the end of February, by which time I had regained my mobility, I was invited to Jayyous village to stay with Shareef Omar's family, famous for their 'STOP THE WALL!' campaigning.

The contentious plan to divide Israel and the West Bank with a continuous barrier had been a twinkle in Sharon's eye since the late 1970s. He, then Minister for Agriculture and already resolved to stymie the two-state solution, declared large areas of the West Bank 'State Lands', permanently at the disposal of the IDF 'for security reasons', therefore available for settlement. New settlers were presented to the world as 'employees on behalf of the army', living in military camps. This chicanery was duly 'legalised' by Attorney General Aharon Barak; Israelis resident in such camps could be employed by the army 'in accordance with needs'. In October 1977, after the government's approval of this arrangement, six army camps were reserved for settlers. Gush Emunim hardliners resented this compromise ('humiliating') but soon those camps had become 'legitimate' civilian settlements.

By June 2002 the rate of suicide-bombings, within Israel, had made it politically possible at last to implement. In October 2003 Israel's full cabinet approved the Barrier's route by a large majority; they had not been consulted sooner because Sharon was awaiting a nod from Washington. This came when the US National Security Advisor, Condoleezza Rice, and Sharon's cabinet chief, Dov Weisglass, had between them determined exactly how much Palestinian land the Barrier would annex. No Palestinian was brought even to the edge of these discussions. As one PA representative acidly pointed out, 'Again we have a situation where Israelis and Americans are making decisions that Palestinians are going to have to pay for.'

Happily the Barrier is beyond sight of Nablus; it would have unhinged me to live for months in its presence. Sharon disliked the final plan because it left many isolated settlements, on the hilltops around Nablus, 'unprotected'. Then he realised (as quoted by Aluf Benn) that enclosing Nablus would mean annexing 'hundreds of thousands of Palestinians who would eventually join up with the Israeli Arabs, and that would become a major problem'. The compulsion to do demographical sums tormented Sharon's last years.

An incisive Al-Haq publication, *The Annexation Wall and its Associated Regime*, explains that this construction's main purpose is to grab more land. About 86% of its length is not on the 1949 Armistice Line (commonly known as the Green Line), the only internationally accepted boundary between Israel and the OPT. In 2002, when suicide bombers were keeping Israelis in a permanent state of terror, the 'security' excuse sounded quite convincing. Yet by now every cat on the roof knows of gaps allowing desperate Palestinians to slip through into Israel to earn low pay as illegal workers. Where they can go, so could suicide bombers. Mercifully they don't, and haven't for a long time, because the Resistance has come to see suicide-bombing as counterproductive. A former Shin Bet director sees the Barrier as equally counterproductive. On 14 November 2003 *The Washington Post* reported, 'Avrham Shalom states that the Wall creates hatred, expropriates land and annexes hundreds of thousands of Palestinians to the State of Israel. The result is that the fence achieves the exact opposite of what was intended.'

On the edge of Nablus our serveece joined a checkpoint queue where the road to Qalqilya emerges from the valley between Jarzim and Ebal. Here five vegetable-laden donkey-carts were being held up, for no apparent reason, beside a working stone quarry. The young man in the front passenger seat suddenly turned to me and said, 'See how it happens? Our rulers like to see dust settle on fresh food!' As we waited, IDs at the ready, Hussein Issa decided to swap seats. He introduced himself as a journalist, grandson of an oil company engineer forced out of Haifa in 1948, son of a Qalqilya-based businessman who had set up a joint enterprise with an Israeli Palestinian – as sometimes happened during the Oslo years. By 1996 Father could afford to buy four acres of land, only to have it seized by the IDF in 2000 'for a transmission mast site'.

We now entered Area C, which has always been under full Israeli control: security, planning, commerce, construction, demolition. A lot of demolition: most villagers were denied building permits and almost always the bulldozers dealt with those (usually young couples) who had rashly invested in an 'unauthorised' home. Area C (72%) covers the OPT's most fertile land, supporting, in 2009, about 150,000 Palestinians and 300,000 illegal settlers. By then 40% of the entire West Bank consisted of settlements, outposts, military bases, closed military areas, settlers' industries including quarries and ersatz 'nature reserves', all out of bounds to Palestinians. That morning I found it hard to enjoy the quiet beauty of Samaria in winter: the low, long curving lines of the hills, the sombre hues of boulder-flecked olive groves and shaggy moorland, the occasional strip of green in a deep *wadi*. All was too still and unpeopled: there should have been mini-tractors and donkeys ploughing, shepherds with their flocks, villagers toing and froing on those faint, winding paths. Checkpoints marked the turn-offs for Sarra, Immatin, Jinsafut, the Israeli flag flying high above the IDF's concrete cubes or stacks of sandbags. Our serveece was going directly to Qalqilya and Hussein warned me that I'd probably have to walk the four miles from Azzoun to Jayyous. 'So many road-blocks in that corner, taxis don't go.'

At one turn-off, for the notorious settlement of Alfe Menashe, a band of ostentatiously armed men stood along the verge awaiting a lift into Israel. 'It's same as mandate days,' said Hussein. 'Then we tried to stop Zionist immigrants and the British let new settlers run their own militias. From the British, Zionists learned how to keep Arabs down – with executions and demolished houses.' He paused, then raised his voice to say that recently he had read *Mein Kampf* in Arabic and 'I only hate Hitler because he didn't kill them all.'

It took me an instant to register his meaning. Then I felt breathless, disoriented, as though I'd been kicked in the stomach: moral shock having a physical effect. A moment later we stopped on the edge of Azzoun and I scrambled out, mumbling a general goodbye.

Huge concrete slabs were jumbled on the verge, an off-duty roadblock, to be replaced before the next anti-Barrier demo. I sat on a slab, feeling chilled, and realised that never before had I met undisguised anti-Semitism. It frightened me – and gave me a new understanding of the Israelis' fear. Despite my never having met another Palestinian who spoke thus, Hussein was certainly not unique. Do I lead an unduly sheltered life? Walking on, I began to feel foolish, to accuse myself of over-reacting. Hussein's sentiment, however upsetting, shouldn't have even slightly surprised me. In the Holy Land Zionism has sown and continues to fertilise the seeds of hatred – as so many Israelis, including

Shin Bet's Avrham Shalom, readily admit. But it did alarm me to think of *Mein Kampf* still being available in Arabic. All my long-repressed authoritarian instincts came swarming to the surface. Surely, in *this* context, *that* book should be banned?

I was late for an appointment with Amneh Bassem in Azzoun's girls' school, where one of Shareef Omar's daughters taught English. Near the school I paused beside a new building, two-storeyed and characterless, identified by a bilingual placard.

Palestinian Economic Council for Development
and Reconstruction (PECDAR)
HAS DONE THE FINISHING WORKS FOR INFORMATION &
COMMUNICATION TECHNOLOGY CENTER IN AZZOUN.
FUNDED BY WORLD BANK.
NOVEMBER 2006

Within the school's spacious yard I chuckled over a colourful bilingual mural extending the length of one wall: 'A fine woman can do without fine clothes'. It was an unexpectedly big school for quite a small town. On the West Bank, two-thirds of pupils attend single-sex schools; only some UNRWA camp schools are co-ed, providing free compulsory education to Grade 10 (age sixteen). After that, ambitious pupils must enrol at a PA or private school. The OPT Palestinians are 99% literate and attach such importance to education that if need be parents will go hungry to pay school fees.

Amneh was a bulky, grey-haired woman who worked at a few local schools as an unpaid psychotherapist. She spoke sadly of the increasing number of pupils with serious behavioural problems and I admired her for sounding sad rather than angry. She was of the generation that did much of its studying in jail. The thousands imprisoned in the '80s were usually being punished for belonging to specifically non-violent student groups, trades unions and Popular Committees. 'We were arrested for being *anti*-terrorist,' said Amneh with just a hint of bitterness. 'I got five years for writing, printing and distributing a booklet about running a long-term transport strike. But how can we expect this generation to value non-violence?' She gestured towards the yard, now a noisy mass of pupils enjoying their mid-morning break.

My mention of BDS brought a deep sigh and a shake of the head. 'Yes, it's grown naturally from the first Intifada's thinking. Problem is, it can't work without wide, direct, consistent support. From our own leaders, from our Israeli friends who come and stand with us to protest the Wall and demolitions, from foreign friends and NGOs and governments. And that sort of support we won't get before we reassert ourselves.'

Amneh craved a return to the '80s spirit of determined unity. In her view, Azzoun's Information & Communication Technology Center was being steered in the wrong direction by its neo-liberal funders. She laid part of the blame for the Palestinians' current lack of a coordinated strategy on the 'international community'. 'We're not short of intelligence or energy. Why not leave us alone to do it our way? So many possible sources of funding aren't helping. Above all we need unity and they divide us into competing groups.' Amneh spoke for many as she excoriated foreigners' control of the Palestinians' destiny.

At the top of the steep main street two taxis were parked under a walnut tree but neither driver had a permit to enter Jayyous. The long walk to the Omar home proved my damaged hip to be serviceable again and so it remained for the next half-year or so.

In this region the Barrier's 'Associated Regime' was then particularly constricting. Al-Haq considers it under four headings:

1) **Gates and Checkpoints.** The 26 checkpoints are controlled by Israel's Border Police (the most feared branch of the security forces) and by private security companies. The Barrier incorporates seven types of gates: agricultural, checkpoint, military, road, school, seasonal and settlement. These are placed irregularly and opened erratically; they drastically reduce Palestinian freedom of movement and access to schools, hospitals, mosques, markets, family and friends.

2) **Permit Systems.** The gates, checkpoints and *ad hoc* roadblocks are operated through a sadistically restrictive permit system. Al-Haq explains:

The application process to acquire a permit is prohibitively complex and arbitrary. Palestinians must submit an application to the District Coordination Office of the Israeli Civil Administration. (The Civil Administration was established in 1980 by a military order issued by the IDF's Regional Commanders.) The process for obtaining a permit has never been clarified by Israeli authorities, nor are there definite criteria for examining a request for a permit. Palestinians are further discouraged from applying because an applicant denied on the basis of posing a 'security threat' is subsequently placed on a security list. The duration of permit validity varies but, typically, permits are valid for between two weeks and six months. The permit duration is a particular obstacle for farmers whose land now lies suffocated between the Green Line and the Wall. These persons must now apply for a 'visitor' permit in order to farm their own land. Essential for obtaining this permit is proof of land ownership coupled with supporting purchase documentation. These documents are difficult to produce for those whose land ownership title dates from the Ottoman, British Mandate or Jordanian periods of rule. A 2007 survey found that less than 20% of those who fall into this category were actually granted a permit . . . Professor Dugard, the former UN Special Rapporteur, described the permit system as reminiscent of South African Apartheid 'Pass Laws'.

3) ID cards. From their sixteenth birthday Palestinians must carry ID cards or risk arrest and a fine. East Jerusalem residents hold blue cards, the rest green, and since 2001 family unification has been denied to the latter who are not allowed to live – or even sleep overnight – in Jerusalem. Along the Barrier's length, this 'colour code' shreds the Palestinians' social fabric and causes immeasurable grief to divided families. To prevent relatives foregathering on festive occasions, or for weddings and funerals, is yet another form of collective punishment.

4) Property Destruction and Confiscation. In some areas – Qalqilya and environs a grim example – this practice has impoverished whole villages whose farmers had prospered for generations on the produce of their land. As Al-Haq puts it, 'Property appropriation and destruction has been the *modus operandi* for the Israeli Ministry of Defence to secure sufficient land to build the Wall inside the OPT.' The confiscation of property by an Occupying Power is prohibited by Article 46 of the Hague Regulations and Article 53 of the Fourth Geneva Convention (1949). Already, in 1986, UN General Assembly Resolution 41/63 declared Israel's numerous breaches of that Geneva Convention to be war crimes and 'an affront to humanity'. There could be no more apt summing-up of the Barrier and its consequences.

*

Azzoun, Jayyous and the neighbouring villages seemed like dying communities. Shops were closed or only half-stocked, streets were too quiet, many homes' exteriors looked neglected and the depleted populations, if visible, lacked vitality. Yet there was some evidence of pre-Occupation prosperity in premises that had been modernised – and much evidence of ancient prosperity in the handsome remains of substantial Ottoman dwellings.

A few of the Oslo years had been kind to these villages. Jayyous's 120 greenhouses, shared with nearby Falamya, yielded 7 million kilos of fruit and vegetables annually, for sale to traders from Nablus, Qalqilya and Israel. Then – disaster! The second Intifada's total closure meant isolation from most of the Palestinian and all the Israeli markets. Two years later came the Barrier – why? At first everyone was bewildered; no suicide bomber had ever been traced to this region. Its farmers, though resolute when attempting to defend their land, were not militants of the calibre found in refugee camps and overcrowded cities. As it became obvious that the Barrier would lie almost four miles east of the Green Line, within spitting distance of some village houses, Abu Azzam (as Shareef Omar is universally known) joined with a few others to hire a lawyer. But the Appeals Committee briskly dismissed their case on the grounds of 'military necessity'. By the end of November 2002 the Caterpillars were at work and 4,000 olive trees had been uprooted.

On the narrow, twisting road from Azzoun to Jayyous I passed only a few youths collecting something unidentifiable from what might have been pastureland before military vehicles and Caterpillars ravaged the surface. Three lengths of weed-enshrouded water-piping caught my eye; these had been lying by the roadside, I later learned, for seven years – awaiting a permit. Abu Azzam recounted other cases of what Robert Fisk calls 'apartheid-by-permit'. Oxfam were not allowed to build an underground reservoir with 700 metres of piping, nor were they allowed to provide above-ground tanks and a booster pump; they must restrict their giving to rooftop tanks. Soon after, in the village of Zbeidat (believed to belong to Area B), a scandalous complication arose when an EU agency spent £80,000 sterling on installing a sewage system and eighteen waste water shafts. In fact one-third of Zbeidat belongs to Area C and, because the donor had not secured a permit, six of the shafts had to be demolished and some £27,000 of taxpayers' money sacrificed on the altar of Israel's 'Civil Administration'. Incidentally,

I never met anybody, Israeli or Palestinian, who could show me the B/C border.

Being above the Western Aquifer makes this region uncommonly fertile. Now Jayyous's six agricultural wells are beyond the Barrier, accessible only through one gate, opened at the IDF's whim. Household water must come from a well shared with another village and is also, as Ray Dolphin has explained, affected by Israeli restrictions. 'At just 23 litres per capita per day, domestic consumption in Jayyous is far below the WHO's recommended 100 litres, let alone the 350 litres per capita consumption in Israel and the settlements. As a result, Jayyous suffers critical water shortages in the long summer months, necessitating the purchase of expensive tankered water.'

Beyond the permitless pipes rose an odd blackish hillock of what might be described as antique garbage, dumped here by settlers during the 1990s. For years it smouldered away, night and day, causing much local ill-health. Only when its noxious fumes began to affect the settlers themselves did they choose another site. Jayyous tries to be responsible about its own garbage. I met one of the binmen who has an honours degree in physics; the Associated Regime puts more appropriate work out of reach.

Being prominent in the anti-Barrier movement, Jayyous sees many Internationals. As I wandered through its maze of old streets an endearing little boy asked 'Abu Azzam?' – then led me to the far side of the village, chattering away in a tantalising English-peppered Arabic. He didn't like going to school because of having to get up so early. Jayyous had a girls' secondary school but no primary schools and the Associated Regime could make it very difficult to reach Azzoun's schools; all depended on IDF moods at checkpoints. Later I heard that USAID had just donated $250,000 for a two-storey primary school. My informant added cryptically, 'Cui Bono?' The PA had earned no trust by sometimes despatching its own police to reinforce the IDF at anti-Barrier demos.

As I arrived in the Omars' new bungalow, high on a steep hillside, three generations were sitting down to lunch (the villagers' main meal). Abu Azzam and his wife welcomed me like an old friend, as is the Palestinian way, and someone fetched a seventh chair from the verandah. Umm Azzam beamed when I showed appreciation of her *musakhan*, a mysteriously flavoured chicken casserole on *taboun* bread. We swopped family details as we ate. Abu Azzam was twenty-four when he married the very beautiful eighteen-year-old sister of a friend. Umm Azzam is still very beautiful, the adored mother of seven university graduates (four girls, three boys) who had already supplied twenty-six grand-children. As I gradually got to know them, it seemed to me the Omar family were typical Palestinian followers of the Prophet, devout in an easy-going way. For 36 years this couple had saved up to build their seven-room home, its design remembering past eras, its furnishings modern but hand-crafted.

A few years ago, when Abu Azzam was too Barrier-preoccupied to think of anything else, his wife went to the bank, asked 'How much is in our savings account?' – then told him, 'We've enough for a new home!' Abu Azzam laughed at the recollection. 'That was clever, it eased Barrier tension!' Later I visited their old village-centre two-storey home – standing in its own shady compound, solid stone, shabby but distinguished and now leased for a token rent to an INGO which monitors IDF behaviour at the Gates.

When we Oldies had retired to the sitting-room to sip thyme tea and nibble baklava I prompted Abu Azzam to wax autobiographical. His activist career began in Jordan where he led a schoolboy protest outside the French Embassy – Algeria the issue. While serving 18 days in an Amman jail a fellow-prisoner asked him to make copies of a Marxist text and 'I became a convert for some years, as a student.' Back on the ancestral land in Jayyous, he soon reverted to the benign (more or less) capitalism which seems natural to Palestinians. His Resistance activism dates from 1967. Already, in 1949, Jayyous had lost much of its land; the Armistice Line ('the Green Line') lies far from the UN's original Partition boundary.

In 1988, when 1,350 dunams were confiscated to build Zufin settle-ment, Abu Azzam led 80 farmers in an appeal to the Israeli high court. At that date his 42 acres, planted with 3,600 mixed fruit trees, made him one of Jayyous's richest landowners. The legal process was pro-longed, perversely complicated and exorbitantly expensive. Over the years twenty farmers dropped out; in 1996 the court ruled the rest could keep their land. Meanwhile, in 1990, the opening of a privately owned Israeli quarry had deprived Jayyous of another 400 dunams.

Then came the Barrier. In December 2002 the IDF and Border Police attacked a non-violent demo of about 100 locals, backed by ISM volunteers. The injuries inflicted did not deter future protesters; scores still rally round at many points along the Barrier. During 2003 the

IDF obliterated five of the six roads leading from homes to farmland, completely isolating all Jayyous farmers from their fields and groves. In September 2003 the IDF closed the only agricultural gate, causing 80% of the guava crop to be lost – a fruit needing collection within a day of ripening. In Falamya, 6,000 citrus and fruit trees died.

Also in 2003 a new settlement, North Zufin, was being planned by Lev Leviev, reputedly Israel's richest man. At that date the use of private contractors left the government feeling free to claim that *it* was not expanding settlements – something 'forbidden' by Bush Jnr's black joke Road Map. The Barrier greatly excited developers by making new Arab-free building sites available. Moreover, the price of insufficiently watered land falls quite dramatically. Abu Azzam showed me a 2004 report by his hydrologist son-in-law, Abdul-Latif Khaled:

> The situation in Jayyous is a microcosm of what is happening all over the West Bank. With such restricted access, it is hard for farmers to maintain their plots and much of the farmland is deteriorating. The neighbouring Israeli settlement, which will cut across the farmers' only access road, will force them to take a longer route – a five-hour or six-hour round trip by donkey-cart. With no overnight stays allowed, there will be no way to cultivate the fields . . . So far 15,000 citrus trees around Jayyous have died because farmers denied access are unable to irrigate and tend their groves. With thousands of trees uprooted and countless trees having to be abandoned, we find ourselves in the midst of an environmental disaster exacerbated by lack of water meaning the loss of our ability to live on our own resources.

Behind the formal language, one senses Abdul-Latif's personal grief. His home region has long been admired for its farmers' industry, skill and enterprise. As another report (United Reformed Church) puts it: 'The best of Palestinian modern irrigated agriculture could be found in that area. This has been deliberately destroyed, and without it Palestine's viability is endangered.'

In 2003 Amnesty International declared that Barrier construction 'must be halted immediately'. In February 2004 the International Committee of the Red Cross condemned it as 'contrary to international law'. Five months later the Hague's International Court of Justice delivered its celebrated Advisory Opinion, rejecting Israel's right to build any part of the Barrier on West Bank land.

Abu Azzam leads the Land Defence Committee for the Qalqilya District and Abdul-Latif is regional director for the nationwide anti-Apartheid Barrier campaign. In 2003 Abu Azzam addressed the Mumbai World Social Forum meeting and gave evidence in The Hague before the International Court of Justice. On his return from Europe the Civil Administration offered him a 'special' permit on condition he gave up campaigning. To punish him for declining this offer, he was denied *any* permit for the next seven months. On another occasion, as punishment for having talked to an *Ha'aretz* reporter who sought an interview, his permit was cancelled for nineteen days.

Until January 2005 permits were granted to most members of an extended family; at that date eligibility was restricted to owners and their spouses and children. Since then it has been further restricted; in 2009 villagers needed *ten* different permits and documents to enable them to set foot on their own land. Only 18 permits were issued in Jayyous (population 2,800) during 2008. Abu Azzam received one but all applications from his children failed though ageing parents so obviously need help on the land. He of course must pay the penalty for being so vocal, durable and mobile as an anti-Barrier campaigner. The IDF give him special treatment – like six- or eight-hour checkpoint delays – as he tries to get his now limited produce to Qalqilya market. In Ramallah a Machsom Watch monitor showed me her photograph of an Omar load of perishable goods which only got through on a mid-summer's day (35°C in the shade) because of her intervention.

During the second Intifada Jayyous lost six men to the IDF and at the time of my visit twenty-three were in jail. Among the twelve in 'administrative detention' was the second Omar son, a university law lecturer now nearing the end of his second six months of imprisonment without due process. No one could guess the outcome of his case-review on 1 April; a neighbour had had his sentence renewed nine times. (Nine sixes: that's four and a half years . . .) Shareef Junior, when arrested (abducted?) had been organising a non-violent students' anti-Barrier demo. Not much has changed since the 1980s when Amneh was jailed for advocating non-violent trade union activities – except that nowadays universities (and some employers) deflect prisoners' salaries to their families. Umm Azzam was allowed a half-hour visit per month – sitting on one side of a bulletproof glass wall. In eleven months Abu Azzam had received only one permit to visit but detainees could make a three-minute telephone call every four weeks and Shareef Junior always spoke to Shareef Senior.

How frail is 'the West's' loyalty to the rule of law! Think Guantanamo Bay, where innocent men have been rotting for years because the US couldn't admit it blundered by paying lavish bounties to impoverished Afghan peasants who pretended to identify 'terrorists'. And think administrative detention, the Zionists' way of 'neutralising' men and women whose only crime is having the courage to resist injustices. As Uri Davis repeatedly reminds us:

> The characterization of the State of Israel as being permanently in a state of emergency . . . is a settler colonial legal statement in that so long as 'the state of emergency declared by the Provisional Council of State in 1948' has not been declared to have ceased to exist, the State of Israel is administered under a dual system of law: civilian law (itself structured as a two-tier apartheid system) versus military law. This legal dualism obtains in all the territories under Israeli rule and occupation.

Also there's religious law, not to be scoffed at because so many settlers heed it. As laid down by a former Chief Rabbi – 'The land is the heritage of the Jewish people and if anyone plants a tree on my place, both the tree and the fruit belong to me.' In the late 1990s Amira Hass was reporting – 'The famous immunity of the olive tree does not serve it in the face of settlers' attacks.' Since then, throughout the OPT, Palestinians have suffered 'the chopping down of thousands of olive trees at night by unknown perpetrators who are never caught and never punished'.

In 2002 Jayyous was the first village to organise weekly anti-Barrier demos – non-violent, large-scale, multinational (including Israelis). Soon many other communities were being equally active and international media attention put Bil'in, near Ramallah, in the spotlight. Many of this campaign's leaders emphasise that supporting BDS is 'the most powerful thing' we outsiders can do to help the Palestinians. So wrote Mohammad Khatib, an articulate and passionately anti-violence member of the Bil'in Popular Committee, in *The Nation* (11 September 2009). He had recently been detained for two weeks, accused of stone-throwing and encouraging others to throw stones. Unluckily for the IDF, his passport proved his presence in Canada on the relevant date. But for that, he might still be imprisoned.

In Jayyous too, some elderly people condemned ritual stone-throwing; they recalled a time when children were cowed by the IDF, now most are implacably defiant despite seeing their schoolmates injured and occasionally killed. But they are also indifferent to the damage done by retaliatory tear-gas and house incursions and Abu Azzam was doing what he could to restrain youngsters. In one recent week thirteen had been injured, six with live bullets. Quite often conscripts tauntingly tell women how much they enjoy 'playing with your children'. (In my journal I wrote: Something symbiotic here? Bored young villagers, bored young soldiers, confrontations breaking monotony for both?)

Throughout the OPT, tear-gas is used indiscriminately against anti-Barrier demos which never threaten the well-armoured IDF with more than stones. That evening five of us sat around the kitchen table nibbling olives and nuts and drinking a memorable vintage of home-made lemon juice. Then Umm Azzam joined us, seeming close to tears. She had been visiting friends who were mourning an asthmatic toddler; the child's roadside bedroom had been filled with tear-gas as he slept. The IDF frequently invaded Jayyous; on the previous occasion, eight hives of bees, five in-lamb ewes and countless hens were killed by tear-gas. A fortnight after my return home, a Bil'in activist, Bassem Abu Rahmeh, was killed by a high-velocity tear-gas canister fired at close range.

The Palestinians' apparent lack of bitterness repeatedly astounded me. When fifty-three-year-old one-legged Jawad called to meet me, Abu Azzam explained that in 2003 his house had been demolished around him – the least of his family's misfortunes. In 1984 an IDF sniper shot his paternal grandmother, through the heart. Ten years later another sniper killed his youngest brother. In 2006 his eldest son was sentenced to fourteen years for possession of a weapon. Now his land lay beyond the Barrier, neglected because so difficult of access. Therefore he was angry – but not bitter.

As Umm Azzad brewed more coffee Jawad told us that nine young men had left the locality in the past week. Some leave Palestine forever (what the Zionists want) if a relative or friend abroad can help them. Others move into already overcrowded Area A. Everybody believes the Barrier is permanent. Jawad quoted a relevant proverb: 'Whoever catches a bird will never release it again.'

*

Early next morning, on my way down to the Barrier, I paused outside chez Omar to watch the sunrise. Only ten miles away, yet always inaccessible to Palestinians, the sea glinted faintly beyond the coastal conurbation: Netanya, Kefar Sava, Herzliyya. Closer, between Qalqilya and Tulkarm, lay more than 27 square kilometres of rich farmland known to the IDF as 'the Seam' – Palestinian territory trapped between Green Line and Barrier. From here one can see how the Barrier had to contort itself to protect various settlements, diving into *wadis* and generally making no topographical sense in relation to Israel's 'security'. (The UN Office for the Coordination of Humanitarian Affairs was then recording more than 1300 permitless Palestinians slipping through the Barrier each week to work in Israel.) The less perspicacious settlers were at first anti-Barrier, fearing it presaged the two-state solution and their own uprooting; then they found the plot and set about using it to speed up land-grabbing. Ze'ev Schiff, a senior military analyst, wrote in *Ha'aretz* (31 October 2003) – 'The hijacking of the settlement fence by the settlers, with the government's help, and its transformation from a fence intended for protection into a political fence, is liable to contribute to the deepening of the occupation.'

I descended briskly through the village, pleased that my disability seemed none the worse for the previous day's exertions. The narrow streets were quiet; farming apart, there's no reason to get up early in Jayyous. Pre-'48 this must have been a handsome, thriving village with its domed and dignified Ottoman dwellings – some now crumbling or shelled – and its bustling markets, long since subdued or closed. Approaching the Barrier, I passed a few solitary houses surrounded by boulder-strewn scrubland and cut off from their groves; each little front garden, once flower-filled, had been planted with compensatory olive saplings. Hereabouts I met the first traffic of the day, an empty rubber-wheeled donkey-cart being driven by an old woman in traditional dress. Her husband, tall but rather bent and wearing an all-white *keffiyeh*, leant heavily on his stick and walked beside the donkey. They were of the Nakba-witness generation, survivors who often carry sorrow in their eyes.

From above I had seen many miles of the Barrier's military road, a thin pale snake undulating across a deserted landscape, blocking the old farmers' track on which I was now walking – and all other similar tracks. However, at its own level the Barrier takes one by surprise. Suddenly there's a massive tangle of razor-wire, and beyond that a wide, deep dyke, and beyond that the IDF road, and beyond that the nine-foot-high electronic fence. Some say the dyke is mine-lined, others say mines lie on the far side of the road. An oblong red and white trilingual notice, embedded in the wire, warns:

MORTAL DANGER – MILITARY ZONE
ANY PERSON WHO PASSES OR
DAMAGES THE FENCE ENDANGERS HIS LIFE

On the gate across the road – supplemented by a pole-barrier – an orange trilingual notice says:

GATE No. ——
Resident:
THE PASSAGE THROUGH THE GATE WILL BE PERMITTED
BETWEEN THE HOURS —— TO ——
IN CASE OF AN EMERGENCY OR A CLOSED GATE
DURING THE OPENING HOURS
PLEASE ADRESS [sic] AT THE LOCAL DCL AT THE
FOLLOWING PHONE No. ——
OR AT THE CIVIL ADMINISTRATION
HUMANITARIAN HOT LINE – 02-9977733

All those blank spaces prove the Civil Administration's cynical contempt for the locals and that 'humanitarian' hotline makes one want to retch. This metal notice's several deep dents are a tribute to some rash stone-throwers' accuracy and vigour.

I walked beside the razor-wire towards Zufin settlement, soon to be expanded by 1,100 housing units. Hundreds of trees had been sacrificed to 'Nofei Zufin'. In *I was Born Here, I was Born There* Mourid Barghouti writes with piercing poignancy of the olive tree. 'Everywhere you look, huge olive trees, uprooted and thrown over under the open sky like dishonoured corpses. I think: these trees have been murdered, and this plain is their open collective grave. With each olive tree uprooted by the Israeli bulldozers, a family tree of Palestinian peasants falls from the wall.' Mourid's lament continues at some length and for those pages alone it's worth buying this book. My own heart was breaking as I gazed across a plain once tranquil in its business, now become the tense tormented 'Seam' where armed Israeli men and women limit the hours

and the spaces Palestinian men and women may devote to their crops
and land. Here I felt I at last fully understood Mourid's other lament in
I Saw Ramallah: 'The Occupation has created generations of us that
have to adore an unknown beloved: distant, difficult, surrounded
by guards, by walls, by nuclear missiles, by sheer terror. The long
Occupation has succeeded in changing us from children of Palestine to
children of the idea of Palestine.' Viewing the settlements, Mourid
wrote: 'These are not children's fortresses of Lego or Meccano. These
are Israel itself; Israel the idea and the ideology and the geography and
the trick and the excuse. It is the place that is ours and that they have
made theirs . . .'

Perhaps travellers from agricultural societies (as Ireland was until very
recently) are more affected than others by the Palestinians' grief at
being separated from land not valued merely as the family's source of
income. It isn't as simple as the *land* belonging to *them*. *They* belong to
the *land* in a way incomprehensible to most urban dwellers, people
many generations removed from the rhythms and bonds of farming.

I had a noon appointment with Mr Saif Sitta – tall, lean and white-
haired, a sad scholarly man with an endearing hobby: collecting eccentric
pebbles. He lived near Qalqilya and, through Karim, had offered me a
guided tour. Around Qalqilya I would see the Barrier's contortions at
their most perverse and malign.

Qalqilya has grown *on* the OPT's border with Israel and is said to be
Palestine's most misfortunate population centre where even at the best
of times tensions remain high. Originally a Canaanite trading village,
it became a large town in '48 when the new State of Israel seized much
of its land. A disproportionate number of suicide-bombers emerged
from this community during the second Intifada and ever since prolonged military closures have isolated Qalqilya from its hinterland,
to the detriment of health care, education and employment. When
Barrier-building began, most of the remaining land was confiscated
without warning and at once people began to organise resistance. A
futile attempt: until December 2003 the town and five nearby villages
had to endure a curfew lifted only one day a week. Hereabouts all the
emotional distresses and material deprivations occasioned by the Barrier
are magnified.

From Jayyous, Mr Sitta and I took a collecteeve to the roadblock
outside Azzoun, then walked to the main road and boarded a Nablus

minibus bound for Qalqilya. On the way my companion pointed to numerous scars on this military-mauled landscape and said, 'If we were walking you'd also see a little beauty. Anemones and cyclamen, coming up between the rubble. For me, they're symbols – tiny blossoms, strong symbols.'

Then Mr Sitta cautioned me to express no opinion to anyone we might meet about anything remotely related to the Middle East. Here 'Fatah versus Hamas' was interwoven with daily life. Qalqilya had elected a Hamas municipality for several years, until Hamas's undisputed victory in the January 2006 Assembly election prompted the 'Leaders of the Democratic World' to label the winning party 'terrorist'.

To me impoverished Qalqilya felt quite friendly and around the souk's lively *shwarma* and *falafel* stalls it had a raffish sort of animation. But that drained away as we traversed a once-crowded shopping street where we saw nobody and only a few poorly stocked premises remained open. 'Take note,' said Mr Sitta, 'Qalqilya shows you a second catastrophe. Terrorised families came here in '48 with so little and worked hard to make another business. Now Zionism expands and all is lost again.'

I find myself not wanting to remember or write about that afternoon. A taxi took us towards the settlement of Alfei Menashe, almost completely 'protected' by the Barrier. Here it's a 25-foot wall of bleak grey concrete unrelieved by the wit of those graffiti activists who operate near Bethlehem and Ramallah. All around, the IDF's obsession with security has transformed farmland into wasteland. Mr Sitta drew my attention to three isolated homes now one-storey because their upper storeys had bothered the soldiers in the watchtowers. We passed areas on the Seam where once the sheep of three Bedouin communities safely grazed; in 2002 all had to be sold – grazing stolen, no shekels for fodder. At one point the space between the Barrier's two arms was scarcely wider than the road. Claustrophobia is not among my problems but for a moment I felt almost panicky.

We parked on an open dusty expanse some 30 yards from a wide closed gate beside a watchtower. Mr Sitta, recognising the lone elderly man waiting to be let through, ground his teeth audibly before informing me, 'Salim's land is 20 yards from his home. This gate is four miles from his home.'

Briefly we fell silent and could hear the four conscripts arguing above

the traffic hum from Israel's nearby motorway. (There is little motor
traffic in this corner of the OPT.)

'They won't let Salim through because it's 2.00 p.m.,' said Mr Sitta.
He opened the taxi door, looking angry. Our driver restrained him. The
unit on duty were known nasties, an intervention might provoke them
into 'punishing' Salim. After only a slight hesitation Mr Sitta shouted
to his friend, offering a lift home. Slowly Salim walked towards us,
explaining that he'd come at this hour having found the previous unit
decently flexible and knowing nothing of the nasties' arrival. I hoped the
presence of an outsider wasn't rubbing salt in his wound of humiliation.
Afterwards Mr Sitta reassured me; Salim wished more foreign writers
would come to report on Zionism in action.

We included in our Misery Tour that spot where the Barrier encloses
Kfar Saba, a place of pilgrimage for Mr Sitta. There, in July 2004, he
attended a rally organised by the People's Campaign for Peace and
Democracy, which seeks to show how many ordinary people on both
sides are hungry for peace. He recalled with joy – and an ember of
hope – the Israeli mayor of Kfar Saba, surrounded by 400 or so
supporters, leading the two rallies in a megaphone conversation across
the Barrier.

The People's Campaign for Peace and Democracy was co-founded by
Sari Nusseibeh, a Palestinian aristocrat, academic and activist, and his
old friend Ami Ayalon, a former Shin Bet director. Karim remembered
the hostility aroused in some Nablus circles by its brave effort (foreshadowing the one-state solution?) to show how many ordinary people
on every side were longing for Peace. 'Maybe peace more than democracy?' mused Karim. 'What had democracy ever done for us?'

Strong feelings had also been aroused in An-Najah University by the
campaign's recruiting drive. Sari Nusseibeh, himself president of Al-
Quds University, was to have addressed a student meeting – prudently
cancelled at the last moment. Instead, the two college presidents debated
their ideal on television, hoping thus to spread its message to every West
Bank home. However, most Palestinians dismissed it as one more offshoot of the peace process that never processed to anywhere. They
noticed that Professor Nusseibeh had long since proved himself a not
very shrewd judge of character. (Example: he once described Mahmoud
Abbas as 'a decent man free of the opportunism tainting so many of his
colleagues'.) Moreover, with an Old Etonian son and a brother (Zaki)

serving as the Sheikh of Abu Dhabi's most trusted financial adviser, Sari has a credibility problem. He admires his brother's contribution to turning Abu Dhabi into 'the Singapore of the Middle East' but most of my friends don't want to live Singapore-style. They want their fertile land back and a fair share of the region's water in an unoccupied Palestine.

Before we parted Mr Sitta advised me to avoid all anti-Barrier demos. International protesters run the risk of being blacklisted, forbidden entry to Israel for at least ten years. And one can't enter the West Bank without passing through Israeli-controlled territory. For the vast majority of its inhabitants the OPT is a 'lifer's' prison and increasingly the prisoners' visitors are being vetted and controlled.

CHAPTER 16

Preparing to Move on

At the end of February, Leila and Karim both advised me to move on to Al-Khalil (Hebron) slightly sooner than I had planned. By then the PA police were beginning to take an unwholesome interest in my movements – innocent movements as far as I knew, but were there too many 'suspects' among my friends? Also, on the practical level, my room had of late suffered from a water shortage and a sewage embarrassment; the drain-away hole in my loo corner tended at intervals to regurgitate all the household sewage and spread it around, creating the sort of stench to which one does not become accustomed.

Balata doesn't do farewell parties and that sewage stymied the gathering I had hoped to organise in my room. As I toured the camp, saying my goodbyes one family at a time, several of the husbands and sons who hitherto had avoided me joined their womenfolk to say farewell.

The husband of my closest Balata friend (a devoted disciple of Edward Said) said, 'You're leaving us all in a trap. Being bullied three ways – by Hamas, the PA, the Zionists.' He asserted that to most Palestinians Tehran's support for Hamas looks as bad as Washington's support for the PA. His wife disagreed, arguing that Iran's interest in matters Palestinian was fickle and its material support probably greatly exaggerated, another symptom of the Zionists' paranoia about the Iranian threat to global survival.

An older husband, Abdul, with whom I had never before spoken at length, discussed the one-state solution with an exhilarating mix of pragmatism and imagination. He could foresee, 'a long time away', the defeat of political Zionism and religious nationalism. And then the emergence, by evolution rather than revolution, of a multicultural democracy, tactfully renamed and encompassing all of historic Palestine including Jordan where the population is more than half Palestinian.

I asked, 'What about political Islam – Hamas, Hezbollah, the Muslim Brotherhood, Islamic Jihad?'

Abdul had a ready reply. 'We don't like that sort of thing. It wouldn't interest us if we could live normal and peaceful. Our tradition is moderate, we're good Muslims but not *politically* religious. Some imams say good Muslims have to be political, Islam should control all of life. Maybe they're right, talking as scholars. I'm only telling you how it's been for us before now. Changes began when settlements grew and military rule got worse and being moderate did us no good. In some mosques hardliners began preaching hatred and violence and much bigger crowds listened, specially youngsters. Now the first lot of those have kids themselves – out throwing stones aged three, with poor chances of a real job. That's the Zionist game, keep us so poor and hopeless we'll give up and go. But we won't. People here all their lives aren't the sort to give in. Maybe we look scared and hungry and sad but under it all we're *proud*. What was bad was suicide bombing, making us look like the Yanks, the way they kill civilians in their wars. The difference is our martyrs are brave enough to die! Yankee pilots flying over Afghanistan and Zionists over Gaza know they'll get home safe! If they use any pilots – the Yanks like using drones when they're killing an ally's citizens. Or is Pakistan an ally of the US? It wouldn't be if its government listened to its people.'

I agreed that suicide bombing was both the Palestinians' biggest mistake and worst crime – worst since the bloody old days of Abu Nidal and his like. Many outsiders thought it justified Zionism's retaliatory excesses and the resultant loss of Palestinian jobs. How else to protect Israel, with Palestinians queuing to blow themselves up?

'Our *only* crime!' said Abdul. 'It's not crime to kill soldiers and settlers on occupied land. But today – isn't it chicken and egg?'

'No,' I said, 'it is not. The colonial seizure of your land laid the suicide bomb egg.'

'That's going far back,' said Abdul. 'I think inside my own lifetime – once it took six months to get a bomber psyched up, then repression increased and that came down to six weeks. More were supporting them emotionally, though we'd never feel good about helping in practical ways. Now, long after that campaign stopped because Hamas saw it harming us, we're still being punished with permits and checkpoints.'

At an al-Yaseen farewell gathering all my An-Najah friends were enraged – quietly enraged, as is so often the Palestinian way. For the next 25 days all males from Tubas, Jenin and Tulkarm, aged between 16 and 35, were forbidden to enter Nablus where hundreds of them studied. 'Why?' I asked. 'Is there another Intifada brewing?'

'We're never told why,' said a first-year language student from Jenin who would now have to doss down in Nablus. 'Not explaining is part of it. You needn't explain to dumb Arabs, only make sure they obey.'

Leila added, 'Orders like that can come from junior officers, don't have to be written down and read out officially. As an occupying force the IDF is decentralised, not like a normal army. It's free to oppress on a whim.'

Dalal spoke then, a third-year medical student from a nearby village. Two days previously, when no taxis were running because of a flying checkpoint, she and two friends set out in mid-afternoon to walk home. They met only one vehicle, an IDF prison van from which four soldiers emerged to surround them, shouting incomprehensibly in Hebrew. The officer pocketed their IDs and mobiles and told them to kneel on the ground. Then the four smoked cigarettes and chatted among themselves – before suddenly ordering their captives into the van. When the girls argued the officer threatened to destroy their ID cards and detain them. Terrified, they scrambled into the van, were driven a mile or so to the foot of a low but steep hill and ordered to climb to the top. There they again had to kneel and for half an hour were questioned about their neighbours, 'with mixed Hebrew, English and Arabic'. Next they were told to sit on a boulder and remain still or they'd be shot. The four returned to the van to play Hebrew folk-music while smoking and laughing. As darkness fell they shouted to the girls to come down and walk back to Nablus – not to go home. Their IDs were returned but not their cell phones.

'Write all that down,' said Leila. 'It's a fine example of a decentralised army making its own amusement.'

I had mixed feelings about leaving Nablus/Balata: a lot of sadness, some relief at the prospect of getting away from the camp's tangled stresses and strains, some anticipatory excitement at the thought of three weeks in Hebron's Old City where the stresses and strains would be *different*. Raja warned me not to be 'too influenced' by Hebron's vibes, to remember that this city is (happily!) unique. It didn't take me long to appreciate what he meant. However, the repercussions of various events in Hebron, from the 1920s onwards, have been so widespread one can't really regard its vibes as merely 'local'.

In seven weeks one accumulates an unwieldy amount of printed matter. Therefore, being still lame and stick-dependent, I had to take a private taxi from Huwwara to Beit Jala near Bethlehem, from where many collecteeves depart. On arrival in Hebron I was to ring Faisal, a UN agency employee who would pick me up in a 4 x 4 and deliver me to my Old City destination.

I now had to study Hebron's geopolitical idiosyncrasy. When the IDF partially withdrew on 15 January 1997 it left a divided city. Sector H1 (80% of the municipality) is autonomous (sort of) under the PA. In Sector H2 – the Old City – live some 40,000 Palestinians and 600 fanatical settlers being controlled (sort of) by 4,000 or so soldiers. According to the Alternative Information Centre in Beit Sahour, 'Israel's settlement policy, which supports the presence of radical Jewish fundamentalists with a strong anti-Arab ideology in the middle of a Palestinian city, is the proximate reason for the high level of violence in Hebron.'

The Old Testament has quite a lot to say about this tortured place near the south-eastern edge of Palestine's central mountain range, some twenty miles south of Jerusalem. See Genesis 13:18 – 'So Abram removing his tent came and dwelt by the vale of Mambre, which is in Hebron: and he built there an altar to the Lord.' In those days, too, local tensions ran high. Abram moved his tent because his herdsmen and Lot's had been quarrelling about grazing rights. Then Lot chose to dwell in nearby Sodom where the men were very wicked and the Lord had to do some collective punishing to sort them out.

Jews flourished hereabout in 1730BC when, as many believe, Hebron was founded. Excavations on Tel er-Rumeida in Sector H2 put its foundation even earlier – around 2000BC – when there was a surge in city building throughout what we now call Palestine. (In Ireland in 2000BC our more innovative ancestors may have been seeking a bigger cave.) A millennium later, David was anointed king in his first capital, Hebron (see 2 Samuel 5:3). When Babylon brought down the Kingdom of Judah, sending many Jews into exile, the way was clear for the pro-Babylonian Edomites, based in the Negev and Sinai, to take over the land as far north as Hebron. In Persian times (sixth century BC) Hebron controlled most trade routes between Arabia and the Mediterranean and had become one of the region's main cities. The Jews returning from exile in sophisticated Babylonia were unimpressed by primitive Jerusalem and many chose to settle in Shechem (Nablus-to-be) or Hebron.

Towards the end of the second century BC John Hyrcanus forcibly
converted the Idumeans, as the Edomites came to be known, to Judaism;
as a result of mass-circumcision, general septicaemia killed many adult
males. Despite the ruling that all converts should be welcome 'to
shelter under the wing of the Divine presence', anti-Idumean prejudice
persisted. Around this time Aristeas wrote to Philocrates, 'The lawgiver
fenced us about with impregnable palisades and walls of iron, so that we
should in no way have dealings with any of the other nations.'

The Romans nominated Hebron as capital of Idumea and the Jewish
Herod the Great, whose mother was a Nabatean Arab, had a special
feeling for Abraham as the ancestor of Jews, Idumeans and Arabs alike.
He believed in the ancient tradition that Hebron's Macpelah Caves
contained the bones of Abraham, Sarah, Isaac, Rebecca, Jacob and Leah.
To honour them he built a massive monument; today its awesome
remains form the outer wall of the Haram al-Ibrahimi.

By the fourth century AD Hebron had dwindled to a mere village but
then the Emperor Justinian paid attention to the Caves' contents, built
a church and proclaimed Hebron a Christian pilgrimage destination.
Three centuries later another Prophet – Mohammad – came on
the scene. In his *Journeys*, Ibn Battuta quotes from the Hadith: 'The
Messenger of God says – "When the angel Gabriel took me on the
Night Journey to Jerusalem, we went over the tomb of Abraham and he
said to me, 'Get off and execute two rak'ahs of prayer, for here is the
sepulchre of your Father Abraham.' Then we went over Bethlehem and
again he said, 'Get off and pray two rak'ahs, for this is the place where
your brother Jesus was born.' Then he brought me to the Rock."'

Islamic tradition identifies Hebron as the first human settlement,
established by Adam and Eve when they became refugees from the
Garden of Eden. The city's Arabic name, Al-Khalil er-Rahman, means
'the Beloved of the merciful One' and ever since that Night Journey
Muslim pilgrims have been praying around the Cave of the Patriarchs –
everybody's Patriarchs, which is why today Hebron feels almost un-
bearably sad. To those who believe in the power of accumulated vibes,
this city carries far too heavy a load of history.

The Crusaders came, drove out all non-Christians and turned the
Haram al-Ibrahimi into a church. Quite soon they went, leaving behind
many blue eyes and not much else. Under the Ayyubids and Mamluks
Hebron regained its importance, became a major textile trading centre

and by the fourteenth century was celebrated for that blue glassware still being blown in a factory on the H1–H2 boundary – seven centuries after Venetian cotton merchants introduced the art.

At the end of the fifteenth century the Iberian peninsula's Sephardic Jews fled Catholic persecution for the safety of Muslim lands. Hundreds of those refugees were made welcome in Hebron. The city had lacked Jews since the first century AD – though many fifteenth-century residents must have been descended from those who did not adhere to Judaism when the Romans overcame all Jewish resistance. Henceforth, in Hebron, the followers of the three monotheistic faiths lived together quite peaceably until the decline of the Ottoman Empire coincided with the birth of political Zionism.

During the second half of the nineteenth century several groups of immigrants in retreat from Eastern European and Russian anti-Semitism settled briefly in Hebron, once again a favourite of refugees. Many newcomers sought protective alliances with the Great Powers, then establishing institutions throughout the Holy Land in preparation for carving up the Ottoman corpse. But in 1920 Hebron's Jewish community numbered only 600 or so, mostly devout, defenceless non-Zionists, part of the Old Yishuv.

In Mandatory Palestine, as political Zionists methodically laid the foundations for a Jewish state, Palestinian unease and suspicion festered. Hebron became particularly fraught; its ultra-religious immigrants were openly hostile to Arabs and condescending towards the Arabic-speaking Old Yishuv. Their refusal to integrate, or even be civil to other communities, was noted but not officially criticised by the British authorities.

In August 1929 trouble broke out in Jerusalem, the catalyst a long dispute about who should control which holy place. Many Jews were attacked with stones and knives and seriously injured. On 24 August the rioting spread to Hebron where 66 Jews – men, women and children – were slaughtered by a hate-fuelled mob and 50 suffered serious injuries. Many more would have died had their Muslim neighbours not courageously protected them. Next day, in Safed, 45 Jews, also part of the Old Yishuv, were murdered within a few hours. The week's death toll was 133 Jews dead and 339 wounded, 116 Palestinians dead and countless wounded. The British at once evacuated the surviving Jews from both towns.

Then, foreshadowing the initial Zionist reaction to the Holocaust, some Israelis-to-be condemned the riots' Jewish victims as a disgrace to Zionism, 'sheep' who 'died an utterly immoral death' because they tried to flee instead of fighting back. So wrote Avraham Shvedron, a Zionist 'thinker'. Ben-Gurion used the massacres to unite the Workers' Party and reinforce the paramilitary Haganah. He declared, 'Our spilled blood cries out not for pity and succour, but rather to increase our strength and our work in the land.'

Fast forward to 1967, when Rabbi Zvi Yehudah Kook (remember him?) delivered a rant still emotionally quoted in certain circles. 'Where is our Hebron? Are we forgetting it? Every clod of earth, every square cubit, every region and piece of land that belongs to the Lord's Land – is it within our powers to relinquish even a single millimetre of them?'

Yigal Allon was listening, a man who began his career before the establishment of the State of Israel commanding the Palmach, the Haganah's quasi-terrorist elite force. Then he became a notorious IDF commander, a Minister of Labour during the Six-Day War and eventually Israel's deputy Prime Minister. He saw the promotion of settlements as a logical sequel to a conquest of territory. In January 1968 he proposed 'the building of a Jewish neighbourhood in Hebron' and when the government said 'No' he resolved to help Rabbi Kook's followers to break the law.

In March 1968 another Rabbi appeared centre stage: Moshe Levinger, who had been closely associated with the Kfar Etzion proto-settlement. He asked Hebron's military governor for permission to hold the Passover seder in an Old City hotel; after 48 hours he and his 60 guests would leave – that was a promise. Israeli citizens were not allowed to stay overnight on the West Bank but for Levinger the governor, Uzi Nrkiss, made an exception. Ever since, crazed Gush Emunim types have been implanted in Hebron's heart like a poisoned arrow. This is the only OPT city afflicted by settlers within its boundary.

In April 1968, the IDF hastened to arm the settlers. Meanwhile Hebron's mayor, Sheikh Muhammad Ali Jabari, was demanding their removal and a few Hebrew University professors were pathetically waving protest placards outside Levinger's base, deploring his sly infiltration as a perilous trend-setter. In the Knesset Moshe Dayan was questioned by Uri Avnery – 'Is it true the group lied to the army about only staying 48 hours?' Dayan promptly replied, 'I don't examine innermost thoughts!' Soon after, he revealed that the group had applied for recognition as permanent residents of Hebron 'and the administration has approved their request in accordance with the government's decision' (*Knesset Protocols*, vol. 29, 12 June 1968). At this stage Hebron's settlement was being amply funded by an American Jew, Shmuel Wang, and by the 'Movement for the Greater Israel'.

Some twenty years later, when Hebron's settlers had become globally infamous, bringing shame on the Zionist project, Uzi Narkiss, the military governor who said 'Yes' to Levinger, wrote *A Soldier for Jerusalem*. In it he referred to the settlers' 'cunning manipulation of the political situation' and noted that 'the little trick they played was destined to go very far'.

CHAPTER 17

Arrival in Hebron

Oldies remember driving from Nablus to Hebron in one and a half hours; my private taxi ride to Bethlehem alone took more than three. Granted, it was only nominally private; thrice we stopped to give short lifts to the driver's friends. He, poor fellow, had an agitating problem requiring him to remain on his mobile even while negotiating this famously hazardous road. The problem was financial (shekels came into every sentence) and he often took both hands off the wheel to gesture expansively. Meanwhile two wide IDF vehicles were causing the main delay; though capable of a normal speed they crawled through Area C, doubtless enjoying the tailback. Many complain about this ploy and I'd wondered – are the Palestinians being slightly paranoid? Those vehicles provided the answer.

Beyond Beit Jala, my minibus front seat allowed a depressing view of Gush Etzion, a settlement wedged between Bethlehem and Hebron. Its more than 40,000 inhabitants were soon to be registered as residents of 'Greater Jerusalem'. This bloc ensures exclusive Israeli control of the precious Mountain Aquifer, said by some to have made possible that 'orchard of pomegranates' celebrated in the Song of Songs. New apartheid roads were being gouged through expanses of rich soil stripped of their olive groves and vineyards. Since biblical times this region has been renowned for its grapes. Some settlers still cultivate vines and make wine for sale in Hebron's Gutnick Centre.

From afar, Herodium rises above the shrunken area of farmland remaining to the Palestinians. An artificial conical hill, as intrusive in its time as Gush Etzion, it supported the most elaborate of all Herod's palace-fortresses, built between 24 and 15BC to mark the spot where his cavalry, in retreat from the Parthians, overcame a large Jewish force. Below the fort a city extended to the base of the mountain and excavations have revealed many wonders. Herodium is in Area C but controlled by the Israeli Ministry of Tourism.

Apart from annexed East Jerusalem, Hebron/Al-Khalil is the West Bank's biggest city. Since Mandate times its population has risen from

16,000 to more than 160,000 and its people are noted entrepreneurs, regarded by some Nablusis with mingled envy and disdain; their uncommon energy has enabled them to overcome many of Al-Khalil's handicaps. At first sight this metropolis seemed to me sprawling, over-crowded and charmless, not to be compared to my beloved Nablus. But that was before I became an Old City resident.

On arrival my plan went all agley. I was to have rung Faisal from the taxi terminus in H2, but extreme traffic chaos tempted the driver to dump his one remaining passenger on a busy pavement in H1. When I asked a passer-by to tell Faisal where to find me, it transpired that for reasons unknown all Hebron's telephone lines and signals were inoperative. The kind young man who had stopped to help me – though carrying a toddler and a bulging shopping bag – made reassuring noises; a five-minute taxi ride would take me to the only hotel, optimistically named Hebron Tourist Hotel.

On the West Bank empty taxis don't cruise around seeking passengers; for a quarter of an hour I stood unsuccessfully beckoning beside my pile of luggage (big rucksack, little rucksack, sausage-bag; all book-heavy). Then another kind young man increased the traffic chaos by stopping his small car to offer me a lift. Angry shouts came from every direction as he adjusted his own luggage before taking on mine. Regrettably, he spoke no English.

Hebron's 30-room hotel was an agreeable establishment with pleasing 1950s décor and no guests (never mind tourists), a friendly staff of two but no heating (understandably, at €24 for B&B). Prudently, I'd brought two bottles of anti-freeze Scotch from Christian Ramallah, having been warned that Hebron lacks a Samaritan village equivalent. Those precious bottles were for emergency use and now, as a gale drove hail against my window, I registered – 'Emergency!'

The knock on my door was unexpected and the visitor unknown. He spoke adequate English and introduced himself as 'Mahmoud' – a middle-aged man, tall, big-bellied, balding and chain-smoking. He claimed to have spent four years on the run and eight years in jail . . . It was his privilege to welcome me to Al-Khalil. I disliked him at first sight.

Mahmoud urged me to move next day to his friend's luxury apartment on Sharia al-Salam Street – only US$70 a night with satellite TV. I said I'd be moving to lodgings on Bab al-Babadiy – only US$5 a night.

Mahmoud expressed shock/horror before showing an interest in my
Balata and Nablus friends, especially those with university links. I made
much of searching for a lost address book, then mumbled vaguely about
not being able to remember Arabic names. My hobbling around the
room, leaning heavily on a stick, completed the image of a doddering
old woman running out of marbles and unlikely to be of use to anyone.

Later I learned that my visitor, when released from jail in 2000, joined
Preventative Security, the PA's FBI-cum-CIA equivalent – 'meant to
find out everything about everyone', said my informant. During the
following weeks I often saw Mahmoud driving around H1 in his 2009
BMW.

At sunset my mobile rang and Faisal apologised for the communication failure but made no attempt to explain it; UN employees feel
obliged to be politically neutral. At 9.00 a.m. on the morrow he would
escort me to the Old City and I was invited to sup with his family that
evening.

An hour later Raouf rang, proposing to call on me next day with
some interesting documents; so began my Hebron collection of printed
matter. Raouf was Karim's uncle, his mother's youngest brother and
one of his closest friends. He too belonged to the honourable tribe of
returnees. In Canada, during the '90s, he had studied social anthro-
pology, economics and psychology – a valuable academic concoction,
he pointed out, in the hell that is Hebron.

On the following day, under a low grey sky, Faisal escorted me across
the 'border' into H2. Here at Bab As-Zawiya, the besieged Old City
begins, now resembling a war zone (which it too often is) rather than a
commercial and residential district (which it once was). Side streets are
barricaded by tangles of razor wire, by metal gates six metres high, by
concrete blocks three metres square. Look up and you see on high roofs
soldiers and guns and sandbags, and Israeli flags and radio antennae
sprouting from Mamluk domes. At street level all is quiet; only settler
and security force vehicles are allowed – and a very few Palestinian cars
with special permits obtained after prolonged hassles. Since the 1994
Goldstein massacre more than half the Old City's shops have been
closed and sealed by the IDF and its resident population has declined
from 30,000 to 10,000. Traditionally, this souk was one of the West
Bank's busiest, employing thousands. Why was a Palestinian city

punished because a Brooklyn-born religious maniac murdered 29 Palestinians?

At the entrance to the medieval souk we turned left up a short, steep, narrow street of eighteenth-century three-storey terraced houses, once the homes of prosperous extended families – Palestinian merchants, doctors, lawyers, government officials. My landlord, Hisham, was awaiting me, looking slightly apprehensive. A would-be tourist guide, he hoped to convert this long-empty house into a backpackers' hostel. But would I now find it too primitive? He couldn't know that by Balata standards it seemed 5-star. The antique gas cooker was a twin of my own model and the lavatory flushed six times out of ten. At first the hall door key defeated me; it was eight inches long and heavy enough to serve as a weapon. (Hebron makes one think in those terms.) Patiently Hisham taught me the subtle technique – how to jerk and wobble it. He was both congenial and, I discovered, very knowledgeable. On his brief daily visits to check on my welfare, he drip-fed me fascinating bits of local lore.

Hisham's was one of many homes attacked by settlers during the '80s and early '90s. Most of the neighbouring houses were empty and one had been half-demolished by settlers in retaliation for the owner's refusal to sell. A large sheet of corrugated iron hung loose from a freestanding gable end and when the wind rose its clattering sounded like protests reverberating through this otherwise silent street. If I leaned out of my iron-barred window I could see – within 100 yards – three separate army posts guarding the bright new settlement buildings that towered above Al-Khalil's ancient souk.

This top-floor, high-ceilinged flat, at the head of a steep winding stairway, consisted of an enormous unfurnished reception room and three locked rooms off a long corridor leading to a pantry-sized bathroom (Ottoman loo, tiny hand-basin). The narrow kitchen's capacious sink suffered from a blocked water-pipe. One corner of the reception room had long since been partitioned off and furnished with a single bed, a large wardrobe, an easy chair and a small table piled with photocopies of academic papers analysing Hebron's distinctive problems. Only this room and the kitchen were electrified. After dark, as I made my way around by torchlight, I fancied happy families had lived here; the ghosts were amiable.

From Raouf, Hisham borrowed a rusty one-bar electric fire which crackled ominously when plugged in and did nothing appreciable to raise the temperature. All day the sky remained low and dark, the wind icy, the thunder loud, the hail showers frequent. I ventured out between showers to forage around the corner, but in this depopulated district of front-room shops with three-quarters empty shelves I could find neither tea nor sardines. On my way home a ragged teenager followed me, begging insistently – 'One shekel, only *one* shekel!' It would have been unwise for a temporary resident to become known as 'a soft touch'. When I said '*No* shekel', kindly but firmly, he trailed me to my door, then grabbed the key as I was about to insert it and demanded, 'Only *one* shekel!' Looking up into his face I could see that he was no threat. When I smiled and seized his wrist while repeating 'No!' he at once released the key. Later, I was able to identify his family and donate an anonymous gift.

That afternoon it tried to snow but only achieved sleet.

The wind was still icy when I set off at sunrise for the Tomb of the Patriarchs/Haram al-Khalil, to Jews and Muslims one of the most sacred places in Palestine, surpassed only by Jerusalem's Temple Mount/Haram al-Sharif. No archaeological artefact has been found to indicate that this particular place was holy before Herod accepted the Cave of Machpela story and built another of his massively magnificent structures to honour Abraham et al. But that's irrelevant. Genesis guarantees the link between the general Hebron area and the Patriarchs.

For fifteen minutes I walked through the silent souk, past scores of shuttered shops, meeting no one. Once, those covered passageways and open alleys would have been as bustling as Nablus's Kasbah – with hundreds of stalls opening, piled hand-carts being pushed by yelling youths, cats queuing while butchers eviscerated sheep, charcoal being lit in tin 'cookers' for the breakfast kebabs, freshly ground coffee being brewed, six-storey metal crates of squawking hens being manoeuvred into Crusader-era alcoves – all noisy and colourful and pungent. Poor Hebron! A few hours later some shops would open but even at its busiest the old souk is now two-thirds 'in abeyance', as one mournful carpet merchant put it.

All exits are aggressively militarised. I found myself confronting thick metal bars blocking a graceful archway overlooked from on high by electronic gadgets. There was just enough space for one person to squeeze into a covered passageway where I had to exert myself to push slowly through a heavy, ceiling-high turnstile admitting me to another short covered passageway lined with shops – their doors welded shut. Beside the next iron grille a soldier in a sentry-box on stilts bent down to take my passport. Eleven other conscripts lounged nearby, all wearing woolly balaclavas and scarves and gloves but looking cold and extra-bad tempered. Beside the final checkpoint, a walk-through metal detector, one elderly Israeli policemen sat slumped in a chair, fast asleep – until my purse full of coins caused the machine to squeal. Scrambling to his feet, the sergeant fell over his weapon and had to grab my shoulder to steady himself. Blearily he groped for my purse, then waved me on before shouting angrily at the conscripts who had sniggered as he stumbled.

Slowly I ascended a long flight of wide granite steps, trailing my right hand along Herod's wall – 20 metres high, some of its blocks measuring 7.5 x 1.4 metres (so says the guidebook). Inevitably I remembered Dr Baruch Goldstein who on another cold foggy February morning in 1994 drove from Kiryat Arba and walked up these steps wearing his IDF uniform and armed with his M-16 rifle. God wanted him to kill as many Muslims as possible while they were kneeling at Friday prayers. His total was 29, but he injured many more.

In the vast twilit vestibule a smiling youth pigeon-holed my boots, draped me in a brown *gabaya* and whispered, 'Welcome! Welcome!' – followed by what sounded like a brief Arabic prayer. Then I was entering the empty mosque where something very odd happened. All thoughts of Goldstein and his immense significance evaporated, as did the anger engendered by Hebron's tragedy – which can feel like the Palestinians' tragedy in concentrated form. A strangeness overwhelmed me: suddenly I seemed to have been transferred to another plane. But by *what*? Maybe nothing more than this Haram's densely complicated history.

Like all the Holy Land's places of pilgrimage, the Tomb of the Patriarchs/Haram al-Khalil is an exciting cultural rag-bag. Herodian stonework, chunks of the Emperor Justinian's church incorporated into an early Ummayyad mosque – itself added to by Ayyubids, before the Crusaders turned it into a church and contributed the stained glass window above the main entrance and the soaring central arches. The Ottomans added and subtracted bits and pieces – nothing of much consequence, certainly nothing to rival the marquetry *minbar* (pulpit) created for the Ascalan mosque in 1091 and exactly a century later moved to Hebron on Saladin's instructions. During all my visits I found myself repeatedly drawn back to the *minbar*. Over the past 900-plus years it must occasionally have been restored yet it allows one to feel close to the master craftsmen who created it.

It was only after the Goldstein massacre that this space was divided into 'mosque' and 'synagogue'. The connecting doors are kept permanently locked, a necessary but sad precaution. Everyone can see, through bars, the make-believe tombs of Abraham and Sarah, fourteenth-century Mamluk cenotaphs resembling decorated tents. The IDF prevent Jews and people with Jewish surnames from entering the mosque. They also maintain a depot, at the far side of the building, where settlers must leave their weapons before entering the synagogue.

For over an hour I was alone in that extraordinary space, its tranquillity so mysteriously unblemished. Then the first local worshippers appeared, soon followed by groups of debating madrassa students and visiting pilgrims led by imams. The welcoming youth, who had remained tactfully in the background while I was alone, identified the arrivals in very broken English. Mosques are not reserved for prayer and religious ceremonies; many also serve as multi-purpose social centres.

The settlers' territory semi-surrounds the Tomb of the Patriarchs and, after a close scrutiny of IDs, foreigners are allowed into it through the barriers. By chance, this being the Shabbat, I now had a close-up view of scores of worshippers returning from their synagogue. Some were in (very large) family groups, some walked alone still reading half-aloud from prayer books. Most men carried heavy weapons and wore the self-designed uniform of those vigilante units which occasionally clash with the IDF if the latter seem 'over-protective' towards Palestinians (a rare circumstance). In general Hebron's settlers are US-born, with a soupçon of newish immigrants from France. I feigned friendliness: big smile, jolly 'Good morning!' Most pretended not to see me (we were within touching distance), a few looked briefly at me with hate in their eyes. Beyond question these people are severely disturbed; some consider them psychotic. If that diagnosis is accepted, one can't blame them for what they do. The blame lies elsewhere.

The settlers' main building dominates the eastern end of Shuhada Street and there a conscript stepped out from behind sandbags to demand, 'What your religion? You Christian?' 'No!' 'You Muslim?' 'No!' 'You Jew?' 'No, I have no religion.'

A long, baffled pause, while the teenager struggled with this vacuum. He had exhausted all known possibilities; Hinduism, Buddhism and other such oddities were beyond range. Abruptly he extended a gloved hand. 'Give ID! ID show religion!' I presented my passport while explaining that it doesn't specify the bearer's religion which is of no concern to civilised governments. This further confused the youth. Gazing down at the passport he asked, 'Which country yours?' provoking me to snap, 'Can't you read?' (Afterwards remorse pricked: possibly the poor fellow could only read Hebrew.) When my passport had been registered in the IDF post another conscript returned it and waved me on my way with warnings. I must not go anywhere near the Jewish cemetery on the hill above or take photographs. But this I'd already done, when passing a symptomatic notice, six feet wide:

> THESE BUILDINGS WERE CONSTRUCTED
> ON LAND PURCHASED BY THE HEBRON JEWISH
> COMMUNITY IN 1807
> THIS LAND WAS STOLEN BY ARABS
> FOLLOWING THE MURDER OF 67 HEBRON JEWS IN 1929
> WE DEMAND JUSTICE! RETURN OUR PROPERTY TO US!

Hebron's 500 or so settlers have always claimed 'This is a *Jewish* city!' – a sacred place to which they have been welcomed back by 'our Patriarch Abraham'. They refer to the 160,000 Palestinian residents as 'foreigners' and all good Jews have a duty to banish them. From the outset Rabbi Meir Kahane's racist Kach movement promoted violence – firstly in New York where he founded the Jewish Defence League, a citizens' militia to oppose 'the spread of Black anti-Semitism in America'. In the early 1980s, when Baruch Marzel arrived to lead the Hebron community, violence increased with daily settler attacks on Palestinian persons and property. Rabbi Kahane, at the 1980 funeral of a US-born settler killed by a Palestinian sniper, proclaimed, 'Anyone who says that vengeance is not a Jewish virtue is simply wrong. Henceforth we shall not pay with an eye for an eye, but rather with two eyes for an eye!' Raouf showed me a 1985 photograph of Moshe Levinger providing cover with his rifle for Baruch Marzel as he wrecked a row of Palestinian cars. In 1990 Levinger was sentenced to five months (!) imprisonment for murdering a stall-holder in Hebron market. Not surprisingly, the settler death toll is highest in the Hebron/Kiryat Arba bloc.

Goldstein belonged to Kach and in 1995 Rabbi Kahane published a book praising his friend's 'act of self-sacrifice for the sanctification of God' and urging others to follow his example. Yigal Amir did so, assassinating Prime Minister Yitzhak Rabin on 4 November 1995. During my first week in the Holy Land, many Israelis were angrily objecting to broadcast excerpts from a furtively obtained Channel 10 TV interview with Amir – in jail since 1995. The prison service allows him no media opportunities and in response to public outrage Channel 10 scrapped the full interview. What interested me was his naming, in 2008, of three Generals (Ariel Sharon, Rehavam Ze'evi and Rafael Eitan) as his main motivators. In 1996 he had told the Shamgar Commission another story – at Goldstein's funeral in Kiryat Arba 'I saw the love all those thousands had for him. I spoke with them and began to understand they are not simply fanatic extremists. They are fighting very hard for the nation. It began after Goldstein. That's when I had the idea it's necessary to take Rabin down.' Amir then drew close to Levinger and worked with those who turned Goldstein's grave into a shrine attracting many 'pilgrims' – until the authorities insisted on the shrine being dismantled.

Shuhada Street died in 2000, at the beginning of the second Intifada. Then a Military Order closed the whole area to protect a few score settlers who live along one side of what used to be the West Bank's most thriving commercial centre. Hundreds of shops employed thousands of helpers and the surrounding villages' prosperity depended on access to al-Khalil's famous vegetable market. Now Palestinian people and vehicles are excluded, checkpoints and military blockades isolate Shuhada Street from the rest of Hebron. To walk its silent length is truly heartbreaking: one can feel the ache in one's chest. Apart from the ever-present conscripts, and an occasional settler, and an even more occasional patrolling army jeep, the whole long street is deserted and desolate. Weeds grow around doors welded shut by the IDF, their rusty panels daubed with jeering Hebrew graffiti or spray-painted menorahs or Stars of David. Once this was a dignified street, its well-proportioned upper storeys adorned with handsome wrought iron casements. The few families still living behind or over former business premises cannot set foot on the street; they must enter or leave their homes through roofs or rear windows. Another few families, who live near Tel Rumeidah, are allowed to cross Shuhada Street at one precise spot opposite the western checkpoint from which a steep street climbs towards Tel Rumeidah. This checkpoint consists of metal containers blocking the wide street fifty yards from where it ends (or begins) in the triangular 'square'. Within the container IDs are checked and Palestinians may not carry anything – however innocent, like a cabbage – through this barrier.

One day, as I approached the gate that comes before the barrier, it surprised me to be overtaken by a small car marked TIPH in large red letters and travelling at walking speed. Two unsmiling civilian observers – male and female, wearing wide TIPH armbands – stared out at me, registering disapproval. They might have been from Denmark, Italy, Norway, Turkey, Sweden or Switzerland, the countries which contribute to a Temporary International Presence in Hebron. According to itself:

> After the Goldstein massacre the UN Security Council called for an international presence in Hebron. The current TIPH was agreed upon in January 1997 after the signing, by representatives of the PLO and the state of Israel, of the Protocol for the Redeployment in Hebron. This document regulates the division of security responsibility in Hebron and both sides commit to maintain normal life in Hebron for all. TIPH is a civilian mission. The two parties agreed it should be the neutral witness on the ground who monitors and reports on the situation. TIPH does not intervene in disputes, incidents or activities conducted by the Israeli or Palestinian side. Typical reports concern violence and harassment around settlements, shooting incidents and misconduct by police or soldiers, house searches, prolonged ID-checks and restrictions of freedom of movement. Its reports are not public. They are legally assessed and presented with questions for clarification to the IDF and the PA police. TIPH follows up violations in order to receive a satisfactory answer. It communicates its findings not only to the Israeli and Palestinian authorities but also to the six member states of TIPH which then can use diplomatic channels to widen the dialogue concerning the situation in Hebron.

TIPH members may be military or police officers, academics or 'experts' in particular fields. They serve for terms from 6 to 18 months, are generously paid by their respective foreign ministries and enjoy special status and immunities – which of course does not deter the settlers from taunting and harassing them. Given the sponsor countries, nothing upsetting to Zionism can be expected to flow through those diplomatic channels. Most of my Hebron friends categorised TIPH as Quartet-like, another ineffectual 'international community' money-waster with neither the will nor the ability to advance the Palestinian cause. They relished TIPH as a fitting acronym; '*tif*' in Arabic means 'to spit'.

No less heartbreaking than Shuhada Street are the 23 half-demolished houses overlooking the road to Kiryat Arba. These superb 400-year-old homes were only half demolished because their sturdy stones demanded so much of the bulldozers. As residences, they would have lasted another 400 years. Their destruction was deemed necessary to protect Kiryat Arba settlers driving to and from the Tomb of the Patriarchs. Kiryat Arba, built in 1970 on 430 hectares of confiscated land, has been described by Professor Idith Zertal as 'the hothouse of the entire settlement project, with its subversion and defiance of the law and of Israeli democracy . . .'

Not far away is a new house which earned many front page headlines during my first visit to Israel. On 17 November 2008 the *Jerusalem Post* reported that the High Court of Justice had unanimously decided against nine settler families who were occupying a four-storey house, known to them as Beit Ha'shalom, on Hebron's outskirts. (Ha'shalom means House of Peace; the Palestinians knew it as House of Contention.)

On 19 March 2007 150 settlers had taken over this new empty property, owned by its builder, Faez Rajabi. His complaint to the police was ignored so he took the case to the High Court, seeking an eviction order. Then came a peculiarly Israeli legal quirk. Beit Ha'shalom is in H2, therefore the High Court hearing had to be postponed for 18 months while 'a separate legal procedure was taking place in a military appeals court on the status of the building'. Finally the High Court announced it was prepared to wait no longer for the military court's decision. One of my Israeli friends said, 'See whose side the army's on? That's a big worry!'

In the High Court the settlers claimed that two of their many generous supporters, a father and son from Brooklyn, had paid almost US$1 million for Beit Ha'shalom. However, a police investigation of the relevant documents detected forgery and the Court gave the occupiers 'three days to leave of their own free will'. On the fourth day the police would be authorised to evict them.

The countrywide reaction didn't surprise my Israeli friends though it shocked me (then a newcomer). The Council of Jewish Communities in Judea, Samaria and the Gaza Strip described the High Court's decision as 'Scandalous!' The Council of Rabbis of the Jewish Communities in Judea, Samaria and the Gaza Strip forbade the settlers to leave the building because 'All of Israel belongs exclusively to the Jewish people. It is forbidden to assist in any way the expulsion of Jews and the sacrifice of a settled area . . . Permission has not been granted to sacrifice any settled area, certainly not a building that is located in the heart of Hebron, the city of our forefathers.' Rabbi Shalom Dov Wolpe offered to reward soldiers who refused to take part in the eviction; for every night they spent in jail he would pay their families 1,000 shekels. Peace Now also issued a statement: 'We are hoping that the Defence Ministry . . . will enforce the law even if it is a challenge for Israeli society and the defence forces.'

The police agreed to obey the court yet took no action when three days had passed and the occupiers remained *in situ*. Meanwhile four new families had joined them (settlers like to operate in family units) and a member of the Knesset, Nissim Ze'ev of the Shas party, had moved in, representing many right-wing and religious politicians. Rabbi Ovadia Yosef, the Shas 'spiritual leader', fervently blessed the occupiers behind their barricades. The court verdict was given on a Sunday and by the following Friday Hebron's settlers had been augmented by 20,000 or so from all over the West Bank – fanatics who gathered annually to hear *Chayei Sara* being read, a portion of the Torah describing Abraham's purchase of the Cave.

Thereafter, gangs of youths roamed the neighbourhood, slashing the tyres of police and IDF vehicles, badly injuring one soldier by pouring turpentine onto his face, spray-painting 'Mohammad is a Pig' on a mosque wall, uprooting vegetable plots, defacing Muslim graves. On Beit Ha'shalom's roof they adopted battlefield postures, ready to repel any rash evictors. From there they stoned all Palestinians who came within range, as many had to, including old people and children. Some of their bruises and cuts were photographed for B'Tselem by Amjad al-Jabari. He told me that when he begged two police commanders to station men on the rooftops they replied, 'It's not possible.' Said Amjad, 'The settlers frighten everyone, not only us.'

As tensions rose nationwide the then defence minister, Ehud Barak, announced the eviction could no longer be postponed and travelled to Hebron with the IDF C-in-C, Gabi Ashkenazi, 'to show muscle'. And still nothing happened. In the *Jerusalem Post* on 28 November 2008 Naomi Chazan wrote, 'Flagrant defiance of the law breeds disorder; the ensuing chaos makes the imposition of any authority impossible. The foundations of Israel's system of government are at stake.' By then the IDF were admitting they couldn't depend on the many soldiers and policemen *who themselves live in settlements* to obey eviction orders. Before I left Israel in early December, OPT roads were being blocked to mark solidarity with the persecuted Hebron brethren, a synagogue had been set up within Beit Ha'shalom and the general public were being asked to inform the squatters about any unusual IDF movements. Obviously quite a large force would be needed for this eviction. Then, suddenly, stun grenades and tear gas were used to 'cleanse' Beit Ha'shalom, as Operation Cast Lead was being planned. 'Clever timing!' said Soufian. 'Attacking Hamas made heroes of soldiers who'd just attacked settlers. They didn't put up much of a fight, Ashkenazi sent so many.'

Next came the post-eviction horror. On my flight home I read Avi Issacharoff's account in *Ha'aretz*: 'Hebron Settler Riots were Out-and-out Progroms' (5 December 2008). When the IDF and police had left Tel Rumeida infuriated mobs attacked several Palestinian homes. More than twenty members of one family were trapped indoors and a yelling gang of masked men surrounded the dwelling, some pelting it with bottles, stones and chunks of concrete, others dousing it with petrol preparatory to burning the Palestinians alive. All the watching journalists – Israeli and foreign – attempted desperate phone calls to the security services but none could make contact. The threatened family's neighbours dared not emerge to try to rescue them; this was an armed mob avid for Arab blood. Only the journalists' immense courage saved those 23 people. With the Israelis in the lead – shouting warnings about dire consequences if any media representatives were harmed – they broke through just in time to rescue the family before matches were struck. Soon the house had been totally destroyed – and then the police arrived, to be greeted with the standard settler jeers: 'Nazis! Nazis!' Some of my friends, Israeli and Palestinian, used this Tel Rumeida saga to illustrate how impossible it would be to impose a two-state solution on half a million settlers.

During the House of Contention stand-off, when everyone felt the local atmosphere couldn't become any more poisoned, the IDF proved them wrong by launching an anti-Hamas campaign likely to be remembered for as long as Hebron's other atrocities. Equipped with six Military Orders, the soldiers began, on Tuesday 26 February 2008, a series of incursions to close or confiscate many long-established Islamic Charitable Society (ICS) enterprises. The ICS has been helping the Palestinian poor, in Hebron and elsewhere, since Jordanian times (1962) and has been endorsed by the EU, the YMCA, Defence for Children International, World Vision, the International Women's Peace Service and former President Jimmy Carter. Now the IDF wrecked – by closure and/or confiscation – a thirty-unit apartment block and administrative buildings, two bakeries that provided subsidised bread to more than 5,000 families, a warehouse holding over US$300,000 worth of school supplies, clothing and food, a new shopping mall, three schools, two orphanages whose closure left 240 children without shelter, two new school buses and a van. They also closed a sewing centre where girls learned how to earn a little money; as that Special Squad left Hebron it tipped all the ripped cloth and smashed sewing machines onto the city dump. A US$2 million school for 1,700 pupils, due to open in September 2008, was confiscated and had its gates welded shut. The IDF accused ICS teachers of 'incitement to violence and hate, promoting Hamas' goals and recruiting terrorists'. In fact all ICS schools on the West Bank follow the PA curriculum and the ICS asked, in vain, for its staff and operations to be investigated by some neutral organisation. It provides no support to families of prisoners, apart from continuing to pay employees who face administrative detention – as do the PA, UNRWA and various NGOs.

These Military Orders deprived the particularly vulnerable ICS beneficiaries of specialised services not otherwise available. They also represented a new threat by authorising the transfer of ownership of private property in the H1 Area (under Palestinian control) to the IDF. As my activist friends pointed out, those closures and confiscations violated Articles 6 and 7 of the International Covenant on Economic, Social and Cultural Rights, Article 39 of the Fourth Geneva Convention, Article 38 of the Convention of the Rights of the Child – and lots more 'Articles', not to mention violating the Oslo Agreement and the Hebron Agreement, signed by Israel in 1995 and 1997, respectively. There is no other charitable or public fund to replace the ICS in Hebron which, since the IDF closures began, has suffered a 70% increase in poverty. Any unblinkered observer can see how neatly this campaign fits into the 'transfer' pattern.

Meanwhile, what was TIPH doing? Neutrally observing, of course – taking care not to intervene.

If you cross-bred Dante's *Inferno* with *Alice in Wonderland* you might get something like twenty-first-century Hebron. About 4,000 soldiers are deployed to protect fewer than 600 settlers. Twice Raouf had seen settlers burning Palestinian cars while soldiers stood twenty yards away, watching. The IDF cannot check any form of settler violence; they are in Hebron to impose military law on all Palestinians and to protect all settlers who are subject only to Israeli civil law – its enforcers rarely visible or accessible.

Where else has a vigorous economy been destroyed and many thousands left jobless – and many precious buildings bulldozed – to safeguard a few hundred fanatics (mostly foreign-born) who have forced their way into the heart of an ancient Arab city? Where else does a whole community bestow hero/saint/martyr status on a homicidal maniac who shot in the back 29 Muslims praying beside the mutually revered Tombs of the Patriarchs? (And who wounded almost 200, some of whom will never fully recover.)

Where else are known criminals allowed to run free, and repeatedly re-offend, while their victims' community is subjected to curfews, closures, sealed roads, mass arrests, mass evacuations from their homes? Where else do civilians on their way to and from divine worship wear loaded sub-machine guns? Where else do shopping streets need close-fitting awnings of gauze and chicken-wire (UN-provided) to protect pedestrians from the settlers who occupy upper storeys? Missiles regularly used include household garbage, broken glass, bricks, metal spikes, canine and human faeces. These awnings are of course no protection against buckets of urine and sprayings of noxious liquids.

At times sheer disbelief momentarily overwhelmed me. Surely all this couldn't be real, true, part of everyday life for the inhabitants of a 'developed' urban society? Where else can a tiny minority of fanatics bend a State – and the 'international community' – to their will? Where else does the UN have to spend its scarce (we're told) resources on buying materials to shield ordinary men, women and children from hate-driven, shit-throwing neighbours?

One of my 'insider' Ramallah friends quoted a Mossad official who conceded that Hamas' decision to launch a suicide-bombing campaign against civilians within Israel was a direct response to the Zionist reaction to the Goldstein slaughter. Hamas' code forbids indiscriminate attacks on civilians but the mosque murders, and the subsequent punishment-without-end of Hebronites, was felt to cancel this taboo and justify revenge. It's an attitude impossible to condone but easy to understand.

Raouf and I often met in Hisham's pleasingly simple Hanthala café in Ein al-Askar Square – overlooked, as is almost everywhere in Hebron's Old City, by IDF posts. Despairingly I asked, 'How can all this have come about, under the eyes of the world?'

Raouf twirled one end of his trim little moustache (which reminded me of my grandfather's) and replied, 'We're not really talking of one city. Here's the tip of an iceberg that could sink Israel as "the Jewish homeland". Can't you see this? You've been living for two months in the bulk of the berg, around Nablus. The spotlight fixes on Hebron. We offer easy access for foreign press, much drama to video with exciting romantic buildings in the background, bloodshed to sob over, raving rabbis to laugh at. Most commentators don't identify what I, personally, see as the likely outcome. Hebron as we know it couldn't exist without official tolerance which it gets because it's only the tip. Elsewhere settlements are supported and encouraged and growing faster and faster. Political Zionism used to want a secular democracy, its own sort of "Jews only" democracy. If it still wants that it can't have it. There's no agreement around the ideal of democracy, no "United Israel". The state's fissured all over. Ashkenazi and Mizrahi, Americans and Russians, Yemenites and Falashas, rich and poor, black and white, liberal cosmopolitans and rabid nationalists, seculars and Haredim. Plus fringe factions like Rabbi Eliezer Waldman's in Kiryat Arba and Rabbi Shalom Dov Wolpe's at Kiryat Gat. Wolpe directs the Chabad educational institutions and has written more than forty books on rabbinical law and suchlike. He says the State of Israel is the enemy of the Jewish people. Outsiders laugh at cranks like him but we see their long-term significance. Some say Gush Emunim is the Zionists' Frankenstein – they forget its instincts were never benign. But it's true the settlements are destroying Israel, have made it ungovernable. That keeps my little ember of optimism glowing.'

On a practical level, the Hebron Rehabilitation Committee (HRC) boosts public morale while giving visitors a pleasant surprise; one doesn't expect to see so many skilfully restored buildings. Said Raouf, 'The settlers have their fantasy about reclaiming Hebron but Al-Khalil won't lie down and die. We're proud and strong, with our HRC to prove it!'

In 1988 several Hebron University architects, concerned about the Old City's deterioration, formed the original HRC with limited resources. Then in August 1996, two and a half years after the Goldstein murders, Hebron's dire needs inspired the PA to undertake rehabilitation in a big way. This new HRC is mainly sustained by the Saudi Development Fund and the Arab Economic and Social Development Fund, with smaller contributions from various European countries. It strives to preserve the Old City's architectural integrity (an impossible task, given the IDF's unstoppable bulldozers), to provide basic social services, to reconnect the Old City to the rest of Al-Khalil and to restrict the settlers' horizontal expansion by encouraging Hebronites to return to abandoned homes. Its initial efforts won the 1998 Aga Khan Award for Architecture, presented biennially to the Islamic world's most successful new project. Then the pace slowed, as proliferating Military Orders (MOs) banned all work on buildings near settlements. Bulky construction material can't be smuggled and every Palestinian motor vehicle entering the Old City needs a special hard-to-get permit; this alone enables the military to curtail rehabilitation. Some returning families were arrested en masse, despite being able to prove residence in the Old City for six or eight generations. Craftsmen qualified to repair ancient archways, domes and walls have been indefinitely detained without charge but much interior work continues to be done furtively, using tools and materials smuggled into buildings behind IDF backs. By March 2009 almost 5,000 had returned to 900 discreetly renovated homes.

One morning near the souk entrance I saw four men unloading sacks of cement from a trailer for an adjacent project. As I peered through the relevant archway four conscripts approached and set about enjoying themselves. Two stood beside the van, demanding to see the municipality employees' IDs and their vehicle's various permits. The others stood at a little distance holding M-16s at the ready. When I moved closer to the van one undersized youth ordered me away. 'Go! Go!' he shouted. 'Get gone, fuck off!'

I beamed at him and said, 'I like standing here.' Angrily he jabbed his gun at my shoulder, repeating 'Go! Go!' I snapped 'Grow up!' and turned my back on him, the better to study his mates' hassling technique. One had taken out a jotter and biro and was insisting on writing down the three rows of numbers on each sack as it was being unloaded. If this infuriated the Palestinians their faces didn't show it. Military occupation teaches one how to keep emotions under wraps – until the next Intifada . . . Half-an-hour later, when the trailer was empty, the IDF sauntered away, giving me dirty looks, and the unloaders shook my hand and said 'thank you' in Arabic and English.

Exacerbating the effects of Military Orders are certain HRC flaws of the sort endemic to committees wherever they sprout. These seem to irritate some Hebronites but it astonished me that any committee could achieve so much against such odds. The HRC also hopes to revive tourism and sponsors three horse-drawn carriages (recalling Cuban equine buses) that stand all day in Bab as-Zawiya, ready to take tourists around the few 'open' streets. I never saw them in action but the plump cobs looked happy and Raouf assured me they get enough exercise when it's their turn to haul loads of mortar and roofing timbers to a restoration site. One horse, caught delivering to an unauthorised site, was arrested and detained for three hours and has had a lyric composed in his honour.

Escape from military surveillance is possible only within the covered souk and even there foot patrols come through at irregular intervals. Although most shops remain shut a few have reopened, being in receipt of small HRC stipends. The Old City souk used to be among Al-Khalil's main tourist attractions, noted for its sheepskin and leather goods, its traditional sweet-shops specialising in lemon- or rose-scented Turkish Delight and its Hebron Women's Co-operative. This last enterprise survives, its 120 weavers maintaining very high standards. Throughout the Holy Land I saw nothing comparable to their carpets, embroidered gowns, scarves, wall-hangings, woollen bags – all made in the members' homes using designs particular to individual villages. The Co-op's two shops face each other across the narrow alleyway, providing unexpected colour and animation. They are run by two infinitely hospitable forty-something sisters, Narwal and Laila, who hold strong views on anything you care to mention.

By Day Two I had been absorbed into what I came to think of as the Co-op Club, an institution valued by countless foreign friends of the Palestinians. Such independent travellers, usually on day-trips from Jerusalem, make up the bulk of Al-Khalil's post-Goldstein tourists. Hebron is kept off the package tourists' itinerary, apart from those coachloads of US settler-supporters who are led through the souk with tiresome frequency, escorted by eight-man IDF units. Their leader (a man infamously rude to all Palestinians) tells them what they want to hear. Without their backing, Jews would be excluded from the Tomb of the Patriarchs by Islamic fanatics. How would those US fanatics react if told that for many pre-Zionist centuries Jews and Muslims met and mingled, amiably saying their separate prayers here and at Rachel's Tomb, Safed and the other sacred-to-both sites?

The IDF tried to deter me from eavesdropping on these tours but they have no authority over foreigners and the guide's Brooklyn voice is loud and clear. He presented the 1929 riot as ample justification for 'reclaiming' Hebron. It is a Jew's *duty* to take over this territory of the Patriarchs and Matriarchs. As Rabbi Eliezer Waldman put it in 1980, 'The voice of our brethren's blood is crying out to us from the Land of Israel, from the earth of Hebron, a cry of innocent blood that has been spilled from 1929 until this day . . . We will no longer be able to block our ears to this outcry. The blood is crying out for the removal of the restraints that are binding the Jewish settlement in Hebron, restraints that are preventing Jewish life at the site of the murders. Only a Jewish presence will prevent the insolence of evil . . .' There's nary a mention of the part played by Hebron's gentiles in 1929. More than 400 Jews were rescued, sheltered and had their wounds tended by non-Jewish neighbours – whose descendants are not allowed to be full citizens of Israel, even if they live within its borders. Yehuda Shaul, a religious conscript who founded 'Breaking the Silence' at the end of his posting to Hebron, one day saw an aged Palestinian woman being stoned by a gang of settler children. By chance, he recognised her. In 1929 her parents had risked their own lives to protect Jews.

A seventh-century Jew, quoted by Shlomo Dov Goitein in *Palestine's Jewry in Early Islamic and Crusader Times*, wrote about those sons of Isaac who had evaded Byzantine persecution and recently returned to Jerusalem protected by the sons of Ishmael – this was God keeping his promise to Abraham, their shared ancestor. Moreover, Jerusalem's Arab conquerors readily agreed to the building of new synagogues and *yeshivas*.

One of the quirkier aspects of Israeli academic life dates from 1936 when the Hebrew University (in other respects conventional) chose to establish two history departments: the Department of History and the Department of Jewish History and Sociology. Israel's other universities, as they were founded, did likewise. For Zionist purposes, Jewish history needs to be studied in its own sterilised space, uncontaminated by gentile methodology. Unfortunately for Zionism, this neat arrangement came unstuck in the 1980s when Israeli universities began to breed those subversive scholars now revered or reviled as 'the new historians'.

Narwal, a woman of great spirit, leads the Co-op; born in a nearby town, she studied at Amman University (economics and history). One afternoon I found her looking slightly shaken; half an hour earlier a foot patrol had invaded both shops and accused the sisters of being TIPH spies. (They must cultivate all expats as potential customers.) Clearly those conscripts were unaware of TIPH's precise role in this miserably muddled enclave. When Narwal quietly pointed out that, given its mandate, TIPH doesn't need spies, one soldier shouted in English, 'Shut your mouth!' Another 'used a very bad word', a third jeered 'You're dirty bitches with foreign men!' The fourth pointed his gun at Narwal's chest and asked, 'Are you scared?' Concealing her anger she replied, 'You can't scare us with guns. We've a better sort of strength.' Then in chorus the quartet used that 'very bad word' – and departed.

'This sort of thing we've had to get used to,' said Narwal.

During Cast Lead, when everyone was even more on edge than usual, the Co-op defiantly sold T-shirts in the Palestinian colours, their illustration an AK-47, and one hung outside the shop among many other items. A patrol stopped, accused Narwal of 'supporting violence' and stole it. Narwal retorted, 'I'm dealing in *pictures*! You're violent with every sort of weapon to kill our people in Gaza!'

Certain foot patrols loot from souk shops, giving no excuse, a practice sometimes (not always) frowned upon by senior officers. As that unit went on its way, Narwal replaced the T-shirt and added three more to the outside display. Subsequently she retrieved her stolen property by threatening a court case, having been advised to do so by a Scandinavian lawyer serving with EAPPI.

The Ecumenical Accompaniment Programme in Palestine and Israel (EAPPI) recruits remarkably brave volunteers. It describes itself as 'an initiative of the World Council of Churches in response to a call made by the Heads of Churches in Jerusalem . . . managed by Quaker Peace and Social Witness.' Its volunteers wear jackets inscribed 'ECUMENICAL ACCOMPANIER' and in the OPT and Israel their main function is 'to offer protection through a nonviolent presence'. Example: on Faisal Street, in H1, I saw four soldiers and two Border Police accusing a poorly dressed young man of driving a stolen car with a false number plate. Their victim nervously but emphatically protested his innocence while his wife cowered in the front seat, a terrified toddler on her lap, being reassured by one EA in broken Arabic while her colleagues spoke sternly to the hasslers in broken Hebrew. All came right, but only after a twenty-minute ordeal while IDs and car papers were ostensibly being checked by radio. Fully to appreciate the cruelty of this common brand of harassment we have to remember that Palestinians can be detained for indefinite periods without charge.

Conspicuous among the family photographs on Raouf's kitchen shelf was one foreigner, an EA – Tom Fox, aged 54 when kidnapped in Baghdad. A few months later his corpse was found beaten and bound with multiple bullet wounds to the head and chest. A US Quaker, he became close to Raouf's family while serving on the West Bank where many remembered him with gratitude. In Jayyous the mayor had told me, 'Tom always sat in front of the bulldozers to delay them, so's people could save things from homes before demolition. We said, "Remember Rachel Corrie!" but he went on sitting.' After Tom's kidnapping, angry meetings demanding his release were held throughout the OPT and in Toronto and Chicago. Palestinian peace activists, politicians and religious leaders of all stripes sent many messages to the 'Sword of Righteousness Brigades' – never before heard of – but Tom became the forty-first foreigner to be murdered by kidnappers since the invasion of Iraq in 2003.

In addition to their IDF-induced tensions, the Co-op sisters had to cope with certain male merchants who regarded an efficiently run all-female enterprise as an indecency. When Narwal spent US$100 on an overhead sign, to be hung between the two shops, those competitors complained that the women already enjoyed an unfair advantage, being a co-operative, and intimidated her into taking it down.

The souk sees much drug-dealing – often in public – between interested conscripts and local petty criminals. As in Balata (but more so) political collaboration is also rife, leaving many mistrustful of their neighbours. In such an environment, problems that should unite communities tend to fracture them and poverty leaves H2's population extra-vulnerable to thirty pieces of silver.

Narwal disapproved of my lodgings, thought Bab Al-Baladiya Street 'too empty' and anyway 'it's sad for a person to live alone'. In fact I valued Hisham's silent apartment where I could unwind in solitude after the day's harrowing encounters. But Narwal was insistent: Radwan and Habsu, who had a spare room, needed rent money more than café-owning Hisham. Radwan was nearly sixty with bad health and no job and a second wife in her twenties. They married in 2000, on Radwan's release from seven years in jail. Their four children ranged from eight years to eight months. A first wife and nine adult children lived in a nearby village. En passant Narwal noted, 'Al-Khalil doesn't show Islam at its best. Some men like two or even three wives and all must do as they're told. Maybe Habsu must also have nine!'

I moved at the end of the week into a late sixteenth-century souk dwelling, restored by the HRC in 2002. Radwan's family had lived within those same walls since the Ottoman Empire was young. In 1998 settler pressures forced them out, in 2003 the HRC coaxed Radwan to repossess his property though it was on the front line. Nearby lived none other than Miriam Levinger whose name, were you Palestinian, would bring you out in septic spots. As Rabbi Moshe Levinger's US-born widow, her legendary campaign to banish Radwan and his neighbours had only recently ended.

From the main souk 'street' a very low arched doorway (even I had to bend) opened into a longish, dimly lit, stone-walled tunnel. Beyond, a small open-air space was bounded by high irregular walls studded with small oblong or oval windows, all barred. A flight of narrow, steep, uneven steps (open on one side: not negotiable after a night out) led to a wide patio off which opened six spacious unconnected rooms, their roofs domed or flat. Each had superbly moulded ceilings, numerous eccentric curves and niches and storage corners, and short flights of steps linking slightly different floor levels. From two corners, steep stairways led to other roofs/patios. No one walking through the covered souk would suspect that on either side, above the shops, people live in a separate world – a secluded world, pre-settlements. In Jerusalem's Old City one sees similar homes but too many have been over-modernised.

Here the HRC had made few changes to the original structures while providing minimal mod cons. All rooms were tactfully electrified: no wires appeared. In the large kitchen, fitted with gas cooker and sink, one curtained corner served as loo and shower-room, its water supply uncertain; Habsu apologised profusely when the loo became obvious. In my room no Western furniture intruded; colourful cushions and folded quilts were piled around the bases of three walls and in the centre of the smooth mud floor stood a home-made coffee-table – two short planks on a wobbly base. As I wrote my diary, pairs of chain-smoking conscripts stared down at me from their fortified post some 40 yards away on a roof requisitioned for 'settler protection'. They did six-hour shifts and sometimes shouted to comrades across the rubble of nearby upper storeys, demolished to clear the IDF's 'field of vision'. At sunset the guard changed and all night powerful searchlights swept to and fro across the Old City, often shining directly into my eyes as I lay on a soft bed of quilts. The room's two round windows, set in a four-foot-thick wall, were shutterless and uncurtained.

Habsu was paranoid about security: I must never leave my room unlocked, even if only crossing the patio to the loo. Four times in the past three years thieves had got away with bedding, kitchen utensils, food (the International Committee of the Red Cross rations) and a thirty-year-old TV set donated by an Egyptian charity. They usually gained admission to Palestinian homes through IDF posts. As Faisal commented, 'It's all part of Zionism's overarching campaign to de-moralise us Arabs.'

CHAPTER 18

The Two Faces of Purim

Going walkabout in H2 one can't expect to be made to feel welcome. To the IDF and the settlers, any foreign woman not with a 'Hebron Fund' group must be undesirable, a friend of the Palestinians. And many Palestinians suspect the same woman of being a settler ally. The contrast with friendly, settler-free Nablus could not be more marked.

One early morning stroll took me out of the souk on an uphill track winding between tall Ottoman houses. In some open cellars goats and sheep are stabled behind crudely contrived gates; these belong to villagers driven off lands officially designated 'for military use', then appropriated by settlers. Where this track becomes precipitous it is lined with low, one-windowed homes, their flat roofs seeming to form a giants' stairway. Most had been abandoned but the HRC was working to entice their owners back. Above them, a faint path crosses boulder-strewn wasteland, then meets a tarred road, curving up from an uninhabited *wadi*. Here looms a massively ugly Border Police post, its high tower affording an unimpeded view of Al-Khalil. Nearby sat an ancient shepherd, his dozen multi-coloured goats feeding from tin troughs of grain. Goats are not fussy but in March that hilltop is seriously arid.

Another stroll to another level ridge-top gave me a clear view of Kiryat Arba and the settler-distressed adjacent countryside. I passed drab, newish two-storey residential blocks near an old Muslim cemetery where weeds half-smother broken and defaced gravestones. Two women, conversing from window to window, paused to stare at me uneasily and a few malnourished children looked scared and disappeared. A man repairing stakes in a small nearby vineyard didn't return my greeting. Pre-settler, Palestinians cultivated grapes on much of the land around (and under) Kiryat Arba; for centuries Hebron was the main exporter of grapes to the Arab world.

Descending to the 'prayer road', I walked unnoticed through a checkpoint; the solitary soldier was asleep, his head resting on the barrier pole. Then I was approaching the devastated area near the Tombs, with bulldozed homes on my right. Because of incomplete demolitions, one could easily visualise the evicted ones moving through those shattered rooms. Al-Khalil often inspires a gut-wrenching mix of sadness and anger. I was already on edge when I saw four little settler boys standing on a high ruin chucking heavy chunks of rock – each carried by two boys – onto the roofs of front-line dwellings. Most Ottoman roofs can survive such assaults and for months – Raouf told me – the residents had been refusing to get the message and retreat to safety.

Purim being imminent, a few kiosks on the edge of the park below the Haram were selling home-made snacks and tapes of Hebrew folk music, played not too loudly and pleasing to the ear. I bought a bag of buns from a handsome young man: very tall and thin with long ear-locks and an even longer beard and pale blue eyes. He spoke American English but preferred not to chat with gentiles. As the sun gained warmth I sat on a bench breakfasting and watching settler children playing on the smooth grassy slope below the synagogue – of course *verboten* to Palestinian children. An elaborate mobile Border Police post had just been put in place and was blocking my view of the Tombs. Navy-blue police vans raced to and fro and four pairs of conscripts patrolled the front-line. At one point a male settler and his two little sons stopped at the nearby junction, awaiting a lift to Kiryat Arba. When an elderly Palestinian appeared, wearing a long gown and *keffiyeh* and carrying a bucket, the father signalled to the soldiers. At once two responded, in crouching battlefield mode, yelling threateningly. The Palestinian had to move away from his bucket and stand still, the guns steadily pointing at him, until a minibus arrived ten minutes later. I asked myself – for how much longer can this viciously grotesque Occupation continue?

My cell phone rang as I stood up to go; an Irishwoman, visiting the Club, was anxious to meet me. Although I then stood no more than forty yards from her, the Co-op was a two-mile walk away – so effectively has the covered souk been severed from its hinterland. The many short connecting passageways are blocked by concrete cliffs, sheets of iron, metal grilles and thickets of razor wire. Being eager to meet my compatriot, this delay annoyed me. When more serious issues are at stake, what must such distortions of their neighbourhoods do to H2 residents?

The uphill walk from Shuhada Street to Tel Rumeida takes one through

H2's most desolate district where only 50 of 350 families have defied
the settlers. On the left are substantial two- and three-storey houses,
now mostly empty. Facing them is a high grey fence, another section of
the front-line, some 100 yards long. An eerie atmosphere prevails. One
rarely sees a human being and no traffic of any sort is allowed, not even
ambulances or hearses; patients and corpses must be person-carried
into H1. Hereabouts are five checkpoints within a one-mile radius and
my friend Fahdi's father's corpse had to be taken through two barriers.
At both, his sons were ordered to put their burden on the ground 'for
examination'. Then Abu Fahdi's body was stripped naked, to the
indescribable distress of the bereaved. This funeral was held up for two
hours while all the mourners' IDs were being checked.

At Tel Rumeida an 18-family settler 'outpost' protects the archaeological dig. There was no one in sight when I paused to photograph a
large bilingual metal sign – much scratched and dented, only semi-
legible. In part it said:

ANCIENT TEL HEBRON. THE ADMOT YISHAI NEIGHBOURHOOD.

This is the site of an important city in Biblical times. King David's
first capital . . . During 1909 excavations an enormous
Early Bronze Age wall was discovered . . . A Jewish city
existed here during the Second Temple period as well . . .

- At the start of the nineteenth century these lands were purchased
by the Jewish community of Hebron. Later on, Arabs seized
control of much of the property.

- In 1984, Jewish life was renewed at Tel Hebron, albeit in trailer-
homes.

- In 1998 Jewish construction was permitted as a result of the
murder of neighbourhood Rabbi Shlomo Ra'anan by an Arab
terrorist.

- In 2005 . . . buildings were dedicated in memory of the Lubavitcher
Rebbe.

The murdered Ra'anan was a grandson of Rabbi Abrahams Isaac
Hacohen Kook, a dotty but alarmingly influential messianic scholar,
and a son of Zvi Yehudah Kook, one of the founders of Gush Emunim.
Suddenly a blonde young woman confronted me, flushed with rage.

'What for you messing here?' and she tried to grab my camera. I
couldn't place the accent (Brooklyn-tinged French?) and I didn't even
try to think of a placatory reply. Hastily I departed, forgoing Tel
Rumeida's meagre archaeological delights. As a foreigner I was in no
danger; Palestinians may be attacked – killed – with impunity but
settlers know where to draw the line. However, H2's violent atmosphere
is of itself quite unnerving.

Several of my Al-Khalil friends lived on Tel Rumeida, on a long ledge
just below the trailer-homes whose occupants flung all their garbage,
including disposable nappies, into the 'Arabs'' gardens and onto window
sills and verandahs. On my first visit to this ledge I had to be guided by
Fahdi, shown where to scramble over awkward ditches and find the
correct path through bramble-threatened olive trees. The road from
Shuhada Street was closed to Palestinians and for their visitors to attempt
to descend from trailer level would have been unwise.

For seven years these ledge dwellers, who so doggedly refused to move
from their ancestral homes, had been denied their crop of olives. Then
they secured a court order allowing them to harvest. Fahdi showed me a
video of settlers stoning an IDF unit which insisted on enforcing that
order – perhaps because a group of Israeli activists, led by Rabbis for
Human Rights, had come from Jerusalem for the occasion. The Israeli
NGO, B'Tselem, also helped by distributing video cameras throughout
the West Bank to ensure the accurate recording of human rights abuses.
Every Palestinian home around Tel Rumeida is raided monthly, often
in the small hours when all children have to be roused because everyone
must stay in one room while soldiers search for weapons. Ownership of
a kitchen knife had earned three-year sentences for some householders.

Fahdi had a scarred face and a shortage of teeth. During one nocturnal
incursion a conscript laid a hand on his wife's breast and when he struck
out another soldier hit him on the left cheek with a rifle butt and he lost
three teeth. Then the offender smote him on the right cheek and he lost
two more. Between my first and second visits to this family stick-
wielding settler children had left their seven-year-old son with a four-
inch cut on his scalp. Fahdi's brother Abdul lived next door and his
nine-year-old son had recently been attacked by a woman who dragged
him into her trailer home, held him down in an armchair – knee on
stomach – then forced a stone into his mouth and manipulated his jaw
until two teeth were broken. The bruises on his face had not yet faded.

As Fahdi said, 'You couldn't make it up.' Abdul's wife had suffered fractured fingers when a mob of women went on a rampage and she tried to shield her five-year-old daughter from their fists.

The Haganah had seized Fahdi's family home in the Galilee ten years before he was born. In 1952 his teacher father chose to be ruled by Jordanians rather than Israelis and moved to Hebron. Sixty years later his sons agreed that for the children's sake they would take refuge in their ancestral region were that possible. As things are, they couldn't even briefly visit their relatives there.

Those who have 'stayed on' in H2 are not all, as some outsiders assume, too poor or debilitated to emigrate. Many are highly educated, clear-thinking, articulate, with nerves of steel and an extra share of *samoud*.

When a two-classroom school was built on the lowest Tel Rumeida ledge, directly opposite the settlement's core, its opening set off a year-long terror campaign. To get to and from school, pupils must use an exposed stairway of twenty unsteady stone steps, attached to the gable wall of the last house on Shuhada Street. Then comes an equally exposed five-minute walk along the ledge. Raouf's niece, disoriented by stone-throwers, fell off those steps, breaking an arm. After a few more such accidents, the authorities were persuaded to provide a railing. They also tiled the narrow path which can become very slippy. Those tiles must be guarded at night; eleven times they have been dug up and smashed.

'Going to school' was such a daily ordeal that a group of parents took their case to court, using videos as evidence. Raouf showed me a selection. At sundown settler children piled up stones at strategic points, ready for the morning. While going into action those children, with their older siblings and mothers, formed howling mobs, the sound quite terrifying. Sometimes babes in arms and toddlers on paternal shoulders contributed their piercing decibels; one toddler became hysterical with fear as the mob seethed around him. A woman taunted two brave mothers who had come to collect their offspring; the words 'bitches and whores' were clearly audible. The attacks on pupils and teachers caused many minor and a few major injuries. Homes, too, were attacked; a soldier could be seen relaxing on a balcony, arms outstretched, while five yards away adolescent girls were shattering windows as their fathers shot holes in water tanks. Fahdi's sitting-room featured; large stones lay on the floor below a broken window. The headmistress was insulted and kicked, then told by a soldier to 'Get out of the way!' The female settlers' garb adds to the air of unreality; one expects women wearing long skirts and sleeves and flowing headscarves to remain in the background, behaving demurely.

The judge dismissed the parents' case for lack of 'sufficient evidence'. When Raouf YouTubed these videos he was threatened with a long jail sentence if he didn't at once take them out of cyberspace.

Then EAs came to the rescue. Every morning two calm, competent women – young but not too young – courageously escort pupils to the school door. One can see how much these guardians are loved by the 128 girls and (pre-pubescent) boys. The building is as electronically protected as any billionaire's mansion, with bullet-proof windows, and one marvels at the cheerful classroom atmosphere. A fourteen-year-old girl, fluent in English, told me – 'In Al-Khalil, here is the *nicest* school! Teachers treat us like friends!' This headmistress is – has to be – an extraordinary person. As Fahdi remarked, she has the resources, both intellectual and material, to be operating at university level far from Al-Khalil. Twice she invited me to her spacious and elegantly appointed home in H1. Sireen deplored the mindless transfer of social workers to another district just as the most needy children were beginning to confide in them about such delicate matters as incest, drug-dealing and domestic violence. We also discussed the Occupation and all that led to it and what might come after it. And what might come next weekend, because Purim was approaching and tensions were rising. Now and for the foreseeable future, this ancient Jewish festival will be associated in Palestinian minds with the 1994 Goldstein murders.

I remembered the Tel Rumeida school when reading an interview given to Yerushalayim (28 April 1995) by Professor Moshe Zimmerman of the Hebrew University of Jerusalem:

There is a monster in each of us, and if we continue to assume that we are always justified, that monster can grow. Therefore, we Jews are obliged to always hold the German example before our eyes. Already today I am addressing a phenomenon which is growing: there is an entire sector in the Jewish public which I unhesitatingly define as a copy of the German Nazis. Look at the children of the Jewish Hebron settlers: they are exactly like the Hitler Youth. From infancy they are pumped with ideas that all Arabs are bad, of how every Gentile is against us. They are turned into paranoids, they think of themselves as a master race, they are exactly like the Hitler Youth. There is a very dangerous tendency of leniency towards that sector.

Professor Zimmerman was internationally esteemed as an authority on twentieth-century German history.

The word 'genocide' is twentieth-century but the idea was around in the sixth century BC during the reign of Ahasuerus (possibly aka Xerxes?). The Book of Esther (quite a cliffhanger) opens with the king throwing big parties to demonstrate his wealth and power.

> And they were invited, drank in golden cups, and the meats were brought in diverse vessels one after another. Wine also in abundance and of the best was presented, as was worthy of a king's magnificence . . . Also Vasthi the queen made a feast for the women in the palace . . . Now on the seventh day, when the king was merry, and after very much drinking was well warmed with wine, he commanded the seven eunuchs that served in his presence to bring in queen Vasthi with the crown set upon her head, to show her beauty to all the people and the princes: for she was exceeding beautiful. But she refused, and would not come at the king's commandment. Whereupon the king, being inflamed with a very great fury, asked the wise men . . . who knew the laws . . . what sentence ought to pass upon Vasthi the queen . . . And they answered, Queen Vasthi hath not only injured the king, but also all the people and princes that are in all the provinces . . . For this deed of the queen will go abroad to all women, so that they will despise their husbands, and will say, King Ahasuerus commanded that Queen Vasthi should come in to him, and she would not. And by this example all the wives of the princes of the Persians and the Medes will slight the commandments of their husbands: wherefore the king's indignation is just . . . Let it be written according to the law of the Persians and of the Medes, which must not be altered, that Vasthi come in no more to the king, but another, that is better than her, be made queen in her place. And let this be published through all the provinces of thy empire (which is very wide), and let all wives, as well of the greater as of the lesser, give honour to their husbands . . . And the king sent letters to all the provinces . . . in diverse languages and character, that the husbands should be rulers and masters in their houses: and that this should be published to every people.

Soon after, several beautiful virgins were brought to the city of Shushan by the king's commandment – among them Esther, a Jewess, escorted by her uncle, Mordechai. Within a year all had become concubines except Esther, the new queen. Meanwhile Haman, King Ahasuerus' favourite, was plotting to kill all Jews in the empire. To choose a suitable date, 'the lot was cast into an urn, which in Hebrew is called Phur, and there came out the twelfth month, which is called Adar . . . And letters sealed with the king's ring were sent by his messengers to all provinces, to kill and destroy all the Jews, both young and old, little children, and women in one day . . . and to make a spoil of all their goods.'

With some difficulty, Mordechai persuaded his niece to risk her life by begging the king to spare the Jews. Nervously, Esther invited Ahasuerus and Haman to a banquet at her palace and 'the king said to her, after he had drunk wine plentifully: What dost thou desire should be given thee? and for what thing askest thou? although thou shouldst ask the half of my kingdom, thou shalt have it'.

By now Haman's plot had become so tangled that Esther dithered and asked her guests to return next day for another banquet at which she would 'open her mind'. 'That night the king passed without sleep', doing important research on security matters. Then, as Haman's wife Zares warned him that things were getting dodgy, 'the king's eunuchs came and compelled him to go quickly to the banquet which the queen had prepared. So the king and Haman went in, to drink with the queen. And the king said to her again, after he was warm with wine: "What is thy petition Esther, that it may be granted thee?"'

Here the pace quickens as Ahasuerus gives Haman's house to Esther and commands that his favourite 'be hanged on a gibbet because he durst lay hands on the Jews'.

Many more letters were written, this time ordering 'the Jews in every city . . . to kill and destroy all their enemies with their women and children and all their houses . . . So the swift posts went out to rulers over the 127 provinces from India even to Ethiopia and the king's edict was hung up in Shushan and all the city rejoiced and was glad . . . Through all the provinces the Jews slew their enemies and persecutors; insomuch that the number of them that were killed amounted to 75,000, and no man took any of their goods.' (Who knows what to make of ancient statistics? Did Xerxes really send 2,641,610 men marching across the Hellespont on that immortal bridge of boats? Or did Herodotus enjoy inventing such improbably precise figures?)

> They that were killing in the city of Shushan, were employed in the slaughter on the 13th and 14th day of Adar: and on the fifteenth day they rested. And therefore they appointed that day to be a holy day of feasting and gladness . . . And since that time these days are called Phurim, that is, of lots: because Phur, the lot, was cast into the urn . . . these are the days which shall never be forgot: and which all provinces in the whole world shall celebrate throughout all generations: neither is there any city wherein the days of Phurim must not be observed by the Jews, and by their posterity, which is bound to these ceremonies.

One wonders, what became of Vasthi? There must be some associated legends. Was she reduced to permanent concubinage? Or did she continue along her pioneering route, perhaps inspiring other, nameless feminists?

Some Jews believe that Queen Esther asked her son Darius to organise her (and Mordechai's) burial near Baram village in the Upper Galilee. That coterie was miffed on 9 December 2008 when the Iranian government added the putative tomb of uncle and niece to their National Heritage List. A simple but conspicuous domed brick structure, of unknown but very distant date, it was first noted by Benjamin of Tudela, a famous twelfth-century Jewish traveller. It stands near Hamadan, supposedly the site of Shushan, some 20 miles west of Teheran. In March 1963 I paused to picnic beside it, on my way to India. Iranian Jews still gather here annually to celebrate Purim.

Over the millennia this minor religious festival has morphed into Judaism's major public event, a noisy, gaudy carnival with floats and bands and parades, and mythical creatures on stilts, and adults and children dancing impromptu all over the place. Traditionally, families improvised their own costumes but by now consumerism has taken over. On 6 March *Ha'aretz* quoted Arik Gabison, CEO of the Kfar Hasha'ashuim toy-store chain, who boasted that 60–79 million shekels were being spent annually on Purim toys and accessories.

This is the one day in the year when devout Jews are not merely allowed but encouraged to drink alcohol. The Talmud directs them to imbibe so freely 'that we cannot tell the difference between cursing Haman and blessing Mordecai'. Yet in H2 I saw few drunks among the settler throngs, from all over the OPT, who had gathered to make merry under the aegis of their Patriarchs and Matriarchs – and to honour their hero/saint, Baruch Goldstein, who on Purim 1994 was 'employed in the slaughter' of 'the Jews' enemies'.

At that date Avirama Golan was reporting for *Ha'aretz* from the Haredi city of Bnei Brak where the mayor had hired a special IDF unit (religious veterans only) to maintain order and modesty. She described how news of Goldstein's crime was received on the streets. A security guard shouted to his mate, 'A Purim miracle, I'm telling you, a Purim miracle! That holy man did something great. Fifty-two Arabs at one stroke, God has helped.' There were many rejoicing that 'God Himself ordained a well-deserved punishment of the Arabs'. Others remained silent. Next evening Avirama attended a concert featuring a famous religious jazz singer, Mordechai Ben-David. 'After the performance some people reminisced that more Gentiles (75,000) had been killed by the Jews in Shushan during the original Purim. They therefore, reasoned that this was the right time to kill a comparable number of Gentiles in the holy land.' (*Ha'aretz*, 28 February 1994.) Dov Halvertal, a relatively moderate member of the NRP, soon after told Avirama – 'This Purim joy epitomizes the moral collapse of religious Zionism . . . If it doesn't undertake soul-searching right now, I doubt if it will ever have another opportunity.' But soul-searching was not on any of the relevant agendas.

Another *Ha'aretz* contributor, Rami Rosen, asked:

> Is it only by chance that Goldstein massacred his victims on the Purim holiday? A check of the main facts of the (Jewish) historiography of the last 1500 years shows the picture is different from the one previously shown to us. It includes massacres of Christians by Jews, mock repetitions of the crucifixion of Jesus that usually took place on Purim . . . assassinations of adulterous women in synagogues and/or the cutting of their noses by command of the rabbis. (15 November 1996)

Most of those mock crucifixions took place in the Middle Ages though a few were recorded in sixteenth-century Poland.

In *Jewish Fundamentalism in Israel* by Israel Shahak and Norton Mezvinsky I read that 'From the eleventh century until the nineteenth, Ashkenazi Jews were more violent and fanatical than were the Oriental Jews . . . The influence of Christian fanaticism on the Jews may have been a cause.'

Rami Rosen, using research by Professor Ze'ev Gris of the Department of Jewish Thought at Ben-Gurion University, recounts the sad fate of Rabbi Avraham Cohen. In 1848, in Lemberg (then part of Austria), this modernist scholar, supported by enlightened Jews, tried to introduce certain reforms. Five orthodox Jewish notables at once resolved to 'take him out' and their campaign gruesomely foreshadowed the prologue to Yitzhak Rabin's assassination.

First [writes Rosen], they put placards in the synagogues inciting Jews to spit in his face and stone him. When the persecution increased, Cohen's friends asked him to agree to his being guarded all the time; he refused, saying he did not believe that Jews would kill him. The next placards said plainly, 'he is one of those Jewish sinners for which the Talmud says their blood is permitted' (that is, every Jew can and should kill them). Another placard asked, 'Will a Jew be found who will liberate us from the rabbi who destroys his congregation?' The fanatics first decided the assassination would take place during Purim in 1848; they even cast lots to determine who would have the honour of murdering the rabbi, but their plans went awry . . . On 6 September, however, a Jewish assassin successfully entered the rabbi's home unseen, went to the kitchen and put arsenic poisoning in the pot of soup . . . Shortly thereafter, Rabbi Cohen and his little daughter died. The Hassids and their leaders did not attend the funeral; they celebrated. No Orthodox rabbi, moreover, uttered one word of condemnation, neither of murderous incitement nor of the murder itself. Many nationalist Jews who were not Orthodox shared in being silent.

In a chapter entitled 'The Real Significance of Baruch Goldstein', Shahak and Mezvinsky tell us what the international media failed to report. We heard much about President Weizman's 'heartfelt shock' on being told of the murders. We heard nothing about his friendly discussions with the criminal's family, and Kach comrades, about how best to organise a suitable cortege. Kiryat Arba's mayor, Tzvi Katzover, warned the President by telephone that unless the funeral was allowed to parade through all of Hebron 'the settlers would make a pogrom of Arabs'. General Yatom, the area commander, in principle had no objection to this route but feared 'disorder'. Weizman announced, 'The army should pay respect to the desires and sensibilities of the settlers and of the Goldstein family.' After further negotiations he decided on a compromise: the funeral could wind solemnly through Jerusalem, where the police would close all main streets to traffic. To win acceptance for this arrangement General Yatom, in person, had to plead with the Kach leaders – not once, but day after day.

Before the funeral began several prominent rabbis praised Goldstein's 'Patriarch's Cave operation'. Rabbi Israel Ariel reminded everyone that 'The Jews will inherit the land not by any peace agreement but only by shedding blood.' Ben-Shoshan Yeshu'a urged young Jews to follow 'the holy martyr's' example. Yeshu'a belonged to an underground terrorist organisation and had been sentenced to life imprisonment for murder but released after a few years' confinement in a luxury hotel.

The cortege was followed through Jerusalem by Kahane disciples continuously chanting, 'Death to the Arabs!' Many of these mourners were identified by journalists as 'wanted' men but the police pretended not to recognise them. In Kiryat Arba Rabbi Dov Lior eulogised 'Baruch Goldstein of blessed memory who dedicated himself to helping others'. A few years previously the Mengelesque Lior had advocated the use of live Arab 'terrorists' for medical experiments.

After the burial, the IDF guarded Goldstein's Kiryat Arba grave. Chief-of-Staff Barak explained, 'The army was afraid Arabs would desecrate Goldstein's tomb and carry away his corpse.'

A journalist, Nahum Barnea, asked Rabbi Moshe Levinger if he felt sorry about the massacre. Gush Emunim's leader replied, 'I am sorry not only about dead Arabs but also about dead flies.' For months after the crime, settler children all over the OPT wore buttons proclaiming 'Dr Goldstein cured Israel's ills'. Concerts of Jewish religious music became semi-hysterical tributes to 'a righteous man'. All such demonstrations were widely reported in the Hebrew media, yet no major politician criticised them.

Teddy Preuss, then one of Israel's most forthright political com-mentators, wrote in *Davar* (4 March 1994):

> Let us not devalue Goldstein by comparing him with an inquisitor or a Muslim Jihad fighter. Whenever an infidel was ready to convert to either Christianity or Islam, an inquisitor or Muslim Jihad Fighter would, as a rule, spare his life. Goldstein and his admirers are not interested in converting Arabs to Judaism . . . They see the Arabs as

nothing more than disease-spreading rats, lice or other loathsome creatures; exactly how the Nazis saw the Jews.

As Shahak and Mezvinsky point out, those familiar with Goldstein's career understand the IDF's subservience. Soon after his immigration from Brooklyn he was posted, as a conscript/doctor, to the Lebanon where he declared, 'I am not willing to treat any non-Jew. I recognise as legitimate only two authorities: Maimonides and Kahane.' He was hurriedly moved to another battalion when three nervous Druze soldiers begged their commander to replace him. In both the conscript army and the reserves he continued to serve as a doctor though he re-emphasised to all his commanders that for religious reasons he could never treat Arabs, however ill or wounded.

Amir Oren, the *Ha'aretz* military correspondent, reported that in 1984 the national unity government's Defence Minister, Yitzhak Rabin, and the Chief-of-Staff, General Moshe Levy, considered Goldstein's refusal to treat gentiles and the wish of the artillery and medical corps commanders to court-martial him. Easily done, those officers thought – but 'Goldstein was then already protected by highly placed people in senior ministries. Those patrons requested that he be allowed to serve in Kiryat Arba rather than in a combat battalion'. Here was 'a bone of contention between the commander of the army's medical corps and its chief rabbi'. Oren gets angry at this stage:

> The issue of what to do with an officer who openly refused to obey orders by invoking Halacha has never been resolved . . . Why was no order to court-martial him ever issued by the entire chain of the army command? . . . Why did they refuse to decide without first consulting the chief rabbi? . . . The fear of publicity time after time prompted the army commanders to give in to all kinds of Goldsteins, rather than to denounce their views and court-martial them.

In Shahak and Mezvinsky's view, outsiders and most secular Zionists are too unworried by Israel's fundamentalists, who are developing more and more political muscle. They cannot be dismissed as a fanatical fringe, tiresomely noisy and occasionally disruptive but a nuisance rather than a problem. The writers remind us that Yigal Amir is a talmudic scholar trained in a *yeshiva*. He and his many sympathisers justified Rabin's murder by referring to two halachic laws: 'The Law of the Pursuer' and

'The Law of the Informer'. The first 'commands every Jew to kill or to wound severely any Jew who is perceived as intending to kill another Jew . . . It is enough if rabbinic authorities announce that the law of the pursuer applies to such a person'. The second law 'commands every Jew to kill or severely wound any Jew who . . . without rabbinical authority, has informed non-Jews . . . about Jewish affairs or has given them information about Jewish property or delivered Jewish persons or property to their rule or authority'. In the months preceding Rabin's assassination messianic agitators incessantly applied both these laws to their Prime Minister. All religious Jews regard all of the Holy Land as Jewish property – and the Oslo Accords, signed by Rabin, purported to give Palestinians some degree of autonomy on the West Bank. Therefore he should be 'pursued' as an 'informer'. Levinger so described him – and all officials willing to negotiate with Palestinians. Pre-assassination, Professor Asa Kasher of Tel Aviv University, a scholar respected throughout Israel, warned the public about the mortal danger implied in the halachic terms being used by Gush Emunim. Everyone ignored him, including Shabak, the force responsible for Rabin's safety; they believed him to be at risk only from Palestinian terrorists.

Shahak and Mezvinsky write:

> The reason for the wilful ignorance of this danger, shared by many Israeli Jews, including Rabin himself, was in our view Jewish chauvinism . . . The chauvinists falsify the history of their nation in order to make it appear better than it really was. They also falsify the current situation by claiming that their nation is the best . . . a claim especially virulent, because the identification between Jewish religion and Jewish nationality has prevailed for so long and still prevails among many Jews. It should not be forgotten that democracy and the rule of law were brought into Judaism from the outside. Before the advent of the modern state, Jewish communities were mostly ruled by rabbis who employed arbitrary and cruel methods as bad as those employed by totalitarian regimes. The dearest wish of the current Jewish fundamentalists is to restore this state of affairs . . . The dangers of their being established in Israel as at least part of the ruling power are great.

By 1984, Gush Emunim had founded the Yeshi Council, launched an official journal, and fostered the 'Jewish Underground'. Since 1977 its core members had been plotting to blow up the Mosque of Omar (the Dome of the Rock) and in 1984 they were caught planting bombs under six Jerusalem buses, bombs timed to explode on the Sabbath when (good) Jews may not travel by motor vehicle. This plot had been given a rabbinical blessing yet Rabin, Shamir and Peres, colleagues in the government, directed the police not to investigate those rabbis.

The authors of *Lords of the Land*, by Idith Zertal and Akiva Eldar, consider the Jewish Underground deserving of attention partly because of

the forgiveness that was granted them by the political establishment and by Israeli society as a whole. This preferential treatment in favour of messianic nationalists . . . accorded with the preferential treatment that the settlers had always enjoyed. The people of the Jewish terror group . . . came from the best families of settler society and the heart of the believing establishment . . . Most of them were funded by the government and held jobs as public officials . . . With the help of the army and with its weapons, the settlers' militias arose . . . When the day came for justice to be applied, these people won far more than the formal pardons and decreased sentences that was granted them. They were heroes, and not only amid their own ranks.

I sometimes wandered through the Avraham Avinu settlement – neat, grimly angular, stone-faced. There I rarely met anyone but was all the time aware of being observed from the windows of this confined, barricaded, fraught neighbourhood. A new Play Center, equipped with too much garish plastic fun-furniture, proclaimed its gratitude to Ruth and Hyman Simon. I was photographing the Shalhavet memorial plaque when a second-floor window opened and a woman yelled angrily, then was replaced by a man pointing an Uzi. I trotted out of their sight with a certain lack of dignity.

A Palestinian sniper killed Shalhavet, the infant daughter of Yitzhak and Oriya Pass, as the family walked towards Oriya's parents' home. That was in March 2001 when settlers were again attempting to seize Abu Snina, a nearby neighbourhood long disputed. The single bullet, fired from Abu Snina, was aimed at a member of the Bat Ayyin terrorist group; it wounded his leg while smashing his daughter's skull. Instantly neighbours grabbed her body; it could not be buried, they said, until the IDF had been allowed to occupy Abu Snina on their behalf. They erected a protest tent and launched a week-long revenge rampage, looting shops and burning *waqf* buildings. Emunah Elon, a settler journalist, elucidated:

> Oriya and Yitzhak Pass decided to delay the burial of their sweet infant because they wanted to donate her dear organs to save the sick body of the State of Israel . . . The settlements, and especially the one in Hebron, are a reflection in miniature of the Jewish state: a tiny island surrounded by a huge and hostile Arab ocean . . . The injury to the dignity of this particular dead child would apparently have been much greater had the adults hastened to bury her body and cover her screaming and weeping blood.
>
> (*Yedioth Aharanoth*, 28 March 2001)

Meanwhile Israel's Foreign Ministry, with Pass family encouragement, was distributing to the international media photographs of Shalhavet's shattered skull, taken immediately after her death. As Akiva Eldar wrote, 'The dead baby was not only a political tool in the hands of the settlers but a propaganda tool in the hands of the State.'

Two months later two Palestinians were killed near Hebron by shots from a passing car. Three days after that shots from another passing car wounded three more. When a third passing car fired at a Hebron firm's commercial vehicle, killing one and wounding two, the Shalhavet-Gil'ad Brigades explained – 'It's a revenge attack.' (Gil'ad Zar, of the sinister Itamar settlement near Nablus, had been shot dead by a Palestinian in May 2001.)

Yitzhak Pass was arrested three months after his daughter's death, following another revenge attack on a car carrying seven members of the Timzi family to a wedding. Three were killed, including a six-months-old baby girl; the rest spent weeks in hospital. For this ambush 'The Committee for the Defence of the Roads' claimed responsibility. Oriya Pass said, 'Never in his life would Yitzhak ask anyone to avenge Shalhavet's death. But we don't weep over an Arab child who is killed and it doesn't matter what the circumstances are. I have no sorrow about an Arab child who is killed. They are our enemies.'

In July 2002 the career soldier Elazar Leibowitz was shot dead by Palestinians as he drove towards Yatta, just south of Hebron, on the eve of his twenty-first birthday. In the car behind his a settler family was killed: Hannah and Yosef Dickstein and their small son, Shuv-El. The settlers' newspaper recalled that Leibowitz was born on the anniversary of the 1929 riot and had repeatedly expressed a longing 'to die in the sanctification of the Holy Name and to be buried as befits a martyr . . . to shock the nation and impel it to act to eradicate the shame [of 1929] and restore confidence and security, pride and tranquillity to the Jewish people'. Leibowitz was buried, as he had requested, beside the '1929 Martyrs' Plot' in the old cemetery. During his funeral an eight-year-old Palestinian boy was stabbed to death and many Palestinian homes and shops were vandalised and looted amidst indiscriminate gunfire which killed a fourteen-year-old girl and wounded ten adults.

At the end of the '90s Natenel Ozeri, a fervent young follower of Meir Kahane and Baruch Goldstein, set up an outpost near Hebron known as Plot 26. He had his own fervent followers among the 'hilltop youth' and he ignored several High Court of Justice orders to move. When two Palestinians shot up his mobile home in January 2003 he died beside his injured five-year-old daughter. His widow, Livnat, was the daughter of a Shaul Nir terrorist who earned a life-sentence in the mid-'80s by helping to kill students in Hebron's Islamic College. (That was in revenge for the killing of six *yeshiva* students outside Beit Hadassah.) Livnat wanted to bury Natenel beside their hero, Goldstein; his father wanted him buried in Jerusalem. By way of compromise, Livnat decided that his remains should rest on Plot 26, to seal 'a covenant of blood with the sacred land on which the Patriarchs trod'. But no – Rabbi Dov Lior intervened in favour of Hebron's old cemetery. The frenzied Ozeri funeral has become legendary. Its start was delayed for hours, until the IDF allowed the illegal Kach movement to play a part. When the CO gave in and the Kach hordes swarmed onto the scene they seized Natenel's corpse from the truck-hearse, insisted it must be buried on Plot 26 and, showing contempt for Jewish law, exposed the face 'because he is a martyr'. For the next twelve hours they dragged their 'martyr' around the countryside, damaging many acres of Palestinian crops and fighting their way through checkpoints and over roadblocks. By midnight 800 soldiers had been deployed, their arrival provoking the customary yells – 'Nazi! Nazi!' When at last the body-snatchers gave in Natenel ended up in the old cemetery, to Rabbi Lior's satisfaction.

These are but a few of many bizarre funeral dramas inspired by the settlers' 'sanctification through bloodshed' death cult.

*

Occasionally I patronised the Gutnick Center, hoping to get into conversation with a few settlers – so unapproachable on the street. 'Diamond Joe' Gutnick, an Australian mining tycoon and enthusiastic funder of settlements, is commemorated by this small café-cum-souvenir shop between Shuhada Street and the Street of Prayer. Above the entrance a misleading notice says 'All are Welcome!' On my first visit, at opening time, the dreary café was empty. A teenage boy, made girlish-looking by long curly ear-locks, scuttled away to find the 'in-charge', a puny little man who wore a striped apron and had hardly enough hair left to accept his kippa's paper-clips. He was distantly polite, with downcast eyes. From the microwave he served instant coffee and a chocolate pastry, then disappeared into the kitchen until another customer arrived, a tall young man wearing prayer gear and a stern expression. He sat with his back to me, as far as possible from the gentile.

An appeal leaflet came with my order – 'Dear Visitor, You have an opportunity to ADOPT A SOLDIER. Buy a coupon in the cafeteria for a Family Size Pizza & Bottle of Drink *for just 65 nis* and give the coupon to a soldier. On behalf of the soldiers, we thank you.' Decorating the margins were seven photographs of smiling conscripts all with the Tombs in the background. A young woman opened the shop as I was leaving. Its souvenirs seem like an overflow from Jerusalem's tourist beat: Judaica such as miniature mezuzas, hand-of-God amulets, messianic bumper stickers, kabbalistic charms, menorah brooches and earrings, havala spice boxes, shofars (when real a luxury, when plastic repellent), posters of (in)famous rabbis, tapes of Jewish folk songs and Sabbath hymns all labelled in English, postcards unblemished by anything Islamic like a minaret, yarmulkes, camel T-shirts (no Bedouins included) and Nike T-shirts inscribed 'Just Jew It!' One can also buy costly but well-regarded local wines which would have tempted me but for their provenance.

Despite my failure to 'consume' on the premises, I was presented with a copy of *Hebron Today* (winter 2009) – in its way a thought-provoking publication. One double-page spread shows the Hebron Fund's 'Gala Anniversary Dinner' attended by 700 guests (exuding respectable prosperity) in the New York Marriott Marquis's main ballroom. The Master of Ceremonies, Mr Ben Brafman, Esq. (*sic*), spoke of 'our debt to the brave people on the front line in Hebron who preserve and protect our heritage'.

David Wilder, 'Spokesman of the Jewish Community of Hebron', commented on the Beit Ha'shalom crisis:

During a radio interview with the BBC, I was asked about our future plans. When I responded that we would continue to purchase property in Hebron, the interviewer asked, 'But won't that just cause more violence?' I answered, 'If I bought a home in London and was told that a Jew purchasing on that side of the city would cause a violent reaction, how would that be viewed? Probably as anti-Semitism and racism. Why then can't a Jew buy property in Hebron, just as people purchase homes all over the world?' It should be clear. Hebron's Jewish community opposes and rejects any and all violence aimed at innocent people, be they Arabs, Jews or anyone else.

Rabbi Simcha Hochbaum, Director of Hebron Tourism, contributed his mite:

We read in the Torah of Moshe's role in redeeming the Jewish people from Egyptian exile . . . 'Moshe grew up, went out to his brothers and saw their suffering' . . . We hope and pray that our elected leaders . . . can feel the pain of their fellow Jews. In Moshe's case, this realisation led to 'He smote the Egyptian and hid his body in the sand'. We expect our leaders to bury the Hamas terror infrastructure deep in the sands of Gaza.

A young woman supplied the main article; she had been awarded a trip to Hebron after working for three years in the Hebron Fund's US head office. Her fantasy-world chilled me.

In Hebron you are not only surrounded by Arab hilltops all around, but the Jews living in Hebron are living amongst the Arabs. Their next door neighbours, walking down the path together, kids going to school, or just playing outside, they are constantly surrounded. The Jews are not called heroes for nothing. Their whole life is filled with purpose. They are living on a higher plane . . . Living in such close proximity to the Ma'arat Hamachpela – what more can you ask for when raising a family and trying to instil the precious values of our Torah young children? The Jewish families living in Hebron truly 'walk the walk' in every sense . . . We must be so thankful and grateful to our brothers and sisters living on the front line, enabling us to come

and visit our Patriarchs and Matriarchs . . . There are truly
no words to describe the spiritual feelings and emotions that one
experiences . . . to breathe in that special air, to live that life of self-
sacrifice for a higher purpose and truth, to stand united and show
courage to those living there on a daily basis!

And there is much more, three euphoric pages proving how well
'Hebron Tourism' does *hasbara*.

Gazing at the 700 donors assembled in New York's Marriott Marquis,
I wondered – why are most of the Hebron/Kiryat Arba settlers US-
born? What makes so many US-born Jews feel a compulsion to invade
Al-Khalil's Old City? Why don't more Israeli Jews hear their brethren's
blood crying out from the earth of Hebron? Then I remembered bits of
Yitzhak Rabin's apparently impassioned outburst in the Knesset three
days after Goldstein's massacre. 'The murderer', said he, 'emerged from
a small and limited political sector in the people. He grew up in a
swamp that has its source in foreign lands as well as here. They are alien
to Judaism, they are not part of us. To him and his ilk we say today: You
are not part of the community of Israel . . . You are not partner to the
Zionist deed. You are a foreign body, you are pernicious weeds. Sane
Jewry vomits you from its midst.'

CHAPTER 19

Into the Hebron Hills

'It won't cheer you up,' said Raouf, 'but you need to see it.' So off we went by taxi, into the South Hebron Hills. I already knew our daring taxi-driver, Mazin, a friend of many Co-op Club members. Not all Hebronites cared to run the settlement gauntlet in a region where several ISMers, EAs and other defenders of the Palestinians have been badly beaten up.

Without the settlements, these austere hills might attract coachloads of tourists to delight in the scattered Roman remains, in Samu''s home-woven carpets, At-Tuwani's traditional embroidery, the Canaanite ruins in underground galleries, the fourth-century synagogue, the Umayyad mosque still in use, the Nabatean-style cave dwellings also still in use – some disguised by the addition of, as it were, a sun-room. And all these treasures are packed into less than 30 square miles at the southern end of the West Bank.

We paused in Yatta, the region's once-prosperous market town (population 40,000). As Raouf led me towards a cluster of famed Byzantine dwellings, destitution was everywhere evident and the atmosphere felt sullen. Since the early years of this century the pace of settlement construction has been quickening, encouraged by the appointment of Ron Schechner, a settler leader, as deputy to the Defence Minister, Shaul Mofaz. This colonel in the reserves lives in Yattir settlement and zealously promotes the IDF–Gush Emunim partnership.

Our destination was Umm al-Khair, a Bedouin community of about 130 refugees living in improvised shelters – not substantial enough to be called 'shacks' – on a flat expanse of stony desert. Less than 100 yards away, beyond a barbed wire fence, stands the new settlement of Karmel, a symmetrical row of red-roofed, mass-produced homes presided over – dwarfed by – a hi-tech water tower. The Bedouin must buy water from a tanker.

Taxis are rare around Umm al-Khair and from within their shelters of tin and sacking hungry-looking children peeked out: half-scared, half-excited. Their mothers didn't appear. The menfolk greeted Raouf warmly but were ill at ease with the unknown female. We sat outside the Sheikh's shelter, the visitors on those ubiquitous white plastic chairs, and gradually Raouf approached his task: to enthuse the young men about a proposed kindergarten. Nearby, a derelict four-room house (very small rooms) had been donated to the community by a local farmer – now living in Al-Khalil, all his land lost. It could become a kindergarten if local labour restored it, using foreign funds to buy the materials. Support had been promised from UNRWA, England, Australia and the Villages' Group who had initiated the project.

The Villages' Group is a joint Palestinian/Israeli organisation founded in 2003 to help the Hebron Hills' most needy communities. In the Club I had heard UNRWA being angrily criticised for its neglect of these Bedouins who have few communication skills of their own and few friends to speak up for them. However, Israeli NGOs such as Rabbis for Human Rights and B'Tselem do all they can – as do several brave Israeli freelancers, people like Raouf's old friend Ezra Nawi, whose decrepit little car we had seen parked near Samu'. Ezra was said to be the most popular Israeli in the OPT. 'It's hard to think of him as an Israeli,' said Raouf. 'Maybe because he was reared by a granny who could only speak Arabic. His parents came from Iraq in '51, the year before he was born. He's a very determined activist and not ashamed of being gay.'

In 2007 Ezra attempted to save from demolition the shelter of a particularly vulnerable Umm al-Khair family. He was arrested and convicted of assaulting two Border Police but only given a one-month sentence; among his vigorously vocal defenders were Noam Chomsky, Peter Tatchell and Naomi Klein. In 1997 he had received a six-month sentence for having an improper relationship with a fifteen-year-old Palestinian boy. Raouf did not mention that fact but it emerged two years later when David Norris was running for the Irish Presidency. He seemed likely to win until someone revealed that in 1997 he had written to the Jerusalem High Court requesting a non-custodial sentence for his former partner. Luckily Ireland had another, equally admirable candidate, but this anti-Norris campaign exacerbated the bad smell coming from the dead Celtic Tiger.

When we left Umm al-Khair Raouf suggested a two-mile détour to introduce me to 'a hero friend of mine in At-Tuwani. A shepherd, old as you and four times beaten up – *still* taking out his sheep! There's no choice of grazing. He must stop shepherding or risk more injuries – he'd get a VC in the British Army!'

Here Mazin went on strike. For him At-Tuwani and the adjacent settlement of Ma'on – and the Ma'on Farm outpost – constituted a no-go area where taxis carrying Internationals were quite likely to be stoned. Although Nablus is surrounded by settlements – some notoriously aggressive – it seemed to me the South Hebron Hills implants were even more pernicious. Perhaps because of that Patriarchal miasma . . .

On our way back (following a newish road built for settlers but on which Palestinians are allowed) Raouf recalled one of his most painful encounters with the IDF. A few months previously bulldozers had arrived to raze half of Umm al-Khair's shelters – the half closest to Karmel – and to extend that settlement's land, moving the fence. Activists had been alerted and Raouf was not the only witness. Two Palestinian lawyers and several representatives of Israeli and international human rights organisations stood impotently watching the IDF-protected bulldozers at work. Video cameras recorded the crime – a futile gesture which amused the conscripts. But it comforted the victims to know that this evidence, shown to the world on YouTube, would corroborate their own equally futile complaints. Raouf said, 'For me this was a torture of frustration. Because I know "the world" doesn't care. And the Zionists know the world doesn't care. That's why the IDF laughs at all those busy cameras.'

Back in H2 I thanked my companion and added, 'You were right, today did not cheer me up.'

(There is a positive footnote. Umm al-Khair's young men made an outstanding success of the kindergarten project; on my brief visit to Hebron in December 2010, Raouf showed me photographs of the inauguration party at which, for diplomatic reasons, UNRWA was given more praise than it had earned.)

Four days later, Faisal invited me to accompany him on a working tour of the Hills, including At-Tuwani.

Faisal is small, slight, pale and a workaholic. He explained, 'I know I can't achieve anything and I'm so crazed that makes me try harder.' He was born in Kuwait of Hebron parents – engineer father, teacher mother. In 1990 the Iraqis invaded and his family had to leave. He graduated from Berkeley just as it seemed (from a distance) that the Oslo Accords might work. Having never seen his native country he found a UN job and chose to work in Al-Khalil, to the delight of his extended family. He and his beautiful wife (much younger, not an English-speaker) lived in a simple but spacious flat over an H1 suburban corner shop. On my last visit I sat beside Faisal's tightly packed bookshelves, making an 'essential reading' list, while a toddler untied my bootlaces. This congenial home afforded soothing breaks from H2's highly charged emotions.

In Faisal's massive UN SUV we took the rough Palestinian road to Yatta. Hereabouts there are few apartheid roads 'for Israelis only'. 'But soon we'll have them,' said Faisal. 'Further north they're important in the "transfer" strategy.' Indicating the grey barren hills, he lamented their dwindling sheep flocks, under threat not only from a four-year drought, which left fodder unaffordable, but from the settlers' poisoning of wells and crops. One scoffs at Christianity's anti-Semitic slanders which include accusing Jews of poisoning wells during the Black Death. Now I said to Faisal, 'Maybe there was a *little* fire, making all that smoke.'

We stopped for an hour or so in a village on a steep mountainside near Yatta. Here Faisal was organising the building of a new hamlet to house six families. Those 45 people, displaced by settlers in 2005, were so unwelcome in this wretchedly impoverished place that serious feuding had developed. They urgently needed to move on.

While waiting I strolled between substantial old houses, now disintegrating, where the half-starved children looked hostile. It astonished me to come upon eight glossy, long-haired nanny goats in a clean, stone-walled enclosure guarded by a bony and xenophobic lurcher. These were communal property, the village's main source of cash.

Back at the SUV, Faisal was being bullied by an angry community leader unprepared to be cooperative about anything. 'It's what settlements do,' my companion observed wearily as we drove on. 'History tells the Hebron Hills were tranquil before the Nakba.'

A narrow bumpy track took us up to the cave-dwellers' district of At-Tuwani, dangerously overlooked by Ma'on settlement, hidden amidst its trees on the nearby hilltop. In times past the caves, and a scattering of small dwellings amidst large boulders, housed about 1,200 wheat and sheep farmers. Now fewer than 250 remain, being protected and supported by North American Christian Peacemaker Teams (CPT). These live on the spot – two at a time – with no mod cons, in a caravan-sized hut on a mountain ledge. When we arrived the pair currently on duty were at the local branch of the Women's Co-op and I regretted not meeting them. CPT volunteers have been working in the Hebron Hills, and in H2, since 1995. They are indomitable defenders of Palestinians and rarely emerge undamaged from their At-Tuwani ordeal. Several have been seriously injured: broken ribs, a fractured skull, a ruptured kidney, usually the result of attacks as they escort children to school. Latterly the IDF, supervised by the CPT, have been acting as escorts, driving jeeps at walking speed before and after the pupils.

Where the track ends, and a footpath to Ma'on begins, a new clinic had been built but not yet opened. It was a neat little structure, blending into the landscape – but the settlers disapproved. Threats had been issued. Anyone brave enough to staff it would need more robust guarding than CPT could provide.

Faisal wanted me to photograph a cave dwelling but I refused. These people have enough to put up with, don't need their homes being gawped at by tourists. None of them speaks English and as Faisal listened to their news (always bad) I sat apart on a boulder, watching a youth brewing tea over a primus stove and brooding on the iniquity of settlers being generously subsidised. They receive unknown amounts of State (and other) funding. Unknown because the World Zionist Organisation and the Jewish Agency collude with government departments to keep things vague. When occasionally precise figures are revealed, many Israeli taxpayers register resentment. For instance, a Tel Aviv University researcher found that OPT local councils benefit from grants worth three or four times more than those awarded to undeveloped 'development towns'. In 2003 the Hebron Hills settlers received bonuses of US$1,360 per inhabitant, as compared to US$390 per Sderot inhabitant. Such bonuses are an investment in Zionism's long-term plan to rid the Holy Land of Palestinians – destroying, as they go, such anciently stable communities as the Hebron Hills shepherds, the fruit farmers around Qalqilya, the fishermen of Gaza.

On our way back to H2 I remarked that it seems to be my generation's fate to witness the sudden death of traditional communities. In Nepal I've seen it, and in Baltistan, Ethiopia, Madagascar, Laos.

'That's globalisation,' said Faisal. 'For us it's happening another way. Not through famine or civil wars or corporate exploitation. Zionism is different – the worst sort of colonialism, like the Spanish in South

America and the English in North America – get rid of the natives!
Zionists must do it more behind-the-scenes, with excuses like "security".
But the mindset is the same.'

Two English-speaking Co-op members, Sahar and Sireen, invited me to
their village ('where things are more calm') for a few days. We left H2 in
mid-afternoon, being driven by Bassam, Sahar's eldest son, in a 1970s
Ford saloon. The compliment misfired when I admiringly remarked
that Palestinians almost equal Cubans when it comes to contriving
vehicle longevity. Bassam yearned for a 2009 BMW.

Our pot-holed 'Palestinian' road, free of checkpoints, wound upwards
into the Hebron Hills at their steepest and rockiest but with some
skilfully terraced slopes. From one deep *wadi* rose thick clouds of black
smoke, polluting square miles. 'Settlers,' explained Sireen, pointing to
Otniel on its distant hilltop. 'They burn tons of tyres to spoil our
grazing.'

Where the Hills receded a long descent took us to our destination,
always referred to as a 'village' though by Irish standards it's quite a
large town, dispersed over undulating and poorly watered farmland. I
was to stay with Sahar's very extended family in an enormous one-
storey dwelling near the edge of a wide *wadi*. This home had gradually
expanded as rooms were added to an eighteenth-century core. Evidently
the pre-Occupation family was quite wealthy but now the Apartheid
Barrier, only a few miles away, has depleted everybody's resources. Yet
Sahar's clan could still grow enough food for domestic consumption
and milked its own goats – their kids bleating pathetically, confined to
a pen instead of bounding around the 'settled' hills. The innumerable
good-looking children were rosy-cheeked, with shiny hair and sound
teeth. As in Balata, I didn't even try to memorise names as they swarmed
in and out – or to unravel relationships. Polygamy gives rise to major
problems. One four-year-old romped happily with his two-year-old
uncle and the grizzled father of a three-month-old girl was also the great-
grandfather of an eighteen-month-old boy. (It's marvellous what a man
can do if he begins at seventeen and keeps it up till near on eighty.)
Two sisters, aged three-and-a-half and four-and-a-half, were among the
most ingenious troublemakers – attractively assertive personalities but
already being treated less tolerantly than the boys.

The adults ate separately, sitting cross-legged around a low table in a spacious inner room. Then we reclined on piled quilts, some sporadically watching TV: an Egyptian soap, Fox News, a Turkish cabaret show which would have poleaxed the most liberal of imams. At bedtime this room became the women's sleeping quarter; seven of us curled up beneath our ample quilts. I hoped my snoring wouldn't keep everybody awake.

While bread was being baked for breakfast I went walkabout, to the general puzzlement. Walking for fun (and with a *limp*, needing a *stick*) is just too eccentric . . .

A short steep track led down to the town's main street, lined with symptoms of a lost prosperity. Substantial two- and three-storey buildings (shops and offices below, homes and offices above) couldn't be maintained, three disused warehouses had been vandalised. Turning down a side street, I was between smaller, older dwellings, some roofs domed. Then came a few overgrown ruins with interesting arches – and amidst them a neglected USAID-donated 'Park and Playcenter', a disconcerting eruption of garish plastic. Why neglected, unused? Bassam had an answer: many Palestinians see USAID projects as condescending gestures, meant to impress people too dumb to see that Zionism couldn't have its way without another sort of US aid. As I photographed, a smiling elderly woman emerged from the nearest house and handed me a hot round of bread, seasoned with salt and herbs. 'Eat!' she said. 'You are welcome!' And before I could say '*Shukran!*' she was gone.

At various points, further on, steep tractor-made tracks led to the new houses of people uprooted from the Hebron Hills – all surrounded by litter and builders' rubble. Some had been abandoned when half-built, a common phenomenon in 'Developing Countries' and now quite common in my own bankrupt country. Later in the day, when I came the same way with my hostess on a round of extended family visits, she listed the main reasons for money running out: unexpected death – overambitious design – uncertain ownership of land causing expensive delays – other arcane legal disputes, with Ottoman roots, needing to be resolved by well-paid Koranic judges. Several of the most imposing villas were – according to Sahar – shoddily finished inside, with rudimentary lighting and plumbing, and ceilings and walls already damp-stained. She gave those details with malicious glee; the owners were either associated with the Ramallah mafia or suspect IDF informers. She identified the owner of a notably pretentious eyesore as an Oslo-enabled racketeer also well-known in Nablus. Such homes are regarded as sound investments by people whose incomes are not open to scrutiny. Given the OPT's jobless rate, labour is cheap and cut-price materials are readily available if you know your way around.

Where the town merged into farmland I sat on a dry-stone wall to eat my warm bread while enjoying the soft patter of unshod hooves on tarmac. The traffic consisted of one mini-tractor and many donkeys, some drawing carts loaded with antique ploughs, some ridden by elderly men going to weed minuscule ancestral olive groves. Soon schoolchildren appeared, walking in segregated groups or pairs, all clean and tidy, the older girls scarved, most of the older boys moustached; Intifada closures and other disruptions set their education back by three or four years. They eyed me uneasily, with intimations of hostility among the males – in marked contrast to the welcoming, interested older generations.

Returning by way of a long, high ridge, I could see how built-up this terrain has become, post-settlements. Three small towns – each ancient centre gathered around a mosque – have been linked by ribbon building achieved at the expense of formerly widespread olive groves. All those square, flat-roofed white cubes, scattered higgledy-piggledy across uneven ground, depressed me. But the displaced Hebron Hills villagers have to live somewhere . . .

We breakfasted on the verandah, a simple meal of new-baked *taboun*, dipped in olive oil and *za'atar* (a mix of freshly ground herbs and sesame seeds). All day a kettle of over-sweet tea was to hand. At intervals the turbulent juvenile tribe tried to teach me complicated card games, a task not simplified by my instructors speaking only Arabic.

The Occupation imposes a variety of disadvantages on everyone. Of the families we visited, most had health problems and couldn't afford appropriate treatment. In one home, the sixty-eight-year-old granny was dying of an undiagnosed lung disease. 'Probably cancer,' whispered Sireen. Her sister, living next door, spent all day lying flat on the living-room floor, immobilised by painfully swollen knees; she needed constant care, being unable to use the squat loo. Of her two resident daughters-in-law, one was slightly retarded. Sahar drew my attention to several congenital defects; she led a group of local women dedicated to the discreet discouragement of first-cousin marriages.

Uphill from my base, in a new 'Western' bungalow, lived a young PA government official whose teacher wife told me she was sad because he didn't want any more children; they only had two. Ahmed had just been presented with a bicycle (a rarity hereabouts) for his sixth birthday. Seven-and-a-half-year-old Hannan, on demanding a bike of her own, was told it's *haram* (bad, wrong, sinful) for females to cycle. She seemed to think a foreigner's intercession might help. As her brother trick-cycled around the concrete yard she held my hand tightly, looked up tearfully and said, '*Please* ask for me a bike!' At that moment Ahmed rode out onto the track, turned towards the motor road and chanced to meet a fourteen-year-old girl cousin. She grabbed him, shouting in alarm. He fought back, kicking and trying to bite, as a granny and an aunt rushed from behind the bungalow. Before they could reach the struggling pair Ahmed had broken free and was hurtling downhill. Then came the horror moment: we could see him speeding across the road only a few yards ahead of a cement truck. As he crashed into an open ditch his mother, aunt and cousin hastened to retrieve him. Granny, standing beside me, swayed and would have fallen if not supported.

The erosion of family discipline is another OPT problem. Sireen's youngest aunt (a fluent English-speaker) remarked that one can't fairly blame today's young parents. Of the Intifada generation, they grew up in a turmoil of violence, fear, tension and hate. A thirty-year-old father and twenty-five-year-old mother, likely by now to have three, four or even five children, were aged eight and three when the first Intifada began. Although that was a largely non-violent movement on the Palestinian side, the routine IDF responses were disproportionate and indiscriminate, not conducive to children's developing self-control and a respect for authority. And then, during that age group's adolescence came the savagery of the second Intifada.

A powerful gale made my afternoon walk across a rocky slope quite hazardous. Nowhere else have I encountered flying litter on this scale – a blitz of bags, bottles, cups, tins, junk-food packs, dried-out disposable nappies, socks, plastic shoes, garments, hunks and sheets of polystyrene. Soon my dust-filled eyes were sore and blood trickled from a slight tin-inflicted cut above my nose. Between the olive and fruit trees lay bits of cars, fridges, cookers, shredded mattresses, furniture – all the detritus of modern living without modern garbage collection. On my descent to the road I was twice mildly stoned, once by half-a-dozen primary school girls. At sunset, before our return to H2, this freakish gale dropped as suddenly as it had arisen.

The morrow was Mohammad's birthday (as authentic as 25 December) when Muslims from all over the region throng to Al-Khalil. Therefore Bassam's mature Ford was sensationally overcrowded: I had two babies on my lap and a toddler on my shoulders. Sahar told me that the UN Human Rights agency had negotiated a deal with the IDF and the settlers – for three midday hours Palestinian children could play on that grassy slope which used to be a public space. The synagogue would be closed, but all appeals to open Shuhada Street, allowing worshippers easier access to the mosque, had been rejected. And Kiryat Arba's 'prayer road' had been blockaded for the day.

Long before dawn thousands had assembled and at 7.00 a.m. an immeasurably long queue began to move through the narrow souk 'tunnel'. All were dressed in their best and many little girls proudly wore adult garb – covered from head to toe like their mothers but in brighter colours. Everybody had to go through the one-person metal turnstile, as slowing a barrier as could be devised, and another identical turnstile lay only twenty yards ahead.

I made my way through empty Shuhada Street to the settlers' area and sat at the edge of the park watching women and girls climbing a long outer stairway, leading to the purdah gallery. Later, talking to Raouf, I inanely marvelled – yet again – at the Palestinians' cheerful tolerance of inherently outrageous restrictions. He shrugged. 'On our happy day, showing anger about queuing would spoil things. And naturally people can seem resigned, after 42 years of repression. For most, this is how life has always been. We don't know about freedom, how it feels. But be aware – the anger is there, and growing.'

It could be said that Kiryat Arba and my daughter share a birthday. On 10 December 1968, as I lay in the labour ward of a Wimbledon hospital, Yigal Allon, the Hebron settlers' champion, was publicly proposing the construction of a Jewish town close to the Cave of the Patriarchs. Fifteen months later the Knesset approved a ministerial decision to establish Kiryat Arba, having spurned Uri Avnery's warning that any such development would 'damage the chances for peace in the region'.

The new town's 23-acre site, on a low hill fifteen minutes' walk from the Tombs of the Patriarchs, had been expropriated 'for military purposes' – illegally expropriated, according to Israel's High Court of

Justice. However – and not for the last time – they announced their judgement much too late, long after the hill had been stripped of its rightful owners' orchards and vineyards and 'cleansed' of their homes. While Palestinian labourers built apartment blocks the future residents were working in Jerusalem and an IDF officer noted, 'When Kiryat Arba is complete, the men will commute to Jerusalem and we'll have to protect the place so's Arabs won't harm the women and children.'

In June 1971 the first 50 families moved into housing units funded by Israeli taxpayers. As long as the OPT's formal political status remains unclear, the IDF's appropriation has no legal validity and tenants cannot buy their flats. Instead, token sums are paid monthly to the Ministry of Housing as 'rent'.

Kiryat Arba was born handicapped, disabled for years by government dissension about political control – Labour ministers versus national-religious ministers. Finally the Labour minister pronounced that all towns in IDF-held territory must be run by a local authority permanently under military surveillance. In those days some saw Kiryat Arba as an Israeli city-in-the-making. The original Hebron settlers wrote to the Prime Minister demanding its rapid expansion to 5,000 housing units for 100,000 Jews 'with industrial projects, a broad road and electricity, to put the Arab town in the shadow of the Jewish town' (*Ha'aretz*, 26 November 1972).

It was not to be. Kiryat Arba's vaunted attractions (pleasant climate, good soil, ample water, nearness to Jerusalem) never outweighed a realistic perception of *danger*. The population grew slowly to its present 6,500, of whom the majority are rabid rabbis and their students – all professional spongers on government ministries, chiefly the Ministry of Religious Affairs. Under the guidance of such teachers as Moshe Levinger, Eliezer Waldman and Dov Lior, fanaticism flourished and in due course several Jewish terrorist gangs were bred in these *yeshivas* and study houses. Residents attributed the construction of Kiryat Arba to a divine plan, reflected in the settlers' 'desire to have the privilege of taking part in the activity of redemption'.

The turn of the century saw many empty flats in Kiryat Arba – soon noticed by Shavei Israel, a privately funded NGO set up in 2004 by New York-born Michael Freund. He had made *aliyah* in 1995 and, while working in the Prime Minister's PR department, during Benjamin Netanyahu's first term of office, he began to fret about new data suggesting that the assimilation rate is 70% among Western Jews. To help compensate for that, while boosting Israel's Jewish population (slow-growing compared to its 'Arab' population), he set up his NGO. It soon had a dozen 'rabbinic educators' in its Jerusalem head office and teams of sleuths were Jew-tracking in nine countries. North-east India provided their major coup. There an unfortunate group of pale-skinned hill people with Mongoloid features somehow became convinced that they were descended from one of the Lost Tribes of Israel. These neophytes, known as Bnei Menashe, don't benefit from Zionism's 'Right of Return'. They must study in Israel (or the OPT) for a year before their 'conversion' and during this time are on tourist visas, ineligible for government assistance. Within Israel, only the under-populated development towns of Mitzpe Ramon and Dimona offered space – but couldn't afford maintenance. Hence the first 1,000 Menashe arrived in generously subsidised settler towns like Kiryat Arba and this enraged Shavei Israel's secular critics. Meir Sheetrit of the Interior Ministry (himself Moroccan-born) accused Freund of 'turning Israel into a foreign legion nation', plagued by 'various refugees claiming to be Jewish'. The next 450 Menashe were despatched to not-very-welcoming new Israeli towns like Karmiel (not to be confused with Karmel) and Upper Nazareth. According to Shavei Israel, another 7,000 longed to migrate to a country they'd never heard of before Freund's sleuths came on their scene. And doubtless there are potential immigrants among the 15,000 Subbotnik Jews, Russian peasants whose forefathers allegedly adopted Judaism at the beginning of the nineteenth century. And what of the so-called Bnei Anusim, whose ancestors were forcibly converted to Christianity by Spanish Inquisitors? Many of those hundreds of thousands may yet be tracked down in southern Italy and Sicily – especially if the recession continues to bite Europeans.

On hearing of my plan to visit Kiryat Arba, in search of a com-municative settlement leader, Raouf advised me not to walk; the security guards at the gate might turn back a solo foreigner without 'accreditation'.

At sunrise, seeing Gutnick's door open, I reckoned there was time for a cup of tea before the minibus arrived. But, as I entered, a dozen swaying men were beginning to chant, wrapped in their prayer-shawls (*tallits*, the corner fringes of which dangle below jackets all day). Hastily I retreated.

The settlers' transport to Kiryat Arba is free and would have taken me all the way to Jerusalem, stopping at other settlements en route. My fellow-passengers were two workmen, wearing knitted kippas, and a long-coated young woman clutching a prayer-book. All three pretended not to see me.

Walking from the bus stop to the centre, my first impression was of quite a pleasant town – wide, steep, tree-lined streets, litter-free grassy verges, three-storey stone-faced apartment blocks overlooking shrub-filled gardens. There was nobody to be seen until I met a clean-shaven man with a Brooklyn accent who responded amiably to my greeting and seemed ready to chat while his bulldog read a letter on a tree trunk. He had made *aliyah* with his parents as Kiryat Arba was being developed and felt drawn back after studying agronomy in the US. When I asked about the settlement's resources he replied, 'Here we grow nothing but we've land nearby for all our fruit and vegetable needs.' There was something artificially jovial about his manner but he seemed much less abnormal than H2's denizens. (In this context 'denizen' is peculiarly apt: 'a wild plant, probably foreign, that keeps its footing'.)

By 7.30 Kiryat Arba was coming to life: commuters driving in small elderly cars to Tel Aviv or Jerusalem, children going to school, their mothers going to a poorly stocked supermarket – and one of the mis-fortunate 'Menashe' imports leaving the bleak-looking 'Absorption Center', carrying a baby in a blanket on her back, pushing a toddler in a US-style buggy and followed by two small girls – identical twins. She wore such a sad expression that I scared her by stupidly trying to start a conversation. As part of her 'Absorption' process, she would be learning only Hebrew.

In the vast Cultural Center, showing no trace of any recent activity, a desiccated woman sat behind a distant desk frowning at a computer. She transferred the frown to me on being shown a letter from my publisher and hearing of my wish to talk with an English-speaking community leader. Returning the letter unread she advised, 'Go to Municipality.'

I asked, 'Where is it? In which direction?' She refocused on her computer and snapped, 'Outside.'

Seeking more precise guidance I approached three settlers who spoke no English but were not unfriendly. The fourth, a shuffling OAP leading an obese dachshund, growled 'Speak it with Hebrew!' then walked on.

The fifth, a young man *sans* beard or ear-locks and shouldering a daughter to play school, pointed to an ugly circular complex looming over the town centre: small shops below, offices above including the Municipality. Many stores were defunct, some with stock draped in dust-sheets. A long grimy stairway led up to a long grimy corridor; in the first open office a sallow, thin-lipped man said, 'No English speak here!' Simultaneously a tall, middle-aged woman appeared beside me speaking the Queen's English. She was dressed and mannered like a senior Whitehall civil servant – perhaps with her I could discuss Kiryat Arba's past, present and future? She invited me into her office, read my letter, then brusquely declared, 'I can give you two numbers, a rabbi in Hebron – a distinguished scholar – and our best known lawyer who lives here. These men may help.' She scribbled in my notebook, then indicated, politely but decisively, that she was a busy woman.

Next I went beer-hunting. In one small shop a friendly girl spoke French-accented English and had waist-length golden braids and corn-flower-blue eyes. When I asked for six bottles she took four from the ice-box and apologised. This was her entire stock – 'It's Purim, our men drink then like no other time.' I tried to prolong our dialogue, with limited success. She volunteered that Kiryat Arba is not a buzzy place but 'to be near our Patriarchs is of most importance'.

It wasn't difficult to find a quiet corner where I could lessen my load. After the morning rush hour, all of Kiryat Arba goes quiet; it has failed to become a normal human community, even by settlement standards. Continuing to explore, I noticed many unoccupied blocks. But how come a town of 6,500 inhabitants can feel so lifeless? The answer is that most men lead a quasi-monastic existence, sitting all day in *yeshivas* studying Talmudic texts and other rabbinic literature.

Towards noon I approached the only person in sight, a fifty-ish blonde with sun-dried skin. She offered to guide me to the bus stop and seemed eager to talk. When I hypocritically referred to Kiryat Arba as 'a fine town' she shook her head and said vehemently – 'No, no! Here is nothing! No industry, no culture, no fun! Here is a *dead* place!'

'So why stay?' I asked. (Her accent puzzled me: Eastern European?)

My guide made a hand-wringing gesture. 'I married a rabbi – all his life is here, teaching. I *must* stay! Our children is different, all want not to stay. The first has gone, I don't know where. They see other ways of living. For me this makes trouble with their father, I must support them.' Suddenly her eyes filled with tears. She turned her face away while extending a hand and saying, 'Goodbye, soon the bus comes.' Our conversation, suspended within mutual anonymity, reminded me of hitchhiking exchanges.

By the bus stop, uphill from the security barrier, a few plastic tables and chairs stood in the sun outside a trailer-café. The grumpy Slavic owner wore an ankle-length woollen skirt and a thick knitted scarf around head and neck. Her husband's headgear, beard, complexion and features were startling: in Peshawar he could have passed for a native. Kiryat Arba enjoys a remarkably wide choice of racial types.

Buses run infrequently so the 'Pathan' advised me to 'go tramp' (hitch a lift). The trickle of traffic was mainly police vans or army vehicles, including two APCs. Yet soon I had been picked up by an inquisitive rabbi with white ear-locks and a beard like an avalanche tumbling down his chest. 'Why you here?' he asked. 'I'm an Irish tourist.' He frowned. 'But why you come *here*?' 'I heard it was beautiful with lots of trees so I wanted to see it.' 'You sleep where?' 'In the Old City.' 'You live with us?' 'No, in the souk.' A very long pause. Then, 'In that place they kill you for visiting Kiryat Arba!'

We were now at the junction where I said, 'Thanks for the lift and don't worry. My souk friends are not killers!'

Back in the Club, I showed the names in my notebook to Narwal and Laila who shuddered. The rabbi was lethal, the lawyer viciously cunning. In H2 a lethal rabbi is likely to be just that – directly responsible for Palestinian deaths. I decided to target the lawyer and looked him up in the *Lords of the Land* index (a book borrowed from Faisal).

Elyakim Haetzni, a vociferously secular Zionist, was among the most forceful proponents of the Kiryat Arba development. The authors describe him as having been 'a radical young idealist, an oppositionist by nature . . . a partner to many anti-establishment efforts in the 1950s'. Ten years before the Six-Day War, which condemned millions of Palestinians to military occupation without end, he helped to found the 'New Regime' movement. This sought 'to break the monopoly on rule by Ben-Gurion and his Mapai Party . . . It called for a constitution that would establish the citizen's basic rights; for the annulment of the laws and regulations that restrict the liberty of the individual; for freedom of speech, freedom of movement and organisation; for the abolition of the military government over the Arabs of Israel; and more. In geopolitical terms, the New Regime movement supported the uniting of the entire land of Israel in peaceful ways, the establishment of federative treaties with Jordan and Lebanon, and a solution to the problem of the 1948 Palestinian refugees'.

That scenario is now known as 'the one-state solution'. Sadly, the New Regime couldn't arouse enough enthusiasm for a peacefully united Greater Israel, in a federation not fixated on *Jewishness*. Instead came the conquest of the OPT and the steadily increasing empowerment of religious Zionism. Haetzni then began to work for another sort of Greater Israel, giving legal advice to the militants (mainly Six-Day War veterans) who were soon to coalesce into Gush Emunim. Later he was briefly a Knesset member, representing the short-lived (1979–92) right-wing Tehiya Party.

When I rang this 'viciously cunning lawyer' I expected him to need time to 'research' the oddity who was living in the souk. But no – he'd be happy to see me at 11.00 a.m. the next day.

The Haetznis' unpretentious two-storey house, in a shady sunken garden, stood near the edge of a bluff. Several fat cats decorated window sills, enjoying the spring sunshine. As the hall door opened I was bonding with a lordly black Persian – very like my own Herbie – and a discussion of feline idiosyncrasies got us off to a good start. Elyakim Haetzni was tall and well-built, still handsome at 82, with a firm handshake. At once I knew I was going to like him, which would have seemed impossible five minutes earlier. And the same went for his wife when she appeared to ask 'Tea or coffee?'

Some settlement spokespersons are famously affable and hospitable, even to antagonistic visitors, and one can spot these smooth PR operators at a glance. Into this category the Haetznis did not fit. They were at ease with themselves, neither arrogant nor on the defensive. Had I been confrontational they would no doubt have tactfully abbreviated our meeting, not feeling it necessary or desirable to argue. In such company my being untainted by anti-Semitism is a considerable advantage, something quickly sensed by people as perceptive as these two. It helped that we shared a primitive sense of humour. When I needed the loo, Elyakim explained, 'Just now it's occupied, in a moment you may liberate it.' Much later in the conversation we agreed that, logically, Jews should find it easier to tolerate Mohammad's message than Jesus's. The former

saw himself as a successor of the prophets and only claimed to have
taken dictation from an angel whereas Jesus claimed to be the son of
God – a God who played rather a nasty trick on Joseph by making his
wife pregnant.

The wide windows of a book-strewn living-room overlooked the
Hebron Hills and were open when I arrived. Then, as Friday prayers
started at the Haram Al-Khalil, Mrs Haetzni closed them. Her husband
said, 'We both speak Arabic and don't like to hear the hate preaching.'
He went on to recall Archbishop Tutu's most recent visit to Ramallah.
There, as the South African – surrounded by PA leaders – delivered an
impassioned condemnation of Israeli apartheid, a giant banner was
unfurled above the platform declaring in Arabic: 'On Saturdays we kill
Jews, on Sundays we kill Christians!' I had already heard about this
incident from embarrassed friends in Ramallah.

In 1939 the thirteen-year-old Elyakim had arrived in Haifa from
Berlin. I know not what his family endured under Nazism; it would
have been uncharacteristic of him to get personal, at that level, with a
stranger. But as he talked on, with quiet intensity, about what the
creation of the State of Israel meant to a people so discriminated against,
in so many ways, for so long, I remembered that faraway time when I
myself, ignorant of the Nakba, was pro-Israel, rejoicing that at last the
Jews had a land to call their own. In the 1950s and '60s, when hearing
of my friends' working holidays on kibbutzim, it was easy to sympathise
with political Zionism. It seemed unrelated to those seeking to redeem
the land bequeathed to them millennia ago by the God of Israel –
people who listen to blood crying out from the earth and feel obliged to
shed lots more blood on the way to 'redemption'. In the 1970s Gush
Emunim set about queering political Zionism's pitch and by now the
'redeeming' settlers have made the Occupation apparently permanent.
Elyakim registered impatience when I mentioned Rabbi Dov Wolpe,
one of the leaders of Chabad's Messianic faction. Wolpe was rapidly
gaining support among the 'hilltop youth' and their kindred spirits who
describe the State of Israel as 'the enemy of the people'.

Standing by the window, my host pointed out certain areas reserved
for a new brand of refugees, should anti-Semitism ever take over in the
US. He had been born into a Berlin community inspired by Moses
Mendelssohn, of whom Ruth had spoken to me so movingly in her Tel
Aviv flatlet. Now he dwelt on the extent to which such Jews had

identified with Germany, how proud they were of having won more than their share of Iron Crosses during the First World War. Then came the 1929 crash, Hitler and the Shoah. Could it be that the 2008 crash would arouse anti-Semitism in the US where Jews feel themselves to be American? Although only 2% of the population they are, he reflected, disproportionately influential . . . And the US is not a nation but an agglomeration of variegated immigrants with a culture of violence. ('Just like Israel!' I thought but didn't say.) An anti-Semitic surge was possible, not of course on the Shoah scale but perhaps like the Russian and East European pogroms . . . When I raised a sceptical eyebrow he opined that low-level anti-Semitism, though rarely discernible among the US elite, still thrives among the masses, only waiting to be activated.

Finding myself in such scholarly company, I sought clarification about Judaism's diverse denominations and the disparate groups within Orthodoxy, so bewildering to *goyim*. As might be expected of an eminent (or 'cunning') lawyer, Elyakim expatiated lucidly for more than an hour, going into various historical and regional developments in some detail, with frequent inputs from his wife. Occasionally they disagreed on minutiae and argued briefly; after fifty-plus years of marriage they were still mentally stimulating each other.

The first Reform temple went up in Hamburg in 1818. Six years later a Reform Society of Israelites evolved in South Carolina. By the end of the nineteenth century Reform was closely associated with US Jewry and for long its adherents were pro-assimilation and anti-Zionist. Then, as Fascism stoked Europe's anti-Semitism, their distaste of Zionism lessened. They sought to preserve Judaism as a 'relevant inspiration' (Elyakim's phrase) for those who found Orthodoxy too hard to reconcile with everyday life in the gentile world.

Conservative Judaism was sired in Germany by Zacharia Frankel (1801–75) and reared to maturity in the US by Soloman Schechter (1850–1915). Conservatives accept modern scholarship in relation to their source documents, including the Bible, and Elyakim reckoned they now form the largest single Jewish denomination in the US. In 1983 most voted for the ordination of women and the few rabbis who objected formed the Union for Traditional Judaism. In Israel, where only Orthodoxy is officially recognised, Conservatives are known as 'Masorti' and generally detested.

Then there are the Reconstructionists, of whom I'd never previously heard. These followers of Mordecai Kaplan (1881–1983) were favoured by the secular Haetznis. They advocate a big rethink, starting with God, Israel, Torah and the Synagogue and Rabbinate as institutions. This movement has always recognised 'gender equality' and – beyond Israel – is gradually, quietly influencing both the Reforms and the Conservatives.

To an extent, this Kiryat Arba encounter reminded me of my friendships with some hardline Boers in the South Africa of 1993, people whose mindset was incomprehensible but whom one had to appreciate, as individuals. There were however significant differences. Unlike the cultivated, cosmopolitan, multilingual Haetznis, those North Transvaal Boers were simple folk, their homes bookless, their horizons limited, their anti-Semitism extreme; several quoted from the 'Protocols'. For me the previous months had been packed with confusions and paradoxes and here was the ultimate confusion: how could this couple have supported Gush Emunim for decades?

My host insisted on driving me to the hitching-spot and on the way pointed out a few new schools – some for children from other settlements – then being built. Drily he added, 'They're expected to enliven Kiryat Arba.' His farewell advice was, 'Waste no more energy on our currently intractable problems. Leave it to *time*. Given *time*, solutions happen.'

CHAPTER 20

What Goes on in the Jordan Valley?

As I was saying goodbye to my Hebron friends, several made warning noises.

'The Jordan Valley is another sort of issue – don't try to see the river.'

'Down there, political Zionism is at its worst.'

'Don't go hiking near Jericho – the Valley's our most militarised bit.'

'Remember you can't ride around in taxis like in the rest of the West Bank.'

And Raouf said, 'Let me know if you need help.'

Leaving Hebron at dawn, I took a serveece for Jericho from Bethlehem's Manger Square. My seat companion was an articulate PASF recruit being US-trained in Jordan and now on his way to the Allenby Bridge. He complained that most PA weapons were Russian, only a few US-made, which led to muddles and quarrels; the trainers were not at ease with the Russian equipment, most recruits envied the minority's superior weapons. He scoffed at the US reluctance to entrust 'state-of-the-art' guns to the PA. 'They still see us like terrorists, even after the Olso big deal.'

The dramatic descent to Jericho, through the naked, curvaceous pale brown hills of Judea, has been inspiring writers for centuries. In our day it is less inspiring; infamous Ma'ale Adumim has been defacing this West Bank landscape since 1976. The first of its Persil-white angular apartment blocks appeared, on land 'cleansed' of those Bedouin who had camped near Jerusalem after their expulsion from the Negev. They now camp opposite Ma'ale Adumim, on sandy slopes above the road, and bus passengers can glimpse their makeshift shelters – too insubstantial to be called 'hovels' – perhaps with a malnourished camel calf tethered nearby. Israeli tour guides like to draw their customers' attention to these quaint links with the Biblical past. The current plan is to include Ma'ale Adumim in a 'Greater Jerusalem' extending all the way through West Bank territories to the Jordan River.

Some archaeologists identify Jericho as the world's oldest as well as lowest city (1200 feet below sea level) – a not uncommon claim in the

Middle East. It is also made by Bethlehemites, though they admit the first historical reference comes latish, in the fourteenth century BC, when a Canaanist prince wrote to an Egyptian Pharaoh about Beit Lahmu's aspiration to become a city state. Indisputably Jericho's Neolithic remains (*c.*7000BC) make it the oldest walled settlement – as distinct from city – yet discovered. Biblical claims took another hit when radiocarbon dating placed the founding of Jericho city in *c.*3100BC, with *c.*2300BC for the destruction of its walls – instead of Joshua's 1200BC. Around 2000BC the city was rebuilt, covering a much wider area, then abandoned *c.*1550BC, after Pharaoh Amosis I's invasion.

In the tenth century AD Al Maqdisi admired Jericho's 'prosperity and calm', the former based on indigo, bananas and dates, the latter on a local dislike for the Sunni/Shia discord then troubling Jerusalem. A millennium later, Jericho was chosen as the first Palestinian city to be visited by Arafat and the PLO on their return from exile. In the nineteenth century, and during the Mandate, this was a favourite winter refuge, a Simla-in-reverse, for Jerusalem's notables and British colonial officials. Several notable families treated themselves to below-sea-level homes a mere half-hour's commute, even then, from Jerusalem. Under Jordanian rule (1948–67) the Jordan Valley – one-third of the West Bank – experienced a remarkable agricultural renaissance, largely owing to the benevolence of one notable named Musa Alami.

Post-Oslo, certain senior PA politicians collaborated with some of their Israeli counterparts, and a few foreign investors, to exploit the tourist potential of Jericho and the Dead Sea area. Where our serveece turned north, I winced to see their most obvious venture. The 181-room, five-star, three-swimming-pool Intercontinental Hotel opened in 1998 and overlooks the Aqabat Jaber refugee camp which has no reliable water supply. Often this development is used to illustrate what the Oslo Accords have done for the Palestinian masses. In Raja Shehada's *A Rift in Time* we read that the Intercontinental's Austrian-run Oasis casino admitted a profit of $54 million at the end of its first year in operation. Between September 1998 and its closing exactly two years later at the beginning of the second Intifada, it registered a daily average of 2,809 players of whom 99% were Israeli. Hitherto, Israel's gamblers had had to fly to Istanbul – as many habitually did. When one of Raja's clients had made a serious bid for the Intercontinental site this entrepreneur was imprisoned in Jericho until he changed his mind:

When I tried to intervene on behalf of my client I was brought before the Palestinian prosecutor and forced to forfeit all links with the case. I was only spared further humiliation by the intercession of well-connected acquaintances. However corrupt the Palestinian Authority might have been during its early phase, society was still closely knit enough for personal relations to put some limits on the immoral behaviour to which bad money might otherwise lead.

In my youth polite people occasionally exclaimed 'Go to Jericho!' when others might have said 'Go to Hell!' One assumes Biblical connotations. But nowadays there's no apparent reason – at least in springtime – for this straggling little city (population 20,000) to be regarded as a punishing destination. My first impression was of an impoverished, undistinguished and rather lethargic town, a place finding it hard to come to terms with its recent history. In the small central square I sat outside a teahouse noting the numerous cyclists – a rarity elsewhere on the West Bank – and the soothing shortage of motor vehicles. (I'm told it's now possible to hire bicycles at 5 shekels per hour.) Raouf had mentioned that here Westerners are not the flavour of the decade so all my pro-Palestinian regalia was ostentatiously displayed: a black and white *keffiyeh*, a Palestinian flag bracelet, a ditto keyring dangling from my watch strap, an oblong Palestinian flag badge, a large circular Mahmoud Darwish 'button'. Elsewhere it had touched me to see faces lighting up when the Palestinians' most beloved poet was recognised – and sure enough a young man, pushing a handcart loaded with cauliflowers, paused to ask, 'You like this poet?'

Then I sauntered along the main street, enquiring about cheap lodgings, and a kindly old man directed me to an enormous nineteenth-century hotel. At 10.30 a.m. its door stood wide open but there was no one in sight. The high-ceilinged, dimly lit foyer was a study in greys and browns. On my way to the long reception desk I tripped over a central strip of ragged, dark grey matting. No one responded to loud thumping, followed by questioning shouts, so I sat in one of several dark brown armchairs (*c.*1950, their guts protruding) and contemplated the empty cigarette packets on the floor and the overflowing ashtrays and empty tea-glasses on chipped and scratched coffee tables.

Ten minutes later a youth came hurrying in. He stared at me in astonishment, then hastened away through a bead curtain and could be heard banging on a door while yelling, 'Mustafa!' Soon he reappeared with Mustafa – tall, neatly bearded and elegant, the sort of built-in elegance unrelated to garb. Yes, a room was vacant (later it became plain that every room was vacant) for 80 shekels without breakfast. When I presented a 200-shekel note Abd, an endearing ten-year-old, went for change while his father excused himself: he worked as a night security guard at the Intercontinental and must now go back to bed but Abd would show me to my room and always be around if I needed anything.

Soon Abd came trotting back with my change, then led me through another bead curtain, up a curving, cracked marble stairs and down a long corridor of bare planks. This building, I could now see, was a semi-ruin; all the rooms to one side were derelict, their high doors replaced by heavy red velvet curtains (a bizarre touch) and each had been stripped of furniture, window frames, electrical and bathroom fittings. My cell-like room, at the end of this corridor, had a balcony overlooking a garbage dump; beyond rose a once-gracious mansion converted to flats. A bulky TV set dominated the cell; Abd apologised because at present the power was cut off, but within an hour or so some of my 80 shekels might have enabled it to be restored. The nearby cupboard-like WC was W-less. Abd pulled the antique chain to confirm this fact, then said 'Tomorrow' with unconvincing confidence. My door had no key, bolt or hasp but that didn't matter; dereliction doesn't necessarily engender bad vibes.

When I went walkabout at noon the sun would have been too hot but for a cool frisky breeze. Away from the new hardlinery of Nablus and Hebron, one notices many more 'uncovered' (unscarved) women, both Muslim and Christian. I even saw one small girl happily riding her bright pink bicycle along the pavement. It also cheered me to see Taybeh beer prominently displayed in shop fridges.

Level Jericho encourages bicycling but makes for dull walking. From the Grand Palace Hotel (my nickname) I followed a wide, straight, mile-long street, passing five large vine-roofed garden-restaurants, relics of Jericho's once-thriving tourist trade. Only two were open and at the first of these I was overcharged by 10 shekels – a novel experience in the OPT. The owner introduced himself as an Orthodox Christian who had spent twenty years in London. He urged me to avoid the Ein Es-Sultan refugee camp – my destination. 'It is too far to walk and no taxi will take you, those people are too rough.'

Before the Bisan Street junction I paused to silently commiserate with a camel tethered on an expanse of rubble-strewn ground overlooked by three gawky, extra-tall, date palms. Behind him sprawled a long four-storey half-built edifice – another enterprise aborted by the second Intifada. Around the corner, on Bisan Street, loomed the deplorable Telepherique starting-point (of which more anon). In its vast carpark stood a solitary yellow-plated vehicle. The only sign of life was a peacock giving a full display, standing in the middle of the tarmac staring directly at me as if to say, 'This is all for you!'

Security was tight at the camp, perhaps because it is so close to Tel Es-Sultan archaeological site marking Jericho's very first (c. 9000BC) settlement. More than 20,000 displaced from Ramlek and Lydda lived here until the Six-Day War when most fled across the river. Only 2,000 or so registered refugees remain; the other houses shelter the poorest of Jericho's poor – mainly jobless and/or in some way disabled. The eight-foot-high wire netting fence was intact and beside the locked gate a faded notice said, 'UNRWA – Construction of Additional Rooms at Ein Es-Sultan CoEd School – Project Donated by USAID'. My rattling the gate went unheard but as I turned away a bareheaded woman cyclist stopped beside me. Afaf was arriving to do her hygiene inspection job and, having glanced at my passport (her duty as a PA civil servant), she readily admitted me.

This camp, too, is plagued by acute water shortages. 'Why my job is so needed and so hard!' said Afaf. I made the inevitable comparison with Balata: Ein Es-Sultan was much less cramped but the poverty seemed even worse – or less well concealed.

'I find their lethargy frightening,' said Afaf. 'But here it's the real refugees have most energy. There's a strong pushy women's co-op – right now preparing for some international competition.' (Months later I heard that Ein Es-Sultan had won that couscous competition in Italy, using their 'Fair Trade' Jericho *maftoul*. And three years later their co-op was exporting 70 tonnes of couscous annually to Europe. As Afaf had said, 'Palestinians, especially women, need only *half* a chance . . .')

Afaf was very unusual; aged thirty but unmarried because she had never met a man willing to adjust to her Women's Lib (1970s model) world-view. Strikingly good-looking, with a soft voice, a gentle manner and a will of iron, she acknowledged that in one important respect she was lucky. 'My father accepts me and loves me as I am. You'd like him, can you eat lunch with us tomorrow?'

Afaf introduced me to some of the camp's teachers; she was very proud of its co-ed school – on the West Bank as unusual as herself – and I suspected she was its behind-the-scenes inspiration. But as so often in refugeeland, the lack of resources was pitiful: or perhaps one should say 'tragic', given so much undeveloped talent.

I rambled back to my 'Palace' through a semi-rural suburb where on open spaces between streets some people attempt market gardening, water supply permitting. Growers unable to afford plastic tunnels improvise with shopping-bags and relevant scraps discarded by settlers, who now monopolise the Valley's fertile land. Apart from Jericho and the adjacent village of Al-Auja the entire Valley lies within Area C and has been declared a Military Zone. Shockingly, when crops have been lifted the plastic bits are ploughed into the ground, leaving it densely flecked with multicoloured fragments. Nearby, tattered strips hang from bushes and wire fences, flamboyant additions to their layers of captured litter. In one field, overlooked by a defunct factory and scattered with the remains of a cabbage crop, twenty or so handsome long-haired goats were being guarded by a Bedouin elder. He stood tall and erect, his white beard bushy, his pale blue *galabiya* and flowing white turban freshly laundered. When I rested on a wall he ignored me. Only his herd mattered; at intervals he had to deprive a goat of its mouthful of plastic. For some reason this unlovely vignette remains imprinted on my memory as an authentic symbol (and symptom) of twenty-first-century Jericho.

At sunset Afaf joined me for a beer. She preferred not to defy convention needlessly – 'It's stupid to be provocative' – so we met at the 'Christian' garden-restaurant. I explained why I had not visited Tel Es-Sultan, beside the camp, and would not be visiting any other of Jericho's celebrated sites: all are controlled by Israel's National Parks Authority in collusion with the IDF. The shekels thus saved could be spent on taxi rides to the Valley's misfortunate villages. For lack of public transport, the taxi would have to be private.

Afaf frowned, gave me rather a strained smile and said, 'That won't work. Our taxis won't drive up Road 90. Checkpoints can be manned by both settler vigilantes and conscripts – a scary mix!'

The next half-hour was instructive. Palestinians living in Jericho city or Al-Auja cannot obtain permits to visit relatives in nearby communities north of the city. Those from other parts of the West Bank, not holding Valley residence permits, may enter the city only by public transport or on foot. The few Jericho vehicle owners (green number plates) may enter the Valley through only two (Hamra and Tayasie) of the four 'border' checkpoints. Another checkpoint controls access to the Dead Sea and Palestinians without Jerusalem IDs can't reach what the Civil Authority oddly describes as a 'recreation water source'. Nor can they enter Israel, therefore Gaza beach has always been inaccessible. Afaf echoed my Hebron friends – 'In this Valley we have military rule at its most ruthless.'

Back at the Palace, a small kerosene lamp glowed on the reception desk and Abd admitted to a cash-flow problem. Tonight there would be no electricity but across the street – he pointed to a café – tourists could watch . . . I assured him that I didn't want to watch and always carried a candle for emergencies and would be content diary-writing in my room. (It's easier to write by candlelight than torchlight.)

That evening Raouf solved my transport problem. Two days hence his friend Salah – employed by an INGO based in Jerusalem – would be collecting statistics in the Valley and would take me along for the ride. Scary checkpoints didn't bother him: his employers was 'toweringly prestigious' – Raouf's phrase.

In 1967, immediately after the Six-Day War, General Yigal Allon revealed an infamous plan to turn the Jordan Valley into a heavily militarised buffer zone. Netanyahu often quotes him, emphasising that no peace agreement should permit an IDF withdrawal from this region. Avigdor Liebermann also beats the Allon drum – 'We cannot secure the State of Israel without maintaining control of the Jordan Valley.' Less expansionist observers point out that twenty-first-century weaponry has radically reduced land borders' significance; Israel won't be obliterated by troops wading across the Jordan. Professor Yaron Ezrahi of the Hebrew University has commented, 'Netanyahu probably knows this though he won't say it because it would weaken his land-grabbing policy.' Then the Professor remembered Al-Qaeda and added, 'Such players work by infiltration and terror. Here borders are important because we see instability in Jordan . . . The King is facing some troubles. Instability does create questions about borders.'

This contentious territory (part of the Great Rift Valley) stretches from the Sea of Galilee in the north to the Dead Sea in the south. It covers more than a third of the West Bank's landmass but 90% of its villages have been demolished and it supports only 2% of the population. Here the West Bank's first settlements appeared in 1968: 17 had been established by 1977. In 2009 there were 36, supporting 9,400 settlers, and by the time you read this there will be several more. The PA controls only 0.5% of the Valley. Throughout the Valley, all areas labelled 'State Land' – whatever their ostensible purpose – are controlled by Settlers' Regional Councils. Now the Valley supports some 56,000 Palestinians; as part of Jordan, it supported 320,000, living between Bisan in the north and Ein Gedi in the south.

As B'Tselem frequently complains, 'Israel has de facto annexed the Jordan Valley.' And according to a characteristically verbose yet under-stated Oxfam International report: 'The Jordan Valley has the potential to be the Palestinian breadbasket . . . but the persistent expansion of Israeli settlements and their impacts on the Palestinians and other restrictions on Palestinian development have made life extremely difficult for Palestinian communities.'

Of the Valley's Palestinians, some 25% are Bedouin; another 15,000 or so live elsewhere on the West Bank. Pre-Occupation these tribes from the Negev found Jordanian rule tolerable enough though spatially restricting. As herders they were able to maintain, on a limited scale, the important rhythms of their seasonal migrations. But 1967 brought a second traumatic upheaval; inexorably the spreading settlements restricted their wanderings. Then came Oslo, for them the ultimate catastrophe. When most of the Valley became Area C the unrestrained Civil Administration (aka the IDF) could treat them as illegal immigrants on their own land. Thus ended a way of life almost unchanged since the building of Jericho's first walls.

From Balata I had visited the Bedouin community of Al-Zubeidat in the northern Jordan Valley. By now the sale of cheese and yoghurt, from roadside stalls along Road 90, is these Bedouins' main source of income. On that February day they told me that six months previously the Al-Zubeidat stall, and four others belonging to neighbouring communities, had been smashed by IDF bulldozers. Also, their dairy products, and 85 large crates of fresh fruits and vegetables, were deliberately destroyed. This was the punishment for setting up stalls without permits – which of course had been applied for but refused. Some of those bulldozers' operations, up and down Road 90, were carried out in full view of UN officials who had come to negotiate with the Civil Administration about supplying electricity to Bedouin communities. Six months after the event, as Al-Zubeidat's elders told me of this crime in voices trembling with rage, several wives were quietly shedding tears and a few sons (my Nablus interpreter told me) were planning vengeance.

Most Bedouin rely for lighting and cooking on small but costly generators and they must buy water at high prices from mobile tankers or from settlements. Despite being twice displaced, few Valley Bedouin have sought UNRWA assistance. They cherish their 'Right to Return' (a real right, in so far as anything guaranteed by 'international law' is real) and many suspect that registration with the distrusted UN would somehow impair that right.

In March Jericho's night temperature drops abruptly and it was almost chilly next morning when I set off to visit Deir Quruntal (the Monastery of the Temptation). Happily a few geographical features are resistant to the Zionists' 'Change the face of Israel' ideology. Looking directly up at Deir Quruntal on its high ledge near the summit one sees nothing but harsh golden-brown rockiness, surely unchanged since Jesus spent 40 days here resisting Satan's dirty tricks. However, it's essential not to look south. There the Telepherique's lamentable terminus has inflicted a large metallic scar near the boulder known as 'Jesus's seat'. By any reckoning this Swiss investment is unnecessary. The path to the monastery entrance is indeed dusty, quite steep, narrow and in places uneven. But even with my dicey hip I made it to the top in 20 minutes. So why desecrate such a hallowed mountain with a cable car?

The Monday–Friday opening hour is supposed to be 8.00 a.m. but at 8.10 nothing happened when I simultaneously used the giant iron knocker and the electronic bell. I relaxed then on the doorstep, close to another sort of desecration; the long deep gullies below me proved how much this Russian Orthodox congregation relished fast-food and noxious pseudo-fruit juices. All that had to be monkish garbage; no one was going to haul their domestic litter up here.

The scene was very still – no movement anywhere, not a person or a bird visible. This immense panorama induces an odd solemnity. For how long has the Jordan River been serving as a border? In the Book of Joshua:

The Lord hath put the river Jordan for a border between us and you, O ye children of Ruben, and ye children of God; and therefore you have no part in the Lord. And by this occasion your children shall turn away from our children from the fear of the Lord.

Slowly my eyes travelled from the aloof Mountains of Moab to a sliver of pewter-coloured Dead Sea to the straggle of Jericho's not-quite-urbanised oasis. In the Holy Land history can taste like some astringent concentrated essence of humanity's experience – imbibe sparingly!

Was it a mistake to keep on rebuilding Jericho? When the walls fell down –

Joshua said to all Israel: Shout: for the Lord hath delivered the city to you . . . And they took the city and killed all that were in it, man and woman, young and old. The oxen also and the sheep, and the asses they slew with the edge of the sword . . . But Joshua saved Rahab the harlot and her father's house, and all she had . . . because she hid the messengers whom he had sent to spy out Jericho. At that time, Joshua made an imprecation saying: Cursed be the man before the Lord, that shall raise up and build the city of Jericho.

At 9.00 a.m. I again rang and knocked, to no effect; perhaps the monks were attending to their complicated business interests in Jerusalem. But my frustration was mild; the ascent, and that silent time on what does feel like a special mountain, were what really mattered. This monastery's foundations date back to the sixth century but for a millennium it was abandoned and the present simple structure is late nineteenth-century and not very exciting.

Back on the Valley floor, a dirt track soon took me onto a long ridge-top overlooking banana plantations, orange orchards and maize fields. I wondered as I strolled, when Mark Antony presented the Jordan Valley to Cleopatra, did she hire consultants to advise on increasing production? Or did life jog on, as before, for the *fellahin*?

Here were small clusters of concrete block homes, one or two-roomed, surrounded by tidy vegetable patches with flower and herb pots on the window ledges. Many of the residents looked more African than Arab and I saw no 'uncovered' woman. Jericho has a high percentage of dark-skinned Palestinians, supposedly descendants of African slaves imported by the Umayyads to work on their cane plantations. To me this sounds

as likely as a Bible story. I had passed one of the derelict mills, between
Mount Quruntal and Tel Es-Sultan; water from the once-powerful Ein
Duyuk spring powered its wheel. Although sugar milling had declined
before the Crusaders arrived they quickly revived the industry because
in Europe sugar was then becoming an expensive luxury.

I had paused to converse with three cats when an elderly man
beckoned me to sit on his balcony; he introduced himself as 'Daoud'
and insisted on my drinking tea. Then, noting my 'button', he tapped
the book on his knee and said, 'Darwish! We still mourn him! But why
are you in this place? You are far from hotels and limping! All my life I
live here, until now seeing no tourist!'

Jericho-born Daoud, aged seventy-five, had never forgotten eye-
witnessing the Nakba – thousands of terrorised villagers struggling to
cross the Jordan, many with only the clothes they wore, many carrying
small children, the unluckiest falling and dying. We've all seen the
photographs. And by now similar scenes have become almost
commonplace in numerous countries. But Daoud's verbal pictures –
brief, stark – were incomparably more moving than any camera-shot.
For his own farming family, the Nakba was not too disruptive though
fear of the Zionist colonists shadowed his youth – and in 1967 was
justified. 'It's not true,' he said, 'that we all trusted other Arabs would
rescue us. My father worked for Musa Alami who said every hour to
everybody, "Palestinians must rescue themselves".'

Pre-Occupation, Jordan and the Gulf States imported 60% of the
Valley's produce. Then, gradually, that invaluable outlet was curtailed
and in 1994 the Jordan–Israel Peace Treaty (so loudly cheered in certain
circles) triumphantly reinforced Palestinian dependence on the Israeli
market. Jordan could no longer import the Valley's bananas and the
resultant price-slump caused widespread hardship. 'It was planned to
make us suffer,' said Daoud, lest I might have missed the point.

As we talked, three younger men joined us, curious about the wandering
granny. Two of them needed crutches; they had been permanently
injured while date harvesting. Valley palms grow to 65 feet or more and
the cranes which elevate the pickers are often operated by unlicensed
contractors who economise on safety checks and provide no harnesses
or helmets. Men are sometimes left to make their own way from tree top
to tree top, or are immobilised in uncomfortable postures when cranes
break down. Then exhaustion and dizziness can take over. (I remembered

the skill with which my unmechanised Cuban friends shinned up even taller coconut palms – which admittedly are not 'armoured' towards their bases.)

Israel's belated minimum wage law (2007) is consistently ignored throughout the Valley and workers lack any form of insurance. Although legally entitled to free medical treatment for work-related conditions the Zionist version of apartheid takes over here and Palestinians must pay their own bills. Yet instant dismissal follows any injury or illness. Daoud believed the sprays used on the trees were the worst hazard, affecting all harvesters – and packers. By this stage his wife, herself a packer from July to October, had joined us. She was angry. Sometimes masks were provided but mostly not and those susceptible to the chemicals suffered rashes, coughs and headaches for months. But her anger was about something else: two of their teenage grandsons had been in administrative detention for almost a year, accused of 'resisting the Occupation'. They had visited Qumran, twelve miles south of Jericho on the Dead Sea coast, to meet a Canadian ISM friend who wanted them to help him make a video of the Essenes' famous cave. And that morning had brought a rumour, horribly likely to be true, about a detention extension . . .

Daoud frowned at his wife, seeming not to want to discuss this family matter. Then he told me, 'The IDF made new rules in 2006. Now we can't sell our produce at a convenient border crossing, must travel as much as 30 miles to the Jalameh cargo terminal. Also, since then, the internal checkpoint waits get longer – *every day* people lose perishable consignments while the soldiers laugh at them!'

I wished I could have a tête-à-tête with my fellow-granny, whose English was even more fluent than her husband's: but soon Afaf would be waiting for me at the camp school gate.

The Sartawi family (now reduced to father and daughter by emigration) lived in a district of fine residences behind high stone walls topped with barbed wire. One expected to hear watch-dogs in the half-acre gardens but there weren't any. In general, Afaf reminded me, Arabs don't like dogs. 'Except Zaluqis for hunting,' she added, 'in feudal times. And don't imagine these mansions are family homes – they're apartments.'

Mr Sartawi was quadrilingual (Arabic, English, German, Hebrew), an agronomist who had retired early when settlements obliterated his workspace. He was small and square (Afaf was small and slight) with a genial manner, penetrating eyes and a firm handshake. He said, 'My daughter is very happy to have you here. For her Jericho is a prison.'

The ground-floor flat, bushy with house plants, was traditionally furnished and lunch came on a communal tray. 'We live Ottoman-style,' said Afaf. 'It's my father's way of making a statement. The settlers come but we don't go.'

When I turned the conversation to the Boycott, Divestment and Sanctions campaign, my host recommended a special focus on the Carmel Agrexco company; it profits hugely from the export of West Bank (including Valley) products needing intensive irrigation only obtainable through the misappropriation of Palestinian water supplies. Afaf quoted Mr Katz-Oz, a Zionist water controller and erstwhile colleague of her father's who prided himself on his logic. To visiting foreigners he pointed out, 'There's no reason for Palestinians to claim that just because they sit on lands, they have the rights to that water.'

Pre-Occupation, Mr Sartawi recalled, 209 wells served the Valley. Now Palestinians may use only 89 and are denied permits to restore old wells or dig new ones. Mekorot, the Israeli water company, sells water to West Bank towns and public bodies and controls 98% of the Valley's water resources. Under Oslo, almost six times *more* aquifer water was allocated for Israeli use: 350 litres per person per day, compared to 60 litres per West Bank Palestinian. My host referred me to Mourid Barghouti's summing up of Oslo:

> The problem was that what took place between our negotiators and the Israeli delegation wasn't so much a negotiation as a series of approvals of proposals presented by a team of Israel's shrewdest politicians and lawyers with highly specialised skills in everything needed to make us fall into their visible and invisible traps.

The Sartawis found Fatah and Hamas equally distasteful. 'Both live on their own myths,' declared my host. His daughter corrected him. 'Lies, not myths. But they've things in common. Most of our politicians won't admit the Zionists easily bought land from us when the price was right. From absentee landlords – you know about them in Ireland! They didn't want to be responsible leaders of a Palestinian nation.' 'Back then,' said Mr Sartawi, 'nations were a sort of Western novelty. Our educated men were locked into the Ottoman paradigm.'

'And we didn't have any educated women!' Afaf reminded me.

Her father continued, 'It's true a few good leaders in 1908 – even *one* really inspiring leader – might have meant no Balfour.'

'But couldn't have stopped Sykes–Picot,' said Afaf.

Her father shrugged. 'We'd have survived that as our neighbours did – in a way . . . Zionist colonialism was the deadly thing. Palestine's tragedy was to be seen as a territory so marginal and powerless it could be given to the Zionists without *nationalist* protest. Voiceless *fellahin* could be smoothly transferred from the Ottomans to a much worse colonial tyrant.'

'Not so smoothly,' said Afaf. 'All that bloodshed under the Mandate sent the British running home in the end, clearing the way for the Nakba!'

It was decided the foreign writer should be shown something cheering and positive, like Jericho's Mosaic Centre, established to create jobs while reviving ancient skills. After lunch Mr Sartawi escorted me on foot to Jerusalem Street. 'I'm sorry we've no transport,' he said. 'It's not worth the running costs when you can't run anywhere. Before retiring I had a permit for Jerusalem, now they punish me for telling *why* I retired . . .'

Naturally I asked, 'And why did you?'

My companion laughed. 'You don't need to know!'

We parted outside the centre where I spent the next few hours watching hand-cut tesserae being made from local stone and talking with two men who had worked with a quartet of my Balata neighbours on the conservation of Nabi Yahya's tomb in Sebastia.

I had seen not one tourist in Jericho and next morning I discovered why. By chance, while seeking the sixth-century Shalom Yisrael synagogue, I came upon their ghetto, a few miles from the centre, reeking of affluence. Here were spacious grounds startlingly litter-free (not a cigarette butt in sight), two long swimming-pools shimmering invitingly, another empty as a concession to the prevailing drought, and tastefully tiled paths winding between high glossy green hedges, trimly shaped. The eight-storey hotel overlooked rows of Miami-style bungalows from which, at 7.30 a.m., aged couples were making their way to an acre-wide restaurant. Behind the hotel a bamboo grove concealed five coaches: Israel-registered, Hebrew-scripted, their passengers' nationalities pasted in English on the windscreens – American, Russian, Japanese, French, British. The lack of security astounded me; I was strolling around with a knapsack on my back having walked unchallenged through the main gateway. Then I visited a 'Ladies' Rest Room' opposite the reception desk where a crimson-faced Texan granddad was having a tantrum about a mistreated shirt, sent to the laundry with all its buttons but returned without any. I spent a long time in the 'Ladies', having a thorough wash-down (the first for days) yet when I emerged nobody seemed to notice my surely unauthorised presence. It would have been easy to plant a bomb or two in waste-bins. From this Jericho Resort Village tourists are driven to romantic Ancient Jericho, then returned to Jerusalem on a main road by-passing the impoverished reality of contemporary Jericho.

Resuming my quest for the synagogue, I came upon a puzzle in the desert. Something massive was being built amidst the sandy flatness with not another building in sight. Many acres had been enclosed by high, precisely constructed stone walls – dazzling white stone, an expensive project, this. I stood staring. All was silent, no works visible – perhaps because the day was Friday? But what could this be? Walking on, I came to an entrance, a pole-bar in front of a black metal gate flanked by low crenellated towers. And above the gate was the explanation, in English and Arabic: 'The Palestinian Security Sciences Academy'. By then the sun was hot but suddenly I felt chilled. Here foreign security services will train PASF recruits, like my Ramallah friends, to do dirty deeds in their post-Oslo role as US stooges. Walking on, I found it hard to combat despair. It did seem the Zionists had it all sewn up.

Shortly after my return to Ireland, in May 2009, General Dayton grievously embarrassed Mahmoud Abbas and his Fayyad-led government by making it plain, in a Washington speech, that US advisers were 'remoulding' the PA National Security Forces 'to strengthen Israel's security'.

Raouf's friends were to pick me up by the Tree of Zacchaeus ('Tow [sic] Thousand Years Old', according to the Tourism and Antiquities Department notice). They arrived at dawn in a classic INGO 4 x 4 fitted with so many electronic 'enhancements' I feared making some clumsy move likely to bring an F-16 screaming towards us.

Salah was tall, bald and tending to corpulence with a permanently worried expression and only one eye. 'Like Dayan!' he noted. 'But we've nothing else in common.' He spoke fluent English, having been INGO-employed for thirty years. His driver, Ahmad – young, thin and cheerful – hoped soon to be fluent and kept a mini-dictionary in his bush-shirt pocket. He had been born, and still lived, in a refugee camp within walking distance of his ancestral village and within sight of Jerusalem. His daughters, aged 6 and 8, wondered why they were forbidden to visit the city where their father worked – though he could never stay there overnight. I mentioned the Jayyous children, who wonder why they are forbidden to visit the beach though the Mediterranean is visible from their home and TV often shows their contemporaries playing with the sand and the sea.

Salah shook his head and sighed. 'Too many children are growing up with too many questions. What are we to say? Honest answers must destabilise them one way or another. Or in different conflicting ways . . .'

By then we were on Road 90 which runs the length of the Valley between the hills of Judea and the invisible river – invisible because of the IDF's fenced and mined buffer zone. In places the rusty '67 vintage wire has been reinforced by an electric fence in which a few gates – long, low and bright yellow – give access to 1,250 acres, once Palestinian private property. This fertile stretch is more than a mile wide and planted with date palms, an exceptionally profitable crop. It was leased to settlers in the 1980s by the World Zionist Organisation to whom it had been presented by the State after the Six-Day War. Oslo-engendered hopes prompted a few of the dispossessed families to return in the mid-'90s but their claims were treated with contempt. The IDF had decreed, 'From a security standpoint, it is unthinkable to admit someone who is not part of the security forces or an armed veteran.' Nowadays, however, selected Thai workers are granted permits – but never a Palestinian. On Road 90 one sees an occasional Thai cyclist; there are few civilian vehicles – and none with green plates. As Raja has noted, 'More than anywhere else in the West Bank, the Valley seems to be devoid of Palestinians.'

Of the IDF's 48 OPT bases, 14 are in the Valley which also holds eight 'Nahal' – mixed military/civilian settlements which never specify their quota of civilians. Road 90 shows a landscape defaced by militarism.

On what should be pastureland tank tracks compact the soil and unexploded mines menace pedestrians. IDF firearms practice targets and gross convolutions of razor wire replace desert scrub. Since 2006 wide trenches have been dug deep to separate farmers from their nearest market. By the roadside wide red trilingual signs, twenty feet high, warn – 'DANGER! Firing Range Entrance Forbidden!' Closed military zones occupy more than one-fifth of the West Bank and some 'Firing Ranges' soon become new settlements. Five Valley communities are now encircled by military zones and animals caught grazing on traditional pastures may be held to ransom while their owners' IDs are confiscated for indefinite periods. Alternatively, owners may be fined or imprisoned. 'Nature Reserves' are another dodge. Israel has set aside almost 50,000 hectares of Palestinian land as 'Nature Reserves' which cannot be cultivated; 30% of that area overlaps with firing zones. Half way up the Valley Salah pointed out a signpost to Ma'ale Efrayim, hidden away amidst one such reserve in very beautiful mountains.

Near Massu settlement we passed acres of greenhouses: commercial farming on an industrial scale. Behind that shiny expanse rose grey-brown rock-strewn slopes, deserted now, where Bedouin herds and flocks once grazed.

'Some Valley settlements with a lot of land have few houses,' said Salah. 'Only one or two families – but all getting fat agricultural sub-sidies, tax breaks, housing subsidies, all sorts of tempting hand-outs. The State admits wanting to double the Zionist population.' Soon after, my attention was drawn to road works in progress – the re-routing of parts of the 'Trans-Samaria Highway' to expedite the delivery of fresh produce to Europe via Ben-Gurion airport.

The IDF frequently stages training exercises near Palestinian com-munities, using live ammunition. One such, in the '90s, left the mayor of Al-Aqaba, Haj Sami Sadeq, paralysed from the waist down. Thereafter he campaigned doggedly until, in 2001, the Israeli High Court ordered the IDF to stop training on Al-Aqaba's land and move their camp from the entrance to the village. Ignoring this, the authorities in 2003 ordered the demolition of most of Al-Aqaba, including the mosque, nursery school, health centre and many homes. When Mayor Sadeq appealed again to the High Court it submitted to pressure ('We don't know from where,' said Salah) and upheld the demolition orders because all those buildings – raised in Area C on Palestinian land – had gone up without

Israeli permission. Yet it was generally known that since 1998 the Civil Administration had been refusing permits to Al-Aqaba families, even for tents and water containers. Salah quoted from a UN Office for the Coordination of Humanitarian Affairs report – agricultural and pastoral communities have endured 90% of the Valley's demolitions.

My companions were engaged in a 'Vulnerability Survey of Herding Communities in the West Bank'. For bureaucratic purposes there are 'Bedouin' and 'non-Bedouin herders', the latter being groups of landless shepherds who for generations have roamed between the high ground and the Valley. Salah and Ahmad were particularly concerned about the Al Hadidiya community who had been displaced five times between February 2006 and February 2009 – all its pitiful shelters, for humans and animals, demolished and their few sticks of furniture smashed. Routinely, the IDF arrive before dawn with bulldozers and sometimes mounted police and dogs. Bulldozers seem superfluous to raze such primitive constructions but, as Salah remarked, 'Soldiers enjoy intimidating.'

Our first visit was to a recently improvised encampment on a strip of wasteland between Road 90 and an aggressively fenced vineyard. Most dwellings were oblong 'tents', some eight feet by four, their torn white plastic laid across unsteady wooden poles. Lengths of old drainpipe served as 'chimneys' when it was possible to scavenge firewood instead of using the costly communal generator. The two mini-tractors surprised me as there is no land to cultivate; Salah explained how essential they are, for fetching water from far-away sources. When I marvelled at these families' obstinate defiance, setting up homes certain to be demolished – including, here, one tiny tin shed – Salah said, 'It's the Arab way to provide new homes when children marry. Once it would've been a goats' hair tent. And by now, with so many structures listed for demolition, people can hope theirs will be at the end of the list and survive for a few years.'

Of these 145 herders more than 50 were children, harrowingly under-fed and dispirited. For the first time I was seeing dirty Palestinians, their persons and garments unwashed. On all faces, strain showed; very likely my inexplicable presence was not helping. As Salah and Ahmad settled down to compile their statistics (a six-page questionnaire to be filled in for each community) I slipped away to commune with settler depredations.

An apartheid road took me past the vineyard, bounded on one side by a row of young palms, stretching as far as the eye could see. Then came an unidentifiable crop protected by chicken-wire and opaque plastic and sustained by an elaborate irrigation system of oddly shaped red and blue pipes and taps, and white oblong windowless structures emitting a low hum – an eerie noise, alien to the Valley. The high, wide metal gates and miles of fencing were all instantly lethal to the unauthorised touch: even to approach too close could be fatal. Only that hum broke the silence and there was no one visible, no movement apart from spraying water. Technology Ruled OK where herders couldn't wash.

Soon I could see in the near distance a newish two-storey, ten-roomed settler school, flying an outsize Israeli flag. At this point the 4 x 4 pursued me and a scared-looking Ahmad yelled, 'Stop! Come back! They see you maybe they shoot!' No doubt he was overstating the case but as his guest I couldn't argue. His turning made a dust cloud and to get off this apartheid road he drove too fast. We wondered why the Valley sees less settler-versus-locals violence than the rest of the West Bank. 'Maybe,' said Ahmad, 'it's about soldiers here always feeling free to attack and harass. Other places have more foreigners watching – like ISM people, sometimes *killed* by soldiers!' (Generations of grateful Palestinians will remember Rachel Corrie and her fellow-victims.) Later, Salah commented more lucidly: 'Many valley settlers are hard-headed agribusinessmen. It's the religious nutters around Hebron and Nablus who stir the worst violence.'

Along Road 90 tall IDF watchtowers mark the periphery of most Palestinian communities. Our next stop was near the military base of Maskiot where new housing units were being built to accommodate an 'outpost' of twelve families for whose sake 80-plus herders were about to be 'moved on'.

Salah foresaw the current drought delivering the *coup de grâce* to all Bedouin and other herders. 'This group, for instance, must pay for fodder with kids and now many don't survive because starved nannies run dry – where to find a more vicious circle? Communities fall more and more deeply in debt until fodder merchants own all their animals. Palestinian Shylocks, I call those guys! To rear a kid or a lamb costs around £20 sterling per head. So parents can't buy children's shoes so no one goes to school . . .'

My companions looked disbelieving when I said the logic of this argument escaped me. In my primary school, in the 1930s, some pupils from rural families walked barefoot to school (a three- or four-mile walk) in weather conditions never experienced by Valley residents.

As we drove on from Maskiot, Salah continued, 'These generations refuse to accept their way of life is over and can't be revived. The twenty-first century is not for nomads. But herding wouldn't have ended so abruptly if the Zionists hadn't become "Lords of the Land".' I realised then that here was another fan of that book.

Near the large village of Al-Jiftlik we came upon an UNRWA 'special delivery' van distributing a meagre six-monthly ration of sunflower oil, flour, lentils, rice, beans and powdered milk to single (widowed) mothers, the handicapped, the old and infirm. Some women had dressed up for this unusual occasion, their long gowns frayed but with richly embroidered bodices. The handicapped lacked all those 'aids' normally provided in 'developed' countries. My companions knew most of the group; local employees of their INGO had helped them to reach this delivery point. 'There can be problems around rations,' observed Salah. 'The disabled can need protection from herder youngsters. Hunger never brings out the best in animals, human or otherwise. I've an American friend loved her dog like nothing else, then got her nose ripped when she moved its bone off some priceless carpet.' Salah acknowledged that for obvious reason Palestine's travelling merchants and settled farmers have not always coexisted happily with the Bedouin. But he emphasised that since the mid-nineteenth century, and in the Valley from 1948 to '67, and even during the pre-Oslo decades, there had been surprisingly little open friction. 'Maybe you could say both lots chose a state of armed neutrality – unless something specific flared up. Over the Green Line, a few Bedouin from unrecognised villages have been taken to international conferences on the rights of indigenous minorities. Not much help but ours don't even have that. The PA didn't include them in their census till 2007 – only then stopped pretending they weren't here! They'll never do anything to lessen prejudice against them.'

Raja Shehadeh agrees with Salah:

Perhaps we in Palestine/Israel . . . should learn from the Bedouin outlook. We haven't yet. Nor are we ever likely to, for one of the tragic consequences of the scramble to possess land following the Israeli occupation was that the Bedouins were pushed out of their traditional grazing grounds. Most of us failed to see that they represent an attractive, alternative way of life and attitude to land that we must all have once shared and from which we still have much to learn.

Within Al-Jiftlik we paused to admire a talented work-party, twelve men young and old co-operating to restore an Ottoman home said to be the Valley's oldest surviving structure. Their dedication to traditional building methods was impressive and by now Al-Jiftlik has a guesthouse accurately described as 'The Jordan Valley's ecologically sound alternative to Jericho's Resort Village'.

Here Ahmad and a local teacher began to argue heatedly about child labour – quite common in the Valley – and Salah later gave me a précis. At least 25% of the dispossessed have to work in settlements and, for their different reasons, it can suit all concerned to ignore the relevant laws. Already Ahmad had shown me photographs of small boys being made to leave their contractor's truck at Hamra checkpoint and parade on the road, stripped to the waist. (Hamra was a notorious checkpoint, between Nablus and the Valley, where I myself had witnessed grown men being forced to remove their shirts and walk slowly from their vehicles to the IDF post. 'That was at sunset,' said Ahmad. 'They'd picked for twelve hours in glasshouses. Three went all weak, had to be helped to walk. The soldiers thought that was very funny.'

Long before this incident, Ahmad had passionately opposed child labour and supported the trade unions who were then campaigning for the closure of a Tubas textile factory employing boys and girls aged ten to thirteen. (Also, they paid their women workers 30% of a man's wage.)

Inevitably the teacher protested that Ahmad, enjoying a secure INGO job plus perks, had no right to meddle in this high-minded way with the lives of the less fortunate. Many Valley children were in no position to refuse a wage, however small and however long the hours. Here was another of those conundrums bred by situations inherently indefensible yet leaving people like myself debating 'the lesser evil'. Those herder children I had just seen, might they not be better off as child labourers? Rather than languishing all day in their encampment, hungry and idle, waiting fearfully for the next demolition order, the next incursion of brutal soldiers.

Salah advised, 'Don't get into it all with Ahmad, it upsets him too much. He says when he looks at his own daughters he feels so bad for not being able to help other kids.'

The Bedouin village of Upper Fasayil, our last stop, lost most of its land years ago but had recently experienced something remarkable and cheering. The process started in Brighton in May 2006 with the formation of the Brighton–Tubas Friendship and Solidarity Group. In April 2007 a few members visited Upper Fasayil where the community longed to build a school for which an ample Norwegian donation was available. The Brightonians urged them to build without the impossible-to-get permit and promised every sort of support. Six months later, when the Bedouin were ordered to stop building, they disobeyed and challenged the injunction in court. Promptly the Brightonians organised an international petition and managed to engage the indignant sympathy of Britain's national press. (No easy task when Palestinians are involved.) Quite soon the Israelis reversed gear and a year later the school opened. By the time of our visit its seven classrooms were packed with eager pupils of both sexes, the girls wearing the standard blue-and-white candy-striped tunics with jeans and headscarves. Moreover, because Upper Fasayil's nearest source of rudimentary medical care is 8 miles away, these Bedouin were planning to build a clinic with the aid of Ma'an Development.

Salah had been busy giving this episode maximum publicity. He said, 'It shows the Zionists' vulnerability to a bad press. Also it shows what a small group of activists can achieve. People may say it's just a drop in the ocean but if there weren't any drops there wouldn't be any ocean.'

The Valley's Palestinians, Bedouin and otherwise, don't lack NGO attention but Salah complained that few if any of the well-known organisations would have dared to intervene as directly, on a practical level, as the Brightonians had done. 'You know why?' he asked rhetorically. 'They'd be afraid of retaliation – being kicked out, blacklisted.'

I remembered those words in 2012 when OCHA, the UN agency most loudly and eloquently critical of Zionist outrages, was attacked from Jerusalem, accused of 'supporting unauthorised building in Area C'. And – 'a clarification of your mandate' was formally demanded. By that date Israel was being reprimanded more often, though always in plaintive clichés. The EU foreign ministers 'called upon' Israel to 'alleviate the living conditions of Palestinians living in Area C', whereupon Oxfam took courage and 'called upon' the EU and its individual member states 'to pressure Israel to end the construction of illegal settlements and comply with its obligations under international law'. Personally I am seriously exasperated (can actually feel my blood pressure rising) by all such references to international law, Geneva Conventions, human rights and so on. These devices for the regulation of mankind's behaviour, which for generations have been flouted with impunity, now look like hypocritical weapons only deployed by the powerful when it suits their particular interests.

On the way back to Jericho we passed the Mehola settlement which produces irises, dates, citrus fruits, rosemary and sage, exported by 'Jordan River Herbs' and 'Arava'. 'They label their stuff "organic" or "bio organic",' said Salah, 'but I'm not convinced . . .' We then discussed BDS. Despite the Valley's dependence on settlement jobs, Salah found most Palestinians fervently pro-BDS. Were the foreign market not so lucrative, the whole hi-tech Jordan Valley agribusiness project would make no commercial sense. Although it would still, alas! make 'security' sense to the Zionists in power.

A cousin of Salah's who lived in the ancient town of al-Auja (in Area A, a few miles north of Jericho) had invited the three of us to supper. In medieval times Al-Auja flourished as a pilgrim centre; people thronged to bathe in the Jordan where St John was said to have baptised Jesus. Thereafter the town's importance gradually declined but it was reduced to poverty only when the Occupiers seized its lands and water and confined its inhabitants within this fragment of Area A.

Where we parked at the end of Tamima's laneway – too narrow for the 4 x 4 – Salah hired an emaciated elder to guard the vehicle. 'Prob'ly no need,' he said, 'but given so much destitution it could be a temptation.'

Tamima was middle-aged and overweight, a childless widow with a keen interest in Friends of the Earth Middle East and a strong hope (since fulfilled) that the organisation would set up a guesthouse-cum-environmental information centre to boost the town's economy while educating visitors about 'crimes against Nature'. In 2001 her husband, a local government clerk (PA) and 'Green' activist, had been killed by an army jeep while cycling home one evening at dusk. 'It wasn't an accident,' said Tamima. 'Witnesses saw that driver going for him.' (Afterwards Salah told me the unfortunate man's bicycle had been unlit.)

We ate in the Ottoman-era bedsit to which Tamima had moved

when widowed; its dingy plastered walls were brightened by long embroidered scrolls – verses from the Koran. Our simple first course of salad, goats' cheese, hummus and hot bread was followed by the luxury pudding Salah had brought from Jerusalem – a baker's tray of baklava and honey-soaked, nut-filled pastries (not suitable for semi-toothless grannies).

Two of Tamima's six sisters joined us and matters environmental concerned all present. Salah confirmed what they had told me in Jayyous – that the Valley settlers dig wells much deeper than the Palestinian norm and their ignorance of what is ecologically sustainable (for all their boasting about 'making the desert bloom!') has further damaged the Jordan River and Dead Sea basin.

Syria and Lebanon contribute numerous streams to the Jordan's head-waters, then Jordan and Israel (mainly Israel) divert so much that the river reaches the Dead Sea as a sluggish trickle containing catastrophic concentrations of chemicals. By now these are gravely endangering the extraordinary variety of migrating birds which until recently made this one of the world's most ornithologically exciting destinations. Also, notoriously, more than 1,500 sinkholes have opened up around the Dead Sea shores, threatening both wildlife and tourist trade earnings.

Tamima explained that since the Dead Sea became a global scandal – its level dropping annually by more than three feet – several Palestinian, Jordanian and Israeli environmentalists have united to run a 'Save the Dead Sea!' campaign. When she insisted, quoting some of these experts, that just enough time remained to avert disaster, her sisters pointed out a big 'if'. If Israel could be induced to release its tight grip on the Jordan, allowing it again to flow naturally into the Dead Sea . . . The omens were not good. Zionist technocrats favoured 'saving' the Dead Sea by pumping in regular replenishments of salt water from the Gulf of Aqaba.

In a verbal flurry of apologies and thanks, we had to hasten away at 7.00 p.m.; the 4 x 4 lived under curfew. On the way to my 'Palace' Salah described himself as a devout Muslim worried about increasing Salafist influences throughout the OPT. 'Some of us are going backwards, in reaction to the Occupation. People seeing no political way forward turn to the religious way and then abuse it. They believe only Allah can help us and one day he will, knowing our cause is just. I believe that too. But I hate the argument that our faith is weakened or betrayed by compromises with Western ways – like bareheaded women on bicycles!'

Only then did I discover that Salah had read my first book (published half-a-century ago) which is about a bareheaded woman on a bicycle. We arranged to meet next day in Jerusalem; Salah's home was not far from my favourite hostel in the Muslim Quarter.

CHAPTER 21

Here and There in Jerusalem

Serveeces fill up quite quickly in most OPT cities but Jericho's taxi service is unpredictable. Although there was no shortage of vehicles – most looking past their drive-by date – few locals are granted permits to visit Jerusalem. On the previous evening one of Tamima's sisters had asked me, 'How would you feel if you couldn't visit Dublin? Or pray in your holiest place . . .'

At sunrise I took a front seat in a resuscitated Volvo, its windscreen sporting a scrap of cardboard saying 'Jerusalem'. The bleary-eyed young driver assured me, 'Soon yes we go!' He had been sleeping in a quilt under the eaves of the main vegetable market; now he rolled up his bedding and disappeared. It seemed that 'soon' was to be loosely interpreted. I opened my book (Maxime Rodinson's *Israel and the Arabs*) and shifted to a sitting posture aligning my buttocks more comfortably with certain defective springs.

An hour or so later Taysir returned. 'Yes we go!' he beamed. But we didn't go far, only to the junction beyond the Intercontinental Hotel. There we waited hopefully: some of the night staff, going off duty, might need a serveece. When all hope had faded Taysir said, 'I am sorry, sorry!' and drove me back to the centre.

Eventually I was advised to take a Ramallah minibus to the At Tur checkpoint. Our middle-aged driver was young at heart and enjoyed speeding in the middle of the road. Near the Allenby Bridge turn-off a Border Police patrol detained us and for the first time I found myself applauding an Israeli security force intervention. Angry recriminations, accompanied by detailed note-taking and radio reporting, delayed us for nearly an hour.

As Ma'ale Adumim loomed on the heights above I recalled Raja's comment – 'We must remember some settlements are so big and long-established it would be cruel to uproot them.' I had retorted, 'Too bad!' But obviously he's right, though I'd momentarily scorned his nice blend of realism and compassion. Hence the fatuousness of pursuing the two-state solution.

I had marked an extraordinary passage in *Israel and the Arabs* –
extraordinary because written in the summer of 1967 a few weeks after
the Six-Day War:

> How is Israel to keep the conquered territories under her dominion?
> Either the system becomes democratic, or even remains simply liberal
> and parliamentary – in which case the Arabs will very soon be in the
> majority, and that will be the end of the dream of a Jewish State
> for which so many sacrifices have been made. Or else the Arabs
> will be treated as second-class citizens, discrimination will become
> institutional, a kind of South African policy will be introduced. This,
> together with the increasingly savage repression of increasingly bold
> acts of sabotage and guerrilla warfare, will lose Israel the support of
> world public opinion.

This Sorbonne professor of Old South Arabian languages was probably
the first outsider to discern the affinity between South Africa's white
Nationalists and the Zionist leaders. But the support of world public
opinion is taking a long time to drain away.

On the West Bank side, the At Tur checkpoint flew a row of Israeli flags
above mocking notices in English – 'WELCOME! ENJOY YOUR
STAY!' To negotiate this sprawling fortification took me one hour and
twenty minutes. There were five long queues, two heavy metal revolving
gates and a vast barracks where the airport-type x-ray procedures deal with
only three persons at a time. Then came iron bars, forming a narrow
corridor, and very slowly people shuffled past windows of opaque glass,
pushing their documents under these to be scrutinised by the invisible
bullies within. But at least these residents of the northern West Bank,
unlike the Valley residents, can visit Jerusalem, if only for a few hours.

Serveeces awaited us on the East Jerusalem side and for a few miles
we drove in the shadow of the Barrier, so close we couldn't see the
rapidly expanding settlement on the far side. On our other side were
the dejected homes of recently impoverished citizens abruptly cut off
from their misappropriated land. After my three segregated months on
the West Bank, it gave me quite a jolt to see Palestinians and Jewish
civilians mingling along Jaffa Road and in the Old City – though never
openly communicating. For my last week I had booked into a ten-
room Zionist guesthouse (popularly known as 'No. 99') close to the
central bus station. Shaul had recommended it as a useful base from

which to observe Mea She'arim, one of the city's more idiosyncratic neighbourhoods where Yiddish is favoured over Hebrew – the latter being regarded as a sacred language.

My fellow-guests that evening were a half-dozen middle-aged New Jersey pilgrims, a dovish lot. As earnest Christians they wanted all groups, tribes, parties, clans, sects, classes and races to pray together regularly. 'That's the fast track to Peace!' proclaimed Mr Woodrow Jameson who asked me to quote him by name. 'We pray every day for the two-state solution and the guys in Washington like it too. It's a fair deal, half the country for Arabs.'

Wearily I pointed out, 'If ever it did happen, they'd have only 22%.'

Several pilgrims spoke at once. '*Why*? Why so little?' But when I tried to explain they lost interest. Do most of us find percentages soporific? Yet I'd kept it brief: 'The UN gave 56.5% of the land to the Zionists in 1947, then during the Arab/Israeli war they were able to grab 78%.'

We were sitting at a long trestle table in the narrow front garden, shielded from the busy junction traffic by tall trees and aromatic shrubs. My companions' plan to tour the West Bank had been thwarted. 'We were told it's too risky for foreigners if they can't afford to hire a bullet-proof coach.' Mrs Jameson sighed. 'Shame our budget's so tight! Shame we can't go talk with the Arabs!'

'You could go,' I said, 'if you chose to ignore Zionist propaganda. And if you spent as long in the OPT as in Israel, you'd stop shouting for two states.'

The threat from Europe bothered my companions. By this they meant a tendency, occasionally detectable in certain European circles, to talk with 'fanatical terrorists' – Hamas. I had the routine reaction, reminding them that many members of Israel's early governments had been identically labelled – men like Yitzhak Shamir (twice prime minister) who boasted of being one of the Stern gang assassins, in September 1948, of UN mediator Count Bernadotte. And what about Nelson Mandela and the ANC? And certain members of Northern Ireland's present power-sharing, peace-building Assembly? The pilgrims looked baffled – then suddenly suspicious. Whose side was I on?

Later I wrote in my journal:

This is when I sink back into a Slough of Despond. Such good guys, kindly, well-meaning, anxious to help everybody including the dangerous Palestinians! But useless as allies, so unwilling to probe the painful complexities of it all. Therefore not armed to apply reasoned political pressure to their own government . . .

Next morning, as we dispersed after breakfast, the pilgrims cheerily chorused – 'Have a nice day!' They looked rather taken aback when I tartly replied that I was braced to have a gruelling day in Silwan.

A Caananite village by origin, Silwan has latterly become a squalid, grossly overcrowded suburb deprived of municipal services and menaced by government-sponsored settlers. On its periphery I prudently re-displayed my pro-Palestinian regalia. The local tension level had risen still higher since my last visit in November; many bulldozers had been busy. The query 'Speak English?' provoked sullen glares, despite English being the *lingua franca* of those stalwart Internationals who rally around 'relocated' families during demolitions. As usual the regalia paid off, yet one could sense much vengeful rage simmering just below the surface. At about this date, the poet Mourid Barghouti was writing in his journal: 'There is a huge explosion coming – I don't know where and I don't know when but the explosion, or explosions, are coming for sure.'

It took time to find Noora, first met in November; her parents' home had recently been razed and her new address was obscure. I had almost given up when a small boy volunteered to help.

In 2007 Noora's husband had died in a building site accident the week after their son's birth. Now she shared a bedsit with another young widow who also had a toddler. Our conversation was fractured by the two-year-olds' compulsion repeatedly to venture down an un-protected outside stairway, too often accessible because neighbours left the door open. As in Balata, I felt very conscious here of the multiple inconveniences – minor yet wearing – of overcrowded living quarters.

Four months previously, Noora had shown me the small olive grove on the far side of the Kidron Valley, cultivated by her family for unrecorded generations. Moments after my arrival, she pointed to where it had been – not a tree left, the land seized 'for common use'. Her father, like many others, had refused compensation; acceptance would be interpreted as an acknowledgement of Israel's right to the compulsory purchase of private property for 'development'. While chopping and grating salads she described the latest schemes, contrived 'legally', to 'transfer' Palestinians, allegedly for tourism's benefit – a benefit never to be shared with those transferred.

Noora's mother and aunt joined us for lunch. Neither spoke English but as skilled toddler-tamers they left my hostess free to consult her files and provide me with more human-rights-related statistics than I could ever use. Not until 3.10 did I notice the time; to keep my appointment with Salah I should already have left.

Noora promptly summoned Jawad, a twelve-year-old cousin who would quickly lead me down, avoiding the corkscrewing motor road – on which few motors travelled. In retrospect, this was an exhilarating experience. Here were none of Nablus' obvious, orderly flights of hundreds of steps, with handrails. Silwan's is an esoteric shortcut, often down steep narrow slithery slopes between gable-ends, sometimes along level, two-foot-wide pathlets between the foundations of one row of houses and the roofs of another, occasionally across flat roofs, sometimes intruding on family balconies (causing alarm), twice down unsteady metal ladders linking hall doors to the corkscrew road. And then the familiar dilemma – to tip or not to tip? Jawad let me off that hook by shouting farewell and disappearing into a wayside shack-café before my arrival on the main road.

Near the Dung Gate I loitered to eavesdrop on the brainwashing of a quartet of elderly US males – tycoon types, the sort who fund settlements. While standing by a 'City of David' signpost, on the edge of the cliff, they were being lectured in Hebrew-accented English by another elderly male with snow-white collar-length hair and two chins. He seemed not a tourist guide but a colleague of the tycoons. Gesturing widely, he asserted that Arabs have always tried to establish a fraudulent claim to East Jerusalem by illegally building houses. 'How would *you* feel,' he demanded dramatically, 'if illegal buildings covered your Central Park?'

I had moved closer, while pretending to photograph, and could see the Americans' faces; they looked grave and understanding. One of them observed that Arab cunning and corruption made peace unattainable. Another believed Israel needs to fight much harder against 'Islamic imperialism'. (In my journal I awarded that comment three exclamation marks.) How to explain the saleability of such phoney analogies as the 'Central Park' to people who, in another context, have enough intelligence to make billions of dollars, often starting from scratch?

As the group moved on, gathering smartphone pictures of the Old City walls, I followed them. Snowy-locks wore a hearing aid which perhaps explains why he spoke loudly enough for me (almost needing one) to continue eavesdropping. We were, he lectured, on a famous battlefield. Then he smoothly delivered Zionism's hoary lies about the Haganah's gallant struggle, on 19 May 1948, against thousands of heavily armed Arabs with tanks in the lead. That effort to protect the Holy Places from Islamic desecration cost many Jewish lives. (Muslims have been efficiently guarding those Places for the past 1,400 years – apart from the Crusader episode.)

In fact, on that date, the Arab Legion deployed fewer than 500 poorly armed men – and its first tank was delivered in 1953. Yet that was one of the Legion's rare victories; by early afternoon they had reached the Damascus Gate.

Zionist *hasbara* spinners excel at such editing of the historical narrative. And the occupational hazards are minimal; not many twenty-first-century tycoons are likely to check on the precise date when the Arab Legion acquired its first tank. However, one shouldn't be frivolous about *hasbara*; it has done incalculable damage over a wide area during the past century. Many regard its spinners as the most talented in their field. Raja has noted how effective they were in 1967, when he and all around him believed that Egypt was not bluffing but seriously threatening Israel – an attack-enabling assertion long-since disproved.

Glubb Pasha (John Bagot Glubb, only begetter of the Arab Legion) had his own brush with *hasbara* in the 1960s when he set off on a US lecture tour. At New York airport a press conference had been arranged and he was taken aback when handed a prepared statement, to be read to the journalists, expressing his admiration for the brave people of Israel and detailing their tribulations. Politely Glubb Pasha explained that he always drafted his own statements. A blunt warning followed: if he didn't comply, his lectures might be boycotted wherever Zionist pressures are felt. Sir John however was not for turning and on that tour his earnings fell way below the expectations of Foyles Lecture Agency.

In 1982 Glubb Pasha wrote in his memoirs:

If only the Israelis had loved the Arabs and tried to do them good, they would by now have held as powerful a position in Western Asia as they do in the United States. But successive Israeli governments have continued to suppress the people of Palestine, to rule them by martial law, to evict them and seize their lands and to deny them any part in government.

Not many successful military careers are based on 'love' as a motivating force. In a quirky way, Glubb Pasha's was – while the diplomats and politicians mocked his naiveté.

Salah's four-room, top floor flat had an astonishingly fertile roof-garden from which one could have scrambled, in an emergency, to Sari's hostel roof. His wife Tarub, employed as a part-time interpreter by another INGO, expected him to carry the tray of coffee paraphernalia and *kunafa* up the medieval stairs to the roof – as is not the Palestinian norm. Salah had told me, 'Her hobby is asking awkward questions' and I soon saw what he meant. From my journal I transcribe:

> Have the Zionists successfully split the OPT? How many West Bank Palestinians will easily forget the Gazan slaughtering and isolation if their own living-conditions improved even a little? Since Oslo, UNRWA have been reducing support until most food deliveries are only annual. Poor education handicaps most refugees, their English language teachers can't make one short correct sentence . . . there's too much nepotism in Ramallah and if you look close it's not a real government . . . Why shouldn't the PA take total responsibility for the camps? They get enough funding from the EU! All the time our drugs problem gets worse, mostly coming from Lebanon, sometimes with Israeli conscripts and our 'terrorists' working as teams. In that way, and a few others, we've the one-state solution already!

Mulling over all those awkwardnesses took time; luckily No. 99 provided each guest with a hall-door key.

When I moved to Hebron my heavy luggage (printed matter) had been left with Sari and as Salah escorted me to the No. 18 bus stop he volunteered to meet me at the Damascus Gate and help me with it on the morrow – my last Jerusalem Friday.

In the Old City Friday is a day of action – holy action. Before sunrise Christians from all continents sing hymns and carry plywood crosses as they follow their priestly guides along the Via Dolorosa. In the early afternoon, getting to or from the Damascus Gate takes patience and a resignation to being jostled as thousands of men leave the al-Aqsa mosque via the souk's narrow covered passageways. After sunset, the otherwise staid Jewish Quarter comes to indoor life and families may be heard cheerfully chanting their Sabbath prayers by candlelight. Given all these devout folk enthusiastically worshipping the same god, one can't help having hackneyed thoughts about the cruel absurdity of their leaders being able so often to recruit Yahweh/Jesus/Allah to cause bloody mayhem.

At the Damascus Gate I sat on a low wall, amidst the usual colourful, raucous turmoil, and treated myself to a litre of buttermilk. Pairs of soldiers and police – one of each – were patrolling the throng, exuding the distinctive arrogance of heavily armed men moving amongst a hostile but defenceless population.

An ill-dressed youth, weedy and spotty, appeared beside me, his head-load a long, shallow wooden box, in one hand carrying a plastic crate. Nearby, he found a space – not much space, but then none of this market's vendors enjoys more than elbow room. I watched him tumbling his merchandise (resembling Christmas tree decorations, which here must serve another purpose) into the box, then using the crate as a stand. Around the box's edges were clipped scores of gaudy plastic hair-grips; it had taken some time to put these in place before he set out to earn an honest shekel. For some children Friday is pocket-money day and he had made quite a few sales when 'security' inter-vened. A Falasha soldier and a blue-eyed, mousy-haired policeman accused him of blocking the pedestrian traffic and demanded to see his (non-existent) licence. Both pointed their guns at him; it seems selling trinkets without a licence may be regarded as a terrorist activity. He must pack up and GO and report next day to the Salah Ed-Din Street police station. He cowered and at once obeyed orders, stuffing the decorative bits and pieces back into the crate. When he made to lift the box onto his head the policeman checked him – he must first unclip all those hair-grips. Then he did protest, whereupon an Uzi was pushed against his chest and the policeman snarled something that made the soldier laugh. I was reminded of the IDF amusement, at Huwwara checkpoint, when those two youths couldn't get their granny's biscuit packages together. Such trivial incidents – but what of their cumulative effect?

Throughout this incident I'd been observing the reactions of those around us. Everyone ignored it, all were engaged in their own affairs – or resigned, for the moment, to being victimised.

Sari understood my motive for moving to No. 99 and bore me no grudge. 'Be watchful,' he cautioned, 'around Mea She'arim. They have crazy people there – not normal fanatics, unsafe people.'

Listening to my impressions of the Jordan Valley, Sari showed scant sympathy for the Bedouin. 'Some, yes, can be good and get very bad treatment in the Negev. Most we don't trust. You should write they're not real Palestinians. They'll work for the IDF as trackers or for Egypt or Lebanon as spies. They don't belong to anyone, only to the desert. In Mandate times Arabs from Iraq and Syria tried to help us. Some were killed when the British used Bedouin, organised from Jordan, to stop them crossing the river. My father remembered a big battle in 1939 when our Iraqi friends killed British soldiers based in Jordan. There was a big celebration for that because it wasn't easy to kill British. My father wasn't pleased – he didn't like any killing. The Mandate was very confusing, he said, the British going two ways at once. Their London government backed the Zionists, some officials and soldiers living in Palestine wanted to back us but couldn't, against London. During the Nakba some Bedouin did fight the Zionists – they were with the British-run Arab Legion.'

I complained 'It's *too* confusing! Weren't your friends from Iraq and Syria who were killed by the Bedouin themselves Bedouin?'

Sari looked puzzled. 'Maybe – there are many tribes. Always they fought each other to steal camels.'

I continued, 'How come the British-led Arab Legion fought the Zionists if London was pro-Zionist?'

Sari stroked his beard and thought for a moment. Then – 'Churchill made a fake country in Jordan when the Ottomans went. Afterward the British pretended the Arab Legion was Jordan's army. That way, they could use – when it suited them – British-trained troops to fight Zionists. That's why we say Israel happened by a mistake. There was all that muddle, nobody thinking in one straight line about Palestine belonging to the Palestinians. Europeans still thought they could fake countries for their own convenience – so many people telling big lies to cover up small lies! And always we came out worst. In the Jordan time there was more confusion, fighting in our camps around Jericho. Our refugees hated the Jordan king who worked too hard for the Zionists through the British. They had protests against him and he used Bedouin very cruelly against them. The British officers liked the Bedouin cruelty. My father heard the Bedouin were treating our poor refugees as bad as Zionists did.'

I would have relished hours more of Sari's rather dodgy version of recent history – its dodginess intrinsically quite fascinating. But Salah had just arrived to help transport my load to No. 99 before 3.00 p.m. when all public transport must stop by rabbinate decree: never mind that a high percentage of Israel's Jews are non-observant and resent this constraint. Not long ago Ireland was rightly seen as priest-ridden – or Paisley-ridden, in the North – but the Holy Land's dominant rabbis ride Israel even harder. There are of course dissenting 'moderates'. When I asked Salah if he thought they might one day gain influence he replied, 'Not in my grandchildren's lifetime!'

Every week at this hour the Israeli masses food-shop almost frenziedly as though preparing for a siege of indefinite length. All sorts and sizes scrambled breathlessly onto our bus, each adult clutching two or three bulging plastic bags, and the rush on the pavements accelerated as three o'clock approached. Here was a bizarre version of 'Grandmother's Footsteps' – where would everyone be when the internal combustion engines must be switched off?

Salah advised, as we said regretful goodbyes outside No. 99, 'Don't do your Mea She'arim survey tomorrow.'

That evening eight of my fellow-guests were Christian Zionists from the Bible Belt who make an annual pilgrimage to check out that all is shipshape for Rapture time. Their literature alerted me to their mission – sheaves of pamphlets and leaflets, prominently displayed in the commonroom where we breakfasted between 7.00 and 9.00 a.m. and relaxed in the evenings. Their appearance was unremarkable; they seemed just another group of easy-going, white, middle-class US tourists, not rich, ranging in age from thirtyish to seventyish. Having been warned that there was a writer in the house they approached me as someone worth cultivating.

A tall thin septuagenarian with arthritic hands introduced herself as Leah and quoted their pastor-in-chief, John Hagee, who preaches – 'All other nations were created by an act of man, but Israel was created by an act of God.' A pamphlet later informed me that Hagee runs 'Christians

United for Israel' and hires professional lobbyists. His eight TV networks claim to reach 100 million homes and he sponsors programmes to encourage Jews from anywhere to migrate to Israel.

Joseph and his wife and adult son belonged to the 'Christian Friends of Israeli Communities' (code for 'settlements'), an anti-Oslo group set up in 1995. 'We've funded more than fifty communities in Samaria and Judea,' boasted Joseph. 'It's our duty to fund others here in Jerusalem, the venue for the Second Coming. The presence of Islamic elements could delay The Coming.'

There was something surreal about sitting at a primly laid break-fast table eating a banal meal of cornflakes, scrambled egg, toast and marmalade while listening to this group's utterances. The woman sitting opposite me was reassuring about such catastrophes as the Kashmir earthquake and Hurricane Katrina – they presage the Apocalypse so must inspire rejoicing. Her husband idolised Rabbi Yechiel Eckstein who founded the 'International Fellowship of Christians and Jews' and annually donates millions of dollars to good causes in Israel where his Fellowship is the second-largest charitable foundation. One occasionally reads about such people but the printed word can't give the full flavour: they have to be met to be believed. It alarmed me to learn that there are millions of them; they're not just a fringe of a fringe as I once imagined. Moreover, they have many powerful representatives in the US Congress; here is an under-emphasised factor in the Palestinian/Israel equation. One young man told me that the Christian Zionists amongst others had lobbied the Bush administration to nuke Iran – thereby bringing about Armageddon, the catalyst for Christ's return. That notorious mindset used to make me laugh. Not any more, having talked for hours with real live examples of this terrifying species. Their contribution to nourishing Islamophobia in their 'homeland' is valued by maniacal militarists, men in positions of power who may be heard on the BBC vehemently asserting that Islamists are plotting to take over the US, to impose Sharia law from pole to pole, to obliterate Israel – therefore we must be willing to deploy all our resources against them . . . *All*, mark you.

That afternoon I met Shaul for a beer outside my favourite Christian Quarter café. In his view, non-governmental financial support for the settlers is as politically influential as the $3 billion dollars given annually by the US government to the State of Israel. Rich and middle-aged

Israelis are, in general, much less fixated on settling the OPT than the impecunious Haredim who are happy – quite apart from religious considerations – to have West Bank homes subsidised by foreigners.

We were joined by three of Shaul's ISM friends, newly released from a week's detention. They had been arrested at Sheikh Jarrah, having insisted on remaining with a family (including five children under ten) while their home was being razed. A tent erected at this site was being occupied day and night by Israelis, Palestinians and Internationals, to the Zionists' fury. Now the three had been forbidden to re-enter the West Bank and they half-expected deportation.

Shaul later voiced reservations about the wisdom of acceding to families' requests for live-in support. 'It's a tricky one. There's evidence the IDF take it out on such families when the supporters depart. Yet it's generally accepted their presence during demolitions puts a brake on physical violence and torture-by-insult. I'm cowardly about this, won't give an opinion unless I know a family personally.'

Two days previously I had met another trio of Internationals on their way to a big Friday demo at Jayyous. They planned to travel on Thursday as no foreigners were being allowed through the surrounding checkpoints on Friday mornings. I'd have accompanied them but for my lameness – one needs to be able to run away from tear-gas. A young Frenchman remarked that the army direct their fire so that activists – blocked by the Apartheid Barrier – must run through clouds of gas to escape. Those who have been within close range of the Barrier alarms suffer from earache for several days. One gets the impression that these brave activists quite enjoy the excitement – taking risks in a good cause! The risks, however, are real – and increasing.

Shaul accompanied me back to No. 99, eager for a close-up of the Christian Zionists. 'I feel I'm on the way to the zoo,' he said, 'except these dangerous animals are not caged.'

As we walked, the first two stars appeared and motor vehicles moved again. Crossing Zion Square, we saw what I momentarily mistook for a school group awaiting transport. Then I looked again and identified a family – a Haredi family, two parents and fourteen children including a babe in arms. We paused to watch them boarding and filling a minibus. 'That's the Haredi way,' said Shaul. 'Some demographers think they're consciously competing with the Muslims, seems to me it's how they feel it's right to live – like wearing 1850s fashions.'

I said, 'Those fashions make them very obvious – in fact how many are there?'

'No more than 15% of our total Jewish population, though they've lately topped 25% of Jerusalem's Jewish population. The worry is their strengthening national political influence – because our electoral system has so many loose screws. We can hope the internet will finish them in a generation and their rabble of rabbis know that's possible – even probable. In 2000 the rabbinate proclaimed – "The internet is 1000 times more dangerous than TV." They never had a problem keeping TV off their scene but they can't catch the quicksilver internet. All over Jerusalem the young males crowd into cyber cafés.'

Shaul didn't spend long at the zoo. When next we met he asked, 'How do you do it? How do you sit there calmly listening to that sort of thing and not get up to slap their stupid faces?'

I said, 'It's my job to listen to all sorts. As for that lot, they need to spend years having some specialist psychotherapy which may not yet have been invented.'

As Shaul put it, 'Mea She'arim was begot as a ghetto.' After the Crimean War, when Europeans – with Britain and France in the lead – were quietly establishing their 'spheres of influence' in Palestine, a philanthropic English Jew, Moses Montefiore, and an equally generous Russian Jew, David Yellin, tried to ease the overcrowded, disease-breeding conditions of Jerusalem's Jews. They bought land near the Old City and Mea She'arim was built as a walled colony, according to strict ultra-Orthodox Torah rules, with its own *yeshivas*, synagogue and market. Even when new, the neighbourhood was described as shabby, introverted and reminiscent of sixteenth-century Poland. During the First World War observers noted that Mea She'arim's elders were filthy, bloated with hunger, their faces and limbs covered with sores. Nobody now looks filthy or hungry but neither does the average Haredi glow with health. Black clad and bearded, or long-skirted and closely scarved, they consistently refuse to deviate from the culture and garb of Central Europe's mid-nineteenth-century Ashkenazi communities. The name 'Haredim', meaning 'awestruck' or 'God-fearing', was adopted at that time by Jews opposed to all modern innovations. The males' attire is as compulsory as religious habits once were for Roman Catholic monastic orders. But only in Israel do the rabbis insist on thick black coats and

heavy fur hats being worn at all seasons, come heatwaves or high
water. The many fractious sects include the implacably anti-Zionist
Toldot Haron who believe no one but God should be regarded as
capable of restoring the Temple. At the end of public meetings certain
political parties arouse anger by praying instead of singing the national
anthem. One sect, with mystical tendencies, is irreverently nicknamed
'the Hasidic hippies'; their worship includes jolly songs and rather
uninhibited all-male dancing.

Less jolly is the IDF's Nahal Haredi unit, admired by some for its
uninhibited attacks on Palestinians young and old. In 1999 the Ministry
of Defence expended much thought and money on overcoming the
Haredi aversion to military service. New barracks uncontaminated by
females were built and a separate routine was devised, allowing time off
for daily prayer and Torah study. Quite soon some sects came to accept
soldiering as not incompatible with the Torah but when this provoked
their rabbis to go on the rampage Nahal Haredi shrank abruptly. Then,
to fill those new barracks, foreign Haredi were imported (from the
US, Britain, France and elsewhere) while officialdom turned a blind
eye on recruits from the illegal Kach movement. This blindness was
soon regretted, as international media spread the news that Israeli
soldiers were stoning Palestinian cars, aiming to cause major accidents.
In 2005, two Haredi recruits angered by the uprooting of Gaza's settlers,
planted a fake bomb in Jerusalem's central bus station. The following
year a US-born Haredi blew himself up in a Jordan Valley mosque; in
Jericho Afaf told me it was widely believed he had fumbled his mission,
had intended to press the switch at prayer-time. In the Valley, she said,
the Nahal Haredi's hatred for Palestinians is repeatedly let off the leash
by officers as irresponsible as their men. The unit, now numbering
about 800, ranks amongst the IDF's most undisciplined. In 2006 they
sped joyfully to the Lebanon to tackle Hezbollah, who soon lowered
their level of joy.

From No. 99 a short walk took me into this sad drab slum where
there was little motor traffic and everything needed repainting. Large
locked buildings, with boarded-up windows, suggested a certain level of
lost prosperity. The Haredi way of life is not conducive to commerce
and most business premises seem ready to go into receivership. Along
the main streets' pavements flowed a slow trickle of shoppers – all
Haredi, mainly women with broods following. It was a very windy

morning and litter swirled through the air, being augmented by toddlers in pushchairs as they finished their ice-cream or ersatz fruit juice. Overhead, laundry flapped wildly on the broken balconies of square stone houses. The men all stared at me with unconcealed animosity, the women with a mix of surprise and scorn. Although seeing no trace of Mea She'arim's original walls, I felt, unsurprisingly, 'here is my first experience of a genuine ghetto'. It's odd to be aware of such intense and general dislike/disapproval of oneself simply because one is not – cannot be – kosher. Usually, in hostile environments, there's the possibility that barriers may be overcome through some chance meeting. Not so in this exclusive neighbourhood. I found myself hoping the internet soon demolishes the walls imprisoning these Haredim.

Near the Kikar Shabbat junction I paused to transcribe a few of the numerous placards, banners and gable-end murals warning against 'clothing that would offend the people who live here' – against linking arms or holding hands – against taking photographs or talking to children. I was wearing a long-sleeved, buttoned-up shirt, a borrowed headscarf and – despite the hot spring sunshine – ankle socks. So my attire can't have incensed the two boys who now raced past, kicking me so hard on the buttocks that I fell forward against a wall, dropping my notebook. They stopped at a little distance, to look back and jeer. Then a third lad darted from behind the wall, grabbed my notebook and joined them. (A tiny notebook, almost new, not a serious loss.) The boys were aged ten-ish with long, curly side-locks. In another ten years they'll have long bushy beards and (probably) wives. And ten years after that they are likely to have nine children, something which greatly concerns their secular, slow-breeding compatriots.

On this quiet street there were only two witnesses, elderly women standing by an open hall door some thirty yards away. They ignored the boys but shouted angrily at me, making 'Go away!' gestures. My plan to wander through the adjacent district of short, narrow streets suddenly seemed like a bad idea; instead I descended a slight slope leading out of the ghetto. Here the road surface was in bits and I walked alone, approaching the Green Line that once separated Jordanian East Jerusalem from Zionist West Jerusalem. Across this territory, the two armies fought fiercely in 1948 when the Haganah captured Mea She'arim on 16 May. To my right rose an acutely slummy 1970s apartment block, beside an expanse of wasteland. Soon I could hear the fast dual-carriageway traffic on King George V Street – and moments later could see my way blocked by army-style concrete chunks. As I turned back, swearing at the IDF, I was stoned from the wasteland – a small shower of biggish stones. One struck a shoulder and could have done damage to my head. I hesitated; I'd only glimpsed the bearded young men but they must still be observing me. It made sense to reconsider the concrete chunks, disregarding their trilingual 'STOP!' sign. Inspired by an aching shoulder, it wasn't too difficult to devise an escape via a mound of rubble at the base of the apartment block.

On my way to the nearby Museum on the Seam I recalled Malise Ruthven's superb summing up of all fundamentalisms: '. . . symptomatic of the spiritual dystopias and dysfunctional cultural relationships that characterise the world of "Late Capitalism".' Given Israel's limited area and population, it has an astounding concentration of 'dysfunctional cultural relationships', not least between its secular and Haredim citizens.

The Museum on the Seam, officially known as the Social-Political Contemporary Art Museum, is not soothing, hardly the ideal unwinding spot after an unnerving episode. However, happening to find myself on Handasa Street, a visit was indicated.

The petite young woman at the ticket desk twitched nervously when I appeared; that mound of rubble had left its mark, an apologetic explanation was needed.

'You're daft!' was the reaction. 'I wouldn't go near that place, not for all the whisky in Scotland!' One's sense of distance is contingent; 'that place' lies scarcely one hundred yards from the museum.

In Jordanian times the Green Line (the 'Seam') could only be crossed through the historic Mandlebaum Gate – historic because here, after dark on 22 March 1949, a Zionist delegation met King Abdullah's representatives and a day later the Armistice Agreement was signed to the permanent detriment of all Palestinians. The Gate (later demolished) stood beside what is now the museum's building. In the 1930s a Palestinian architect, Anton Baramski, designed this stone mansion, giving it impressive ornamental columns and tall arched windows – defaced by concrete walls with firing slits when the Haganah took over in December 1947. The Baramski family and all their middle-class Palestinian neighbours were quickly forced into exile, hardly given time to pack a suitcase. Since then this mansion has been known to

Israelis as the Tour Jeman Post; it served as a military base until 1967 and its façade remains war-scarred.

The museum was established in 1999, sponsored by the German von Holtzbrinck family and 'initiated by the Curator and Artistic Director Raphie Elgar'. Many of its exhibits are so emotionally powerful and relentlessly factual that children under fourteen are advised to disport themselves on the roof-top while their elders confront what the Curator defines as '. . . the reality surrounding us, the rampant violence that has crossed all barriers and red lines . . . the truth lying deep in our heart and the bitter frustration accompanying it . . . the embarrassment, the confusion and the anxiety hovering above this house and its past, as they hover above the entire country'.

My two-hour tour left me so shattered that Raphie Elgar stood me a beer and we talked on the roof, overlooking the Old City walls and the intervening savagely 'updated' cityscape. In his development of this museum – its exhibits change annually – the Curator looks to Michel Foucault as one of his main guides. I found him the most exciting and *encouraging* thinker I had met in Jerusalem. Although free of false optimism, he gives one the *courage* to believe that both sides could eventually 'foster values of mutual respect'. He believes it is not too late to 'take the first steps of this long journey that should have started long ago'. All concerned must search, he believes, for 'an equality of thought that enables opposites to exist side by side'. In his introduction to the catalogue he explains, 'The works I chose for this exhibition . . . aspire to move the spectators' hearts and raise their consciousness with the use of realism rather than abstract qualities.'

I hardly slept that night, my consciousness had been raised so high.

When Jacob and his household were on their way from Shechem (Nablus) to Hebron they

> came in the springtime to the land which leadeth to Ephrata; wherein when Rachel was in travail, by reason of her hard labour she began to be in danger and the midwife said to her: Fear no, for thou shalt have this son also – And when her soul was departing for pain, and death was now at hand, she called the name of her son Benoni, that is – the son of my pain – but his father called him Benjamin, that is, The son of the right hand. So Rachel died, and was buried in the highway that

leadeth to Ephrata, that is Bethlehem. And Jacob erected a pillar over
her sepulchre: this is the pillar of Rachel's monument, to this day.

Genesis 35:16–20

Throughout the centuries what is generally believed to be the site of
Rachel's grave has been revered by Jews, Christians and Muslims; Jews
regard it as their third holiest shrine after the Temple and the Hebron
Tombs. It has always been respected and protected, by the Byzantines,
Crusaders, Ottomans and British. One of the Apartheid Barrier's most
shocking offences is its desecration of Rachel's Tomb.

The restoration of this monument was the first of Sir Moses Montefiore's philanthropic enterprises in and around Jerusalem. In 1841 he
funded a new dome and vestibule for the Bilal Ibn Rabah mosque – a
tactful move, to lessen friction between the local Muslims and the
increasingly numerous Jewish pilgrims whose praying was, to Muslim
ears, unnecessarily loud. Childless women of all faiths, including Sir
Moses' wife Judith, hoped to conceive after seeking Rachel's help. Those
rituals didn't work for the Montefiores though the octogenarian Sir
Moses was still siring – on the last recorded occasion, with an adolescent
maidservant. By then he had built a mausoleum for himself and Judith
in Ramsgate, an exact replica of Rachel's Tomb.

Until 1977 the shrine was administered by a *waqf* and open always
to all faiths. Then began a creeping annexation of this part of the
autonomous district of Bethlehem. In 1995, the Oslo Accords forced
the IDF to withdraw from Bethlehem town, and across the road from
Rachel's Tomb they built a camp incorporating an early section of the
Apartheid Barrier with high watchtowers. In 1998 the Montefiore-
funded dome and mosque vestibule were razed and Palestinians were
excluded from the mosque courtyard and from their nearby ancient
cemetery. As the Apartheid Barrier was extended, all nearby shops and
homes were requisitioned. What had been a rural wayside shrine was
transformed into an impregnable military base. An entire neighbourhood had been thoroughly 'cleansed' and Rachel's Tomb purged of all
Christian and Muslim associations.

I had been invited to revisit Irina's kibbutz and when I pleaded 'no
time' she decided on a day-trip to Jerusalem – 'We can do something
together.' By cell phone I proposed Rachel's Tomb as the 'something'
and Irina panicked. 'It's in the West Bank! I can't go there with an

Israeli ID – they could kill me, they do kill Israelis who cross the line!'
Even at a distance her fear was palpable: her daughter would be appalled
to think of her crossing the line at the behest of some reckless foreigner.
As an Israeli who never encountered Palestinians – apart from a few
labourers compelled to be back over the line by nightfall – she had
developed a paranoid fear of 'them'.

Soothingly I explained that Rachel's Tomb is now on the 'safe' side
of the line, the Barrier having annexed it to Israel. (In some conversations I deleted 'Apartheid'.) There wouldn't be a Palestinian in
sight, I assured her; all are excluded from one of their most hallowed
places of pilgrimage. Irina said she'd think about it, consult friends,
look for internet guidance, come back to me . . .

Two days later she and I took a taxi from the central bus station, our
driver briefly reactivating panic by remarking, in Hebrew, that he had
no special permit and must leave us at the checkpoint – we'd have to
walk the last mile or so.

The main Jerusalem–Hebron road crosses mangled, Zionised territory
where farming villages flourished pre-Nakba. A conspicuous signpost
directed us towards the electronically supervised checkpoint. There was
not a human in sight as our driver turned quickly and sped away,
unaware that he had misinformed us. Only security forces may walk
in this zone; wide signs in several languages said 'Private Vehicles
Forbidden!' and 'Pedestrians Not Allowed!'

'Let's go!' I said. 'They won't shoot at two old biddies carrying nothing.'

Irina protested, only half-jokingly. 'Some twenty-second-century
digital gun might get us! Israelis invent magic weapons!'

An awkward dispute was averted by a small car sporting a large
permit stopping beside us. The friendly young woman driver beckoned
us in. She was a First Aid worker; occasionally female pilgrims faint in
reaction to Rachel's Tomb and elderly men have been known to
collapse, buckling under the weight of their own piety.

Here the Barrier consists of two walls, equally high, and the narrow
road is a snaking, imprisoning corridor. Under an almost cloudless sky
we seemed to be driving through darkness. My companions were
chatting and chuckling; perhaps, given time, I too would toughen up.

We emerged onto a bleak plaza. At the far side a solitary limousine,
parked at the base of the Barrier, emphasised its height (8 metres). In the
centre of this concrete space bedraggled tulips grew around the giant

stump of an immeasurably ancient olive tree. Near the grossly militarised entrance to Rachel's Tomb stood a half-dozen pilgrims and a few over-armed security men. Our kind driver asked one of the policemen to place us on a pilgrim coach for the journey back to the main road.

The sepulchre itself is approached through a long, new passageway with separate entrances for men and women. Of this site's Islamic links, few visible traces remain. For our excursion we had inadvertently chosen a Jewish Holy Day (non-observant Irina didn't know why it was holy) and the inner sanctum was packed with women of all ages, the majority Ashkenazi, many bareheaded, several carrying placid babies, most rocking to and fro as they fervently chanted, *sotto voce*, from their prayer-books. Watching them, I visualised the scene on the far side of the Barrier, mere yards from where we stood. A scene of desolation, dereliction, deprivation – even more stricken economically than Hebron's Old City. Empty homes, rows of closed shops, cafés, little family industries – a scene of which those around me knew nothing and were not allowed to know anything. Like Irina they accepted the Barrier as an ugly construction essential to protect them from the killers across the line. Israeli citizens cannot walk behind Rachel's Tomb where I, as a foreign tourist staying in Bethlehem, could walk and observe and lament.

There is of course a variety of merchandise on offer. It didn't tempt me. Instead I photographed a brand-new wall plaque as my souvenir:

Thus saith the Lord: A voice was heard on high of lamentation, of mourning and weeping, of Rachel weeping for her children, and refusing to be comforted for them, because they are not.

Thus saith the Lord: Let thy voice cease from weeping, and thy eyes from tears, for there is a reward for thy work, saith the Lord: and they shall return out of the land of the enemy.

And there is hope for thy last end, saith the Lord; and the children shall return to their own borders.   Jeremiah 30:15–17

On the eve of my departure Shaul suggested a farewell beer in the American Colony Hotel, a surprising venue, I thought, given his Spartan leanings. The explanation was Uncle Ben, Shaul's mother's brother, who had read a few of my books. We sat in a cosy, shadowy corner of the discreetly opulent bar, enormous and crowded yet not noisy. Shaul looked around, then winked at me. 'We're surrounded by diplomats, entrepreneurs, journalists, contractors, politicians, mediators and spies – so they all keep their voices down!'

Uncle Ben was short and stout with a bulky moustache and a monocle. Recently retired and even more recently widowed, he was planning soon to migrate – maybe to England, or Austria or Canada. He had fallen out, painfully, with his only son, a young man corrupted – in his father's view – by military service and now intent on a career in a combat unit celebrated for shooting first and never answering questions.

Uncle Ben condemned Israel's post-Six-Day War euphoria, uncontrolled by Zionism's leaders and allowed to become unthinking triumphalism, soon morphing into ruthless expansionism. He remembered being a twenty-year-old infantryman swept up in it all, rejoicing to have conquered Judea, Samaria, the Strip. After that, the army he'd gladly served in 'began to rot from the head down'. Now, in old age, he couldn't see the State of Israel surviving because too many of its citizens are psychologically damaged. Then he corrected himself: 'No, I mean more than its citizens, I mean everyone, Israelis, '48ers, OPT Palestinians – all demoralised and led astray by bad leadership.'

Shaul demurred. As a devotee of the venerable Jeff Halpern, he made himself look forward to the day when Israel, having accepted the demographic inevitability, will be reborn as a secular, multicultural democracy.

Uncle Ben adjusted his monocle and growled, 'Dream on!'

Shaul smiled affectionately at his uncle. 'OK – I'm sleepwalking! But don't wake me up. Because you can't get hold of what you don't believe in . . .'

I set the drinking pace and we were on our second pint (half-litre) when Uncle Ben admitted, 'The Intifadas, one on either side of the Oslo debacle, pushed me into pacifism. No, not exactly – but into anti-militarism. Especially the second one and Defensive Shield. Then that so-called war on Gaza – you can't have a real war between a lion and a gazelle!'

To me 'gazelle' didn't match Hamas. Nor did 'lion' seem right – I *like* lions. But of course I knew what Uncle meant.

Shaul said, 'The IDF PR gang like to control our – and everyone else's – vocabulary. Also to censor it – "occupation", for instance, is *out*. And now our education ministry is about to ban "Nakba". The term was introduced into the '48ers' textbooks two years ago and the

ministry says it's "spreading anti-Israel propaganda". Worse still, they're
threatening to stop government funding for any group "acting against
the principles of the country". By which they mean commemorating
the Nakba.'

Ben snorted into his beer, spraying his moustache. '*Principles!* What
principles?'

'My group's involved,' continued Shaul. 'We're contesting legislation
that would criminalise the Palestinians' "right to remember".'

(Shaul's group lost their prolonged battle; in May 2010 the Nakba
Law was passed.)

'And still the Nakba continues,' I said, remembering a photograph on
the front page of *Ha'aretz* showing a Sheikh Jarrah mother, carrying a
toddler, being forced out of her home by a tall, burly skull-capped settler.
The despairing anguish on her face so harrowed me that I couldn't finish
my breakfast. That was sixty years after S. Yizhar wrote, in *Khirbet Khizeh*,
of a mother whose village house was dynamited by Haganah.

The woman leapt up, burst into wild howling and started to run
holding a baby in her arms, while another wretched child, who could
already stand, clutched the hem of her dress, and she screamed, pointed,
talked and choked . . . Her world had come to a full stop, and everything
had turned dark and was collapsing . . . and there was no going back.

The only difference, six decades later, is that Palestinians have learned
the futility of screaming, pointing, talking, choking. According to
Shaul, *Khirbet Khizeh* was written within months of its author's active
participation in the Nakba.

While Shaul went outside to make an important phone call about
another of his settler-threatened friends, Uncle Ben listened patiently to
my rant about that Sheikh Jarrah mother. For anyone interested in
justice, she and her thousands of co-sufferers represent the central reality
of today's Holy Land. Forget all those convoluted 'think piece' articles
by such commentators as Aluf Benn and Robert Grenier who can sound
admirably balanced and considered while skirting the real issues. They
may never intend to mislead, but from a certain vantage point certain
issues of necessity remain invisible.

Uncle Ben nodded and half-smiled. 'I guess you wouldn't talk like
that if you'd never lived on the West Bank.'

Shaul, who had rejoined us, added, 'That's where the Zionists win.
It's hard to disentangle the overlapping layers of political/military/

commercial duplicity. No matter how much people love Palestinians, they don't have that sort of time. Therefore few eyebrows are raised when plausible pros, writing for prestigious papers, promote Abbas as a reliable partner for peace.'

Uncle Ben chuckled. 'A very fine exercise in alliteration! Was it by chance?'

'Of course,' replied Shaul, 'it's one manifestation of my genius.'

We were on the way out when Mordechai Vanunu, famous for exposing Israel's nuclear programme in the 1980s, came hurrying through the crowded bar, eyes cast down. As Shaul had remarked, you get all sorts in the American Colony Hotel.

Six hours later, at 3.00 a.m., the gallant Shaul collected me from No. 99 and drove me to the airport. My luggage was light, all that printed matter had gone ahead with DHL – an essential precaution. When the passport officials noted my three-month sojourn in the Holy Land they alerted the customs officials and two tight-lipped young women set upon my rucksack. Every obscure pocket was emptied, every noisome item of unwashed underwear shaken out – in search of what? Drugs? Films of IDF misdeeds? Coded messages from Hamas to the President of Iran? I smiled at them and made friendly noises (unreciprocated) and drew their attention to the most obscure mini-pocket which contained tiny pebbles collected from significant (to me) sites. It was politic to leave a good impression; I planned to return quite soon. Alas! that plan went agley. The lameness demanded a new hip and my return had to be postponed for eighteen months.

PART THREE

CHAPTER 22

Impressions of Yad Vashem

On the Geneva to Tel Aviv flight in October 2010, I had a window seat and the elderly New Jersey couple beside me were both too tall to be comfortable travelling tourist class. Olga and Paul were on their first visit to Israel at the end of a European tour that had taken them as far as Russia 'to look at Putin's AIDS issues'. They were retired physicians and enthusiasts for Obamacare but not sanguine about its chances.

Paul had kind eyes and a slow soft voice. Olga wanted to know all about me; then she expatiated on their three-week, go-slow, self-drive tour of Israel. 'We're not *typical* Americans, we like *time*, for absorbing.' A tendency to talk in italics gave Olga's sentences a peculiar bounciness.

Experimentally, I offered a list of West Bank contacts and agreeable hotels like Al-Yasmeen in Nablus. The couple looked aghast. After a moment of recovery Olga said, 'We can't go *there*! Our *insurance* – it's too *dangerous*!'

Apologetically, Paul added, 'We're sorry for those poor Arabs, especially the crowds in camps. They'd surely be better off if they transferred, went somewhere else, left those areas to the Jews.'

Olga nodded vigorously. 'That makes *sense*! Jews only have Israel, Arabs have *vast* countries all *over* the place – space for *millions*!'

I looked down at Cyprus, counted ten and began to talk about climate change.

Olga bounced on – they were looking forward to staying with her niece's family. A decade ago Judith and Jake had made *aliyah* to bring their children up in the wholesome atmosphere of Hashmonaim, a settlement where the dominant ethos was Moderate Orthodox. 'You *must* visit us there,' said Olga. 'It's *just* round the corner from Jerusalem. And Judith is *passionate* about travel books!' She handed me a card which revealed that Jake is a legal consultant.

'Thank you,' I said. 'For me Hashmonaim will be a treat. It must be
very unlike the national-religious hilltop settlements.'

'I suppose so,' Olga said vaguely. 'I don't know anything about those.'
At which point our descent began.

In Sari's hostel a flattering chorus of 'Welcomes!' was followed by
anxious enquiries about 'your sore leg'.

When I asked Sari about buses to Yad Vashem he compressed his
lips and sighed heavily before replying, 'No. 18 from Mamilla. I hear
it's a strange place, full of sadness and fear. Americans tell me it's very
American too and they go on expanding it, spending more dollars. Be
careful there, don't talk about " '48-ers". Zionists and their friends say
"the minority" or "Israel's Arabs" – as if we were slaves, their property.
They never say "Palestinians" – all must remember there's no place
called "Palestine"!'

I nodded. 'And never was such a place, only "the Land of Israel"
recently infested by Arabs.'

Sari smiled slightly and said, 'Don't get all upset tomorrow. We've
seen guests coming back not able to sleep – or waking everyone else with
their nightmares!'

In Dublin and London my Jewish friends had reproved me for evading
Yad Vashem (the Holocaust Memorial Museum) during two longish
stays in Jerusalem. They exclaimed, 'It's insulting to ignore it!' Or, 'You
must go to understand Israel!' I conceded the first point and promised
to be polite on my next visit.

During the bus ride from Mamilla I thought about terminology. In
the Holy Land context, many words raise hackles. Claude Lanzmann,
the Jewish-French film director, objects to 'Holocaust' because its literal
meaning is 'a burnt offering to a god'. He prefers the Hebrew 'Shoah',
meaning 'catastrophe'. However, the Arabic name for Zionism's 'War
of Independence' – al-Nakba – also means catastrophe. And so I've
been urged to retain 'Holocaust'; one must avoid any suggestion of an
equivalence between the fates of Hitler's and Zionism's victims.

The Palestinian philosopher, Joseph Massad, has strong feelings about
'conflict'. He sees his people engaged in a liberation struggle against
European colonisers – hence 'conflict' is misleading and 'terrorism'
scurrilous. Aida Touma-Sliman, General Director of the '48-ers'

'Women Against Violence', also rejects 'conflict' with its implication of equal forces. The mighty IDF, she points out, is deployed in an on-going *conquest* of the defenceless Palestinians. In like vein, Avi Shlaim had protested, 'Operation Cast Lead, to give the war its bizarre official title, was not really a war but a one-sided massacre.'

Then there's Rabbi Zvi Yehuda Kook, whose use of 'purify' alarms. Gush Emunim's spiritual leader formally lamented the slaughter of six million Jews but preached that bloodshed on that scale was needed to purify God's people – so foully contaminated in the twentieth century by the sins of other nations!

From the bus stop a short resin-scented walk took me to Yad Vashem on its 45-acre site near the base of Mount Herzl. At 8.50 I joined a waiting sextet of Australians, newcomers to Israel and astounded by 'All that's been achieved since Independence!' Although the guidebooks advise at least three hours for this 'experience' their minicab would fetch them at 10.00 a.m. – 'Some of us can't take too much cruelty!' As we were admitted, two coachloads of schoolchildren arrived. No matter – even during the noon 'rush-hour' the vastness of Yad Vashem felt uncrowded.

In 1953 the Knesset proposed a memorial to the Holocaust victims and to all gentiles who had risked their lives to protect fugitive Jews. The most recent of several developments is a history museum opened in 2005 in the presence of forty national leaders plus Kofi Annan, then UN General Secretary – who might have excused himself, citing the innumerable UN Resolutions scorned by Israel since 1948. This building, designed by Moshe Safdie, is 180 metres long, has ten underground chambers and cost US$40 million. Another Safdie creation, dug into the bedrock, commemorates 1.5 million murdered children. Here a solitary flame is reflected in hundreds of mirrors, a weirdly moving conceit marred by gimmicky voices intoning children's names.

Another jarring note is struck by an invitation to parents to 'twin' a son or daughter with a junior Holocaust victim. 'At the end of a customised tour of Yad Vashem, accompanied by a professional photographer, an enhanced twinning ceremony, with the participation of a senior representative of Yad Vashem, will take place in the Syna-gogue. At the conclusion of a meaningful ceremony, designed especially for you, a framed commemoration certificate will be presented to the Bar/Bat Mitzvah child marking his or her pledge to perpetuate the memory of a child who perished in the Holocaust. A beautifully bound personalised photo album recording your family's experience will provide a unique memento of the day's visit.' There follows an e-mail address, 'for pricing information'. Most 'twinners' are US residents.

Observing those around me, I marked a generational difference; the under-40s seemed on the whole more detached than the over-70s. To the young all this is (or should be) in the past, inexpressibly tragic and evil but 'history'. To my age group it is a tangible part of our 'now', though so distant. And perhaps, by Irish standards, I am exceptionally Holocaust-aware because a close friend of my father's spent six years in Dachau. (Anton was a gentile but implacably and vocally anti-Nazi.) In 1938 I heard one of Hitler's tirades live on the wireless; my mother took an interest in current affairs and understood German. She remembered my being so scared of what was coming over the airwaves that I retreated under a table, whimpering. One doesn't always have to speak the language to get the message. Now it was eerie to hear again Hitler's voice and the multitude's savage response when he vowed to free the Reich from all Jewish influences.

Seven years later the Allied forces liberated the camps and I have never forgotten those press photographs, especially that picture of bulldozers shovelling emaciated corpses into a deep wide pit. Another seven years later Anton came to stay with us in Ireland for two months. When we went swimming I saw the numbers on his forearm and felt a frisson of horror. He never sat down to a normal meal: had to eat little and often. And he never spoke about Dachau, not even to his wife who became a close friend of my mother's. He apparently concentrated on his academic work, to the exclusion of everything else. Then in 1959 he took an overdose. In Yad Vashem his shade walked with me.

I remember cycling past Dachau only five years after its liberation and gritting my teeth and pedalling faster when I saw the signpost. Yad Vashem taught me that this first concentration camp was set up, in March 1933, to silence political enemies: trade union leaders, Communists and social democrats like Anton. The SS initially claimed to be holding these people in 'protective custody' while 'educating' them to 'think Nazi'. By the time of Anton's imprisonment, in April 1939, several of his friends had been locked up for years amongst thousands of Gypsies, homosexuals and clergymen. Later came POWs, mainly Russians and Poles. And of course Jews, usually in transit, as Dachau was not a death camp. Exact statistics don't exist; the generally accepted estimate is

200,000 held between 1933 and 1945, of whom 41,000 or so died – of diseases, starvation or lethal medical experiments. Those last involved prolonged and extreme suffering and were carried out by brilliant physicians/scientists. One evening Anton's wife recalled how many such 'researchers' escaped punishment and were then – even as we spoke in 1952 – respected senior faculty members at German universities. I've never forgotten that evening; the sheer hatred in her voice unnerved me.

In my 1985 book on race relations in Britain I severely shocked many readers by suggesting that successful extermination camps could be set up in Britain, given a peculiarly unfortunate convergence of socio-economic crises with a Cliveden Set/Mosley-flavoured leadership. Although presented by Zionism as a unique anti-Semitic crime, that Holocaust is potentially repeatable. Only the technology and bureaucracy were unique; to that the Armenians and Tutsis can bear witness. Recognising this, in 1948 Raphael Lemkin coined the term 'genocide' and pressured the UN to introduce the Convention of the Prevention and Punishment of the Crime of Genocide. Unfortunately, as so often happens with UN Conventions, no teeth have yet come through and by now dim-witted journalists are depriving 'genocide' of its meaning by applying it to mass killings in general, whatever their motive.

One grim truth is prominently displayed on a Yad Vashem wall, above relevant photographs. 'In the 1930s the rest of the world considered the persecution of the Jews to be an internal German matter.'

Another grim truth is glossed over. In the 1930s the persecution of the Jews elicited little sympathy from Palestine's Zionist colony. Under Ben-Gurion's leadership the Yishuv, with considerable help from the mandatory power, was narrowly focussed on nation-building. Political Zionism was all about breeding a 'new man' who would have nothing in common with degenerate Diaspora types. Therefore the Jewish Agency (JA) was consistently logical as it chose who to rescue from Nazism. 'Sound human material' was sought – young, vigorous, hardworking individuals capable of nourishing the embryonic Israeli state. Ben-Gurion's Yishuv had not time for dependent refugees needing physical and/or psychological support. Even after September 1939 the JA insisted on selecting 'the good' from amongst 'the rabble'. (So Moshe Sherett expressed it, in his diary.)

In 1945 Yishuv envoys began to tour the hellishly overcrowded Displaced Persons (DP) camps, helping to organise the flow of God's

Chosen People to their Promised Land. It alarmed these officials to
find that most of these people, feeling let down by Zionism, longed to
return to their homes instead of being shipped off to Palestine where
they were now very welcome. As widely publicised survivors, on their
behalf the Yishuv could expect to do well in the US fundraising arena.
(So much for the myth that Diaspora Jews had spent 2,000 years
yearning to return to Abraham's bequest.) Several envoys describe the
majority of the displaced persons as 'defective human material' – a
chilling phrase, often used in JA reports. Some foresaw such people
'poisoning Zionism', undermining its wholesome socialist-agricultural
foundations. When one envoy referred to them as 'scum' Ben-Gurion
did not disagree. Then, being desperate for an increase in Palestine's
Jewish population, he quickly calculated – 'Yes, they will make trouble,
but at least the troubles will come from Jews.'

Of the 90,000 who arrived in Palestine during the latter half of 1945
some were concentration camp survivors and all had endured Nazi
occupation. Over the next three years, the British would admit only
60,000 more, lest the Palestinians' rage might run out of control.
However, as the mandatory power weakened, the underground Zionist
militia smuggled boatloads of destitute Jews past British coastguards.
The Yishuv could have done more for those hundreds of thousands still
languishing in European camps but Ben-Gurion and his officials were
determined not to antagonise their British allies.

The first year of Israel's existence saw 200,000 arriving and by the end
of 1949 Holocaust survivors made up about one-third of Israel's Jewish
population. During the Nakba, one in three fighters was a survivor
(22,000) – usually enlisted, before leaving a DP camp, by Yishuv agents
who promised 'a warm home in their new country'. Because they spoke
no English most were deployed, after a few days' training, as front line
combatants and found themselves killing Palestinians against whom they
bore no grudge in 'defence' of a country of which they knew nothing.

Those Yishuv leaders responsible for newcomers' welfare noted how
few long-settled Zionists opened their homes to refugee relatives. Tom
Segev has described the Nakba's stark drama:

> Hundreds of thousands of Arabs were expelled from their homes. Entire
> cities and hundreds of villages left empty were repopulated in short
> order with new immigrants . . . Free people – Arabs – had gone into

exile and become destitute refugees; destitute refugees – Jews – took the exiles' places as a first step in their new lives as free people. One group lost all they had, while the other found all they needed – tables, chairs, closets, pots, pans, plates, sometimes clothes, family albums, books, radios and pets. Most of the immigrants broke into the abandoned Arab houses without direction, without order, without permission. For several months the country was caught up in a frenzy of take-what-you-can, first-come, first-served . . . Immigrants also took possession of Arab stores and workshops, and some Arab neighbourhoods soon looked like Jewish towns in pre-war Europe, with tailors, shoemakers, dry-goods merchants – all the traditional Jewish occupations.

Studying Yad Vashem's displays of enlarged 1930s photographs, and reconstructions of street scenes in Eastern European villages, I wondered how many of those depicted had escaped and been able to benefit from the Nakba desolation. One slightly blurry film recorded in some detail the Allies' shameful refusal to put the whole Auschwitz complex and its rail links out of action though they were bombing targets only five miles away. Both Roosevelt and Churchill coldly emphasised their one objective: the total defeat of Nazi Germany. No side-issues could be taken into account. Those crematoria a side-issue . . . ? Significantly, Churchill had always cheered for Zionism. To my universalist Jewish friends, Zionists 'are among the worst anti-Semites'. Back to terminology – one measure of the reach and power of the *hasbara* machine may be found in Webster's *Third New International Dictionary* (1961, reprinted 2002) where anti-Semitism is defined as 'opposition to Zionism: sympathy with opponents of the state of Israel'. Truly this is immoral – to equate anti-Semites with those who seek justice for the Palestinians.

On my way out I passed one of the original cattle-wagons in which Jews were close-packed: for me by far the most disturbing exhibit, its material presence – so much more immediate than any film, DVD or panorama – inducing a moment of physical nausea.

Outside, I slowly paced around the 'Valley of the Communities' where, on a two and a half acre site, the names of 5,000 erased Jewish communities have been carved out of the valley floor. When will the Palestinians be free to commemorate their hundreds of erased villages in a similar manner? Some of those stood for many centuries on the now-forested slopes of Mount Herzl. Up there, amidst the cedars, lies

Theodore Herzl who begot what is now being seen as a major international problem. Really it's all a bit freakish. A Hungarian-born, secular, Swiss-based Jew, shaken by the Dreyfus trial and infected by the European nationalist virus, decides Europe's Jews need their own nation. He and a few other seculars get together and three years later the first World Zionist Congress is held in Basle. It all went on from there, the socialist/secular ideal readily adapting to Judaism the religion, as expediency dictated. When Herzl died young in 1904, he couldn't possibly have foreseen the nightmare that would evolve out of his dream.

Finally I paid my respects to the Righteous. In 1963 many trees (they remain rather spindly) were planted along the Avenue of the Righteous, a dreary concrete walkway commemorating those gentiles who risked their lives to save Jews. This encouraging cross-section of heroes and heroines includes Muslim Albanians, Armenian Christians, Polish housewives, German nannies, an Italian diplomat, a Dutch farmer, an Egyptian doctor, a French railway porter, a Danish king. Saluting their memories, I recalled Zygmunt Bauman's concluding reflections on the Holocaust:

> One lesson is the facility with which most people, put into a situation that does not contain a good choice, or renders such a choice very costly, argue themselves away from the issue of moral duty . . . adopting instead the precepts of rational interest and self-preservation. *In a system where rationality and ethics point in opposite directions, humanity is the main loser* . . . Evil needs neither enthusiastic followers nor an applauding audience – the instinct of self-preservation will do . . .
> Another lesson of the Holocaust is no less important . . . It tells us that putting self-preservation above moral duty is in no way predetermined . . . One can be pressed to do it but one cannot be forced to do it, and thus one cannot really shift the responsibility for doing it onto those who exerted the pressure. *It does not matter how many people chose moral duty over the rationality of self-preservation – what does matter is that some did.* Evil is not all-powerful. It can be resisted. The testimony of the few who *did* resist shatters the authority of the logic of self-preservation. It shows it for what it is in the end – *a choice.* One wonders how many people must defy that logic for evil to be incapacitated. Is there a magic threshold of defiance beyond which the technology of evil grinds to a halt? (Author's italics)

CHAPTER 23

Polite Settlers and Traumatised Conscripts

A free minibus service is one of many concessions available even to the affluent settlement of Hashmonaim. This twenty-year-old intrusion into the West Bank is a mile or so east of Modi'in, just beyond the Green Line. From a discreetly guarded entrance barrier (guns not obvious, as on the hilltops) I walked between the bright monotony of identical red-roofed three- or four-storey houses, some gardens furnished with gaudy plastic play-aids. The only people in sight were two jogging young women – plump and sweaty – who seemed happy to stop and talk in Brooklyn English. Yes of course they knew exactly where Judith and Jake lived – first to the left, then second to the right beyond the Yemenite synagogue. So said the redhead. Her blonde companion decided, 'Best we walk you there.'

They oozed friendly curiosity. I came from where? Was I enjoying Israel? Where did I stay? Where was my family? Would I be around next week to join their Walk for Rain? Having foreigners in the group gave a real boost to such events.

I showed a reciprocal curiosity and learned that Hashmonaim is a settlement of fewer than 600 families (normal-sized families of two, three or four children). More than half are recent immigrants from the US: scientists, doctors, lawyers, engineers, IT high-flyers. The place is a sort of Paradise, so stress-free and near the beach and for entertainment you couldn't do better than Tel Aviv. Only Hebrew made for complications, there weren't enough fluent speakers around and it's a tough challenge. American kids coming suddenly into the state school system can get frustrated and angry, losing self-esteem when they mess up their *bagrut* (matric). The Absorption Ministry had promised to organise a new 'Hebrew Enrichment Programme' for day-care centres and the element-ary school. Most parents figured the best integration programme was army service. That sorted out the average teenager's feeling of alienation.

At the Wilens' gate we could see Judith hanging bedding over a balcony and she greeted my guides by name, inviting them in for coffee. But they were only halfway through their daily run which was part of a soul-balancing regime involving root vegetables, short bouts of concentrated meditation and one pint of spring water drunk quickly every four hours. (When Judith later told us this her aunt exclaimed, 'The surest route to acute colic!')

From the balcony Judith called down, 'Take the side path, they're in the garden.' This three-storey house was not among the minority with a pool – and anyway all pools now lay empty and most shrubs looked parched.

Olga and Paul sat under a beach umbrella playing with Scooter, a seriously teething emperor poodle puppy who had drawn blood from both their hands. Neither physician was fussing about infection so they rose steeply in my estimation. Olga seemed to have undergone a diminution of ebullience since our first meeting. When I remarked on this she half-whispered, 'I think it's the *Wall*!' Less than a mile of drought-yellowed grass separated this garden from the menace and ugliness of the Apartheid Barrier.

Soon Judith joined us, bearing a coffee tray. She gestured towards the field and the Barrier and declared, 'It makes me want to cry!' Briefly I misunderstood, then she added, 'Next week we march and pray for rain. Something organised by the US Centre for Religious Tolerance, all walking and praying together – Jews, Druze, Christians, Muslims. Everyone needs rain and my dad says praying together is firing on all cylinders!'

Judith looked more Irish than Jewish: shoulder-length raven hair, cornflower-blue eyes, pink cheeks. Jake had enjoyed some of my books and would be sorry to have missed me, he was back home on a business trip, he commuted quite often. ('Back home . . . ?' So as yet Hashmonaim wasn't home – would it ever be?)

Before lunch – a Filipino was busy in the kitchen – we talked dogs and cats, AIDS and travel writing, US domestic politics (skirting AIPAC) and paedophilia in relation to rabbis and Christian priests. Over lunch I learned a new word – 'telecommute' – a process enabling many Hashmonaim settlers to continue earning at US rates. Hence those high property prices which in certain circles cooled the welcome for dollar-cushioned newcomers. The non-earning sort, subsidised by Gush Emunim supporters, settled on the hilltops or in places like Kiryat Arba. Later Olga told me that the Wilens' house had recently been valued at $650,000; its location – one of a row directly overlooking the Barrier – kept the price down.

When Olga and Paul had retired for their siesta Judith proposed a
tour of 'the facilities' and with some difficulty we persuaded Scooter to
accept his harness; he still regarded it as suitable for chewing rather than
wearing.

This settlement's nine (or is it ten?) synagogues cater for a variety of
tastes including Chabad, though I was assured, 'Our few Lubavitchers
keep their heads down.' In an amply stocked community library English-
language volumes (not thought-provoking) predominate. Two large
stern buildings accommodate the boys' *yeshiva* and in a jolly Oldies'
Centre fellow-grannies invited me to 'stay for a Scrabble'. There was a
youth centre, too, and a *mikva* (ritual bath). 'For conversion ceremonies,'
explained Judith, 'because some make *aliyah* with non-Jewish spouses.'
Proudly she emphasised that Hashmonaim had been created at minimal
cost to the Israeli government. Funding came from the US, mainly,
with sporadic donations from far-flung Diaspora billionaires. Israel's
taxpayers provided only the religious-stream elementary school.

Quietly I asked, 'Who provided the land?' (Ominously quietly;
instinctively I lower my voice when in danger of losing my temper.)

Judith looked puzzled. 'The *land*? I suppose – yes, that would have
been given to the founders by someone like the JNF. The founders
came from Jerusalem and Petah Tikvah. A few gutsy pioneers lived
rough in shacks till the funding came.'

We had completed our circular tour and were back in the garden,
looking down at the Barrier. Beyond it dwelt the villagers on whose land
we stood. Palestinians were living in poverty while rich US citizens
reared their children in Hashmonaim's wholesome Modern Orthodox
atmosphere.

At this point my silence must have seemed significant. Judith was
looking at me uneasily, uncomprehendingly. A decent kindly woman,
keen on religious tolerance – 'Let's all pray together for rain.' How
could she and her like be so unaware of the realities around them? I
hesitated. Should I attempt to discuss those realities? Could any breakthrough be achieved? But then the children came – four of them, all
making different demands on their mother, all members of B'nei Akiva,
the religious-Zionist movement.

Olga and Paul were soon to take the minibus into Jerusalem to fetch
their self-drive and Judith looked genuinely disappointed when I
decided to accompany them. 'Can't you hang out a while longer with

the kids? They love foreigners!' I refrained from asking, 'Does that include Arabs?'

The four (two of each) formed a rather endearing brood, high-spirited but polite, the eldest aged ten, the others efficiently spaced at eighteen-month intervals. In an orderly row they sat at the counter, being topped up with fruit and nuts, competing to tell me about their hobbies, worried lest Scooter might have a bad reaction to his next inoculation. Here and now they seemed an excellent advertisement for the Hashmonaim ethos. But later on . . . ? Growing up to accept an Apartheid Wall, going on emotional school trips to Europe's death-camp sites, doing military service in a notoriously ill-disciplined army – surely New Jersey offered a less uncivilised ethos?

At the bus stop Judith hugged me and said, 'Come again when Jake's here. You'd like his plans for helping Arabs, he wants to invest in Fayyad's industrial parks.' The bus came then, just in time to prevent my saying something unprintable about Fayyad.

When we had settled into the back seat Paul turned to study my face and said, 'You're upset!'

'It's the *Wall*,' deduced Olga, gesturing towards the Barrier's dark curving bulk. 'It's so *ugly* and it *feels* wrong!'

'But it's essential,' pronounced Paul. 'We do need protection.'

It was time to let my anger off the leash. 'If the Barrier is for Israelis' protection, why build Hashmonaim and hundreds of other settlements on the Palestinian side?'

'Good question!' said Olga as her husband hastily retreated to his 'transfer' theme. The ugliness could come down if the Arabs pushed off, had the wit to see Israel as the only safe spot on the globe that Jews could call their own.

Acidly I asked, 'Were Hashmonaim's settlers being endangered, persecuted, discriminated against in the US?'

'Another good question!' exclaimed Olga. Evidently this first visit to Israel was threatening marital harmony.

Paul raised his voice and stared into my eyes. 'You don't get it! American Jews are in transit, knowing their own country is somewhere else. Homesick people, insecure, needing possession of their own land!'

Olga, too, was hotting up. 'Couldn't Arabs say *all* Americans are in transit? All their *roots* somewhere else – except the *natives* in reservations who don't count.'

'That's it!' said Paul. 'You make my point! All others have a "some-where else" recognised. Until we took Israel – because it was ours – Jews had nowhere else!'

We were approaching the Jaffa Gate. I asked the driver to stop there (illegally) and so our goodbyes had to be conveniently hurried.

Walking towards George's Bar in the Christian Quarter, I pondered Paul's sense of his own identity. At the age of seventy, he was on his first visit to the land 'we need'. He and his father before him were US-born; grandfather came from Russia as a youth in the 1880s. Yet US Jews are 'in transit'. A phrase leaped to mind: 'He's caught Zionism!' – as people catch chickenpox or measles. Sitting at my favourite corner table I took out my journal and wrote:

> It's less enraging to observe the crazed religious-national settlers who believe God wants them to replace Palestinians all over the OPT. They *are* crazed, living within sick messianic fantasies, counting the days to the Apocalypse. Legally they must go in the 'diminished responsibility' category. In contrast, the Hashmonaim settler type is at least outwardly normal, wouldn't dream of uprooting olive groves, burning mosques or emptying chamber-pots on passing Palestinians. Enjoying lucrative careers, they function as conventional cogs in Western society. Yet on a Zionist whim – not of necessity – they make *aliyah* as part of a merciless ongoing Nakba. They pay no heed to those dirty deeds that must be done to create space for all illegal settlements. How to interpret this detachment from the realities around them? It looks like arrogance, old-fashioned colonial racism; having conquered the territory, you needn't consider the natives. Yet one couldn't meet anyone less arrogant on the surface than Judith and her jogging friends. There's something else going on here, not explained by colonial racism.

A South African friend, Betty, had arranged for me to stay with her cousin Amos. He still lives on the kibbutz where he was born in 1936, a few years after his pioneering parents left Cape Town. Betty e-mailed: 'They were fervently socialist Zionists, shattered in '77 when Likud came to power. I suspect their son is still a socialist but too craven to say so in Start-Up Israel! His wife died last year, he's lonely, do visit him. His daughter Anna lives in Tel Aviv and she'll give you a lift. You'll like her.'

I did like Anna, who had graduated as an anthropologist, then decided to do social work. According to Amos, 'My daughter lives dangerously! Always challenging government ministries on behalf of development towns. She tries to shame them into supporting social-welfare programmes inside Israel instead of funding settlements.'

Amos was tall, trim, silver-thatched and immediately congenial. His kibbutz, not far from Jerusalem, was very unlike Irina's in the Negev. Having discarded the founders' silly socialist notions, it had become an agribusiness, also offering expensive holiday accommodation to urban Israelis seeking a quiet time. Amos and a few other unprogressive septuagenarians were tolerated as harmless irrelevancies.

When we arrived Amos was looking worried. That very morning all farmers had gone on strike because of a government reduction in the number of foreign temporary workers to be admitted annually. (These are mainly Thais.) No farm produce, however perishable, would be delivered to the cities. Cattle would be cared for but the fate of the day's milk yield remained in doubt.

As we went walkabout I ventured to comment, 'Aren't the farmers biting off their noses to spite their faces?'

Anna scowled and I noted again that the scowl of a beautiful woman can be particularly eloquent. 'It's all insane!' she fumed. 'We don't need a foreign workers' issue. Over the Green Line are swarms of Palestinians aching for permits to work here.' (She was one of the few Israelis I heard speaking of 'Palestinians'.)

Amos asked her, 'Why won't your Mizrahi friends do farm work?'

Sharply Anna retorted, 'You know why! They're Israeli citizens, they want a fair wage.' She looked at me. 'When employed on kibbutzim they're usually excluded from dining-halls, swimming-pools and schools. Israel as a united Jewish state has never got beyond Herzl's drawing board!'

We had come to the enormous, dismal cattle enclosure where scores of cows were milked thrice daily. All had grotesquely enlarged udders and looked in poor condition; several near the fence were lame. To grow their fodder, waste water from Jerusalem is specially treated – though not specially enough to irrigate crops for human consumption. Amos admitted, 'It's no life for a cow, downgraded to milk-producing machines.' As a youngster he had observed, with a sense of communal achievement, the transition from hard slog farming to scientific agribusiness. 'I was excited by chemical "aids" and hi-tech machines. Now I'm lamenting the damage done to a very fragile environment.'

When the 'pioneers' arrived, this land had looked unpromising: clay, chalk, a stony surface. Then gradually it had been persuaded to produce grapes, wheat, barley and a little cotton (cotton is very thirsty). By now, however, the environmental damage was taking its toll. Recently the winery, established by Amos' parents, had been abandoned to the horror of Diaspora customers who could only drink wine untouched at any point by gentile hand.

Amos lived in a ground-floor flat, spacious but ill-lit, overlooking the awkwardly angular former dining-hall, now a restaurant. As I helped Anna to assemble an instant lunch she said, 'Pa lost his driving licence – eyesight failure – soon after Ma died. Such bad luck when he needs more mobility, more distractions. After lunch we'll go see my brother on his kibbutz – quite near but there's poor public transport.'

I had to sing for my lunch. Unusually (*very* unusually!) father and daughter wanted a detailed account of my time on the West Bank. As we went out to the car Amos said, 'It would be good for Martin to hear all that . . . But if Helen's there best talk about other things.'

Anna observed, 'They're a clever couple, they've developed a tolerance for each other's prejudices. Which works fine if certain topics are avoided!'

Originally Martin's kibbutz had stood on the hilltop site of a village razed in 1950 by order of Yosef Weitz, then the JNF's Head of Settlements. In that village of more than 1200 Palestinians only the Sheikh's large house had been preserved for Zionist use. Crude breeze-block cubes went up on its ruins but quite quickly these Polish refugees tired of the long climb home at the end of a hard day's work. A majority of members then voted to descend to their present site, semi-surrounded by a conifer plantation. Because of the summer heat that move, too, was soon regretted but by then the members lacked energy for a second rebuilding. As Shaul (and others) often reminded me, those destitute newcomers, the majority debilitated by harsh years in Europe's displaced persons camps, had not chosen to settle on Palestinian territory. They were TINA cases, to be disposed of as the JNF thought fit.

Unfortunately Helen, warned of the imminent arrival of an author, had googled me and put up her defences. So our visit had jagged edges and lasted no more than an hour. I'll never get used to this novel method of snooping on strangers with one or two clicks. To me it seems deplorable – excessive – utterly unlike looking someone up in the laconic pages of *Who's Who*.

Helen walked down to the road with us and invited me to admire the dreary conifers. 'Have you noticed how we've redeemed Israel's forests? Millions and millions of trees planted and more every year in special ceremonies. Before, the country was stripped naked. Wanton felling – the Ottomans for ships and railways, the Arabs for fuel. And *no* replanting!'

'Let's go,' said Anna. 'I need a few things from the shop.'

On the far side of the kibbutz a friend of Anna's ran a second-hand jumble shop where I bought sturdy denim jeans for the equivalent of 7 euros and Anna bought an astonishing range of children's toys including three mini-bikes and two dolls' prams. Seeing my puzzled expression she explained, 'They're for the Palestinian kids in the hospital. If you'd like to come tomorrow I'll pick you up after breakfast. I'll be on my way back from Kiryat Gat.'

Left to ourselves, Amos and I settled down to a fuddy-duddy evening, as one of my granddaughters would put it. In the 1930s kitchen (resembling my own) we ate a rudimentary lamb casserole prepared by the teenager who came daily. 'She's soon off to the army,' said Amos, 'and how to replace her? Not easy! Full-time Filipinos are too costly, young Israelis shirk lowly jobs. Anna could find someone in Kiryat Gat but the buses are too irregular.'

When we moved to a book-lined sitting-room the beer continued to flow and the conversation gained weight.

On a low bookcase stood a large group photograph with Table Mountain in the background: Amos's parents and their parents – the men tall and handsome, the older women tubby, everyone looking serious. 'That's the farewell photo,' said Amos, 'taken before my parents boarded the liner. Both families had run from the Pale pogroms, wandered a bit around Europe, sailed for the Cape in 1890. All our elders opposed my parents' leaving. They'd prospered and settled happily on the Cape and didn't believe in Zionism. Hitler had just taken power and childhood memories of Cossacks slaughtering relatives and friends never faded. No one foresaw death-camps but some feared he'd hunt down Jewish refugees in Palestine. My father admitted being impatient with his parents, laughing at their fears. He imagined the man who *talked* about Jews as Hitler did would never take *action*. He was only twenty-two and that was before the Nuremberg Laws. I remember his mistake when it's argued Israel will never attack Iran because we're so vocally paranoid about their bomb. Insane delusions can trigger insane actions.'

I asked, 'Did Zionism then have much support in South Africa?'

'In Jo'burg, yes. Not in the Cape. My father wanted to emigrate because he feared the underground Afrikaner Broederbond. They admired Hitler so much he couldn't understand why they didn't scare the older generation. Also he knew Britain was using its Mandate to help Zionism grow an independent state for Jews. A state to be *their* place, where no version of anti-Semitism could operate. The day my parents sailed, refugees were arriving from Germany. They saw angry crowds of poor Afrikaners on the dock, shouting against Hoggenheimer, the caricature hook-nosed capitalist. The year I was born thousands of protesters, led by Verwoerd's Nazi Greyshirts, met another ship. Malan's Purified National Party was encouraging young Afrikaners to study in Germany and some met Göring, Goebbels and Hitler himself.'

'*Purified*!' I exclaimed. 'D'you suppose those students took lessons in "purification"? How big at that time was the Jewish population?'

'By 1938 it was above 90,000, double the 1911 figure. At first none of them rejoiced when by chance, in May 1948, Malan's coming to power coincided with Israel's Declaration of Independence. Immediately more than 4,000 South African Jews took ship to fight for Israel. Then of course official Apartheid changed everything. Suddenly we were up there with the master class. To Malan every white vote was precious. That's when my father's ancient parents left a beloved home by the sea to die in Israel – in this very house. And it's why a remarkable number of Jews worked and suffered with the ANC.'

I looked again at the group photo. Once immersed in the Palestinians' miseries, it's too easy to forget all those pogroms, strewn over so many centuries in so many Christian countries.

The other photo on the bookcase showed Amos and Magda on their wedding-day in 1959. Anna strikingly resembled her beautiful mother. Said Amos, 'My wife escaped from Vienna when too young to know she was escaping. Both her brilliant parents did a lot for the Hebrew University. It upset them when she chose me and the kibbutz life – she'd have gone far in an ivory tower!' Amos paused, sighed, fetched more beer – then continued. 'I'm the back-story. A decade from now, there'll be no one around to recall the pipedream – what Israel was meant to be. Since the Six-Day War it's been drifting further and faster from the founders' ideals. My sort were reared on a vision of a secular, socialist democracy formed and protected by self-sacrificing Jews, liberals, dedicated to cultivating the best of their traditional culture. Instead, the rabbinate has eroded our civil authorities, the army has eroded our morals, the Start-up state has eroded our socialism and our democracy never really existed. Ask Anna about that. Maybe you think the democracy deficit only hurts Palestinians but she knows otherwise.'

'People can read the back-story,' I said, 'if they're interested.'

'*If!*' echoed Amos. 'Why would they want to spoil what they have by reading about what should have been? Most don't realise what they have is on shaky ground. Outsiders complain nothing here ever changes, we're gridlocked, everyone too scared to move forward. That's not entirely true, undercurrents are always changing – the pace quickening since the second Intifada. You were on the West Bank during Cast Lead, you saw how that shifted global opinion – *and* internal Palestinian alliances. As did the Flotilla killings while settlement expansions got more aggressive by the day. It all adds up, making for international isolation. When Netanyahu whines about enemies trying to "delegitimise" Israel he sounds crazed. We've delegitimised ourselves time and again giving two fingers to UN Resolutions. Not many say it out loud, but this can't go on much longer . . .'

Swiftly I suggested, 'One state? With BDS leading the campaign!'

Amos nodded. 'Of course – I think *inevitably*, in the end. But that's a very big bull and where are the leaders to take it by the horns? Maybe not yet born!'

On which realistic note we wavered away to our beds.

Anna arrived at sunrise. While we were enmeshed in Tel Aviv's rush-hour, I asked, 'Were the pre-state pioneers always chasing a rainbow?'

Anna glanced at me, frowning, and sounded irritated. 'Isn't that a silly question? Or are we simply talking Jews now? Going along with Golda Meir – "There are no Palestinians . . ." OK, given no Palestinians and no Holocaust, maybe Zionists could have achieved some version of their Utopia. Run by immigrants like my grandparents . . . But how many of those were there, *in fact*? My father clings to Zionism's foundation myth. In his heart he blames the Occupation for where we are now. He shies away from the reality that the Holocaust aborted Zionism. Its Ashkenazi founders wanted a state run by and for the incinerated elite of European Jewry. Serviced by an industrious working-class from the shtetls' peasants who could be educated away from backward beliefs. Last night I stayed in Kiryat Gat, a development town considered "lucky". Ten years ago Intel set up a chip factory there and the Mizrahi are supposed to be grateful. They shouldn't be angry about all Intel's white-collar highly paid R&D jobs going to Ashkenazi cities. When I go abroad I realise how few foreigners know about this skeleton in Israel's cupboard.'

We turned into a Tel Aviv side street and Anna explained, 'One of my workmates, Daisy, is joining us – she wants to meet you.' Astonishingly, it transpired that, unbeknownst to Daisy, I was carrying a letter of introduction to her from a mutual London friend. She had become a kibbutznik shortly before the Six-Day War, had been infected by the subsequent euphoria and impulsively married a taciturn *sabra* with whom, to her Hampstead family's bewilderment, she has been living happily ever since.

Daisy – sun-faded but lean and fit – questioned the carload of toys and looked unenthusiastic about the explanation. 'Why,' she wondered, 'are there so many Palestinian kids in our hospital?'

'They're not here by choice,' Anna crisply replied. She belonged to a small group of women who regularly visited this ghettoised ward, bringing what cheer they could.

In a monumental newish hospital, bright and sparkling, floral fragrances replaced the traditional odours. While Anna parked the car underground, Daisy and I piled the toys beside a lift and my companion marvelled at the State's generosity, making such expensive equipment and highly trained staff available to sulky Arabs who rarely say thanks.

On our way up to the top floor, reserved for children from the OPT and Gaza, Anna was informative. The PA pay in full for all medical expenses and for the patients' food but the carers must find their own sustenance. Unable to afford hospital shop prices, they are dependent on Anna's group or on packaged meals handed in by '48-ers to a sympathetic staff member. The support group also donates clothing, and advanced medical aids needed for special cases but judged unaffordable by the PA – which never lacks money for its own 'expenses'.

Palestinian doctors decide who qualifies for treatment beyond the Green
Line; sadly, as I had observed in Balata, the most urgent cases are
not always those nominated. For admission to an Israeli hospital the
paperwork demanded is so extreme that death sometimes renders it
superfluous.

Outside the lift a very young '48-er security guard rather rudely insisted
that our big items (dolls' prams, bikes, scooters) were forbidden – here
was no space for such luxuries. A ludicrous assertion: he was arguing
with Anna at the end of a long, wide corridor between wards and there
were others like it. Later Anna approached the ward manager but she too
vetoed those luxuries.

News of Anna's arrival quickly spread and we were surrounded by
excited mobile patients. A few used old-fashioned crutches or newfangled walking aids. An eight-year-old boy with severe facial burns led
a blind seven-year-old-girl. Several were heavily bandaged or testing new
limbs. One lad's drip was being gingerly wheeled beside him by an
adolescent brother. A grandmother with downcast eyes pushed her
emaciated granddaughter's buggy. Two of the bed-ridden, in single
rooms, wore oxygen masks; they were querulous and scared, having to
be pacified and restrained by their carers. Others were comatose, their
carers sitting by them, looking harrowed and lonely. In whispers, Anna
identified seven victims of IDF attacks on Gaza or on OPT homes.

As we distributed the goodies, after consultations with staff nurses, it
amazed Daisy to hear Anna speaking enough Arabic to be supportive. I
always feel uncomfortable doing the Lady Bountiful thing and here the
strangers' reception was mixed. When not too ill to respond to visitors,
the children were typical little Palestinians, affectionate and outgoing.
In contrast, with Daisy and me most of their carers hovered tensely
between superficial deference and veiled hostility. Anna of course was
welcomed by all; to each encounter – several quite heartbreaking – she
brought an imaginative sort of respectful compassion. Daisy tried to be
amiable in Hebrew but the effort was painfully apparent. Walking
between wards, I speculated about the possibility of helping a legless
five-year-old boy (an IDF cluster bomb) – whereupon Daisy muttered
a warning against trusting the lad's father with money. I could see that
she was being genuinely upset by this medical ghetto, but anti-Arab
emotions run deep. She questioned Anna about the carers' status when
a nurse invited us into her office for tea.

The IDF issues permits for only one carer per child, usually a parent or grandparent (commonly a granny), occasionally an older sibling. In general, carers are confined to the children's ward; a rare exception may obtain a concessionary permit to walk daily for half-an-hour in the hospital's cramped and vehicle-polluted grounds. A second family member – even a mother – may not visit under any circumstances. Nor may different relatives share in the caring; whoever originally accompanies the child cannot be replaced. Few of these cases are short-term; many patients and carers are imprisoned for four, six, eight months or even longer. Yet no child may ever leave the ward, though their condition might benefit from fresh air 'n' exercise. Anna knew of only a single easing of the 'one carer' rule; after a father had spent eight months tending a daughter blinded by a brain tumour, the mother was allowed a three-week visit. 'Next month,' Anna told us, 'that father and daughter can go home to Gaza at the end of their thirteen-month ordeal. Braille schooling will be privately provided by a British NGO.'

Anna's cogent account of the IDF's permit control spotlit the *military* nature of the West Bank's occupation. For these peasant carers – not reared to be self-entertaining, accustomed to the to-and-fro of daily life in a gregarious, close-knit community – this prolonged isolation with a sick dependant, surrounded by other damaged children and anxious relatives, is surely a form of mental torture.

To Daisy I said, 'You look shocked and confused.'

'I *am*! Aren't you?' By now she was wringing her hands, cracking her knuckles.

I shook my head. 'Remember, I've lived on the West Bank. This carer regime is consistent with a long-standing policy to humiliate and degrade Palestinians.'

An angry (or embarrassed?) flush brightened Daisy's cheeks. 'You mustn't generalise! All the Arabs' friends do that and it's not fair!'

Anna beckoned us to follow her to the corridor and went on her way like an unseasonal Santa Claus, humping a big plastic sack. Daisy loitered behind us, then disappeared. Later she was found sitting silently with the red-eyed mother of a boy entangled in tubes.

At noon it was time to go and as we waited for Anna to retrieve the car a disturbed Daisy decided to challenge the senior security officer on duty in a kiosk. Why weren't the Arab children allowed out to play? Why weren't their carers allowed to shop nearby? I could see him replying politely – were permits not strictly controlled, someone might morph into a suicide bomber prepared to die because threatened with their whole family's execution if they didn't obey orders.

When Daisy had translated she added (sounding like any pro-Palestinian activist) – 'Stupid man! And he didn't even *try* to explain how crippled kids could morph into bombers!'

We said goodbye to Anna outside the elegantly landscaped campus of Tel Aviv University and spent the afternoon in the superb Diaspora Museum. This displays no ancient artefacts but, through a stunning combination of images, exhibits, models and music, it presents what Amos called 'the best of the Jews' traditional culture'. I thanked Daisy for guiding me around Tel Aviv's most impressive tourist attraction. And I promised myself I'd return; half a day was not long enough.

As we stood at a bus stop, overlooking that green and pleasant campus, I wasn't too surprised to hear Daisy saying quietly – 'I think I'll join Anna's group. For me today has been an epiphany experience.'

I was on my way to West Jerusalem to stay with Esther, a psychotherapist who had been concentrating, since 2000, on an expanding category of IDF victims: Israeli youngsters emotionally destabilised by army service. Shaul had introduced us in 2008 and, as we sat in George's Bar back then, Esther had boasted, 'My ancestors never left Palestine – no Diaspora for us! Let the Ashkenazis throw their weight around, we're the never-lost tribe, the *bona fide* Israelites. Yet the rabbinate detests us – generations ago we went secular, possibly corrupted by Moses Montefiore. My great-a-few-times-grandfather spent thirty years chopping people up in his clinic.'

'A charitable foundation,' explained Shaul. 'In those days philanthropic foreign Jews competed with the proselytising Christian powers. Who could provide the most tempting free amenities for a half-starved Jewish minority?'

'Like famine Ireland's Protestant soup-kitchens,' said I. 'Benevolent bribery!'

Refuseniks were in the news just then and Esther recalled, 'As a school-leaver, I took the Occupation for granted. Israel had to be defended, I had to do my duty. The destructiveness of the situation, for us and for them, only came into view when I was at Harvard. My sponsors were AIPAC "philanthropists" and their discourse alerted me to what was really going on, behind the political scenes. Back home, after a decade in the States and England, the changed military ethos shocked me.'

'Changed in what way?' I asked. 'And why?'

'In my day, in the mid-'80s, conscripts were not deliberately brutalised – or not often. That change must be linked to the army leadership being so influenced by religious-national extremists. The IDF was never famed for discipline or fair-mindedness but what's going on in the twenty-first century is something else . . . Also of course the global military ethos has changed. That's another story and I've no time for it now. Could you come to stay when you're back from Balata?'

Five months later this invitation was repeated and it came with a warning: 'I won't be an entertaining hostess, our Gaza war crimes have taken their toll.'

Esther lived in the post-Ottoman Talbiya district of West Jerusalem, in the garden flat of a dignified Arabic villa sporting fanciful wrought-iron gates and balconies. Talbiya was developed by rich Palestinian Christians, soon to be dispossessed. Now lesser diplomats favour this quietly charming neighbourhood, their security devices looking incongruous.

Sustained by Taybeh and Scotch, we discussed Balatan reactions to the war crimes. Then Esther said, 'Millions all over the world were shocked during those weeks by Israel's allies' silence. I'd predicted it. The bloody brotherhood *admired* that attack on a "rats' nest" of "terrorist resistance". It was the same in 2002: those attacks on Nablus and Jenin were studied, in the US and UK, as fine examples of "Military Operations on Urbanised Territory". Our generals bragged that their example was followed in Afghanistan and Iraq – the pupils had overtaken the teachers! And after Gaza our political leaders bragged about having fought "the war of the future". A mere 13 Israeli casualties and four of those through "friendly fire". Adding the number of post-combat suicides would have given a different score. And are our traumatised patients not casualties? I've heard IDF chiefs blaming parents, saying kids are being reared too soft, can't handle real life. They won't accept the obvious: ratchet up the brutalising and you get more damaged youngsters and more domestic violence – often hidden till it's too late . . .'

Then I heard the other story. 'There's a horrible intimacy between Israeli, US and UK "urban warfare specialists". Together the bloody brotherhood study systematic repression and state killing – known to Palestinians as "collective punishment". They have their own research centres, conferences, journals – it's a discrete techno-scientific discipline. I've been to one of those conferences, wearing my professional hat. The atmosphere alarmed me. There were sadistic, almost porno strands running through the exchanges as they watched PowerPoint slides. They talked excitedly of "the new reality of combat" and *annihilating* whole cities described as "terrorist nests". And of shooting dead unarmed males of military age – fifteen to fifty – and "speeding to kill" before the media could get to the scene. It was like watching kids getting high on dangerous drugs, as they stoked each other's racism and Islamophobia. You could see how groupthink works, how the bubble is constructed. Ignoring enemy death rates is part of it all – why bother to count dead rats? If you've done your dehumanising job properly, who cares? Just get on with the killing! And remember, all our dead soldiers are noble heroes who sacrificed their lives to defend our homeland and our values . . . Of course not all the old guard are happy about this "new reality of combat". Here in Israel a few retired generals – some my own relatives – say they enjoyed leading their troops into danger and that's what soldiering is all about. They look away and shuffle their feet when there's talk of "taking out" unarmed men – and boys – and not wasting resources by moving the wounded to hospital. As a Jew I must look back to the Holocaust and ask myself – where are the roots of this techno-scientific discipline.'

The bus from Tel Aviv dropped me off at the end of Esther's street and I found her in a rose-bed, harvesting the season's last blooms. In the hallway, crates were stacked.

'I'm merging into the Canadian Diaspora,' said Esther. 'My son and his family live in Vancouver – last month I retired.'

I asked, 'Why so early?'

Esther asked, 'How long could you survive in the land Netanyahu promises?' She broached a Taybeh six-pack and said briskly, 'Let's go to the kitchen. A niece is coming to join us, I must be creative.' As I peeled potatoes she continued, 'Spot-and-Shoot proved the last straw. This camel's back is quite strong but for all there *is* a last straw.'

By then many rumours were circulating about Spot-and-Shoot, the latest triumph of Israel's armaments industry. For anyone of normal sensibility, one could easily believe in it as the last straw. Esther had recently been coping with one of its side-effects – an anguished twenty-two-year-old woman who, having stoically done her duty as a remote control killer, became psychotic in civilian life.

Spot-and-Shoot has an official name: 'Sentry Tech'. Its greatest advantage – it can be operated by women, aged nineteen or twenty. A social taboo protects them from conventional combat; S&S operators are not at risk. Sitting safely in front of a TV monitor, nowhere near a danger zone, they use a PlayStation-type joystick to kill Palestinians – usually Gazan farmers going about their lawful business on the narrow strips of land remaining to them. Or perhaps a teenage boy scavenging for scrap iron in the rubble – who would be labelled an 'incriminated Arab' after his murder. No other IDF weapons system is operated only by women. 'That's crucial,' said Esther. 'Dying on the battlefield has lost its appeal for most of the population. Combat units are desperately short of recruits. And these kids just out of school, who've always had their Sony PlayStation, don't need much training. When they see some-one on the monitor who might be a "terrorist" they contact a CO – probably only a few years older – and he can authorise pressing the joystick button. Shooters are sitting far from the machine-gun in the watchtower but they can hear the shot through the tower's audio sensors. That leaves some with intolerable memories. A UN Special Rapporteur [Philip Alston] has reason to be worried about what he calls "a PlayStation mentality to killing".'

When I winced Esther said soothingly, 'I know, I know it's painful. But UN-speak doesn't do precision.'

I recalled that Gaza City, post-Cast Lead, had replicated the invented, overcrowded Muslim country of Zekistan, shown in *America's Army*. This video has been delivered free to millions over the Internet, by America's army – one of the world's biggest developers of video games, none concerned with the non-violent resolution of conflict.

Esther nodded. 'In our time, children played at being adults, equipped as doctors, cooks, carpenters, cowboys. Now adult men have adapted children's games – how to kill without ever being at risk. Our govern-ment gloats over their "remote killing" inventions. Rafael [a government armaments company] markets them around the world as "the face of the future". By 2020, if all goes according to plan, at least one-third of IDF weaponry will be unmanned.'

We were cheered by the arrival of Esther's thirty-year-old niece, Lydia, a fluent Arabic-speaker. She worked with Shaul in the most tormented districts of East Jerusalem and was an advocate for the one-state solution. 'Some call me an escapist because I'll only allow myself to think positive. On the West Bank, among my generation, the mind-shift has started. Forget slogans, banners, flags and ritual Friday confrontations with soldiers. Those are proud pathetic gestures, futile defiance, by now all meaningless. The notion of a "liberation struggle" belongs to the grandparents' generation. Most young Palestinians know the score, even if they won't admit it. They see how it is – literally *see* it, all around them. The half a million Israelis planted on their soil have made an independent, separate Palestine impossible.'

As a nineteen-year-old, Lydia had refused to serve in the OPT, been jailed for 30 days, then deprived forever of various government subsidies and 'aids to promotion'. Her father, Esther's brother, wanted her to accompany Aunty to Vancouver and promote the Boycott, Divestment and Sanctions movement from a safe distance. She, however, was committed to promoting 'one-state' among her contemporaries on both sides of the Green Line. Esther supported her – 'If all the pioneer thinkers migrate, how can the reform happen? That's my dream, too – a *re-formation* of this state to make space for everyone, all equal before the law.'

Lydia continued, 'Political education is urgently needed, straight-thinking leadership taking people in a new direction. On our side a silent minority hates the Occupation. They need de-brainwashing. They're scared by stories about what would happen if Arabs controlled the OPT – rockets every day on Jerusalem and Tel Aviv. Most of them would feel differently if Arabs were openly claiming ANC-type rights. Now they're forgotten because so silent.'

Esther added, 'Or the few not silent are threatened as post-Zionist traitors. But from where are the new leaders to come, on either side? In general, Mammonism is more powerful than any other ism. And the Zionist Alliance uses it to maximum effect. Any innovative young West Bank leader can't expect genuine support from the PA leadership – its mammonly needs are too well cared for by the US and EU. Their representatives never breathe a whisper of support for one-state, not even when their noses are rubbed in the "facts on the ground". BDS activists don't give enough exposure to foreign collusion with the

Occupation. How many EU taxpayers know their money props it up? Partly through funding the PA security forces, training them to collaborate with the IDF.'

Lydia laughed and said, 'Look ahead and think positive! Those forces could be useful in our re-formed state. Really that's the black joke. Amidst Zionism's War on Terror, aka Palestinians, a sort of one-state is evolving. Even the OPT's Apartheid roads could become a benefit for all. Also, with an unrestricted native workforce, there'd be no need for thousands of imported labourers. We could spend all night calculating the reformation's advantages!'

Which we almost did . . . How long is a piece of string – especially a piece of tightly knotted string? Such discussions, often continuing into the small hours, made me feel slightly melancholy because I'll never know whether or not our various predictions come true.

CHAPTER 24

The Complexities of Safed

Safed felt like a muddled place with conflicting vibes: laid-back yet uneasy, tourist-conscious yet individualistic, attractive but in a not-quite-genuine way, long associated with Kabbalistic Judaism and now half-cowed by ultra-Orthodoxy. You could say I caught the place with its pants down: tension was unusually high.

I approached Safed from Acre – a ninety-minute bus journey on a quiet non-motorway that ascended gradually through conifer plantations and drought-stricken fields. Twice we paused briefly in dejected development towns, their edges blighted by failed factories. Then it seemed Safed on its mountain-top was close – but no, we were on another summit from which our road had to wriggle far down before climbing to the Holy Land's highest city (about 3,000 feet: population 28,000).

On the steep walk up from a rudimentary bus station the most obvious structure is sadly symbolic – a lone minaret, all that remains of Sheikh 'Issa Mosque, built in 1648. Exactly three centuries later it was almost completely destroyed, as was its surrounding area, once known as the Little Market.

Safed is tightly packed on a summit chosen in the second century BC as a beacon site; the chain extended to Jerusalem and the fires were lit to mark holy days or a new month. During the First Revolt (against the Romans: 66–73AD) the Jewish leader Josephus fortified the town, by then an important trading centre on the road to Damascus. The Old City on the west side of Mount Canaan is an agreeable jumble of alleys and stairways but with many reminders of '48: the shells of Palestinian homes.

As the cost of accommodation reflects Safed's popularity with rich Kabbala devotees, Anna had arranged for me to lodge in the Synagogue Quarter, in a long, narrow, cobbled street of terraced houses. My Australian hostess, Suzy, who made *aliyah* fifty years ago, was a wee wisp of a woman, soft-spoken and gentle in her manner but a cast-iron Hasidic. When the warning siren sounded twenty minutes before the Sabbath sunset she locked up all electrical appliances and room lights had to be left on. Lest I might absent-mindedly switch mine off, it was sellotaped for the duration.

This was an odd house – damaged in the 1837 earthquake, Suzy said, 'and it's never been the same since'. From the cramped hallway two short steep staircases ascended, one to a large kitchen-living-room, the other to my cell-like bedroom with a small, deep-set window overlooking an untidiness of tiled and tin roofs and an immense expanse of hilly country. The kitchen's French window gave access to a loo/shower cabin ingeniously built onto the neighbour's roof.

Safed might be described as 'involuntarily pedestrianised', its layout discouraging wheeled transport. Strolling through the down-at-heel Synagogue Quarter, I noticed many doorways protected by heavy Kabbalistic amulets. In the seventeenth century there were 61 synagogues in Safed, now there are 30 or so, not all easily identified by the foreigner.

Some say the Kabbala cult took root in the northern Galilee in the first century AD. Later, it slowly developed on the Iberian peninsula from where it returned to Safed after the expulsion of the Jews by the conquering Christians. Those who took refuge in Palestine at that time seem to have met with little opposition and several seventeenth-century rabbis went over to Islam, including two leaders of the Ari Sephardi community, Shabbtai Ze'ev and Nathan of Gaza. By then Safed had been established as the Kabbalists' main centre.

Towards the end of the eighteenth century, numerous Hassidim arrived from Russia but most died in 1837. Throughout the eighteenth and nineteenth centuries a series of earthquakes and epidemics severely depleted the population. The 1880s saw the arrival of several groups of Orthodox from Russia and Central Europe. These newcomers did not wish to merge with the locals; insistently they proclaimed their differences in clothing, food, customs. Come the Mandate, increased Zionist immigration and was increasingly resented by the Palestinians – then fiercely resisted throughout the 1920s and '30s. The murderous riots of 1929, which spread from Jerusalem to Hebron and Safed, sowed seeds which flowered horribly in 1948. The Haganah isolated Safed, having forced all the surrounding villagers to flee. For two weeks the besieged Palestinians resisted alone cowering in the Citadel, Syria and Transjordan having ignored their desperate calls for help. On 12 May, three days before the UN recognised the State of Israel, the surviving defenders were executed. Their families, Muslim and Christian, then had no choice but to flee into Syria.

Slowly I climbed a wide, steep flight of steps decisively separating the Synagogue Quarter from the Artists' Quarter – a barrier constructed after the 1929 riots to keep Palestinians and Jews apart. The Artists' Quarter occupies what for many centuries was Safed's main market area. A fortified *han* for merchants' caravans later became Ottoman government offices and is now the Wolfson Community Centre where immigrants learn Hebrew and musicians develop their talents with generous assistance.

Two Mameluke buildings are closed to the public; the Red Mosque is quietly crumbling away, the Banat Hamad Mausoleum is a masonic lodge. Several intact Ottoman public buildings, and the private homes of notable Palestinian families, have been converted to other uses and the newish (1902) Al-Younis Mosque proclaims itself to be the 'general Exhibition Hall of the Safed Artists' Colony'. Palestinians are painfully aware of the fate of such 'disrespected' mosques. To them it feels like a planned jeer, a triumphalist flourish. In Nazareth one young man said to me, 'It's worse than burning a mosque; it goes on forever!'

Within three years of the Nakba this Artists' Quarter had been instituted to screen Safed's violent 'cleansing'. Studios and galleries became available (as in Jaffa and Ein Hod) and subsidised craftsmen and artists gladly moved to this picturesque haven overlooking a historic landscape where famous battles were fought. For a light-hearted quarter century all went well, nobody caring how 'observant' anybody else was. But things changed in the 1980s as Gush Emunim gained power and influence out of all proportion to its actual membership. Safed then received the wrong sort of reinforcements, with offspring in sufficient numbers to prove their piety. These came from Jerusalem, where some felt 'repressed', or from North America – mainly the US. This largely State-funded influx caused a housing shortage and many galleries have now been reconverted to accommodate the reinforcements, who brought with them infected baggage. Safed is no longer light-hearted.

Suzy told me that a local rabbi regularly foretells another major earthquake as punishment for the Nakba (though she didn't put it that way). He may well be right; hereabouts the earth is thin-skinned and every century or so collapses disastrously. In 1927, Beisan and Jericho were half-demolished and in Nablus three large houses disappeared.

After the 1837 'quake a Hungarian rabbi, Moshe Teitelbaum, attributed the thousands of deaths to God's annoyance – too many Jews had recently migrated to Palestine. He declared: 'It is not God's will that we should go to the land of Israel by our own efforts and will.' Rabbi Rafael Hirsch, then leader of Modern Orthodoxy in Germany, agreed with him. 'God has commanded Jews never to establish a state of their own by their own efforts.' In the mid-eighteenth century another illustrious German, Rabbi Eibshutz, had reminded his followers that major migrations to Israel were forbidden until the Messiah had arrived. Five centuries before that, Rabbi Ezra of Gerona had warned against moving to Palestine because God is only present in the Diaspora where most Jews live. Only one Jewish leader, throughout the centuries, proposed that Jews should conquer the land of Israel. His name was Nachmanides and he died in 1270. In 1970 Gush Emunim nominated him as their patron saint.

Safed nowhere feels like a city, perhaps because all its tall buildings (grotty apartment blocks) are invisible from the centre. The main thoroughfare – a few miles long, motorable and circular – begins and ends at the bus station. Much of its length overlooks a huddle of old roofs and beyond stretch vineyards and orchards with Mount Meron's smooth bulk in the near distance. Here on Jerusalem Street one finds a mini-supermarket, a tatty shopping centre, five more synagogues, several restaurants redolent of drastically recycled cooking-oil, a variety of souvenir shops (Safed Candles the most worthwhile) and Eliezer's House of Books.

In a small, shiny plastic café, imaginatively named Kappucino and run by a young US couple, I noted the jar of 'instant' and ordered tea. The wife looked teenaged and was shyly welcoming. Her mother, sitting in a corner rocking a baby, showed friendly in a hesitant way. I enquired about the infant's age, sex and nocturnal habits (babies are useful ice-picks) and at once its mother began to unwind. But then its father appeared, glared at me and ordered his wife to fetch the croissants. He was clean-shaven, curly haired, blue-eyed and, given a different expression, might have seemed handsome. The grandmother, bewigged and long-skirted, hurriedly followed her daughter.

As though on cue, Daniel and Moshe appeared, casually dressed but wearing what I think of as exhibitionist watches. Seeing me and my open notebook, Moshe asked, 'Journalist?' They introduced themselves, shook hands vigorously and sat at the next table. Both had dual passports (Moshe's Argentinian, Daniel's Canadian) and were based in Safed having made *aliyah* some twenty years ago. I gathered they drifted in and out of Israel doing unspecified jobs for people who found it hard to go abroad. Neither was religious but they liked Safed because as residents you could hang out whichever way, just doing your own thing. Moshe added, 'It's changing, though – has been for a while. More of the Hairies, trying to bully everyone else. And someone has started a college for Arabs – we never had them around before. Why bother trying to teach them? Why they've never had a country? Too fuckin' stupid to run it! And those Mizrahim aren't much better – you seen how they keep their towns?'

I stood up, murmuring about an appointment and opening my purse. 'No! No!' said Daniel. 'Our pleasure! Maybe see you tomorrow?' 'That would be nice,' I lied.

Back at base, Suzy introduced me to my enigmatic fellow-lodger, Gordon, who looked and sounded like a British army officer (Rtd) but this didn't quite jell with his devout Orthodoxy. He had travelled widely and seemed happy to discuss world affairs without revealing any detail about his personal background. Next morning Suzy – respecting his privacy – merely told me, 'He's been here five years.'

Gordon and I relaxed in a small, high-ceilinged room I hadn't previously noticed – leading off the hallway, windowless, with a long ladder giving access to Gordon's bedroom. The bookshelves held only religious volumes, in Hebrew and English. Between them hung Suzy's inherited watercolours: her mother's strangely dark impressionistic Australian landscapes with hints of human forms in the background. Gordon admitted he had at first found them 'a little unsettling'. It soon emerged that he was a 'one-stater'. 'But in Safed,' he said, 'one doesn't hold public meetings about that.'

The city's most recent blow-ins – Russian and Ethiopian – have been ghettoised in outlying apartment blocks and Anna had given me an introduction to one Falasha family. When I mentioned this Gordon frowned, hesitated, then advised, 'I think not – not at the moment. In that direction we have too many friction points. All to do with our deplorable Chief Rabbi. He's against Arabs enrolling in our Academic College.'

I asked, 'How does that effect the Falasha?'

'They're already on edge,' said Gordon. 'It's like separate little bush fires with different causes – when they join up you're really in trouble. And that could happen here quite soon. The State rabbinate has started one fire, been trying for some time to do away with the Kessoch – what the Ethiopians use instead of rabbis. It's said they still sacrifice animals and they've never been allowed to preside at weddings. Last week the government agreed to go on paying them the standard stipend, so the rabbinate wants them completely abolished. Therefore the Ethiopians are angry – *very* angry.'

The student accommodation 'fire' was even more dangerous, Gordon explained. The city's Chief Rabbi, Shmuel Eliyaku, had forbidden all Jews to rent rooms or flats to Arabs, a command that even in Israel was of questionable legality. But the panic seemed general; countrywide, Palestinian students were being accused of shoplifting, burglary, playing inappropriate music too loudly in public places, treating the Sabbath like any other day and (the panic button) eyeing up Israeli girls. Not all Safed Jews are ultra-Orthodox; many lead Western lives and the panic suggests their daughters are normally susceptible to handsome Arabs. A week previously, three Palestinians had been arrested and accused of 'molesting' teenage girls – a common charge, since the college opened. Always these charges were denied and Gordon believed most of the denials. 'For one thing, Arab youngsters are too hungry for education to risk expulsion. For another they're too scared of being killed. In Safed sex is not just dynamite – more like a nuclear weapon. Earlier this year the wives of 27 leading rabbis sparked a major controversy. They published a complaint about the 25,000 Jewish women who've married or moved in with Arabs – good for our one-state future! Those rabbis' wives warned that Arab wives must endure a lifetime of curses, beatings and humiliations. I'm happy to say my rabbi, Gilad Karive, denounced the letter.'

Later I heard that Gordon had set up a defence group for an eighty-nine-year-old hero of the Haganah campaigns (Eli Tzvieli) who lived alone; he had received several death threats and his property was being attacked by Haredim thugs who spoke openly of punishing him for letting rooms to Palestinians.

Next morning in Eliezer's House of Books I was welcomed almost effusively by Becky-behind-the-till who apologised for the lack of English-language newspapers; it was no longer worth supplying them, everyone got their news online. She herself had given up papers and magazines years ago when she left New York, apart from her Lurianic Kabbala journal.

One could deduce Safed's high density of North Americans from these shelves; about half English-language, US-published and expensive, with shorter shelves for other European languages and the rest Hebrew. Scores of volumes gave advice on family life – obsessively warning against intermarriage – and on child-rearing techniques compatible with Judaism. Other scores dealt in English with Jewish mysticism in general and the Lurianic Kabbala and Hassidism in particular. As I browsed uneasily through these, another customer entered and I overheard:

Becky:	Anything today about Rabbi Eliyahu?
Elderly Customer:	Nothing new, only what the media invent. It's all over . . .
Becky:	I doubt that. Too many people want to keep stirring it. The delegitimisers – it suits them.
Customer:	Our mayor has it all under control. I heard him last night on the radio saying Safed is a symbol of coexistence between Jews and Arabs.

A young mother arrived with three bibliomanic small children each of whom was allowed to buy one book. They wanted English books but were told they needed to read Hebrew because they were Israeli citizens and that was their language.

Standing in a corner, between ceiling-high shelves, I chanced to be invisible to the next customer and soon heard familiar names. But why were Becky and the youngish Haredim so excitedly discussing Shapira and Teitel of Yitzhar? That settlement near Nablus, whose members terrorise all the surrounding villagers – and who curtailed my walks from Balata – is led by Rabbi Yitzhak Shapira. It also shelters Jack Teitel who has admitted to the murders to two Palestinian farmers and the posting of a bomb to Ze'ev Sternhell, a liberal historian.

On realising that Shapira was being castigated I joined the two by the till. Becky readily explained that Shapira had published a criminally controversial book and been hunted by the Shabak, the secret police. 'Is he in custody?' I asked eagerly.

My companions looked uncomfortable and glanced at each other before Becky replied, 'No, I'm afraid not. He and two of his buddies were ordered to attend an interrogation session but refused. The buddies had been all over the place, promoting the book.'

I asked, 'What's this book about?'

'Killing people,' replied Becky. 'When it's OK to murder non-Jews. And certain sorts of seculars like Sternhell. It's called *Torat Ha'Melech* which sounds innocent – "The King's Torah". I doubt it'll be translated – I hope not!'

The House of Books is strictly non-secular and I had been able to find only one slightly interesting volume, *Faith Under Fire: 33 Days of Missiles and Miracles*. As I paid, Becky invited me to drink coffee with her at 6.00 p.m. I had to say no: Naomi was expecting me to spend the rest of the day with her very extended family. It then transpired that Naomi and Becky were old friends. Safed's like that . . .

Later, over our beer nightcaps (Suzy disapproved but pretended not to notice), I asked Gordon what he knew of *Torat Ha'Melech*. He told me that despite the national uproar neither Netanyahu nor the Attorney General had made any comment.

'A common pattern,' said I. 'Weeks before Netanyahu became the Prime Minister, I remember ten of Shapira's followers being arrested on suspicion of setting fire to a village mosque. After his election they were released. My friends in that village had photos of the arsonists but the police weren't interested.'

'Now it's even worse,' said Gordon. 'Two years ago the NRP was officially dissolved but it's still around in new clothes and Netanyahu's coalition depends on it.'

From the House of Books, a two-mile walk took me along Jerusalem Street, through the Artists' Quarter to Naomi's apartment. When the rich and famous took up a version of Kabbala, as one of their escape routes to 'Higher Things', religious tourism became Safed's main industry. There are three English-language *yeshivot* for Jewish foreigners, while the Ascent Institute offers short courses in Torah teachings, Jewish mysticism and Kabbala – including 'Kabbala and Love'. At Eliezer's you can buy *Safed: Six Guided Tours in and Around the Mystical City*. In one gallery I watched 'modern conceptual artists' being inspired by Kabbala and in the David Friedman gallery a lugubrious middle-aged man urged me to stay for a (free) introduction to Kabbala.

There's something falsely reassuring, in a fuzzy way, about what the *Lonely Planet* describes as 'Safed's rich heritage of Jewish mysticism'. Surely mystics must be harmless if a bit scatty, living in another space, making weird calculations – in the Kabbalistic case – about letters and numbers. Which leads us back to Shahak and Mezvinsky, who explain:

> Shelves groan under the weight of books on Jewish mysticism in general and the Lurianic Kabbala specifically . . . . The people who read only these books cannot suspect that they contain basic ideas about Jewish superiority comparable to the worst forms of anti-Semitism. The scholarly authors have wilfully omitted reference to such ideas. These authors are supreme hypocrites, analogous to many authors of books on Stalin and Stalinism. Until recently, people who read only the books written by Stalinists . . . would have false notions of the Stalinists' regimes and their real ideologies.

It's worrying that this Kabbalistic cult has unwittingly become such a dangerous racket – dangerous because it compounds the confusions barring the way to any understanding of the Holy Land's core problems.

Naomi lived in one of several 1960s five-storey apartment blocks. The imposition by secular Zionists of such ugliness on Safed's sacred ground, so near the revered graves of Rabbi Isaac Luria and his fellow-mystics, had aroused much impotent resentment. Most hall doors were unnamed and unnumbered, but eventually I found the Metzgers' corner flat on the top floor – facing Mount Meron, the reward for negotiating so many steep unswept stairways and long drab galleries. I found Naomi alone, scouring the four small rooms in preparation for the morrow's Seder.

I'd heard Naomi's story from our mutual English friend. She was born in Cardiff in 1950, to long-assimilated secular parents. Her brother's name was John, because of a quirky family custom. For generations, all first-born sons had been named after King John who, in the early thirteenth century, reminded the mayor of London that Jews had to be protected throughout the kingdom. (Much good that did: English Jews were soon given the usual choice – 'Baptism or death!')

While training as a nurse, Naomi married a talented and ambitious young doctor and in 1974 the pair migrated to New York. Within two years, to the husband's great distress, his beautiful wife was 'born again' as a Haredi. Sitting with me by the Mount Meron window, Naomi was very clear about her rebirthing process and, oddly enough, I could see how it had worked. As a woman she felt belittled by the most obvious (to her) results of Women's Lib: the commercial exploitation, at every level, of female sexuality. When by chance she became involved with a Haredi community their *tznuit* (Jewish law of modesty) attracted her. She saw female dignity being preserved and within the Torah she found what appealed to her as a durable foundation for family life. A year later she had divorced her high-earning husband and made *aliyah*. Ever since, she had been living apparently happily in Safed with low-earning Monie. Theirs was an arranged marriage, between a widower whose wife had died giving birth to their third child and an 'elderly' (aged 30) divorcee with few Israeli connections. Despite such a late start, and the burden of Monie's three, Naomi had eight children. I realised then that the next-door flat, though quite separate, was part of this family home, serving as a dormitory.

Naomi's offspring were four of each and for the males an austere life of prayer and Torah study lay ahead. 'Possibly this may soon change,' said she in a neutral voice. 'Our *yeshiva* education is more and more criticised for neglecting most subjects. But it does train pupils to dispute, organise thoughts logically, analyse arguments – all one-to-one. So if any want to join the modern world they can catch up quickly.'

Two days later, when our friendship had developed, Naomi told me about their eldest son Ran, who as a nineteen-year-old had opted out. 'He loved us, we never quarrelled, but he did want a wider education. Because of his younger sisters we had to put pressure on him. If he disgraced the family they could never marry.' Before news of her brother's defection could spread, the seventeen-year-old had been hastily married off. Then Ran repented, not wanting to wreck his other sisters' prospects.

'Our daughters,' said Naomi, 'are more adventurous. In these times they can work abroad from the age of seventeen in a Jewish centre – you find them all over the world. But they must be home, ready for marriage, by their 23rd birthday at the latest.'

Naomi had had to struggle for her daughters' right to travel. Monie couldn't approve of this trend; too many girls never came home. Then the family might lie about a tragic death and find themselves doubly disgraced when the 'deceased' appeared ten years later in her new incarnation as a modern woman.

Safed-born Monie was tall, well-built, long-bearded and courteous in a distant way to the foreign female. He augmented the Haredim government subsidy (family allowance) by teaching Hebrew online to newcomers from Eastern Europe. Once he had many Russian pupils, but now there seemed to be something of a backwash; an estimated 60,000 Russian Jews (or putative Jews) were said to have returned whence they came.

Naomi said, 'I want you to meet all sorts here – my friends will pass-the-parcel, with you as the parcel.' And so it was, except that Naomi's circle could hardly be described as 'all sorts'. My diary records:

> Everyone refers to Abraham & Co as though they were recently deceased beloved relatives, whose words and actions naturally and properly influence or determine the course of their descendants' lives. It would seem unkind as well as futile to argue about the absurdity of apportioning land in the twentieth century on the basis of what a god in whom most human beings don't believe said 3,000 or so years ago to a dominant figure in a Holy Book.
>
> Leah appalled me by recalling a recent visit to Hebron's settlers. Her coachload heard (and believed) many accounts of Internationals egging Palestinian children on to stone the IDF so that when soldiers retaliate the media can get pix of Arabs being attacked. Also, Palestinians often disguise themselves as Haredim women and attack their own children to make propaganda. And she showed me an English-language magazine bought in the Gutnick Centre – it claimed that Internationals regularly collude with terrorists in numerous (unspecified) ways.
>
> Miracles are widely credited. Thrice I was told about the wondrous power wielded by Rabbi Shmuel Eliyahu – he who forbade Jews to have Arab tenants. When a bedroom fire threatened a family because the house key couldn't be found Rabbi Eliyahu walked up to the door and opened it. 'He didn't break it,' I was assured. 'He opened it through spiritual power.'
>
> During the wholly unjustified 33-day attack on Lebanon in 2006 Safed was the third most shelled city in Israel. 'We were all in grave danger,' said one woman. 'Only prayer saved us.' A few Safed residents lost their lives. No one would say how many but much was made of the 500,000 Israeli 'refugees' who fled south as Katyusha rockets fell on the north. Some saw this shelling as God's punishment for Safed's failure to defend the Gush Katif settlers when they were compelled to

leave Gaza in 2005. I remarked that this made no sense because the same political leader had initiated the removal of those settlers and the bombing of Lebanon which provoked the shelling of Safed. Everyone looked blank. What could Sharon have to do with it? Those Katyushas came because Islamists hate Jews.

In another household a seven-year-old boy asked his mother, 'Ima, why do the Arabs want to kill us?' She replied, 'Because we're Jews.' Then she recalled Rabbi Eliyahu and a large group from his synagogue dancing under the stars on a Sabbath evening though rockets were falling. 'He knew our Creator would protect them on the Sabbath.'

Naomi's friends are no less 'ultra', ideologically speaking, than the thugs who are tormenting poor Mr Tzvieli. Yet they're among the kindest and most welcoming people I've met in Israel and are greatly upset by the OPT settlers' violence. Their ingrained *fear* of Arabs, though so evident, seems not to have engendered the contemptuous prejudice (shading into hatred) displayed by some irreligious and more intellectually sophisticated Israelis. As my grandfather used to say, 'Put that in your pipe and smoke it.'

When Hassidism was founded in Ukraine by Israel ben Eliezer (*c*.1700–1760) it shocked the Jewish Establishment by promoting Kabbalistic notions among the masses, putting much more emphasis on miracles and 'mystical studies' than on Talmudic learning while encouraging men to sing, dance and even have a snifter in the synagogue. As the movement spread, it gradually compromised with its small 'c' conservative opponents, but the Haredim clothing and beards and wigs, and their dancing to the popular music of Klezmer bands, survive as changeless links with eighteenth-century Ukraine and Poland. It seems darkly ironic that in twenty-first-century Israel some Hassedim sects have become the champions of inflexibility, fostering a frightening – sometimes lethal – intolerance.

That evening I found Gordon listening on his portable radio to an account of the latest flare-up between the Hassidic Gerer sect (the biggest in Israel) and the Shlomei Emunim, leaders of a coalition of smaller sects. Somehow a member of the United Torah Judaism sect had become involved by chance and was thrown to the ground and beaten up in Mea She'arim – allegedly because he wanted to found a newspaper to rival the Gerer-controlled daily.

I asked, 'How come all these sects in such a small population?'

'It goes with the territory!' said Gordon. 'Literally, so you get Bratslaver Hassidim, Belzer Hassidim, Gerer Hassidim and so on – depending on where their hereditary rebbes come from. *Rebbes*, not rabbis – they like to keep these little distinctions. It does seem unlikely that our civil disturbances can have their roots in long-forgotten Eastern European urban rivalries. But so it is.'

'Scary!' I said. 'To think such people now hold the balance in the Knesset!'

'Yes,' said Gordon, 'where they can and do dictate to the secular majority. You have to wonder, when all these experts come here to negotiate – politicians, diplomats, UN representatives – do they have any idea what they're dealing with? Do they realise Kabbalistic spells are being laid on them as they fly towards Ben-Gurion airport?'

I laughed. 'That would be the least of their worries!'

'Quite so,' said Gordon. 'That's what worries *me*. You can't deal with Israel's political right if you don't understand the essence of Haredi politics.'

Monie's sister Sheba invited me for the Sabbath Seder. She and Chaim spoke eccentric English but were uninhibited about this; we communicated easily. Their ground-floor flat was gloomy; it looked across a straggle of puny shrubs to the gable end of yet another block. Every door (except the bathroom) had its *mezuza* – verses from Deuteronomy, written with ink on parchment and enclosed in a little box attached to the door frame on the right as one enters. The living-room bookcase was dominated by a lavishly bound twenty-volume set of the Babylonian Talmud. Suzy had told me why one sees it in almost every Observant (and some other) households: competing Israeli newspapers offer it at '50% Off!' or as lottery or quiz prizes.

Naomi told me how happy it made Sheba to have thirty-year-old Miriam and her husband Moses regularly bringing their brood to celebrate the Sabbath with the maternal grandparents. Four of six married children had moved to Jerusalem or the Hassidic town of Bnei Brek.

I arrived first, to find Sheba placing trays of *matza* (unleavened bread, hot from the oven) on a long table, then carefully covering them with tea-towels. Miniature silver goblets, delicately engraved, marked the fathers' places. Everyone else drank from tiny plastic medicine measures – filled with a local home-made wine for the adults, with grape juice for the children. The seven-branched menorah stood in the centre of the table and around it, on coffee-cup saucers, were several extra candles – one for each family member and close friends. In the cramped kitchen a disproportionate amount of space was taken up by the obligatory two sinks; dairy products and anything even vaguely meaty must be strictly segregated.

Cheerful squeals, yelps and giggles heralded the arrival of Miriam, three daughters – aged eight, six and four – and baby Israel, at fifteen months still on the breast though his mother was five months pregnant. Moments later Moses and nine-year-old Marcus, both in full Sabbath gear, came into the hallway calling for Chaim. The males then took off for a ninety-minute synagogue session; sons participate as soon as they are controllable.

It always irritated me to see small girls (or, indeed, big girls) constrained by *tzniut* whatever the weather – wearing tights, long sleeves, high necks. Now I told myself not to be narrow-minded; Miriam's trio were exceptionally attractive, both high-spirited and well-behaved. Her own English was quite fluent and she longed to teach the girls but Moses felt it would be easier to protect them from 'new dangers' (the Internet) if they spoke only Hebrew. Naomi worried about the company Moses was keeping. He had recently joined a confraternity who were trying – with some success – to bully El-Al into cordoning off certain sections of a plane for 'Male Haredim Only'.

Gordon had warned me that contentious issues must be avoided on the Sabbath – sound psychology, I thought, to have a soothing, reinvigorating Day of Rest when nothing stressful is discussed, domestic, national or global. However, those temperamentally short of small talk may find exchanges of views on bread-making and nappy rash set up another sort of stress.

After the males' return came the moving ritual of both mothers lighting the candles. For this, perfect silence reigned, the children sitting motionless. Then everyone passed around a two-handed ablution ewer and silence fell again between that ceremony and the breaking of the bread. The *matza* was cut in a certain prescribed way and dipped in bitter herbs before its board was turned for each portion to be cut smaller while the mothers fetched a deliciously dressed salad, a hummus

concoction and several nameless culinary wonders. The males were
served first, including the nine-year-old boy, before the seventy-nine-
year-old guest. (Naomi had admitted that as a Haredi neophyte this sort
of thing formed her highest cultural hurdle.) During the meal the males
sang loudly and tunefully, slapping the table; the girls were allowed a
play-break between courses. A vodka toast preceded the four rounds of
wine poured for the adults. A fifth glass was left in the middle of the
table 'for the prophet Elijah' – to be tossed back later by Chaim, as my
father used to toss back Santa Claus' brandy.

After the meal short extracts were read from a beautifully illustrated
Haggada, a book of religious commentaries suitable for children. Then
my host and his son-in-law returned to the environs of the synagogue to
sing some more and dance a lot while their respective wives got on with
the washing of dishes and the bedding of children.

Left on our own, Sheba and I talked until nearly midnight. When the
Sabbath embargo on contentious issues had been forgotten, I heard a
lot about my hostess's worries – all to do with increasing Hassedic
extremism.

Walking home through a dark and soundless Safed, I saw only one
citizen, a clean-shaven man who had had more than four thimblefuls of
wine and needed the wall's assistance on his way to bed. That afternoon
I had passed the Ha'Ari Ashkenazi synagogue, swallowed by the 1852
earthquake, then rebuilt and made famous by a magnificently carved,
olive-wood ark. Now I heard a most unsettling chant coming from
behind this building, a haunting sound, distressed yet rather beautiful.
Gordon, who could hear the chanting from his bedroom, identified its
source: a maverick rebbe being destabilised by his own version of the
Prophecy of Micheas. This prompted me to read Micheas for my
bedtime story – an oddly eerie experience, in the stillness of the night,
so close to the site of Morasti.

What is the wickedness of Jacob? Is it not Samaria? and what are the
high places of Juda? are they not Jerusalem?

And I will make Samaria as a heap of stones in the field when a
vineyard is planted: and I will bring down the stones thereof into the
valley, and will lay her foundations bare . . . Therefore will I lament
and howl: I will make a wailing like the dragons, and a mourning like
the ostriches . . .

For evil is come down from the Lord into the gate of Jerusalem . . .
And they have coveted fields, and taken them by violence, and houses
they have forcibly taken away: and oppressed a man and his house, a
man and his inheritance . . . and them that passed harmless you have
turned to war.

Two days later, at the bus station, I met an Academic College Palestinian
student from Karmiel, one of the development towns between Acre and
Safed. His subject was English and he seemed pleased to be approached
by a friendly foreigner. Karmiel does not have a good reputation among
'48-ers but he was finding Safed much more frightening. Four of his
class mates had been badly beaten up the previous evening, following an
emergency convention of 18 Northern Area rabbis – all backed Rabbi
Eliyahu's ban on student tenants. He praised Karmiel's mayor who had
sacked the deputy mayor for his repeated insulting of Arabs in public.
Why hadn't someone sacked Safed's mayor who openly supported
Eliyahu? A rhetorical question – and anyway the departure of the
Karmiel minibus was about to end our too brief conversation.

CHAPTER 25

Harrowed Again by the Barrier

Anna had said, using her sociologist's voice, 'You could do with some exposure to unreconstructed Zionists, average citizens, no way extreme – like the non-observant Kohns. Limor and Kobi enjoy foreigners – you'll find them interesting.' And so it came to pass that on my way back from Safed I spent two days being pampered by the Kohns.

Limor sells her pottery, aimed at the under-tens, in a souvenir shop overlooking Netanya's seven miles of tourist-friendly beach. Kobi does lucrative things in cyberspace. Their Tel Aviv-based son contrived to skip army service and launch himself, as a nineteen-year-old entrepreneur, into another dimension of cyberspace. His sister Shirley was still at school.

The Kohns' home is a few miles from the nearest town, in what began as a kibbutz where Kobi was born. Lately it has developed into a hamlet of two-storey detached houses, within hailing distance of the Barrier. This whole region is grossly built-up, criss-crossed by a surfeit of motorways and dominated by mega-pylons.

At the bus stop Limor awaited me and was easily recognisable from Anna's description: 'Small, soon-to-be-fat, with a grey ponytail and a caricature Jewish nose, more often seen among Arabs.' During our walk to the car park I fished for her biography, as is my way.

In 1920 Limor's father's family migrated from Poland to London's East End – 'So Pa grew up with the Mosley threat.' Her mother was born that same year to parents who had left Ukraine after its terrifying (for Jews) Beilis Affair – almost the equivalent of the Dreyfus Affair. Her father was apprenticed to a Moldovan tailor who had made good and, recognising the boy's remarkable aptitude for maths, sponsored his grammar school education. Cambridge followed, a stable academic career and a move to Golders Green.

As we sped along the motorway, Limor pointed to a small signpost. 'That was my kibbutz, where I spent a year after school. Then I was lucky, got a training place with a famous Dorset potter. But I missed Israel so much I had to come back – this was my *home. Goyim* who figure all is well for assimilated Jews in England, France or wherever have it wrong. The fully assimilated are a minority. OK, most in England weren't too bothered by anti-Semitism even in the '30s. But we knew it was never far below the surface. We were eternal foreigners, not in our own country. To my parents' generation Israel didn't feel like our own either. Some far-off land – strange languages, foods, clothes, habits, climate. Yet when Zionism presented the possibility more and more came to like it. Then after the Holocaust millions had nowhere else to go.'

Limor slowed as we approached a typical '48-ers' town, shabby and littered. 'See this,' she said. 'Here's a hotbed of crime – drug-ridden, rotting with nepotism. Kobi is afraid even to drive through. The clan warfare is so bad some streets are blockaded and controlled by snipers on roofs. The Interior Ministry appointed a reliable Arab mayor, meant to straighten things out. Seems he's too scared to make improvements.'

Five minutes later we were turning towards the hamlet, visible beyond a few parched hectares of farmland. Limor continued, 'I made *aliyah* in '73, a week before the Yom Kippur war. The next six months were tough, in a government-run Absorption Hostel, learning Hebrew. A year later I was married to my *sabra* – all his folks came in the First *Aliyah*.'

Thinking of Daisy's husband, I asked, 'D'you suppose an English upbringing predisposes young women to fall for *sabras*?'

Limor laughed. 'Could be! A glorification of the strong and silent empire-builder, lean and bronzed . . . Except that always Kobi was chubby and pinkish.'

My host wouldn't appear until after dark; Limor complained that his province of cyberspace made unreasonable demands on the individual. Although the Kohns' alcohol intake was restricted to Purim, large bottles of Gold Label crammed their fridge – as though I'd come to stay for a month.

While brewing coffee Limor pointed to a photo on the dresser, a cheerfully grinning young man playing with an enormous dog of indeterminate breed. 'Kobi's nephew Ben, now a paraplegic. The French Hill bomb . . .' (19 June 2002: 7 killed, 50 injured.) 'The coincidence was eerie. Two weeks before, Ben actually saw from far away the Megiddo bus attack – 17 killed and 38 injured. He said to us then, "The dead are the lucky ones." He didn't know his own worth. Not fazed by eight years in a wheelchair, he's busy every day teaching fellow-victims what IT can do for them.' Limor marvelled, as well she might, at Israel's extraordinarily rapid recovery from that hellish five-year suicide-bombing campaign. By October 2005, 975 Israelis (mostly civilians of all ages, going about their humdrum business) had been killed by Palestinians. And 3,695 Palestinians, mostly civilians of all ages also going about their daily affairs, had been killed by the IDF.

A decisive suicide bombing happened in Netanya on 27 March 2002 when 29 oldies, gathered in the Park Hotel to celebrate Passover, were slaughtered by a Hamas bomber with a specific purpose: to derail the new Arab League peace plan. Hamas lacked the wit to see that this plan, being a dud, would soon have come off the rails without assistance. For some time the IDF had been slavering to launch Operation Defensive Shield and the Park Hotel atrocity provided ideal PR cover. That colossal bomb injured hundreds including a close friend of Limor's, seventy-six-year-old Clara Rosenberger who had survived 3½ years in Auschwitz. Shrapnel killed the friend sitting beside her and severed her own spinal cord. Limor said, 'From the armpits down she's paralysed – must stay in a care home. A cruel end for one of the most energetic oldies I've ever met – active for all sorts of good causes.'

I made appropriate – and sincere – noises. It seemed tactful (but was it moral?) to say nothing about the numbers of Palestinian civilians permanently crippled and/or grievously traumatised by Operation Defensive Shield – not to mention all the rest . . .

Sauntering down the road to visit a neighbour, Limor and I discovered we'd something significant in common. As lifelong disbelievers, we'd both, until very recently, respected all religions – yet now we were becoming *anti*-religion. Has the growth of fundamentalism (Jewish, Christian, Muslim, even Hindu) made what once seemed to us harmless foibles, or a touching confidence in a Good God, into a menacing influence? Said Limor, 'Around the world, political, economic and social turmoil is being used by power-hungry religious leaders – if not created by them.' I told her I'd noticed this shift, from tolerance to impatient exasperation, among other humanist friends in other countries. She nodded – 'Yes, same here. But I'm working at not becoming *hostile* to any religion.' She hesitated, then added with her attractively crooked smile – 'I do occasionally talk to someone in my head!'

Fanny lived with her daughter, son-in-law and an inscrutable Manx cat. She too had come to Israel as a kibbutznik and a few years later, in 1963, felt a compulsion to make *aliyah*. 'Not for any religious reason, I'm outrageously non-observant, but because I knew I belonged here. And I've gone on feeling that way, through the worst of it.'

'We've been talking religion,' said Limor. 'It baffles me that everywhere and always human beings have constructed some form of belief system, however zany.'

Fanny, like myself, had long since concluded that those systems are death-dodging ploys.

'That can't work for Christians,' objected Limor. 'I'd be much more scared of death if I didn't know whether I was going to their Heaven or Hell!'

Fanny said with a bleak smile, 'Unfortunately we know it works for Muslims.'

I thought, 'Oh no! Not those seventy virgins!' Happily we were spared them.

Soon Fanny was mocking the publicity-seeking Freedom Flotilla fools who knew nothing about Gaza. Nobody could blame the IDF for killing nine of them, in self-defence. Gaza would have no problems but for Hamas who stole most of the donated millions. It was not occupied territory, Israel pulled out in 2005 leaving it free to rule itself and get its economy organised as the settlers had done before Sharon so cruelly uprooted them.

I had often noticed that Zionists are extra-touchy about condemnations of the blockade. Do they, at some level, know the truth and feel proportionately guilty? Or, as is more likely, have they swallowed the *hasbara* without stopping to taste it and so feel hard done by when the 'withdrawal' is not praised?

I have yet to meet a Zionist who has voluntarily read the Goldstone Report on Cast Lead. Many, like Fanny, condemn the author as 'a self-hating Jew' who took all his evidence from Arabs and their pesky International friends. Even Israelis who in other contexts scorn their government seem content to echo it in relation to Goldstone. I decided to be provocative and said, 'Reading that Report would help Israelis. It shows why Cast Lead, and the official reaction to Goldstone, so damaged your image.'

Limor was beginning to look uneasy. Fanny stood up to find the previous day's *International Herald Tribune*, then read aloud from a

Thomas Friedman op ed: 'Had Hamas decided – after Israel unilaterally
left Gaza – to turn it into Dubai rather than Tehran, Israel too would
have behaved differently.' Laying the paper aside, Fanny shrugged and
said, 'There's the truth of it! What no Arab will admit!'

'Let's talk literature!' said Limor brightly. 'How do we think e-books
will affect real books? I love my Kindle but some say it's bad for one's
sight – could that be?'

A little later, as we walked home, Limor conceded that a refusal to
read Goldstone weakens the Zionist case; Thomas Friedman is no
substitute. And Fanny is a retired teacher who mentions reading as her
favourite recreation: the excuse 'No time, it's too long!' gives the game
away. I didn't voice my next thought – that resistance to any criticism of
its military is a salient and unsurprising symptom of Zionism's mass
paranoia. Meanwhile the IDF's high standing in what Esther dubbed
'the bloody brotherhood' must burnish its awareness of impunity.

Down at sea-level it was still possible to sit out after sunset: then Kobi
arrived and we moved in to eat. He looked considerably older than his
wife and very tired. The Kohns knew of my months on the West Bank,
yet our conversation followed a too-familiar pattern. When I ventured
to share a few of my observations (editing them drastically and choosing
my words carefully) the subject was quickly changed. Bizarrely, Kobi
treated me as a newcomer to Israel in need of advice. I must remember
that Arabs have no respect for human life – 'They'll kill their own
women and children if that helps them to kill more of us!' People who
don't live with them can't understand – 'They're cruel by nature, another
sort of creature. Any female who doesn't do what she's told will be
murdered by a father, a brother – even a son!'

Limor said, 'They're not really natives of Israel, they came crowding
in when our pioneers – Jews like Kobi's folk – promised development
and jobs. You've read Mark Twain? Without us the land would be back
to the grey, stony barrenness he hated!' (This passage is so often quoted
it must be on the Zionist school curriculum.)

Kobi's English was limited and he soon excused himself; nowadays
office work tends to overflow into the home.

In my bedroom that night, I stood at the uncurtained window gazing at
the Barrier; it stretched north and south as far as the eye could see,
faintly glimmering by the light of its watchtowers. The green minaret

lights of Qalqilya's eleven mosques seemed very close and the sheer
perverseness of the Occupation struck me anew. Here I was, less than
ten miles as the crow flies from my Jayyous friends – but no crows fly
over that Barrier. The sense of imposed distance, of implacable, artificial
separation from all my OPT friends, aroused equal measures of
anger and sadness. Zionists' determination *not to know* what motivated
Palestinian suicide bombers was another sort of ugly barrier cutting
them off from any understanding of a shared 'problem'. Suddenly the
fragility of the State of Israel presented itself to me more acutely
than ever before. And our collusion in that dangerous 'not knowing'
continues decade after decade. Martin Kemp sums it up neatly – 'For
the West to concern itself with the lived experience of the Palestinians
would be to challenge an Israeli psyche in part held together by a
refusal to acknowledge those realities.'

George Awad is equally relevant:

> A powerful oppressor can, more often than not, afford to wait things
> out and take his time; an occupation or an embargo can slowly yet
> effectively destroy the soul and the body of 'the others'. The powerful
> can kill without dirtying their hands or exposing themselves to
> imminent danger . . . Many Arabs and Muslims, even as they are
> horrified by the nature of the suicide bomber's attacks on innocent
> civilians, do not see such attacks as being any more horrible than the
> slow, methodological killing of *their* innocents by the powerful.

At breakfast Limor announced a dual purpose excursion, a day out in
Bet Guvrin-Maresha national park to entertain the guest while helping
Shirley with her school project – on the ancient cities of Maresha and
Bet Guvrin, the former frequently mentioned in the Bible. Shirley had
been staying the night with her boyfriend's family, we'd pick the young
up on our way. First Limor had to do some shopping in the nearby
town and change her books at an Anglo-US Club reminiscent of colonial
or UN clubs in Far-flungery. This was a library of donated volumes; the
small non-fiction section contained none of the books Israelis need to
read. A club noticeboard told of coming 'events', their flavour more US
than Anglo. While Limor shopped I sought *Ha'aretz*, in vain. My hostess
explained, 'There's no "lefty" readership here, *The Jerusalem Post* keeps
us happy!'

Shirley was an effervescent seventeen-year-old brunette, taller than her parents, inexpertly made-up and accoutred with electronic devices I couldn't even name. Her friend Elie – equally outgoing – had recently returned from a Young Judea pre-army trip to Uganda, its highlight a football game with a Jewish tribe, the Abayudaya. As we sped south on Route 6 he informed us that this tribe, numbering fewer than a thousand, had until a year ago been united with the Pulli Jews. Then rival rabbis arrived from the US, insisting on conversions. Rapidly the Pulli became Orthodox while the Abayudaya became Conservative; now they can no longer share the same synagogue hut.

I asked, 'What were they before the US invasion?'

Elie laughed. 'Who knows? Could be they didn't realise they were Jews! Maybe any day now they'll find themselves in Kiryat Arba!'

Outsiders are puzzled by tiny Israel's abundance of parks and nature reserves: sixty-six in all. Many were created to hide Nakba scars, others are the result of JNF machinations to appropriate still more Palestinian land. That said, the Israel Nature and Parks Authority is supremely efficient, its educational displays and multilingual brochures models of scholarly research and – I'm told – clear writing, whatever the language. Of course there's always a flaw: the marginalisation of Arab and Islamic components. Only in a final terse paragraph did our Guvrin-Maresha booklet admit, 'An Arab village occupied the site until 1948. In June that year, the Egyptian Army occupied the British Taggart Fort. On October 27, 1948, Israeli forces recovered the area and in May 1949 Kibbutz Bet-Guvrin was established on the site.'

Resolutely I banished all negative broodings and set about enjoying myself. Within the discreetly wire-fenced park boundary we had 500 hectares to ourselves, a silent undulating expanse in the Judean foothills. Here, midway between the coast and Hebron or Jerusalem, a thriving traders' crossroads became urbanised in Biblical times. A kind breeze tempered the almost-too-hot sun as Shirley and Elie wandered off across the grey-brown barrenness; everything exciting is subterranean. Limor commented, 'I wouldn't put my shirt on this project.' Like other Anglo-Israelis of a certain age, she often used phrases I hadn't heard for decades.

Between caves Limor and I walked for miles on pleasingly simple paths not prinked for tourists as is too usual in Israel. These vast caves – some are 82 feet deep, most 40 to 50 feet – were dug out of soft lime-stone and are quite overwhelming, truly awesome. In the columbarium (*c.* fifth century BC) 2,000 pigeon-holes housed flocks used for religious ceremonies and for food; their droppings were rated the best fertiliser on the market. Each complex of caves has its own distinctive, unpredictable features and some are linked by bewildering networks of corridors.

At intervals we came upon the young – Elie photographing with a real camera, Shirley sketching the more architecturally dramatic vistas, such as the Hellenistic bath-house and its adjacent olive oil press. To Limor I said, 'See! Your shirt may be safe!'

Most memorable of all, for me, are the Sidonian burial caves (third to second centuries BC), a series of long, magnificently gabled chambers discovered in 1902. Several of the original paintings above the burial niches – including a group of musicians looking appropriately solemn – were skilfully restored in 1993.

A day was not too long for this sightseeing exercise. The western cloud banks turned from crimson to gold as we drove down to the road, everyone recalling their favourite cave. Since a dawn spat about OPT ambulance delays, Limor and I had eschewed awkward topics – but halfway home Elie chose to enlighten the visitor. There is too much sparring in the Territories between settlers and Arabs, settlers who have to be on the hilltops for security reasons though keeping order overtaxes the military. He didn't want to serve there, being a target all day for Arab snipers, yet within months or perhaps weeks that's where he'd be.

'And I'll be there next year,' said Shirley in a consoling voice.

In Elie's view – shared, he assured me, by most of his contemporaries – a land swap should be the solution. Give fenced-off stretches of the Negev to the Arabs – who are desert people, really, so they could make a good living growing fruit and vegetables for export as many Israelis did in the Jordan Valley. Quietly I pointed out that those crops were grown with water illegally diverted from Palestinian sources and not likely to flow were non-Israelis needing it in the Negev. My three companions flatly denied that Israeli farmers ever did anything illegal. And Elie demanded – 'Why do you call them "Palestinians"? They're *Arabs!*'

We were nearly home, speeding along Route 6 where the Barrier shadows the road and Qalqilya is within earshot and Jayyous almost so. If Elie felt disputatious, so did I. Gesturing towards the Barrier I said, 'Because of that monster Qalqilya is a town in its death throes. And friends of mine have lost 70% of their land, 500 fruit trees, six underground water sources. Their livelihoods . . .'

Shirley interrupted. Her expression had changed and she looked much older as she snapped, 'We don't want to know anything about them!'

Again I thought of '. . . the psyche held together by its refusal to acknowledge realities'. Also I remembered Amos' speculation – 'Was this one reason for leaving Gaza? To make it easier to pretend those millions don't exist . . .'

Turning off Route 6 Limor said, 'We've also got our Arab friends, a few work for us and sometimes we shop in their towns. They can be so nice and polite, honest about money and easy to get on with.'

I asked, 'Do you visit each other's homes?'

Limor shook her head. 'I know in Jerusalem a lot of that goes on but here it's too dangerous. We daren't go into their houses. It's all about security, it's not that we dislike *individuals* . . .'

That evening I wrote in my diary:

As irrational generalisations come thick and fast, I'm reminded of conversations with 'average' white South Africans in the bad old days. How can I still be so taken aback by this sort of thing? Dehumanising the enemy is the standard preparation for eliminating him/her by one means or another – death or destruction or demoralisation. It's common knowledge that a majority of Israelis hold such views yet on hearing them plainly expressed one's first reaction is an absurd incredulity. Always it throws me to hear otherwise intelligent, kindly people providing proof that dehumanisation has worked. This fear-driven prejudice is quite unlike the yobbish racism to be found at certain levels in most (all?) European countries. It would indeed seem illogical to accuse Israel of racism; its government readily issues passport (full citizenship) to black Africans, Mongoloid Himalayan hill tribes, brownish Aymara campesinos and any other group definable – however implausibly – as Jews. To Anna, those Ashkenazi prejudices against which she battles are more akin to social snobbery than to racism. But it's probably silly to try to disentangle the two, especially in a Middle East context.

To nourish my hopes for one state, I reflect on Daisy's reaction to our brief hospital visit. That shows what can happen when a free-standing Israeli personally glimpses a corner of the Palestinian tragedy, gets a whiff of Military Occupation as it distorts everyday life. Clearly direct experience is what counts. For me – or any third party – to tell Daisy or

Fanny or Limor about how Military Orders affect sick children and their families would have no effect. Hence the socio-political pressures that keep the majority of Israelis apart from the majority of Palestinians. As Esther wearily observed, 'There are no simple antidotes for *hasbara*.'

EPILOGUE

'Seventy years on, the Holocaust plays a complicated but profound role in the deadlocked politics of Israel/Palestine and, I believe, in a moral confusion in the face of it.' So wrote Martin Kemp, an English psycho-analytic psychotherapist, in a hugely important paper entitled 'Psychic Structure and Public Space: Dehumanisation, Guilt and Large Group Dynamics with reference to the West, Israel and the Palestinians'. Despite its formidable title, this text is free of both academic jargon and political euphemisms.

For long the Palestinians and their supporters have been angered and baffled by the West's refusal to challenge Zionism, an issue Martin Kemp bravely tackles. The West feels guilty about its blatantly obvious but never openly acknowledged contribution to the Holocaust. The Zionists feel guilty about their unadmitted brutality, as they dispossessed the Palestinians by death or exile, then imposed a ruthless military occupation and organised on-going land-grabbing. Dr Kemp sees those two guilts interacting to create an agonising tangle not amenable to standard political/diplomatic negotiations.

To explain the West's bias towards Israel, numerous socio-political theories are on offer. Since my first visit to Israel, the psychological factors have seemed to me much more important. Dr Kemp proposes, as part of the explanation –

... an unconscious pact by which Israel and the West, with their distinctive but linked histories of dehumanisation – the West towards the Jews and the Israelis towards the Palestinians – have each allotted roles to the other ... which in turn have enabled them to avoid, in their large-group ways of thinking, the profound guilt that other-wise threatens them. In doing this they have established a kind of couple relationship the unconscious terms of which have prohibited a relationship emerging between the West and the Palestinians. It has prevented a genuine triangulation between these three entities from taking place. This has led the West, as a whole, into a repetition of the 'bystander' position that characterised its response to fascism two generations ago ... To maximise our potential to contribute towards a just and peaceful future I believe we need to make our own 'sober assessment of the situation', as Freud did in 1930, unencumbered by misplaced guilt or misguided notions of neutrality, and informed by an explicit universalist ethic.

(Dr Kemp is referring to Freud's letter to H. Koffler, refusing to promote Zionism.)

Reading Martin Kemp's essay, I felt myself to be stepping out of a dimly lit dungeon, thronged with unsettling half-formed notions, into a bright open space where a few salient facts are plain to be seen. When new to the Holy Land, my ambition was to write as 'neutral' a book as possible. A mere month later, sitting in Ben-Gurion airport, I confided to my diary – 'This is a sick society! As at present constituted, Israel can't survive.' Even as I wrote those words I reproached myself for being so categorical at the end of a brief visit, before I had set foot in the OPT. Yet, while continuing to feel uneasy, I've never been tempted to moderate that first strong reaction. Therefore I was comforted by Martin Kemp's reminder that 'neutrality can provide a cover for amorality disguising itself as "fairness" or "impartiality"'.

Dr Kemp has learned the hard way that 'discussions about Israel / Palestine raise more complex emotions than other comparable situations'. This difficulty is familiar to all the Palestinians' friends and it's to be expected when one considers that, 'The proximity and nature of the Holocaust led to the splitting off and projection of European anti-Semitism by mainstream Western society, leaving an ineradicable unconscious link between any negative effect felt towards "Jews" and the horrors of the Nazi genocide.'

On first reading the Kemp essay a coincidence slightly took me aback – until I saw how it arose from the 'complex emotions' phenomenon. Martin Kemp returned to London eager to share his impressions with all who would listen or read; but soon he felt 'a deep apprehension', an awareness that this plan 'ran counter to professional and wider social expectations'. Then – 'I found myself turning to psychoanalysis to understand the emotional ramifications of the visit for myself.' Happily this therapy worked and when the Kemp paper was being peer reviewed for the *British Journal of Psychotherapy* its author was well able to protect it from 'delegitimising' criticisms.

For me, at the end of my residence on the West Bank, the 'emotional ramifications' were such that, back home, I didn't want to talk to anyone about my impressions – much less write about them. Normally, at journey's end, I at once settle down to work – remaining mentally and emotionally in the place I'm writing about. But for weeks I shirked remaining with the Palestinians. Instead, I spent a solitary fortnight listening to music while frenziedly pulling docks from between the cobbles in my yard – so frenziedly that I damaged a neck muscle. Then a few friends, themselves familiar with the OPT, devised a cunning therapy, reminding me that the Palestinians need people with access to the media to expose their sufferings and honour their quite extra-ordinary courage and resilience. I counter-argued that very many books, well written and carefully researched, explain how Israel came into being and describe the consequences for the Palestinians. But my amateur-psychotherapist friends insisted that a travel writer's book might reach a readership uninformed about the Middle East and disinclined to study political tangles. I hope (faintly) the sales of this volume will prove them right.

HOLY LAND CONFLICT TIMELINE

1897 First Zionist Congress in Switzerland establishes the World Zionist Organisation to secure a 'home for the Jewish people in Palestine', in response to European, and particularly Russian, anti-Semitism.

1917 Balfour Declaration. Britain's Foreign Secretary, Lord Arthur Balfour, announces his government's support for the establishment of 'a Jewish national home in Palestine', in a letter to Lord Rothschild. The British had already made an ambiguous promise of independence for an Arab nation covering most of the Arab Middle East in exchange for Arab support against the Ottomans.

1920–48 Mandatory Palestine. In the aftermath of World War I, Britain is awarded a legal commission to administer Palestine, confirmed by the League of Nations. Arab discontent with aspects of British rule and increasing Jewish immigration leads to clashes between all parties.

1939–45 Some six million Jews are murdered in the Holocaust. Hundreds of thousands are displaced, fleeing Nazi persecution.

1947 Britain announces that she will withdraw from Palestine in 1948 and hand over responsibility to the newly established UN. UN Resolution 181 recommends dividing the territory into separate Jewish and Palestinian states and is accepted by the Jewish Agency but rejected by the Arab Higher Committee. The plan was aborted, overtaken by civil war on the ground.

May 1948 The State of Israel is proclaimed in Tel Aviv. British troops withdraw and Palestinians face al-Nakba, the Catastrophe. By the end of the year Israel occupies some 75% of what had been the British Mandate. Almost three quarters of a million Palestinians are forced from their homes and settle in refugee camps in Jordan, Gaza, Syria, Lebanon as well as in the Palestinian 25%.

1949–67 Gaza is ruled by Egypt, initially under the auspices of the All Palestine Government.

June 1967 During the Six-Day War, known to the Palestinians as an-Naksah (the Setback), Israel doubles its land-holding, taking Gaza and the Sinai peninsula from Egypt, the West Bank and East Jerusalem from Jordan and the Golan Heights from Syria.

1973 Yom Kippur War. To try to regain territory lost in 1967, Egypt and Syria launch attacks against Israel on the festival of Yom Kippur. Three weeks later Israel has reversed all her initial losses.

September 1978 Egypt and Israel sign Camp David accords, leading to the return of the Sinai Peninsula to Egypt in 1982.

1987–93 First Intifada. The Palestinian uprising against Israel's military occupation of Palestinian territory consists largely of well-organised, non-violent resistance.

Hamas, an Islamist party whose charter denies Israel's right to exist, emerges.

1993 Oslo Accords. During secret talks in Norway, the Palestinians recognise Israel's right to exist within her pre-1967 borders, and Israel agrees to gradually cede control of the Occupied Palestinian Territories. Yitzhak Rabin and Yasser Arafat shake hands on the White House lawn after signing the Declaration of Principles, but the most difficult issues, such as the status of Jerusalem, and the right of return of Palestinian refugees, are undecided and have proved impossible to resolve ever since.

July 2000 Camp David Peace Summit, hosted by US President Bill Clinton, ends without agreement. In the seven years since the Oslo Accords, the expansion of Israeli settlements in the West Bank and Gaza provokes many Palestinian suicide bombings.

2000–05 The Second Intifada is characterised by an intensification of suicide bombings in Israel, and of targeted Israeli assassinations of Palestinian militants, as well as widespread collective punishment of Palestinian areas. Israel begins to build a wall dividing the West Bank.

2005 Israel withdraws troops and settlers from Gaza while maintaining remote control of the strip.

January 2006 Hamas wins a majority in closely supervised Palestinian parliamentary elections and forms a government, but Israel, the US and the EU refuse to negotiate with it.

March 2007 Hamas and Fatah form a national unity government, headed by Hamas' Ismail Haniya. Israel still refuses to negotiate, calling Hamas a terrorist organisation. Behind the scenes, Israel, Egypt and the US conspire with Fatah to isolate, weaken and topple Hamas.

June 2007 Battle of Gaza. As trust between Hamas and Fatah breaks down, Hamas seizes power in Gaza, ousting Fatah officials.

2007 Blockade of Gaza. Israel and Egypt seal most border crossings, ostensibly to prevent Hamas obtaining weapons to attack Israel. Egypt maintains that recognising Hamas by opening the border would undermine the Palestinian National Authority and permanently divide the Palestinian factions.

December 2008–January 2009 Gaza War. The Israel Defense Forces' Operation Cast Lead begins on December 27th, ostensibly to stop rocket fire into Israel. A ceasefire is agreed on January 18th, after the death of at least 1300 Palestinians and 13 Israelis, four of the latter from friendly fire. The UN Goldstone Report, released in September 2009, accuses both sides of war crimes.

September 2011 Palestine Authority moves a resolution in the UN for recognition of Palestine statehood, which is put off due to lack of support in the Security Council.

November 2012 Israelis launch Operation Pillar of Defence against Gaza, during which 79 Palestinian militants and 53 civilians are killed. Hamas fires over 1456 rockets into Israel, killing 6.

November 29th 2012 UN General Assembly upgrades Palestine to non-member observer state status in the UN.

June 2nd 2014 Hamas and Fatah Palestinian unity government sworn in, in response to which Israel states that it will not negotiate any peace deal with the new government and will push punitive measures. On June 4th tenders are published for 1,500 settlement units in the West Bank and East Jerusalem.

July 8th–August 26th 2014 The Israelis launch Operation Protective Edge against Gaza, with the stated aim of stopping rocket fire into Israel. Within fifty days over 2,100 Gazans (including at least 577 children) are killed, while 72 on the Israeli side of the border (including 66 soldiers, one child and one Thai worker) die. In addition, over 12,500 Gazans are wounded and homes of one third are levelled by bombs.

GLOSSARY

'48ers
Palestinians who stayed on in the newly created State of Israel in 1948

aliyah (Heb.)
the immigration, by members of the Jewish diaspora, to Israel

Amidar
State-owned housing company in Israel, providing subsidised housing, often in former Palestinian properties

Ashkenazi
Jews of, and descended from, the communities of central and eastern Europe

Bedouin
traditionally nomadic Arab peoples of the desert

B'Tselem
the Israeli Information Center for Human Rights in the Occupied Territories

Chabad
see Lubavitcher

collecteeve
a minibus or shared saloon taxi

Eretz Israel
all the territory of Ottoman Palestine (Greater Israel)

Falasha
the Jewish community from Ethiopia

fellahin (Ar.)
a peasant or agricultural labourer/farmer

galabiya (Ar.)
long, collarless robe worn by Arab men

goyim (Heb.)
those not of Jewish descent

Gush Emunim
a political movement, no longer officially in existence, committed to establishing Jewish settlements in the West Bank, Gaza and the Golan Heights

Haganah
Jewish underground paramilitary organisation during the British Mandate (1920–48)

halacha
the body of Jewish religious laws

Haredim
adherents to a strictly Orthodox branch of Judaism, which rejects modern secular culture in favour of strict adherence to Jewish religious law

hasbara (Heb.)
propaganda

hijab (Ar.)
a headscarf worn in front of men and in public to cover a woman's hair

imam (Ar.)   the leader of worship in a mosque

Intifada   a period of intensified Palestinian struggle against occupation. The first Intifada ran between 1987–93, the second from 2000–5

keffiyeh (Ar.)   chequered black and white scarf, worn either around the neck or on the head, a symbol of Palestinian nationalism and those who support it

kibbutz (pl. kibbutzim)   collective communities, originally agricultural, established in Israel throughout the twentieth century as an important aspect of secular Zionism, often with a utopian socialist origin. The inhabitant of a kibbutz is a kibbutznik.

kipa (Heb.)   small cap worn by Jews, mostly men

Lubavitcher   member of an extensive Orthodox Jewish, Hasidic movement which began in Belorussia in the eighteenth century, also known as Chabad

Lurianic Kabbala   a school of Kabbala named after the Jewish rabbi Isaac Luria who developed it in the sixteenth century

Mizrahi   a Jew whose family migrated to Israel from an Arab country

muezzin   the man who recites the call to prayer from a mosque

Nakba   literally the catastrophe; used to describe the 1947–8 uprooting of the Palestinians from their homeland

Naksah   Israel's seizure, in June 1967, of the West Bank from Jordan, the Sinai from Egypt and the Golan Heights from Syria

narghile   a waterpipe for smoking flavoured tobacco called shisha

Olim (Heb.)   those who have made aliyah, Jewish immigrants to Israel

Operation Defensive Shield   large-scale military operation conducted by the IDF in the West Bank in 2002 during the second Intifada

Oslo Accords   agreements signed in 1993 and 1995 between the PLO and Israel

Palmach   the elite fighting force of the Haganah (see above)

qadi	judge ruling in accordance with Islamic religious law
sabra	a Jew born in the historical region of Palestine (Eretz Israel)
Salafist	Muslims who emphasise their rigid adherence to seventh-century Islam
Sephardi	Jews descended from the ancient community expelled from the Iberian peninsula in the late fifteenth century
serveece	a communal taxi
Shin Bet (Shabak)	Israel's internal security service
samoud (Ar.)	fortitude (sometimes defined as a mix of courage, obstinacy and pride)
taboun (Ar.)	a flatbread
wadi	river bed, which fills after heavy rains
waqf	Muslim charitable endowment
yeshiva (Heb.)	a Jewish college for the study of religious texts, often Orthodox
Yishuv	the original Jewish population of Palestine, before the establishment of the State of Israel
za'atar (Ar.)	a popular condiment containing sesame seeds and salt, with a combination of thyme, oregano and/or marjoram

ABBREVIATIONS

AIPAC	American Israel Public Affairs Committee
APC	armoured personnel carrier
BDS	Boycott, Divestment and Sanctions campaign
EAPPI	Ecumenical Accompaniment Programme in Palestine and Israel, volunteers for which are known as EAs
ELAD	Hebrew acronym for City of David, also the name of a settler group in the Palestinian area of East Jerusalem called Silwan
GA	the General Assembly of the United Jewish Communities
HRC	Hebron Rehabilitation Committee
IAF	Israel Air Force
ICRC	International Committee of the Red Cross
ICS	Islamic Charitable Society
IDF	Israel Defense Forces
INGO	international non-governmental organisation
ISM	International Support Movement
JNF	Jewish National Fund
MK	Member of the Knesset, Israel's parliament
NRP	National Religious Party
OCHA	the UN Office for the Coordination of Humanitarian Affairs
OPT	Occupied Palestinian Territories
PA	Palestinian Authority, renamed PNA – the Palestinian National Authority
PASF	Palestinian Authority Security Forces
PCRP	Palestinian Centre for Rapprochement between People
PLO	Palestine Liberation Organisation

TINA	there is no alternative
TIPH	Temporary International Presence in Hebron
UNESCO	United Nations Educational, Scientific and Cultural Organisation
UNRWA	United Nations Relief and Works Agency for Palestine Refugees in the Near East
WHO	World Health Organisation
WMD	weapon of mass destruction
WSG	Nablus-based Women's Study Group
YCC	Yaffa Cultural Centre

BIBLIOGRAPHY

PRIMARY READING

Abunimah, Ali, *One Country: A Bold Proposal to End the Israeli-Palestinian Impasse*, Metropolitan Books, New York (2006)*

Aloni, Udi (ed.), *What Does a Jew Want? On Binationalism and other Spectres*, Columbia University Press (2011)*

Armstrong, Karen, *A History of Jerusalem: One City, Three Faiths*, HarperCollins (1996)

Carey, Roane and Jonathan Shainin (eds), *The Other Israel: Voices of Refusal and Dissent*, The New Press (2002)

Cook, Jonathan, *Disappearing Palestine: Israel's Experiments in Human Despair*, Zed Books (2008)

Fromkin, David, *A Peace to End All Peace: The Fall of the Ottoman Empire and the Creation of the Modern Middle East*, Avon Books, New York (1989)

Hilal, Jamil (ed.), *Where Now for Palestine? The Demise of the Two-state Solution*, Zed Books (2007)*

Ingrams, Doreeen (ed.), *Palestine Papers 1917–1922: Seeds of Conflict*, John Murray (1972)

Khalidi, Rashid, *Palestinian Identity: The Construction of Modern National Consciousness*, Columbia University Press (1997)

Kimmerling, Baruch, *Politicide: Ariel Sharon's War Against the Palestinians*, Verso (2003)

Masalha, Nur, *The Bible and Zionism*, Zed Books (2007)

Mearsheimer, John J. and Walt, Stephen M., *The Israel Lobby and US Foreign Policy*, Penguin (2007)

Nimni, Ephraim (ed.), *The Challenge of Post-Zionism*, Zed Books (2003)*

* supporting the one-state solution

Nusseibeh, Sari, *What is a Palestinian State Worth?* Harvard University Press (2011)*

Pappé, Ilan, *The Ethnic Cleansing of Palestine*, Oneworld (2006)

Qumsiyeh, Mazin B., *Sharing the Land of Canaan: Human Rights and the Israeli-Palestinian Struggle*, Pluto Press (2004)

Ruthven, Malise, *Fundamentalism: A Very Short Introduction*, Oxford University Press (2004)*

Said, Edward W., *Peace and its Discontents*, Vintage Books (1996)

Schneer, Jonathan, *The Balfour Declaration: the Origins of the Arab-Israeli Conflict*, Bloomsbury (2010)

Segal, Rafi and Weizman, Eyal, *A Civilian Occupation: The Politics of Israeli Architecture*, Verso (No pub. date given)

Shahak, Israel and Merzvinsky, Norton, *Jewish Fundamentalism in Israel*, Pluto Press (1999)

Shehadeh, Raja, *Strangers in the House: Coming of Age in Occupied Palestine*, Penguin (2002)

———, *When the Bulbul Stopped Singing: A Dairy of Ramallah Under Siege*, Profile (2003)

———, *Palestinian Walks: Notes on a Vanishing Landscape*, Profile (2007)

Shlaim, Avi, *War and Peace in the Middle East*, Penguin (1994)

———, *The Politics of Partition*, Oxford University Press (1998)

———, *The Iron Wall*, Penguin (2000)

Whitelam, Keith W., *The Invention of Ancient Israel: The Silencing of Palestinian History*, Routledge (1996)

Zertal, Idith and Eldar, Akiva, *The Lords of the Land: The War Over Israel's Settlements in the Occupied Territories* (translated from the Hebrew by Vivian Eden), Nation Books, New York (2005)

BACKGROUND READING

Achcar, Gilbert, *The Arabs and the Holocaust: The Arab-Israeli War of Narratives*, Saqi (2010)

Abdel Hamid, Dina, *Duet for Freedom*, Quartet Books (1988)

Anon. (ed.), *The Seventh Day: Soldiers' Talk About the Six-Day War*, Andre Deutsch (1970)

Arendt, Hannah, *Eichmann in Jerusalem: A Report on the Banality of Evil*, Penguin (1963)

Bar-Zehar, Michael, *Ben-Gurion: The Armed Prophet*, Prentice-Hall (1967)

Barghouti, Mourid, *I was Born There, I Was Born Here*, Bloomsbury (2011)

Bat-Haim, Hadassah, *Travels with Hannah: A Galilee Family Saga*, Turtledove Press (1981)

Beinart, Peter, *The Crisis of Zionism*, Henry Holt, New York (2012)

Ben-Ami, Shlomo, *Scars of War, Wounds of Peace: The Israel-Arab Tragedy*, Phoenix (2005)

Bettelhiem, Bruno, *The Informed Heart: The Psychology of the Concentration Camp*, Paladin (1961)

Bin Talal, Hassan, *Palestinian Self-Determination*, Quartet Books (1981)

Black, Ian and Morris, Benny, *Israel's Secret Wars: A History of Israel's Intelligence Services*, Grove Press, New York (1991)

Bowen, Jeremy, *Six Days: How the 1967 War Shaped the Middle East*, Simon & Schuster (2006)

Brown, Nathan J., *Palestinian Politics after the Oslo Accords*, University of California (2003)

Butt, Gerald, *The Arab World: A Personal View*, BBC Books (1987)

Carter, Jimmy, *Palestine: Peace Not Apartheid*, Simon & Schuster (2006)

Cheshin, Amir S., Hutman, Bill and Melamed, Avi, *Separate and Unequal: The Inside Story of Israeli Rule in East Jerusalem*, Harvard University Press (1999)

Cohen, Reuven, *The Kibbutz Settlement: Principles and Processes*, Hakibbutz Hameuchad (1972)

Cook, Jonathan, *Israel and the Clash of Civilisations*, Pluto Press (2008)

Daniel, Jean, *The Jewish Prison: A Rebellious Meditation on the State of Judaism*, Melville House (2005)

Dayan, Yael, *My Father, His Daughter*, Weidenfeld & Nicolson (1985)

Davis, Uri, *Apartheid Israel: Possibilities for the Struggle Within*, Zed Books (2003)

Di Giovanni, Janine, *Against the Stranger: Lives in Occupied Territory*, Viking (1993)

Dolphin, Ray, *The West Bank Wall: Unmaking Palestine*, Pluto Press (2006)

Dor, Daniel, *The Suppression of Guilt: The Israeli Media and the Reoccupation of the West Bank*, Pluto Press (2005)

Eisenstadt, S. N., *Israeli Society*, Weidenfeld & Nicolson (1967)

Elon, Amos, *The Pity of It All: A Portrait of the German-Jewish Epoch 1743–1933*, Picador (2003)

Faqir, Fadia, *Nisanit*, Penguin (1988)

Finkelstein, Norman G., *The Holocaust Industry: Reflections on the Exploitation of Jewish Suffering*, Verso (2002)

Beyond Chutzpah: On the Misuse of Anti-Semitism and the Abuse of History, Verso (2005)

Fisk, Robert, *The Age of the Warrior*, Fourth Estate (2008)

Furlonge, Geoffrey, *Palestine is my Country: The Story of Musa Alami*, John Murray (1969)

Furneaux, Rupert, *The Roman Siege of Jerusalem*, Hart Davis (1973)

Garfinkel, Jonathan, *Ambivalence: Crossing the Israel/Palestine Divide*, Penguin (2007)

Grant, Michael, *Herod the Great*, Weidenfeld & Nicolson (1971)

———, *The Jews in the Roman World*, Weidenfeld & Nicolson (1973)

Hazelton, Lesley, *Where Mountains Roar: In search of the Sinai Desert*, Gollancz (1980)

Julius, Anthony, *Trials of the Diaspora: A History of Anti-Semitism in England*, Oxford University Press (2012)

Kamel, Mohamed Ibrahim, *The Camp David Accords: A Testimony by Sadat's Foreign Minister*, Routledge (1986)

Kannaneh, Hatim, *A Doctor in Galilee: The Life and Struggle of a Palestinian in Israel*, Pluto Press (2008)

Karpin, Michael and Friedman, Ina, *Murder in the Name of God: The Plot to Kill Yitzhak Rabin*, Henry Holt (1998)

Kaufman-Lacusta, Maxime, *Refusing to be Enemies: Palestinian and Israeli Nonviolent Resistance to the Israeli Occupation*, Ithaca (2011)

Kelner, Sahul, *Tours that Bind: Diaspora, Pilgrimage and Israeli Birthright Tourism*, New York University Press (2010)

Kidron, Peretz, *Refusenik! Israel's Soldiers of Conscience*, Zed Books (2004)

Kinzer, Stephen, *Reset Middle East: Old Friends and New Alliances*, I. B. Tauris (2010)

Koestler, Arthur, *The Thirteenth Tribe: The Khazar Empire and its Heritage*, Hutchinson (1976)

Kossoff, David, *The Voices of Massada*, Valentine, Mitchell (1973)

LeBor, Adam, *City of Oranges: Arabs and Jews in Jaffa*, Bloomsbury (2006)

Leigh, Jeremy, *Jewish Journeys*, Haus (2006)

Lerner, Michael, *Healing Israel/Palestine: A Path to Peace and Reconciliation*, Tikkun Books (2009)

Lind, Jakov, *The Trip to Jerusalem*, Jonathan Cape (1974)

Litvinoff, Barnet (ed.), *The Essential Chaim Weizmann: The Man, The Statesman, The Scientist*, Weidenfeld & Nicolson (1982)

Lunt, James, *Glubb Pasha: A Biography*, Harvill Press (1984)

Mitchell, R. J., *The Spring Voyage: The Jerusalem Pilgrimage in 1458*, John Murray (1954)

Montefiore, Simon Sebag, *Jerusalem: The Biography*, Phoenix (2011)

Morris, Benny, *Righteous Victims: A History of the Zionist-Arab Conflict, 1881–2001*, Vintage Books (2001)

Nicholl, Donald, *The Testing of Hearts: A Pilgrim's Journey*, Marshall Morgan (1989)

Nusseibeh, Sari with Anthony David, *Once Upon a Country: A Palestinian Life*, Haban (2007)

Oikarinin, Jarmo, *The Middle East in the American Quest for World Order*, Suomen Suera (1999)

Oz, Amos, *A Tale of Love and Darkness*, Vintage (2005)

Parfitt, Tudor, *Operation Moses: The Exodus of the Falasha Jews from Ethiopia*, Weidenfeld & Nicolson (1985)

Pearlman, Moshe, *The Zealots of Masada*, Hamish Hamilton (1967)

Pedazur, Ami and Perliger, Arie, *Jewish Terrorism in Israel*, Columbia University Press (2009)

Perry, Mark, *How To Lose the War on Terror*, Hurst (2010)

Pike, Diane Kennedy, *Search: The Story of a Disappearance in the Judean Wilderness*, W. H. Allen (1970)

Raheb, Mitri, *I Am a Palestinian Christian*, Fortress Press, Minneapolis (1995)

———, *Bethlehem Besieged: Stories of Hope in Times of Trouble*, Fortress Press (2004)

Raphael, Chaim, *The Road from Babylon: The Story of Sephardi and Oriental Jews*, Weidenfeld & Nicolson (1985)

Reinhart, Tanya, *The Road Map to Nowhere: Israel/Palestine since 2003*, Verso (2006)

Rejwan, Nissim, *The Jews of Iraq: 3000 years of History and Culture*, Weidenfeld & Nicolson (1985)

Ricca, Simone, *Reinventing Jerusalem: Israel's Reconstruction of the Jewish Quarter after 1967*, I. B. Tauris (2007)

Rodinson, Maxime, *Israel and the Arabs*, Penguin Special (1968)

Rose, Jacqueline, *The Question of Zion*, Princeton University Press (2005)

Roth, Joseph, (trans. Michael Hoffman), *The Wandering Jews*, Granta (2001)

Sabbagh, Karl, *Palestine: A Personal History*, Atlantic Books (2006)

Said, Edward, W., *Out of Place: A Memoir*, Granta (1999)

Sand, Shlomo, *The Invention of the Jewish People*, Verso (2009)

———, *The Invention of the Land of Israel: From Holy Land to Homeland*, Verso (2012)

Schiff, Ze'ev and Ya'ari, Ehud, *Israel's Lebanon War*, Allen & Unwin (1985)

Segev, Tom (trans. Haim Watzman), *The Seventh Million: The Israelis and the Holocaust*, Hill & Wang, New York (1993)

———, *One Palestine, Complete: Jews and Arabs under the British Mandate*, Little, Brown (2000)

Selby, Bettina, *Riding to Jerusalem*, Sidgwick & Jackson (1985)

Senor, Dan and Singer, Saul, *Start-up Nation: The Story of Israel's Economic Miracle*, Twelve, Hachette Group (2011)

Shabi, Rachel, *Not the Enemy: Israel's Jews from Arab Lands*, Yale University Press (2009)

Snow, Peter, *Hussein: A Biography*, Barrie and Jenkins (1972)

Steckoll, Soloman, *The Temple Mount*, Tom Stacey (1972)

Tahiri, Amir, *The Cauldron: The Middle East Behind the Headlines*, Hutchinson (1988)

Talal, Hassan bin and Polakow-Suransky, Sasha, *The Unspoken Alliance: Israel's Secret Relationship with Apartheid South Africa*, Pantheon Books, New York (2010)

Thomas, Gordon and Morgan-Witts, Max, *Voyage of the Damned: The Voyage of the St Louis*, Hodder & Stoughton (1974)

Wasserstein, Bernard, *Vanishing Diaspora: The Jews in Europe since 1945*, Harvard University Press (1996)

White, Andrew, *The Vicar of Baghdad: Fighting for Peace in the Middle East*, Monarch Press (2009)

White, Ben, *Israeli Apartheid: A Beginner's Guide*, Pluto Press (2009)

Williams, Emma, *It's Easier to Reach Heaven than the End of the Street: A Jerusalem Memoir*, Bloomsbury (2006)

Zweig, Stefan (trans. Anthea Bell), *The World of Yesterday*, Pushkin Press (2009)

GUIDE BOOKS

Irving, Sarah, *Palestine*, Bradt Guides

Kohn, Michael (ed.), *Israel and the Palestinian Territories*, Lonely Planet

Various, *Palestine and Palestinians*, Alternative Tourism Group, Beit Sahour

INDEX

Note: Dervla Murphy's friends, contacts and helpers have been gathered under the heading 'contacts' and the abbreviation DM = Dervla Murphy.